DISCARD

OFF-PREMISE
CATERING MANAGEMENT

OFF-PREMISE CATERING MANAGEMENT

Bill Hansen

JOHN WILEY & SONS, INC.

New York • Chichester • Brisbane • Toronto • Singapore

This text is printed on acid-free paper.

Library of Congress Cataloging in Publication Data:

Hansen, Bill.
   Off-premises catering management / Bill Hansen.
     p.   cm.
   Includes bibliographical references.
   ISBN 0-471-04528-4
    1. Caterers and catering—Management—Handbooks, manuals, etc.
I. Title.
TX921.H36   1994
642'.4—dc20   94-12474

Printed in the United States of America

10 9 8 7 6 5 4 3 2

Foreword

Off-Premise Catering Management is a child born of experience. It is a hands-on book written by one with a sound educational, professional, and teaching background used to develop a masterful art in catering. Up to now there has been no book written that covers in detail all aspects of catering. It is the first book to do a complete job of clearly explaining the total picture from getting started in the catering field to running a successful catering business.

Bill Hansen is a graduate of the School of Hotel Administration at Cornell University and holds a Masters in Hospitality Management from Florida International University. After considerable experience in managing military and private clubs as well as public eateries, he branched into catering. In a short time he became known not only as the leading caterer in Florida but also the best. He has served with amazing excellence groups numbering in the thousands. When Pope John Paul II visited Miami, Bills' Catering was selected to serve the function held for the meeting of the Pope and President Ronald Reagan.

To this firm background, Bill Hansen, in the writing of this book, additionally drew upon his teaching experience at Florida International University's School of Hospitality Management where he is a professor teaching catering, one of the school's most popular and outstanding courses. It is thus not only a manual for those who aspire to learn the art of catering but also one that can serve as a strong textbook for the teaching of catering.

It has been my privilege to see this book develop and to see how well the educational, professional and teaching experience of the author has been brought into it. It is indeed an important contribution to the literature in the field of hospitality management.

LENDAL H. KOTSCHEVAR, PH.D.

Distinguished Professor
Florida International University

Preface

More and more people are entering the off-premise catering arena. Interest in this field is at an all time high, as more and more motivated individuals enter the field. Enrollment in catering management classes at colleges and universities continues to grow as students recognize the advantages of entering the catering field.

The motivation for this book is to provide caterers and anyone aspiring to the business, including college and university students, with a comprehensive resource addressing all important aspects of the business. Anyone with a knowledge of food preparation will be able to apply the principles and techniques herein, and start their own successful, small off-premise catering operation.

The germination of this book began in 1990 as I took on the assignment of teaching catering management at Florida International University. There was so much for students to learn, and little had been written about catering that would make a suitable text. While operating my own off-premise catering and consulting business in South Florida, and teaching year round every Tuesday and Thursday morning, I somehow found time to write.

ACKNOWLEDGMENTS

My partner in life and in business, my wife Terry, has assisted me immeasurably with her input regarding content, style and grammar. I wish also to thank Mindy Schwartz-Angress and the National Association of Catering Executives, who currently help support the catering curriculum at Florida International University. Their support is greatly appreciated.

Others who have offered support, guidance, and assistance include:

Bill Hendrich, Bills' Catering, Inc.
Anthony Marshall, Dean, School of Hospitality Management, Florida International University
Rocco Angelo, Associate Dean, School of Hospitality Management, Florida International University
Professor Charles Ilvento, Florida International University
Dr. Elio Bellucci, Florida International University
Dr. Lendal Kotschevar, Florida International University
David Talty, Florida International University

Ted E. White, Florida International University
Dr. Jeffrey Wachtel, Florida International University
Robert Porter, CPA
Irwin H. Schwartz
Dr. Mary Tanke, Florida International University

BILL HANSEN

Contents

Chapter 1

Introduction to Off-Premise Catering Management

Off-premise catering is serving food at a location away from the caterer's food production facility. One example of a food production facility is a freestanding commissary which is a kitchen facility used exclusively for preparation of foods to be served at other locations. Other examples of production facilities include, but are not limited to hotel, restaurant, and club kitchens. In most cases, there is no existing kitchen facility at the location where the food is served.

Some off-premise caterers completely prepare food and simply deliver it to the event location, while other caterers may cook the food at the party site, serve it with uniformed staff, arrange for beverage service, obtain the necessary equipment to execute the event, and engage subcontractors for other services such as floral design, music, and entertainment.

Off-premise catering can be serving thousands of box lunches to a group of conventioneers, barbecuing chicken and ribs for fans before a collegiate sports contest, serving an elegant dinner for two aboard a luxury yacht, or providing food, staff, and equipment for an upscale fundraiser with hundreds of guests.

Off-premise caterers meet the needs of all market segments, from the low-budget customer who looks for the most quantity and quality for the least amount of money, to the upscale client with an unlimited budget who wants the highest level of service, the ultimate in food quality, and the finest in appointments such as crystal stemware, silverplated flatware, and luxurious linens. Between these two extremes is the midscale segment, which requires more quality than the low-budget market, but less than the upscale market.

Off-premise catering is an art and a science. The art is creating foods and moods, as the caterer and client together turn a vision into reality. The science is the business of measuring money, manpower, and material. Successful off-premise caterers recognize the importance of both the art and the science aspects and are able to work at both the creative and the financial level.

In off-premise catering, there is only one chance to get it right. Many events, such as wedding receptions, occur only once in a person's lifetime. Other events are scheduled annually, quarterly, or on a regular basis, and the caterer who fails to execute all details of the event to the satisfaction of the client will seldom have another chance.

Off-premise catering can be like living on the brink of disaster, unless you are experienced. Uninitiated amateurs do not recognize a volatile situation until it becomes a problem, and later they realize that they should have recognized it earlier.

Catering off-premise is very similar to a sports team playing all of its games away from home, in unfamiliar surroundings, with none of the comforts of home to ease the way. There is no homefield advantage, but there is a minefield disadvantage! As caterers plod their way toward the completion of a catered event, there are thousands of potentially dangerous exploding mines that can ruin an otherwise successful affair. Some examples follow:

> *Already running late for a catering delivery, the catering van driver discovers that all vehicle traffic around the party site is in gridlock. The traffic has been at a standstill for over an hour. The police say that it will be hours before the congestion can be eliminated, and the clients and their guests are anxiously awaiting dinner.*
>
> *A cook wheels a container filled with cooked prime ribs down a pier toward a yacht where the meat will be served to a group of eighty conventioneers in thirty minutes. Suddenly the cook is distracted, and the prime rib container tumbles over the edge of the pier into forty feet of water.*
>
> *The table numbers have vanished, and the guests are ready to be seated for dinner.*
>
> *The fire marshall arrives at a party site twenty minutes before a catered event and refuses to allow guests access to the party site because the space had not been authorized to be used for a party.*
>
> *The catering crew arrives at the party site with a van full of food exactly one week early.*
>
> *A customer calls who is not known to the caterer and asks that food be delivered to a home where family members and guests have gathered prior to funeral services. The caterer sends the food, and upon arrival is told that the person with the checkbook is at the funeral home and to please stop back in an hour for the money. The delivery person leaves without obtaining a signature. Upon returning, there is no one home and no one from whom to collect payment.*
>
> *After catering a flawless party at a client's home, and loading the catering truck to capacity, the caterer is shocked to learn from the client that all fifteen bags of garbage must be removed from the client's property due to local zoning ordinances.*
>
> *The caterer's rental company representative calls the caterer on the morning after an event at a client's home and advises the caterer that the $600 rented chafing dish is missing. It was there the night before when the caterer left the client's home.*

Seasoned off-premise caterers agree that these are only a few of the thousands of possible obstacles that stand in the way of completing a catered event. This text will address the various ways to professionally and successfully deal with these and other difficult situations.

With all of these very real potential problems, why are there over fifty thousand off-premise caterers in the United States? Why are so many young people studying catering at the two-year and four-year college and university levels? Why are thousands of people starting their own catering companies, risking their savings on their dreams of future success? The reasons are numerous: They love the adventure of working in new and exciting places. They look forward to the peaks and valleys of the business cycle. They love the intense feeling of satisfaction, after having successfully catered a spectacular party. They love the myriad challenges of this very difficult profession. Many are their own bosses with no one to answer to but the client. Many pick and choose the parties they wish to cater. Many make six-figure incomes each year, while others cater occasionally, just for the fun of it.

COMPARING OFF-PREMISE WITH ON-PREMISE CATERING

What are the differences between off-premise and on-premise catering? Let's examine these differences both from the client's and the caterer's viewpoint.

From the Client's Viewpoint
Most clients fail to consider the cost of the rental equipment such as tables, chairs, linens, china, glassware, and flatware when they consider engaging an off-premise caterer. They think that it will be less expensive to entertain in their homes or at unique off-premise sites than in hotels. In fact, it can be more expensive due not only to the cost of the rental equipment, but other costs such as transportation of food and supplies to the site, the costs of special labor and decor, and the need for tenting, air conditioning and/or heating, and other expenses. They may save some money by buying their own liquor, but this can be insignificant compared with the additional costs. For many clients, the additional costs are far outweighed by the benefits of the privacy of their own homes, or the uniqueness of special off-premise locations such as a museum, state-of-the-art aquarium, antique car dealership, or historical site.

From the Caterer's Viewpoint
Off-premise caterers must plan menus that can be prepared successfully at the location. For example, foods to be fried should not be cooked in unventilated spaces such as small kitchens in high-rise office buildings. On-premise caterers are not as limited in this regard, and they are generally supported by built-in equipment that can support a wider variety of menus.

On-premise party personnel are more familiar with the party facilities than those who work at a variety of unfamiliar locations. Off-premise catering generally has greater seasonal and day-to-day swings in personnel needs, which can create a greater challenge for the off-premise caterer. The caterer is constantly recruiting and training staff (turnover is usually high since work is on an "as-needed" basis).

Off-premise catering definitely has a greater potential for oversights. Forgotten backup supplies, food, and equipment can be miles away or even inaccessible when catering aboard a yacht miles from shore.

In spite of the uncertainties, off-premise catering offers the opportunity to work in a greater variety of interesting locations. Work is more likely to be different each day, resulting in less boredom and more excitement. For those looking for unlimited challenges and rewards, off-premise catering may be the answer.

ADVANTAGES AND DISADVANTAGES OF OFF-PREMISE CATERING

Among the numerous advantages of catering are:[1]

Advance deposits
Limited investment to startup
Limited inventories
Controllable costs
Additional revenues
Business by contract
Direct payment
Advance forecasting
Free word-of-mouth advertising

Most off-premise caterers require some form of advance deposit prior to the event. This deposit provides the caterer with some security if the event is canceled, and also can be used to purchase some or all of the food and supplies for the party.

There is no need for large amounts of capital to get started since most off-premise catering operations are started utilizing an existing kitchen in a restaurant, club, hotel, church, or other licensed facility. (It is common knowledge that many start their catering businesses in their home kitchens, but it is imperative to state that this is in direct violation of most local zoning ordinances.) Additionally, all of the necessary catering foodservice equipment such as china, glassware, flatware, tables, chairs, and linens can usually be rented, thus avoiding the necessity to invest in expensive equipment inventories.

Food and supply inventories, as well as operating costs, are much more easily controlled since clients must advise the caterer in advance as to the number of guests that are expected. Off-premise caterers need buy only the amounts necessary to serve the event, unlike a restaurant where there are large variables from day to day regarding the number of patrons and their menu selections.

Off-premise catering generates additional revenues for existing operations such as hotels, clubs, and restaurants. Also, off-premise caterers can generate additional revenues and profits by providing other services such as rental equipment, flowers, decor, music, entertainment, and other accessory services.

Both the client and the caterer have expectations regarding the outcome of the party. These expectations should be written in a contract. Payment for the event is normally made directly to a manager or owner, eliminating the cashier or waiter/waitress. This form of direct payment provides for better cash control.

Advance forecasting is more accurate for off-premise caterers, since parties are generally booked weeks, months, or years in advance. Also, each part of the country has seasonal swings which when known assist in revenue forecasting. For example, in the South, the summer months are generally less busy, while in the North, these are the busy months.

Off-premise events generate tremendous amounts of free word-of-mouth advertising that can produce future business without the necessity of advertising.

Many off-premise caterers feel that satisfied guests at one party will either directly or indirectly book another party, by talking favorably about the event and the caterer. In other words, one party can create one or more future parties.

Off-premise catering does have some disadvantages: Catering managers, owners, and staff undergo periods of high stress during very busy periods. Deadlines must be met. There are no excuses for missing a catering deadline. Stress is compounded since work is not evenly spread out over the year. For most off-premise caterers, 80 percent of the event work comes in 20 percent of the time. For most, weekends are generally busier than weekdays. Certain seasons, such as Christmas, are normally busier than others. Of course, caterers must also maintain general business hours too!

Many have left the catering field, burned out by the constant stress and high energy demands. The seasonality of the business makes it difficult to find staff at certain times. Revenues are inconsistent, making cash management very difficult, particularly during the slower periods when expenses continue yet revenues do not.

For caterers who operate hotels, restaurants, clubs, and other businesses, the time spent operating and managing the off-premise business, while away from the main operation, can hurt the main business. For some, it is very difficult to be in two places at the same time.

Many hoteliers and restaurateurs find the rigors of off-premise catering too much. Some quit after realizing the difficulty of catering away from their operations. They feel that the benefits to themselves and their operations are insufficient compared with the rigorous efforts required to stage an off-premise catered event.

ELEMENTS OF SUCCESSFUL OFF-PREMISE CATERING

What does it take to become a successful off-premise caterer? What experience is necessary, and what personality traits are desirable?

Work Experience Prior experience working within the catering profession or the foodservice industry is important. Experience in food preparation and service (back-of-the-house and front-of-the-house) helps enable caterers to understand the procedures and problems in both areas, and how the two areas interface. Those with a strong kitchen background, for example, would be wise to gain some front-of-the-house experience, while front-of-the-house personnel should learn the kitchen routine.

Many successful off-premise caterers have started out working as accommodators. Accommodators are private chefs who are hired to prepare food for parties. Many assist the client with menu planning, purchasing the food and even arranging for kitchen and service staff. The food is prepared and served in the client's home or facility, eliminating the need for a catering commissary. Accommodators receive a fee for their services. The party staff is paid directly by the client.

Entrepreneurism   Entrepreneurism is a trait that is highly desirable for off-premise caterers. An entrepreneur must be willing to spend extraordinary amounts of time and energy to make the off-premise catering business successful; possess an inherent sense of what is right for the business; have the ability to view all aspects of the business at once rather than focusing only on one or two parts; and demonstrate a strong desire to be one's own boss and become financially independent.

Basic Business Knowledge

❑ *Accounting and Bookkeeping.* This is necessary to understand the financial aspects of operating a catering business. The background and ability to prepare and interpret financial statements is essential.

❑ *Laws that Affect Caterers.* These laws include those regulating licensing, contracts, labor, and alcoholic beverage service.

❑ *Human Resources.* Off-premise caterers must know and understand how to recruit, train, motivate, and manage personnel.

❑ *Marketing.* Off-premise caterers should be knowledgeable in how to develop and implement a marketing plan.

Ability to Plan, Organize, Execute, and Control   These are the four basic functions of management. To plan, a caterer must visualize in advance all of the aspects of a catered event and document these plans so that they may be readily understood by the client, and easily executed by the catering staff. Organizing is simply breaking down the party plans into groups of functions that can be executed in an efficient manner. Execution is the implementation of the organized plans by the party staff. Controlling is the supervisory aspect of the event. All well-organized and executed plans require control and supervision. The adage is: "It is not what you expect, but what you inspect." The premier off-premise catering firms in the United States insist on excellent supervision at each event.

Ability to Communicate with Clients and Staff   Listening is the key to good communications with clients and prospective clients. Off-premise caterers must listen carefully and attentively to the client to determine what the client needs. A client who calls and asks "Are you able to cater a party next Friday?" should be dealt with differently than one who calls and asks "How much will it cost for a wedding reception?" The first caller is ready to buy your services, whereas the second caller is shopping. Astute caterers must be able to respond to client requests in such a manner that the client will immediately gain confidence in the caterer.

Communicating with staff is a complex issue. In simple terms, it is the ability to tell staff what is expected so that they understand, and the ability to receive their feedback regarding problems both actual and potential. The result of effective communications is an off-premise catering staff that professionally executes a well-planned party that meets or exceeds the client's expectations.

Willingness to Take Calculated Risks   Off-premise catering is a very risky business. It is not for the faint-hearted who are afraid of the unknown. For example, it is more risky catering a corporate fund raiser at the local zoo under a tent than serving the same group in a hotel ballroom. Off-premise caterers must know when the risk outweighs the gain. In the above example, catering the event at the zoo without adequate cover in case of rain would probably be too risky. The event could be ruined. The tent makes the risk of rain a calculated one.

Sound Body and Mind

Off-premise catering means working long hours without rest or sleep, lifting and moving heavy objects, intense pressure as deadlines near, and even long periods of little or no business, which can cause concern. Successful caterers should be in good physical shape, have a high energy level, and be able to mentally deal with the seasonal business cycles ranging from nonstop activity to slower periods with little or no business.

Off-premise caterers must be self-confident but at the same time realize that they must always find ways to improve the quality of their food and services. In this profession, a fondness for people and feeling comfortable in crowds is important. A "cool head" when under pressure will keep both staff and client calm, while potential problems are resolved professionally and efficiently.

Creativity

Creativity is the benchmark of all outstanding caterers. Creative caterers are able to turn the client's vision into reality by creating the appropriate look, feel, menu, service, and ambience. Those who are not terribly creative can learn to be, or they can employ those who are creative.

Dependability

Dependability is a major cornerstone of success in off-premise catering. When a caterer fails to deliver what is promised, the negative word-of-mouth travels fast among clients and potential clients. Even in those situations where circumstances change, making it more difficult to perform as promised, the outstanding caterer will find a way to deliver, rather than use the changed circumstances as an excuse not to deliver.

Open-mindedness

Open-minded caterers are always keeping up with catering trends and trying new recipes and menus. They are willing to prepare unfamiliar dishes requested by clients, after thoroughly testing and understanding the recipes. They discover and try new dishes. They are always learning better ways to run their businesses.

Ability to Meet the Needs of Clients

The needs of the client must always come first. Success in this business comes from identifying these needs and satisfying them. Unsuccessful off-premise caterers get lost by trying to satisfy their own needs for money, equipment, and greater self-esteem. They forget that the primary goal is to serve the needs of the client. When a client's needs are met, the caterer's needed revenues, profits, and positive feedback will automatically follow.

Ability to Project a Favorable Image to Prospective Clients

Clients hire caterers based on their perceived image of the caterer and what the caterer will provide. Caterers are selling themselves more than they are selling their food. Off-premise caterers must be able to project a favorable image to the client, one that will be in accord with the client's expectations. For example, a caterer whose image is sophisticated and upscale will be hard-pressed to sell a Little League banquet with a low budget. Successful caterers understand their projected images and target their marketing efforts at those clients who desire that image.

Sense of Humor   In this pressure-packed, deadline-oriented, and stressful business, it is easy to become carried away with the magnitude of the undertakings, and become so tense and uptight that work ceases to be fun. Laughter at the right time can relieve that tension and stress, and reinject a sense of fun into the work at hand.

How do caterers serve shrimps? They bend down!

MANAGING THE OPERATION

Even those who possess these qualities that indicate off-premise catering success must know how to effectively put these talents to use. Off-premise caterers should be hands-on managers who are constantly customer focused. They must be able to lead staff and clients alike, while conducting business in a professional manner. They must be able to make timely, ethical decisions, while understanding what makes for a successful event. They must also avoid those situations that cause a business to fail.

Hands-on
Attention to Detail
Management

Success in off-premise catering comes from being involved in all of the details of the business and knowing how to perform all of the jobs such as cooking, serving, selling, and bookkeeping. Great restaurateurs and caterers are involved in the basic details of their businesses and they know how to perform the various jobs. Bern Laxer, owner of Bern's Steak House in Tampa, which has won *Florida Trend*'s Golden Spoon Award for 24 of the past 25 years, attributes his success to paying attention to the details, making everything the best it can be and giving the customer a fair deal.[2]

Many catering amateurs think that a business can be run from a desk while reading computer printouts and delegating all tasks. This is a false belief. Off-premise catering companies must be run from the center of the action, whether it be with the guests or preparing foods in the kitchen. It comes from checking and rechecking every detail to ensure that it meets the highest of standards. It comes from inspecting for the best and expecting the best. Some call this management style "management by walking around." In one sense this is true; but there is more to it than walking around. Astute off-premise caterers must:

❑ Obtain feedback from the client and guests regarding the food and service.
❑ Oversee the catering staff to ensure that they are performing as directed and as expected.
❑ Help out when a table needs to be cleared, or when the bar suddenly becomes very busy. Help in the kitchen during critical times such as hot

food dishup and even help in the dirty-dish area at the end of the evening when the majority of dishes are returned for cleaning.

❑ Never be totally satisfied with the way things are. Always look for new ways to present food, make food more flavorful, and find better and more efficient ways to do things.

Customer-Focused Management

An off-premise caterer's full-time mission must be satisfying the needs of clients.

> Companies that are 100% customer focused make the customer's satisfaction their only goal. They do not have as goals, increasing sales by a certain percentage, raising a profit margin, or reducing debt. They believe . . . that if you strive to sell only the highest quality product and strive to please every customer, sales, profit and success will follow. This is a difficult concept for many of us to grasp. It means letting go of a financial accounting structure passed down from generation to generation of Harvard MBA's who've instilled in us that the only way to build your bottom line is to raise your top line and squeeze the middle. . . . That can work. . . but wouldn't you rather make the quality of your food, the dining experience and your customer's satisfaction your primary concern?[3]

The moral is simple: If you satisfy your customers while charging a fair price and controlling costs, profits will follow.

Managerial Decision Making

Off-premise catering managers must make decisions that keep their operations running smoothly. They realize that some decisions will be better than others, that there is no perfect solution to every problem, and that the best decision-making goal is to find the best possible solution with the least number of drawbacks.

Connie Sitterly, noted management consultant and author, states that to be a good decision maker you should "plan ahead so when problems crop up, you're prepared to act, not react. Control circumstances, instead of allowing them to control you. Take the initiative by anticipating and solving business problems."[4]

Although hundreds of books have been written about decision making, the following tips from Ms. Sitterly should be helpful to the reader when trying to decide.

> Remember that there's seldom only one acceptable solution to the problem. Choose the best alternative . . .

> Make decisions that help achieve the company objectives . . .

> Consider people's feelings. . . . You need to consider feelings whenever people are involved. Even if you must make an unpopular decision, you can minimize repercussions . . . if workers know you have taken their feelings into account . . .

> Allow quality time for planning and decision making . . . pick a time when you are energetic and your mind is fresh . . .

Realize that you'll never please everyone. Few decisions meet with unanimous approval . . . the appointed authority, not the majority, rules . . .

Make time for making decisions . . . in business, delaying a decision can cost thousands of dollars . . .

Put decision-making in perspective. Every executive feels overwhelmed at times by either the enormity or the number of decisions made during a business day. . . . Accept for peace of mind that you are doing the best job you can with the time, talent and resources you have . . .

Don't wait for a popular vote. Rallying your colleagues around your decision before you take action or waiting for their vote of confidence before deciding anything may cost too much in time. There are times when you just have to *do* something.[4]

Leadership   Owners, managers, and supervisors in off-premise catering are expected to lead staff, and sometimes clients. To some people, leadership comes naturally, but for many, leadership techniques need to be learned. Some guidelines and tips for leaders in off-premise catering follow:

- ❑ Guide people, instead of dictating in order to gain cooperation.
- ❑ Give the credit to others.
- ❑ Stand staunchly for what you believe.
- ❑ Never lower your standards.
- ❑ Be humble.
- ❑ In the face of controversy, seek out the truth.
- ❑ Win your points tactfully without arousing antagonism.
- ❑ Have faith in others.
- ❑ Lead by example. It is not what you say, it is what you do that counts.

Professionalism and Common Business Courtesy   Off-premise caterers who are not professional in their business practices will never reach the pinnacle of success in the field. Before we address the technical aspects of catering in the succeeding chapters, it is of utmost importance that we define professionalism. Some guidelines follow that are adapted from an article by Carol McKibben in *Special Events*, November 1991.[5]

- ❑ Become known for doing what you say you are going to do.
- ❑ Only give price quotes and commitments when you know everything about the event.
- ❑ Treat clients and staff with respect.
- ❑ Build relationships with clients. Do not look at them as accounts or projects.
- ❑ Be on time, or a bit early for appointments. Be prepared for the appointment.
- ❑ Be honest; don't play games.
- ❑ Stand behind your work. If it is wrong, make it right.
- ❑ In the face of abuse from others, don't respond by becoming abusive. Try to detach yourself from it emotionally and handle it logically. Of course, do not use your position of power to abuse others.

❏ Dress professionally.

❏ Enjoy your work as an off-premise caterer. When work ceases to be enjoyable, it is time to quit and find a new career.

Ethical Management   Ethics is one of the most talked-about topics in today's business world. We read and hear of illegalities, scandals, and other forms of questionable behavior. Off-premise caterers are in no way exempt from ethical concerns. Even the smallest caterers deal in issues of fairness, of legal requirements, and of honesty on a daily basis. Some examples include truth in menu, misleading advertising, unexpected and unjustified last-minute add-ons to the party price, and even underbidding a competitor when the client has disclosed your competitor's price.

The truly ethical caterer will assume responsibility for the host to ensure that the host plans an event in the best interest of the guests. A host who wishes to serve alcohol to underage guests or barbecued ribs to a group of very senior citizens is out of line and needs to be advised that this will not work. A truly ethical caterer will refuse to cater an event that is not planned in the best interest of the host or guests.

There are times when a caterer is given a free hand in planning a menu. Perhaps a grieving client calls for food after the funeral of a loved one, and says "Please send over food for fifty guests tomorrow night. You know what we like!" The ethical caterer will not take advantage of this situation by either providing too much food or overcharging the client.

Another temptation arises when the caterer is pressed to cater more events on a certain day or evening than the caterer can reasonably accommodate. The extra money looks good. Unethical caterers will rationalize that they can handle all of the events, even if an inexperienced supervisor or staff must oversee these events, or even if the kitchen staff will not be able to prepare food of the caterer's usual high quality due to lack of time and personnel. Caterers who take on more work than they can reasonably accommodate are greedy, and are considered by many observers to be unethical.

In the foregoing situation the caterer should decline the work, and perhaps recommend another caterer to assist the client. Some caterers refuse to recommend another catering firm since they feel that the client may not be pleased with the other firm, and will then blame them for recommending the other firm. Other caterers freely recommend one or more firms when unable to cater events.

There are times when it is very tempting to speak badly about competitors. Unethical caterers will do this. Those that are ethical would rather point our their own strengths than downgrade the competition.

It can be very tempting for self-employed caterers to underreport income and overstate expenses. They rationalize that no one is going to know if they accept cash for a party and fail to report it as income and pay the associated taxes; no one is going to know if they charge personal expenses illegitimately to the business. Some caterers who are licensed to sell liquor by the drink or by the bottle are tempted to overcharge the client for beverages that were not consumed. These practices are not only unethical, they are illegal.

Other ethical violations may occur when caterers receive under-the-table cash kickbacks from suppliers, misrepresent their services to potential clients, and bid on party plans and ideas stolen from other caterers.

Ethical management needs to be stressed within the catering profession. Those entering this profession need to be aware of ethical standards and comply with them if they are to be considered true professionals. The Jefferson Center of Character Education has set forth ten "universal values." These are honesty, integrity, promise-keeping, fidelity, fairness, caring for others, respect for others, responsible citizenship, pursuit of excellence, and accountability.[6] These values should provide some guidance for those off-premise caterers wishing to develop ethical standards for their operations.

Managing Catered Events

Mona Meretsky, President of COMCOR Event and Meeting Production, Inc. in Ft. Lauderdale, Florida is recognized as one of the leading special event producers in the nation. Her work has won numerous awards given by Special Events magazine each year. Many Fortune Five Hundred firms engage her services for planning and executing their premier events all over the United States. Her "Rules for Producing a Successful Event" capture the basic philosophy of managing special events. Those wishing to become better off-premise catering managers as well as those who are just beginning to learn about catering will benefit from her philosophy.

- ❑ Don't assume anything.
- ❑ When in doubt, check it out. Never say you know something if you don't. Find out the answer.
- ❑ Always think safety first.
- ❑ Give your client all you promised and more.
- ❑ Communication is the key to a successful party.
- ❑ Determine your client's needs and desires, and if they are unreasonable, don't be afraid to say "no."
- ❑ Every problem has a solution. Remain calm, and take the necessary time to resolve it.
- ❑ Be organized by providing diagrams, maps, schedules, and confirmations.
- ❑ Learn to delegate properly. You cannot do it all yourself.
- ❑ Do your homework.
- ❑ Finish as much as you can ahead of time.
- ❑ You grow by agreeing to do new things. Take some calculated risks.
- ❑ Murphy's Law applies to everything. Be prepared for the worst, and have a contingency plan.
- ❑ Details make the difference. Pay attention to them.
- ❑ Learn from past mistakes. The biggest mistake is failure to recognize the first mistake.

As you study this text, you will learn specifically how these rules relate to various catering situations as well as how to make them part of your managerial arsenal.

Separating Yourself from the Competition

Gary Player was playing in a senior PGA tour event one afternoon. He came up on a par four, selected his club and drove the ball right down the middle of the fairway. As he approached the ball in the middle of the fairway, he could feel the excitement of the gallery. He wanted to get that ball on the green on his next shot. So he carefully selected an iron and smashed the ball.

Next, coming down the fairway was Arnold Palmer, who shot his ball right down the fairway. As he approached his ball, he, too, could feel the excitement of the gallery. As he stood there deciding what club to use next, someone in the gallery shouted out, "Use a five iron: That's what Gary Player used." So Arnold Palmer picked his five iron and smashed the ball right into the lake. As soon as his ball made a big splash, the same person in the gallery shouted out, "That's exactly what Gary Player did!"[7]

Of course, the moral of this story is that copying the competition is not always the right course. There are distinct advantages to caterers who "separate themselves from the competition" by offering a unique menu, a unique service, or perhaps a unique location. In south Florida for example, the most successful caterers each have a quality of uniqueness. For example, one caterer specializes in catering for doctors through his hospital foodservice management job. Another caterer has an exclusive off-premise contract for a sports facility; another was the on-premise caterer for a city club (which resulted in off-premise jobs for the club members); another catered for a hotel; and another catered from a restaurant that is part of a condominium development.

Each one of these caterers offers or offered unique services that helped separate him from the competition. These caterers are successful within their market areas. This same pattern seems to be true in other parts of the country.

PERSONAL MANAGEMENT

Off-premise caterers need to also understand how to deal with principles of stress management, time management, and personal organization if they are to manage at peak efficiency. Time is our most precious commodity, and to waste it being overstressed or disorganized will inevitably result in less-than-desirable results.

Managing Stress

Stress comes from interaction with others and meeting deadlines. According to John Soeder, this might happen when "a customer is screaming, the brioche is burning, your loan officer is on the phone and the dishwasher just quit. . . . Clearly, stress is no stranger to the foodservice industry. Each day brings a torrent of small tragedies from disgruntled customers and stubborn employees to over-boiling pots and broken ovens. Long hours, a breadth of responsibilities, and the fact that the professional and personal lives of many restaurateurs are inextricably intertwined frequently take their toll."[8]

A certain amount of stress and tension is necessary to achieve the best results. Those who are too laid back generally do not maximize their potential. However, too much stress and tension cause chronic fatigue, irritability, cynicism, hostility, inflexibility, and difficulty in thinking clearly. Catering managers who are overstressed are unable to perform at their maximum capabilities.

Stress can often be controlled through:

❑ Daily exercise such as brisk walking, jogging, or other pursuits that raise the pulse, and take the mind off work.
❑ Mental relaxation techniques such as meditation.
❑ Writing down those issues that cause stress, identifying those issues that can be controlled, making a sublist of how to deal with the controllable stress-producers, and simply making the best of those uncontrollable stress-producers.
❑ Reading articles and books on how to reduce stress.

To conclude this section, it is important to remember that some stress in catering is good. An arrow would not be propelled from a bow if the bow was not stressed. However, too much stress can break the bow, as well as ruin catered events.

Managing Time   Another area of personal management important to off-premise caterers is that of time management. There are only 168 hours in each week, and the greatest rewards come to those who accomplish the most meaningful things during this fixed amount of time. Off-premise caterers realize that if they can accomplish more meaningful production in less time, they will have more time for families, friends, and personal pursuits. They also realize that working smarter, not harder, through effective use of time will produce greater results.

The key to effective time management is to set goals for a lifetime, for five years, and for each year, month, week, and day. Without written goals, off-premise caterers cannot effectively manage their time. Since time management involves choosing how to spend time, it is impossible to make proper choices without knowing your desired goals. The captain of a ship without a destination cannot choose the proper course. He will cruise aimlessly at sea, never reaching his port-of-call.

Off-premise caterers can choose from an array of timesaving techniques and technical advances to help them efficiently manage time. These include:

❑ Making daily, detailed lists of goals and objectives.
❑ Utilizing technical advances to speed up paper handling, such as fax machines and computers with word processing and accounting software.
❑ Using cellular phones to stay in touch while away from the office. These phones are invaluable at off-premise catering locations when emergency and other calls are necessary. Additionally, phone calls can be made while traveling by car, waiting in line, or at any other time when it is impossible or inconvenient to use a public or private phone.
❑ Handling incoming papers only once. Either do it, delegate it, discard it, or file it.

❏ Doing the most important work at times when most alert. Some people are larks and are most alert in the morning, while others are owls who are at their best in the evening.

❏ Taking a seminar or course in time management to learn more about the effective use of time.

❏ Qualifying incoming calls for catering services by first learning from the caller the event's location, date, number of guests, and budget. Time can be wasted talking about a party with a prospective client without realizing that the party is not feasible due to a scheduling conflict, that the number of guests is too small or too large for the catering firm, that the budget is insufficient, or that the proposed location is already booked for another event.

❏ Focusing on results by asking, "Does this activity help achieve my objective?" Prioritize tasks in order of their importance. Most people waste countless hours, days, weeks, and years on things that offer little reward such as chit-chatting on the phone, shuffling papers, running errands, and other things that are easy to do, but offer little payoff. The high achievers in catering and in other fields minimize their time on these low-priority, low-payoff tasks, and maximize their time working on things that will bring the greatest rewards. These tasks are usually very difficult to accomplish, take a large amount of time, and do involve at least some risk. For example, a caterer could spend the entire day showing a prospective client numerous suitable locations for a major event. The caterer would then spend the next three days preparing written proposals for events at all of the various locations, with no guarantee that the event would even take place. However, if the caterer does secure the event, the profits would be five figures. Another high-payoff task might be to completely write a new catering menu. Both of these tasks take large amounts of time and involve some risk, but they more than likely will produce major rewards in increased revenues and profits.

In summary, off-premise caterers who best manage their time in the long run will be the most successful. They become the leading caterers in their communities, in their states, and in the country.

Getting Organized   When projects, tasks, catering kitchens, and offices are organized, things run much more smoothly and efficiently. The wasted time spent looking for things and jumping from job to job could be put to much better use. Many off-premise caterers have found various methods that work for them, such as the following:

❏ Establish a filing system using hanging folders and Manila folders. Categories include upcoming events, projects to do, and projects pending. Files should be kept vertically, rather than stacked one on top of another, for greater accessibility.

❏ Keep those items that are used frequently close by.

❑ Focus on one project at a time, rather than jumping from one thing to another. This can be easily accomplished by blocking out some time during the day to work on major projects and arranging for no interruptions.
❑ Either at the end of each day, or first thing in the morning, prepare a list of things to do for the day.

Summary of
Personal
Management
Those off-premise caterers who can effectively deal with stress, who properly manage their time, and who keep things organized will lead their peers into the twenty-first century. They will set the standards for others to follow. They will accomplish more and will be in a position to receive the greatest rewards.

MANAGING INTO THE TWENTY-FIRST CENTURY

As this century ends, and as the next century approaches, changes occur at ever-increasing speed. Off-premise caterers must manage within this changing environment. They must recognize the differences between food trends and fads, the movement toward more nutritious foods, the decline in alcoholic beverage consumption, the aging of the baby-boom generation, the need for catering in all major markets from budget-conscious to upscale, the need for basic and continuing education in the catering profession, the impact of the computer on catering, the need for industry organizations that will help ensure that professional standards are set and met, the impact of the ever-changing economic picture, and the fast-moving changes within the international marketplace.

There is a growing realization that there is strength in numbers when caterers band together for a common purpose. In Colorado a group of seven off-premise caterers formed a coalition and contracted to cater services at the Colorado Convention Center.

Restaurants, hotels, clubs, and even hospitals are entering the off-premise arena in order to generate additional revenues. However, many who enter this demanding field quickly learn that off-premise catering is much more difficult than serving guests on-premise. Many of these first-timers quickly retreat to the safety and security of on-premise catering. Others become majors in the marketplace.

Nowhere is this more evident than at San Francisco's Westin St. Francis. For nearly a century the property has carved out a tradition of staging spectacular planned affairs and coping even more impressively during disasters. "We fed hundreds of people in Union Square following the 1906 earthquake," said hotel spokesman Michael Stark, "And following the 1989 quake, our catering outfit went into motion immediately. Though we had no power, we brought in our own generators and refrigerated trucks, set up candelabras and ultimately served more than 4,000 hot meals to guests and San Franciscans who couldn't get home.". . . With a bit more advance notice, the hotel can do even more impressive presentations. According to Larry Dean, the hotel's Director of Catering, these range from high-society functions such as feeding . . . opera or symphony patrons under tents set up in conjunction with opening-night festivities; staging off-site receptions for dignitaries . . . ; feeding thousands of diners at the Moscone Convention center; or staging a party for the Police Athletic League in a cell block at Alcatraz.[9]

Hyatt Hotels operate Regency Caterers by Hyatt, which handles off-premise catered events. Other hotels that successfully compete in the off-premise market include the Four Seasons in Vancouver, the Boston Harbor Hotel, Jean-Louis at the Watergate Hotel in Washington, Omni Hotel in Charleston, and the Westin Resort on Hilton Head Island in South Carolina.

Unless top and middle management is highly committed to off-premise catering for hotels and restaurants, the chances for success are limited. Off-premise catering places unusually high demands on staff and equipment. Many operators prefer to do what they do best, which is to produce exquisite catered events within the walls of their hotels and restaurants.

Certain hotel chains are building meeting and banquet facilities without supporting kitchens. They save money on expensive kitchens, yet still offer guests banquet and meeting rooms. How do they do it? Quite simply: They engage the services of off-premise caterers who cater for the hotel's guests. This creates a win-win situation for both hotels and the caterers. Forward-thinking off-premise caterers should look to this market for future business.

The catering business, like most businesses, experiences cycles where business first prospers, then suffers, and then returns to prosperity. Astute off-premise caterers of the future should not be afraid to don the apron when times are difficult. Many caterers, in order to save their businesses and survive downtimes, will need to roll up their sleeves and perform jobs that were formerly performed by employees. The money saved may mean the difference between success and bankruptcy.

During tough times, and even good times, certain regular clients may make unrealistic requests such as:

"Will you cater my party at cost? I will give you all my future business."
"Please cater my Christmas party this year, but defer payment until the following year."
"Please give me a special price, and I will see that all my friends buy from you!"

These requests are unfair, and off-premise caterers should be extremely wary when approached in this fashion. As a general rule of thumb, clients who do not pay their bills in a timely manner, or who are not willing to pay a fair price for catering, are not worth the headaches they cause.

CONCLUSION

To conclude this introductory chapter to off-premise catering management, let's examine some additional techniques, philosophies, and real-life ways to be successful as off-premise caterers.

Five Keys for Success in Off-Premise Catering

In his book, *Positively Outrageous Service*,[10] T. Scott Gross outlines ten commandments for managers of service establishments. Five of these truly mean the difference between success and failure in off-premise catering.

"Be a Quality Fanatic." Every catered affair should be done to the best of the caterer's ability. Good enough seldom is. Every menu item should be continuously improved. Strive to make it even better than the last time!

"Look for Ways to Say Yes to Your Customers." Many companies create policies and procedures that do more to serve the system than the customers. Staffers and bureaucrats who sit behind desks, and who never deal with the customers, create rules and regulations that make it difficult for customers to do business with a firm. Successful off-premise caterers do everything possible to make their businesses user-friendly. It could be something as simple as accepting personal checks or credit cards, or more complicated such as creating a special dish from the client's family recipe file.

"Do the Right Things." Managers in all fields are so intent on doing things to perfection. There is no such thing as perfection. One can only do things to the best of one's ability within the allotted time frame. Rather than be consumed with perfection, off-premise catering managers should strive for excellence by "doing the right things." This means spending one's time on things that will bring the greatest rewards. When faced with a decision of whether to call on a prospective client who is planning a gala event, or to reconcile the business checking account, the astute caterer will call on the prospective client first, and handle the checking account reconciliation later. Another example would be when an important client calls who is visiting from out of town and must see the caterer in thirty minutes to discuss a major, last-minute event. The caterer was just leaving to deposit the quarterly federal tax, which is due at the bank. The caterer cannot do both. Should the caterer see the client or make the deposit? Is it worth it to pay the late deposit penalty? Can someone else make the deposit? Most managers would agree the client is more important, and would make other arrangements for the deposit. Doing the right thing is seeing the client.

"Be a Visible Standard of Excellence." Off-premise catering managers must set the standards. A manager who dresses sloppily sets the stage for his or her staff to dress the same way. People learn by imitating. The smart manager is in the kitchen and with the guests, seeing that all food is excellently prepared and served. This manager sets the tone for the highest quality of food and service.

"Manage First; Labor Second." Top bosses are not afraid to get their hands dirty when necessary; however, they also know that by spending too much time laboring, they can be spending too little time leading and managing. Off-premise catering managers, who find that they are continuously performing work that should be done by their employees, need to make the necessary changes to free their time to manage. Solutions could include hiring additional staff, training existing staff, better organizing the workplace, or even reducing the number of catered events to a more manageable number, eliminating those that are least profitable.

How Does An Off-Premise Catering Business Gauge Success?

There are a number of signs to look for when evaluating an off-premise catering business. Healthy companies rate highly in all of these areas. Those that are unhealthy or are ready to fail will not rate nearly as well.

❑ Management thoroughly plans, organizes, executes, and controls each catered event.

❑ Proper controls are in place over costs, accounts receivable and payable, and liquid assets such as cash and inventories.

❑ Food and service quality is well controlled and meets or exceeds clients' approval.

❑ Pricing for food and services is fair. Clients are neither over- nor under-charged.

❑ The catering firm enjoys good working relations with both clients and suppliers.

❑ There is sufficient working capital to operate the business.

❑ The firm can make loan payments as they become due. Excessive credit is not extended to clients.

❑ Budgets are prepared and followed. Business records are kept up-to-date. The information derived from these records is used to provide data to help manage the business.

❑ Sales growth is controlled. There are sufficient financial and personnel resources to operate the catering business as it steadily grows.

❑ The off-premise firm competes fairly with other firms in the marketplace.

❑ Market trends are anticipated.

❑ Management and staff have a good working knowledge of the off-premise catering field.

❑ There are good relations between management and staff. Staff members are well-trained.

❑ The firm has sufficient insurance and is properly licensed.

❑ Management works closely with a qualified accountant to plan for payment of income and other taxes.

❑ Management is willing to seek qualified professional assistance when problems arise.

This text will show the reader how to build an off-premise catering firm that will meet or exceed these standards. The reader will be exposed to all of the aspects of off-premise catering as outlined in the table of contents. This book will provide all of the necessary information to those who are motivated to start their own firm, or develop an off-premise catering business as part of an existing food-service operation. By studying and learning the contents of this book, the entrepreneurially motivated reader should be well on the way toward success in the off-premise catering field.

The Off-Premise Catering Model

Exhibit 1-1 is an illustration of all the factors that enter into the off-premise catering arena. It shows how managerial philosophies and techniques, as well as laws regarding personnel, business, serving of alcoholic beverages, and sanitation and safety must all interrelate in the off-premise catering business.

It then depicts how marketing efforts produce clients, which in turn creates the need for *site inspections and logistical planning*, including:

Menu planning
Beverage planning

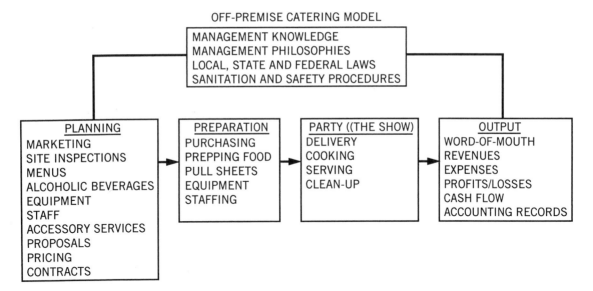

OFF-PREMISE CATERING MODEL

| MANAGEMENT KNOWLEDGE |
| MANAGEMENT PHILOSOPHIES |
| LOCAL, STATE AND FEDERAL LAWS |
| SANITATION AND SAFETY PROCEDURES |

PLANNING	PREPARATION	PARTY ((THE SHOW)	OUTPUT
MARKETING	PURCHASING	DELIVERY	WORD-OF-MOUTH
SITE INSPECTIONS	PREPPING FOOD	COOKING	REVENUES
MENUS	PULL SHEETS	SERVING	EXPENSES
ALCOHOLIC BEVERAGES	EQUIPMENT	CLEAN-UP	PROFITS/LOSSES
EQUIPMENT	STAFFING		CASH FLOW
STAFF			ACCOUNTING RECORDS
ACCESSORY SERVICES			
PROPOSALS			
PRICING			
CONTRACTS			

EXHIBIT 1-1   Off-Premise Catering Model

Equipment planning
Personnel planning
Planning for other services

Once the planning is complete it is possible to provide clients with *written proposals* that include all of the aforementioned plans along with pricing. Normally, proposals are modified. Once modification is complete and all provisions meet the mutual satisfaction of both the off-premise caterer and the client, a contract is prepared that contains all of the conditions outlined in the proposal.

As the party date approaches, certain *operational elements* occur, such as:

Hiring and scheduling staff
Purchasing and prepping the menu items
Ordering the necessary equipment from a party rental firm
Preparing a pull sheet detailing all items supplied by the commissary necessary tc
    produce the party
Coordinating all beverages and accessory services with the client

All of the preplanning elements culminate on the day or night of The Show. At The Show, all of the staff, equipment, food, and other services meet at the party site, and the event is executed.

After the event, there are *outputs* that include:

Positive and/or negative word-of-mouth about the event
Revenues, expenses, profits, and cash
Accounting records

By reading and studying this text, the reader will gain a thorough understanding of how all of these elements combine to interreact in the off-premise catering arena.

NOTES

1. Manfred Ketterer, *How to Manage a Successful Catering Business*, 2nd ed. (New York: Van Nostrand Reinhold, 1991).
2. James R. Hagy, "Art in Steak," *Florida Trend*, September 1991, p. 46.
3. Mike DeLuca, "Is Customer Satisfaction Your Only Goal?", *Restaurant Hospitality*, © 1992 Penton Publishing, July 1992, p. 22.
4. Connie Sitterly, "Making the Right Decision," *The Meeting Manager*, August 1990, pp. 34–35.
5. Carol McKibben, *Special Events*, November 1991.
6. Frank Havran, "Why Ethics? Why Now?", *The Meeting Manager*, May 1993, p. 52.
7. *National Caterers Association, CommuniCATER*, April 1992. Reprinted with permission from the CommuniCATER, official publication of the National Caterers Association.
8. John Soeder, "Handling the Heat," *Restaurant Hospitality*, © 1991 Penton Publishing, April 1991, p. 124.
9. Robert Selwitz, "Outside Catering," *Hotel and Motel Management*, March 25, 1991, p. 55.
10. T. Scott Gross, *Positively Outrageous Service* (New York: Mastermedia Limited, 1991).

Chapter 2

Getting Started—Legalities, Location, and Contracts

The first steps toward establishing an off-premise catering business include understanding the legal ramifications of operating a business and finding a suitable location. Many off-premise caterers operate illegally from their homes with no licenses or insurance. It is imperative that readers understand that this is in violation of local and state statutes and violators may be prosecuted and fined. Professional off-premise caterers follow the laws of each municipality, state, and the federal government. Illegal caterers not only damage the reputation of our profession, but make it more difficult for licensed and insured caterers to compete with those who do not have the expenses of licenses and insurance.

The purpose of this chapter is to inform readers of the legal ways to establish an off-premise catering business in order to help elevate the standards of our fast-growing profession.

Each municipality, county, and state has specific regulations regarding the operation and licensing of businesses. It is impossible in this text to address specific laws for specific locations. Each prospective off-premise caterer is advised to contact local and state authorities first, before selecting a location and starting a business.

LOCAL AND STATE REQUIREMENTS

Zoning. Most municipalities require zoning permits to ensure that businesses conform to local laws. For example, zoning laws prohibit off-premise caterers from building catering commissaries in residential neighborhoods. Many require a certificate of use and occupancy before business may be conducted.

Businesses located in an existing structure previously used for similar purposes will usually have few zoning problems. Off-premise caterers who construct a new facility, convert an existing building used previously for other purposes, or extensively remodel an existing facility will need to carefully check zoning regulations. A zoning variance or conditional-use permit are required to operate a business on land not zoned for that purpose. Filing fees can exceed $1,200 and it can take 90 days or longer for a decision. To change zoning can take six months or longer and require extensive legal work.

Occupational License. After receiving the zoning permit, off-premise caterers must apply for the appropriate occupational licenses required by the municipality, the county, and the state. In South Florida for example, an off-premise caterer located in the City of Miami needs two occupational licenses, one for the City of Miami and one for Dade County.

License to Sell Food to the Public. Many states require this license, which normally is obtained through the state's Department of Business.

Health Permit. Businesses dealing with food must have a health department permit. Prior to issuing a permit the health department will inspect the off-premise caterer's facilities. Readers should refer to the chapter on Sanitation and Safety to gain an understanding of health department requirements.

Fictitious Names. If a business uses a name other than the first and last name of the owner, it must be registered with the state as a fictitious name so that the owner's name can become a public record. Each state has legislation for this purpose and caterers should contact their state's Department of Business Regulation for details.

Local and State Sales Tax. Off-premise caterers should contact the department or division of revenue for their state and municipality for requirements. Sales taxes are further discussed in Chapters 10 and 14.

Workers' Compensation. This is a state requirement for those who employ staff, including part-time staff and corporate officers. This topic will be discussed in Chapter 7.

Other Local and State Permits and Taxes. There are numerous other permits that may be required, but are not limited to fire department permits and sign permits. To avoid costly mistakes regarding signs, it is imperative to check local ordinances and also obtain written approval from the landlord. Many states have corporate income taxes, intangible asset taxes, personal property taxes, and unemployment taxes. Readers interested in starting an off-premise catering firm should contact an attorney.

FEDERAL REQUIREMENTS

Employer Identification Number. Off-premise caterers who employ staff must obtain an Employer Identification Number (EIN) using IRS Form SS-4. Employers are responsible for four types of federal payroll collections and payments:

1. Income taxes withheld from employee wages.
2. Employer/employee Social Security Tax (FICA).

3. Employer/employee Medicare Tax (MICA).
4. Federal unemployment tax (FUTA).

Employment Taxes. Off-premise catering firms and other businesses are required by law to withhold federal income and social security taxes from wages paid to employees, and to file a quarterly return, IRS Form 941. Self-employed off-premise caterers must pay self-employment federal income and social security taxes.

Monies withheld from employees must be paid when due to the federal government. New businesses with insufficient cash to pay all creditors may defer paying the government, so that they can pay suppliers. Penalties are severe: A $10,000 tax liability can increase to $14,050 in six months.

> A corporate officer who is held to be a responsible person and willfully fails to account for or pay the federal government the payroll taxes due will be personally liable for the unpaid taxes. . . . Payroll taxes can be a liability nightmare for the unsuspecting corporate officer or employee. However, careful planning before the business opens and while it is in operation can help minimize and reduce personal liability.[1]

Off-premise caterers should also be aware of federal reporting requirements for employees receiving tips. This will be discussed in Chapter 7.

Unemployment Taxes. Off-premise caterers are also required to pay federal unemployment tax. IRS Form 940 is used for this purpose. In those states that require state unemployment taxes, the amount of federal unemployment tax required can be reduced.

Income Taxes. All off-premise catering firms are required to pay federal income tax in addition to state and municipality taxes in accordance with local laws.

Immigration Requirements. All employers are required to verify the immigration status of all new hires on form I-9. Please refer to Chapter 7 for more information.

Further information on these requirements can be obtained from local Better Business Bureaus, Chambers of Commerce, and the Small Business Administration.

LEGAL FORM OF OPERATION

The four main legal forms for businesses are: sole proprietorship, partnership, limited partnership, and corporation. Each have their advantages and disadvantages.

A sole proprietorship requires no legal papers other than the applicable licenses and the fictitious-name filing. The major disadvantage is that creditors can attach personal property and bank accounts when the sole proprietor is unable to fulfill financial obligations.

In a partnership, two or more people become responsible for each other's actions. In a legal action, each partner will be sued personally. Assets contributed to the partnership by all partners become equity in the partnership. Each partner's share of the profits is reported on the individual tax return of the applicable partner.

Limited partnerships are commonly used for real estate syndications, and are used very infrequently for off-premise catering firms. The legal costs for starting a limited partnership can be very high since these partnerships are very complex and involve a number of investors.

Most off-premise caterers choose incorporation as a realistic form of operation because the corporation is a separate legal entity from the caterer. The corporation alone is generally responsible for its own actions and debts. Under a corporation, off-premise caterers are protected in most situations since they are just an employee of the corporation. A corporation must be operated in a correct legal manner, or protection may be forfeited. A special form of incorporation is the Subchapter S corporation, which is recommended for most caterers since profits are not double-taxed, as they may be in a regular corporation.

It is advisable to consult with an attorney when forming a business venture, but ambitious off-premise caterers may wish to complete the necessary paperwork for incorporation on their own, thereby saving the attorney fees for incorporation.

When selecting an attorney, it is imperative to look for one who has experience in working with hospitality industry clients, who is available when needed, and is dependable.

FINDING A FACILITY

There are basically three scenarios for off-premise caterers when considering facility options:

A. Operate an off-premise catering business from an existing operation where the caterer currently works such as a hotel, restaurant, club, or similar facility. This scenario is excellent since there are few additional expenses for startup; however, it is only an option for existing operators.

Aspiring off-premise caterers may wish to look toward the corporate world for startup assistance. "Today many corporations are finding it more convenient and more economical to hire their own chefs or bring in caterers for on-site meetings. Amy Greenberg, president of the Society for Foodservice Management . . . believes new business-meal deductibility rulings 'will encourage the use of in-house facilities' "[2] (President Clinton's 1994 budget bill lowers business-meal deductibility at restaurants from 80% to 50%.)

Startup caterers may wish to affiliate with a corporation and with its permission, utilize its facilities as a commissary for off-premise events. The added benefit in this scenario is that corporate in-house diners will become off-premise catering clients.

B. Operate from a commissary used exclusively for off-premise catering. This can be an expensive venue, and should be reserved for off-premise caterers who already have an established business.

C. Find an existing facility that has an underutilized kitchen, and arrange to use this kitchen in exchange for a rental fee and/or providing the facility with needed food service. For example, a church kitchen that is only used occasionally would be an excellent option. The off-premise caterer would pay the church for the use of the kitchen on a monthly or "as-used" basis. Part or all of the rent could be paid for in services rendered. The off-premise caterer may cater some of the church functions at a reduced fee in exchange for rent credit.

In summary, the best and most cost-efficient facilities are those that require no initial investment and may even offer a built-in client base. One south Florida caterer developed a two-million-dollar-per-year catering business with a small investment, by offering catering services to a downtown businessmen's club. The caterer served lunch to the members at a reduced fee and, in exchange, was able to cater functions at the club and off-premise, for club members, using the club's facilities. The profits were retained by the caterer.

SELECTING A CATERING COMMISSARY

Not all prospective off-premise caterers will be operating from a restaurant, hotel, club, or other regular food service operation, or from a kitchen located in a church or other facility. This section is directed at off-premise caterers who are evaluating commissary locations.

Ability to Pay The best values are found in the industrial areas, located near expressways or major thoroughfares. Rents in industrial areas are fairly inexpensive and accessibility to major highways facilitates deliveries. The site should be clean and safe, but it need not have a prestigious storefront, or be located in the center of town, since few (if any) clients will visit the commissary. Most off-premise catering sales are made with the client at the location of the event, or in the client's home or office.

A good rule of thumb is that the total annual rent not exceed 10 percent of projected annual sales. For example, a new off-premise caterer who expects to generate $100,000 in sales during the first year of operation should keep rent for the year at $10,000 or less.

Most small-to-medium off-premise caterers can operate in facilities ranging from 1,000 to 2,000 square feet.

Key Points to Negotiate The best leases are those that are short-term with renewal options. For example, a lease for one to two years with two five-year renewal options would be ideal for most off-premise caterers.

Leases should be assignable, meaning that if an off-premise caterer wishes to allow another party to assume the lease, the landlord will allow this.

When inspecting the proposed site, consider the following:

Are there any leaks in the roof or elsewhere?
Where will the staff park?
Is there a delivery door for receiving and shipping foods?
Is there plenty of lighting?
How is the nearby traffic during rush hours?
Who pays for remodeling?
Are there adequate storage areas?
Is there accessibility for a dumpster?
Is it secure?
Is the air conditioning and ventilation acceptable?

Engaging an Attorney It is imperative to hire an attorney who will review the lease as well as ensure compliance with all legal requirements such as zoning, signage, and other matters. Above all, never commit to a lease agreement until all aspects of the lease have been thoroughly reviewed. This is one area where haste can result in huge financial obligations.

CATERING CONTRACTS

Overview Off-premise caterers should develop a catering contract prior to starting an off-premise business. An attorney should review the contract to ensure it meets basic requirements.

Before discussing the specific elements of a catering contract, there are some elements that are critical to an off-premise caterer's understanding of and involvement with contracts, according to Donald A. Blackwell, Esquire.[3]

1. "Have a working knowledge of what constitutes a binding contract and how a court is likely to construe its terms." A contract is a definite agreement between two or more competent people or parties to do or refrain from doing some lawful thing. The difference between a contract and pure negotiations is that there must be a meeting of the minds on all essential terms and obligations. For example, a caterer's proposal to perform service only becomes a contract when signed and agreed to by the client.

2. "Be specific." Each contract should be clear and unambiguous. No one should ever sign a contract that contains blanks. The failure to be specific about what an off-premise caterer plans to do could be very embarrassing on the night

of the event if the client expects something different. A roast beef dinner to the caterer might mean top round, while the client may be expecting beef tenderloin. The caterer should be as specific as possible regarding quantity, quality, and method of preparation.

3. "Know the three general theories upon which caterers can be held liable."

Breach of Contract—Caterers agree to perform a service and they do not do so.
Third-Party Liability—Caterers must use reasonable care, or they can be charged with negligence.
Statutory Violations—Caterers fail to follow laws such as adherence to fire codes or service of alcoholic beverages.

Off-premise caterers may be involved in assisting clients with site selections, as well as subcontracting for certain accessory services such as music, entertainment, flowers, decor, valet parking, and other services relating to the party. Legally, as a general rule, off-premise caterers have a duty to exercise reasonable care for the safety and well-being of the guests attending the event. Although courts have not yet clearly defined the parameters of that duty, it can be safely assumed that they encompass:

The duty to investigate prospective party sites to insure that they are reasonably safe
A duty to investigate the service and safety records of prospective subcontractors of accessory services
A duty to warn clients and guests of known or reasonably foreseeable dangers

Off-premise caterers who fail to make a thorough safety inspection of a proposed party site before recommending its use, or recommend its use despite knowledge of certain potentially hazardous conditions, do so at their own risk. Similarly, caterers who fail to investigate the safety and service records of subcontracted suppliers substantially increase their risk of liability.

Introduction   A catering contract is a blueprint for performance of a catered event. It creates an obligation on the part of the caterer to perform certain services, and an obligation on the part of the client to pay for these services. A contract requires a degree of trust, but it also provides for legal recourse. Signed contracts may even be used as loan collateral.

Most off-premise caterers prepare proposals for catering, which spell out in detail all of the services that the caterer will provide at the party. Proposals will be discussed in depth in Chapter 9. For the purpose of this chapter, suffice it to say that a proposal that has been "agreed to" and signed by both the client and the off-premise caterer becomes a contract. Some caterers use separate formats for proposals and contracts, but this is not necessary in most cases.

Components of an Off-Premise Catering Contract

Off-premise catering contracts should include the following items as appropriate for the event.

1. *The caterer's name, address, phone, and fax number.*
2. *The client's name, address, phone, and fax number, and any other pertinent phone numbers.*
3. *The date of the contract.*
4. *The day and date of the catered event.*
5. *The starting and ending times for the party, as well as for other important events, such as dinnertime.*
6. *Minimum number of guests.* This is the fewest number of guests to which this contract price will apply. When a caterer quotes a price per-person for a minimum of 100 guests, this means that the per-person price will apply for 100 guests. If there are fewer than 100 guests, this minimum guarantee clause will give the off-premise caterer the right to raise the price per person. An extreme example of this would occur when a client and caterer agree to a price per person for a group of 100 guests, but one week prior to the event, the client advises the caterer that there will be only 25 guests in attendance. Reasonably, the caterer cannot be expected to cater this party for the same price per person. This clause gives the caterer the right to charge more per person.

   The number of guests attending an event is always an estimate. There are always last-minute changes that will affect the attendance. Approximate attendance figures can be determined by such factors as:
   ❑ How many attended the same event last year?
   ❑ Is it a business-related event where attendance is mandatory, or is it purely social where attendance is optional?
   ❑ Will there be celebrities or prominent guest speakers?
   ❑ Are there competing events held at the same time?
   ❑ Is there a charge for attending?
   ❑ What type of food and beverages are to be served?
   ❑ When is the event? Morning, afternoon, or evening?
   ❑ How long is the event?
7. *Date for final guarantee.* Four to seven days prior to the party date is standard for off-premise caterers. Many caterers require that their clients provide this guarantee in writing. Once this final guarantee is made, the client is required to pay for at least that number, even if fewer guests attend than guaranteed. This clause is essential to protect the off-premise caterer if fewer than expected guests attend. The caterer should not suffer financially when the client overestimates guest counts.
8. *Location of the event.* This should include as much detail as possible such as street address, building name, floor number, and any other information that will clarify the event's location.
9. *The menu selections.* This section should include all menu details discussed with the client. Nothing should be left out or assumed. Major menu or other changes should necessitate a new contract.

10. *Beverage arrangements.* This section should include a listing of the nonalcoholic beverages provided by the caterers, as well as verification of those alcoholic beverages to be supplied by the client. Of course, in those states where off-premise caterers may sell alcoholic beverages, this section would be modified as appropriate.

11. *Equipment.* This will include all equipment to be supplied by the caterer such as tables, chairs, linens, china, glassware, flatware, and other miscellaneous equipment such as dance floors, stages, bars, and tenting. This section should also address who is responsible for the loss or damage of equipment.

12. *Staffing.* Most off-premise caterers include in this category the number of staff to be provided, the hours they will work, how they will be attired, and the applicable charges for their services.

13. *Floor-plan and seating chart.* This is necessary for major events, which include many details.

14. *Accessory services.* This area of the contract will deal with items such as floral decor, music, valet parking, and other details that may be provided by either the off-premise caterer or the client.

15. *Other details.* This section may include services to be provided other than those already mentioned. For example, will the caterer provide meals for the band and other persons working the event?

16. *Method for determining headcount.* Headcounts for billing purposes can be determined in a number of ways, such as taking tickets, counting plates or napkin-rolled flatware, or keeping track at the door with a handheld counter or, in some larger events, by a turnstile. For those larger special events where this could be a sensitive issue, the method of determining the headcount should be included in the contract.

17. *Charges for additional guests above the guarantee.* This is generally a per-person charge, and in some instances may be less per person than for those included in the base price because the cost of serving these additional guests is generally less, since certain expenses may be fixed whether there are 100 or 150 guests. These expenses may include rental equipment such as bars, and buffets and kitchen labor. Sometimes, a caterer suspects that the client is underestimating the number of guests, only to raise the guarantee substantially on the day of the event, or the day before the event, creating undue hardship for the caterer and staff. In this situation, the off-premise caterer may wish to charge a higher per-person rate for those extra guests who are added at the last minute. This action will generate additional income, if not (hopefully) discourage clients from making last-minute additions.

    Some off-premise caterers agree to plan for a certain percentage over the guarantee. This percentage should be addressed in the contract.

18. *Deposit Policies.* Normally, off-premise caterers require an advance deposit upon signing the contract. This should be spelled out in the contract, along with the amounts and due dates for future payments. Deposits are a way of life in the social and corporate marketplace. They assist cash flow, and are

particularly helpful during the slower seasons when parties are minimal. Deposits are vital to a good contract. Deposit policies vary from caterer to caterer. In general, the larger and more expensive the event, the larger the deposit. Also, contracts signed many months or years prior to the date of the event will require smaller deposits than for those signed only a few weeks or months in advance of the event.

19. *Charges for extra hours.* Normally, the labor charges for extra hours are at a premium rate, since in many parts of the country catering staff are paid at a rate above their regular rate when parties go longer than planned. The astute off-premise caterer will always approach the client or person in charge of the event prior to going into extra hours. Entertainers should be instructed by the client and/or the off-premise caterer not to go into extra hours without first checking with one or the other.

There are some factors that affect overtime:
- ❑ Certain locations such as museums and historical sites have curfews that may eliminate the problem of overtime.
- ❑ A caterer who is slow serving a meal through no fault of the client cannot in good conscience charge overtime.
- ❑ Clients who are in high-rise office buildings should be advised that overtime charges will apply if the off-premise caterer is significantly detained from leaving after the event when elevators are not available (usually cleaning or moving people use them exclusively in the evening).

20. *Special instructions.* This section could include details such as:
- ❑ "Surprise party"—Use care when calling client.
- ❑ "Give special attention to Uncle Joe."
- ❑ "Serve Aunt Mabel light drinks."

21. *Off-premise caterer's policies regarding:*
- ❑ Leftover food
- ❑ Serving alcoholic beverages to minors and those who appear to be getting intoxicated
- ❑ Other applicable policies

22. *Certain legal statements such as:*
- ❑ "The signee has full authority to legally bind the client."
- ❑ "The client has read and understands the contract."
- ❑ "The off-premise caterer is not responsible for the personal property of the client and guests."

23. *Cancellation and refund policy.* This topic will be discussed in detail later in this chapter. Suffice it to say that the cancellation and refund policy should be clearly spelled out in the contract.

24. *Detailed list of charges.* This should include all charges pertinent to the contract including those for food, beverages, equipment, staff, accessory services, service charges, miscellaneous charges, gratuities, sales taxes, and totals.

25. *Signatures of the off-premise caterer, as well as the client.* In the case of weddings where brides, grooms and their families are involved, according to

Dr. Elio Belluchi, Professor of Law at Florida International University, "It is advisable for off-premise caterers to obtain as many signatures as possible on the contract, from both sides of the family, in case it is necessary to proceed with legal collection procedures. In most states, only contracts in writing are enforceable." Also, Dr. Belluchi advises that all changes in menu, other arrangements, and guaranteed counts be made in writing. "If it is not in writing, it never happened. Oral agreements are not enforceable if over certain amounts, which are determined by state statutes, or if they are not performed within one year from the making."

In conclusion, an off-premise catering contract should contain all of the necessary details in order to execute the catered event. Caterers should use care to include some legal details, but a contract that addresses every possible legal contingency would become a virtual volume of "legalese." Too much legalese may result in lost business with those clients who understand that catering an event involves some degree of mutual trust.

CANCELLATIONS AND REFUNDS

Cancellation policies should be spelled out in the catering contract. Most off-premise caterers at the time of a cancellation will have a client's deposit. Should all, some, or none of the deposit be refunded? There are no clear answers to this, but there are some questions that can be asked on a case-by-case basis that should lead to a reasonable solution:

Why is the cancellation occurring?
When is the cancellation occurring?
What are the "real losses" to the caterer in terms of food, other costs, and turned-away business?
How much is the caterer's time worth for planning the canceled event?

The main objective should be to maintain goodwill with the client. Most clients are understanding as long as they feel the caterer is fair and is not trying to take advantage of the situation.

In those circumstances where the cancellation is a year or more prior to the event, a good policy may be to refund the deposit as soon as the date is rebooked. In fact, a recent court case in New York ruled that unless the caterer could substantiate damages, the caterer was obligated to return the advance deposit, since the event was over three years away, and the court felt that this was plenty of time for the caterer to rebook the date.

Where bad weather threatens the event, the off-premise caterer should call the client two or three days beforehand and advise the client that it is necessary to procure and start preparing the food now. At this point, the caterer can give the client the option of cancelling or going ahead with the event with the realization that if the event is cancelled after the food has been purchased, the client will be charged for the food and related expenses at cost to the caterer. Under no circumstances should the caterer charge more than cost in this situation.

Where an event is canceled at the last minute due to a tragedy involving one of the principals, it is best to wait a period of time before discussing refunds.

It is inevitable that caterers will sooner or later fail to live up to the clients' expectations, and there will be a need for some form of refund or credit. It is always good policy for off-premise caterers when they make a mistake to bring it to the client's attention prior to the client bringing it to the caterer's attention. For example, a caterer during the busy holiday season forgot to bring one of the eight hors d'oeuvres to be served at a Christmas party. Assuming there is no time to correct the situation, it would be best for the caterer to advise the client of the problem prior to the party, offer some form of refund of credit, and make arrangements to augment the menu with another item that could be obtained perhaps from a local supermarket. The worst thing to do is say nothing and hope that the client does not notice. This is suicidal, and will most definitely result in loss of future business with that client, as well as perhaps receiving even less for the party than from simply offering a credit in advance.

CONCLUSION

An understanding of legalities and contracts is essential for success in this business. One mistake in this area can cost a caterer his or her business or livelihood. This chapter advises readers of many legal requirements; its intent is not to replace professional legal counsel, but only to make readers aware of the myriad legal ramifications in the off-premise catering arena.

It is always smart to obtain professional legal advice before undertaking any business venture.

NOTES

1. Darrell VanLoenen and Joseph W. Holland, "Payroll Taxes and Personal Liability," *Florida International University Hospitality School Quarterly*, Spring 1993.
2. *Food Arts*, December 1993, p. 63.
3. Donald A. Blackwell, Esq., Anania, Bandklayder and Blackwell, Miami, Florida, from a speech given in 1992.

Chapter 3

Menu Planning

According to Jerry Edwards, National Off-Premise Liaison for the National Association of Catering Executives, "Planning a menu that is creative, cost efficient, and a crowd pleaser is what subtly separates the great caterers from the good ones. To be a great caterer you must serve great tasting foods that can either be innovative or traditional."[1]

A properly planned menu is a major segment of an excellent catered event. An improperly planned menu can ruin it. Caterers who serve only half a tea sandwich for lunch to a collegiate football team will more than likely find themselves being used as tackling dummies after the meager repast.

In this chapter, you will learn ways to avoid unfortunate situations, as well as acquire a complete arsenal of menu-planning principles and techniques.

It is important to state at this juncture that this is not a cookbook. There are thousands of wonderful cookbooks available in libraries and bookstores that overflow with recipes that can be adapted for use in off-premise catering. This chapter will help train you to know what to look for when selecting recipes from these cookbooks for use at off-premise events.

PLANNING PRINCIPLES

Once the party site has been selected, the party-planning process starts with the menu. The menu determines the following:

Foods to be purchased
Staffing requirements
Equipment requirements
Off-premise facility layout and space utilization
Decor for buffets and food stations
Food production and preparation requirements
Alcoholic and nonalcoholic beverages

Since the menu generally starts the party-planning process, where does a caterer start? Most caterers agree that the first stage of menu planning involves asking the clients questions about how they perceive the menu, such as the following:

"How many guests are you expecting?"
"Is there a kitchen or other area for cooking?"

"Who are your guests? Are they male, female, or couples? What are their ages? Where do they reside? Are they sophisticated partygoers? Are there any socioeconomic, ethnic, or religious factors that might affect the menu?"

"Would you like your guests served while seated at a table, or would you prefer a buffet or food stations?"

"Are there any foods that you would particularly want served, or do not want served? Are there any special dietary needs?"

"What is the purpose of the event?"

"What will your guests be doing before and after your party?"

"Have you had this event in the past? And if so, what did you like and dislike about the menu and the food at prior events?"

"What would you like your guests to say about the menu and food after the event?"

"Are there any association affiliations?" (You would not serve chicken to the Cattlemen's Association.)

"Are there any corporate affiliations that might determine menu items?" (You would not serve Pepsi at a meeting of Coca Cola executives.)

"Are there any budgetary considerations?"

By asking these and other related questions, the off-premise caterer should be able to create a dialogue that will begin the menu-planning process. This dialogue, coupled with the caterer's knowledge of foods, will result in a menu for the event.

Menu planning can go from one extreme, where the client tells the caterer, "You know what I like; send me a menu," to the other extreme where the client already has a desired menu and is simply asking the caterer to provide a price. Most menu-planning scenarios fall between these two extremes. Most clients have some menu ideas but are looking for the caterer's opinion and advice.

As stated previously in this text, it is imperative to first qualify the client in terms of the date of the party, the number of guests, the location of the party, and the budget. By asking these questions first, the astute off-premise caterer will avoid using precious time discussing a menu for an event that is not feasible in the first place.

Another main consideration is the location of the event. An off-premise catering menu cannot be planned until the caterer knows the event's location, and the type of available kitchen facilities, if any. Lack of refrigeration, water, electricity, adequate cover, and ventilation will most definitely determine what type of cooking can be done at the site. For example, frying foods to order in a high-rise office building in an office without ventilation will fill the office with the smell of grease.

BASIC MENU CATEGORIES

Catered foods can be served at any hour of the day or night. Off-premise caterers are asked to serve before-sunrise breakfasts, midday lunches and brunches, evening dinners, post-theater desserts, box lunches, and myriad other types of foodservice. Menus vary depending on the caterers and the markets they serve. Menus also vary depending on the style of service; whether buffet, standup, or seated. The style of service will definitely be influenced by the purpose of the event, the allotted time for dining, and the location of the event, among other things.

Here are some basic types of special-event service:

Seated, served meals
Buffets
Food stations (action stations)
Standup cocktail parties
Combinations of the above

Seated, Served Meals   In planning menus for these events, caterers must serve foods that are suitable for serving at a table, either individually plated or from platters. Served meals may be preceded by cocktail receptions that may or may not include various hors d'oeuvres passed by servers, or appetizers presented at food stations and buffets.

The basic courses for a seated, served meal include:

Appetizer/soup course
Salad course
Sorbet (intermezzo)
Main course—entree, starch (optional), one or more vegetables and garnish
Cheese course
Dessert course
Coffee, decaf and tea course

There are endless variations to this format. In European-style menus, the salad is served after the main course, but prior to the cheese course. Many menus eliminate the appetizer course if there are many hors d'oeuvres. Some menus include a fish course in lieu of the appetizer or salad course. A sorbet course should be served only if there are two or more courses served prior to it. Many main course menus eliminate the starch, and include two or more vegetables.

Some clients prefer a combination of served and buffet-style courses. For example, a chilled soup appetizer could be served or preset at the tables, and then guests are served the main course buffet style. Another interesting variation is to serve at the table all courses except the dessert and coffee course. Many groups prefer to have their guests get up for dessert and coffee, so they can mingle with those guests from other tables. In this situation, desserts should be the sort that can be easily eaten (bite-size) while standing. Coffee should be served in some type of attractive mug to eliminate the need for a saucer.

Buffets   In buffet service, the guests are directed to the buffet table(s) where a variety of foods may be selected. Guests may help themselves or may be served by attendants. The advantages of offering a variety of foods, plus the need for fewer service staff make buffets very popular at off-premise events. When the client wants variety, this service system is more practical and cost effective than providing a served meal during which guests order à la carte from the menu. It is safe to say that buffet menus are the most popular for off-premise catered events due to budgets, client preference, cost, and facilities.

One of the most frequently asked questions by clients is: "Which is more expensive, a buffet or a served meal?" The answer to this varies from caterer to caterer. However, it can be stated that buffets require less labor to serve the food, but require more food quantities. A buffet table should be continuously replenished during service so as not to be empty after the last guest eats. Many caterers simply reply that the cost will depend on the menu choices, the level of service required, and other factors. There is no simple answer to this question. A buffet table filled with expensive seafood and beef tenderloins will cost more than a simple three-course chicken dinner. Conversely, a seven-course served meal including caviar, lobster tails, and crepes suzette cooked tableside will cost more than a buffet consisting of one simple salad, a chicken dish, rice, and a basic vegetable.

Buffets may or may not be preceded by hors d'oeuvres. If the latter is true, it is wise for the caterer to be prepared for guests to place more food on their plates than they would if they'd eaten a bit prior to the buffet.

A minimum presentation for the buffet would include one salad, one or two entree choices, one starch such as rice, potato, or pasta, one vegetable or a medley of vegetables, rolls (bread) and butter. Desserts and coffee may be put on a separate table, or on the same table, or may be served directly at the dining tables.

Food Stations   Food stations work well when food needs to be offered on different floors within a building, when international foods are offered, when the client wants people to mingle and move about, or when the client simply wants something different.

> Using the station concept allows (the caterer) to divide the food presentation into smaller components and still have impact; each station can make a statement of its own with decoration, colors, and menu. The station concept makes it possible to offer diverse menu items that you might not be comfortable placing on a single buffet table. It also divides the space and the guests so that the traffic flows smoothly and there are shorter lines. And finally . . . using stations will give the party a more casual feel.[2]

Some popular food station menus are the following:

Stir-fry. Raw and blanched vegetables and several types of marinated meats and sauces are cooked to order in a wok by a trained chef.

Fajitas. Thin strips of beef or chicken sauteed with green peppers and onions are served in a soft tortilla with condiments.

Pasta. Various types and shapes of cooked pasta are heated up on table-top stoves with a variety of sauces such as marinara, pesto, and cream. Italian bread and Caesar salad go well with pasta.

Gourmet Pizza Stations. Pizza crusts with a variety of toppings are cooked to order in a small oven or pizza oven.

Carving. One or more meats are carved to order as guests approach the station. Beef tenderloin, turkey breast, loin of pork, and rack of lamb are popular. Many caterers serve these meats on rolls or breads as sandwiches with appropriate sauces.

Dessert, Coffee and Cordials. A variety of pastries, fresh fruits, tarts, eclairs, cookies, and chocolate desserts are served with a variety of coffees. (Cordials and cognacs may also be served in accordance with state liquor laws.)

These are but a few of the hundred of station possibilities, which include Cajun foods, potato skins, fritters, Southwestern foods, Greek foods, Mexican foods, seafood raw bars, sushi, quesadillas, tempura, satay, Danish smorgasbord, crepes, ice cream and yogurt, hot or cold soups, miniburgers and hot dogs, and large tables filled with cut and whole imported cheeses, fresh fruits, and vegetables.

Many clients prefer to offer a limited number of food stations, with or without passed hors d'oeuvres, prior to a served meal. Others prefer to offer station foods throughout the evening, keeping the party less formal. Seating for all guests at a food station party is optional. Some clients prefer to have no seating, or seating for only a portion of the guests, which encourages more socialization. Other clients prefer that each guest has an assigned seat, with each place setting prepared with all of the necessary flatware and glassware.

Standup Cocktail Parties   In the United States, hors d'oeuvres are customarily served at cocktail parties which may or may not precede lunch or dinner.

> Russians call them *zakuski*; Greeks *mezze*; Spaniards, *tapas*; Italians, *antipasto*; Mexicans, *antojitos*; and Chinese, *dim sum*. Hors d'oeuvres is French for 'outside of work,' or food prepared 'outside' of the main course. . . . Hors d'oeuvres should be a feast of flavor, color and texture to be savored in one or two bites. Selections range from savory canapes to lavish spreads of crudities (raw seasonal vegetables), accompanied by a dipping sauce.[3]

Hors d'oeuvres may either be passed by food servers or may be placed on buffets. They should be bite-size and should be easily eaten. Cookbooks are filled with thousands of hors d'oeuvre selections. The location of the party will influence the hors d'oeuvre selection. For example, where cooking space is limited, cold selections are more practical. Honey coconut shrimp, which is a fried item, cannot be cooked to order and served in a high-rise office building with no ventilation. (Although, once a client insisted on conch fritters for a cocktail party on an office building's sixteenth floor. The fritters were cooked to order on the loading dock, transported up the passenger elevators, and served within minutes of cooking.) Please note that with fried foods it is important to serve them quickly since they quickly become dry, cold, and tasteless.

CATERING MENUS

Truth-in-Menu laws require that caterers and other menu planners correctly describe and represent their menus. Descriptions of portion sizes, grades of meat, brand names, points of origin (Maine lobster/Florida stone crabs), fresh versus frozen, and dietary terms such as *salt-free* must be accurate and not misleading. Frequently, guests who are allergic to certain foods will ask a server about the ingredients in a particular dish. It is of extreme importance that servers possess the proper information regarding foods and their ingredients. They should be instructed to ask the kitchen staff or management prior to answering ingredient related food questions, since some people might become ill, or even die from eating certain ingredients.

Caterers who choose to make nutrition-content claims on menus must be able to support these claims in accordance with FDA guidelines. For example, if a caterer claims that a particular menu item is "light," the caterer would need to be able to prove that this particular menu item contains at least one-third fewer calories than the regular item. To support this claim, the caterer may need an expensive laboratory nutrient analysis. Before making claims, off-premise caterers should be aware of the costs involved in supporting these claims.

Most off-premise caterers prepare some form of preprinted menu. These may or may not be priced, depending upon the caterer's market. Usually, those caterers who market to the budget-conscious, lower-priced market will preprint prices. Upscale caterers who prepare food at the party location, and who prepare custom menus for each client, will generally not preprice their menus, but will provide price quotations for specific menus upon request.

Preprinted menus offer advantages such as the following:

1. The client can respond quickly by reading the menu and making selections without long consultations with the catering sales staff. This also minimizes the number of required sales staff.
2. These menus help "control" clients by giving them specific choices, rather than allowing clients the freedom to choose items at will.
3. The kitchen staff will be familiar with the menu, so they will work more efficiently.

Before off-premise caterers decide whether or not to preprint a menu, they should consider that printing can be very costly. Preprinted menus are certainly not as personal as a custom-prepared menu, and some customers may even perceive those caterers with preprinted menus as being uncreative. For those caterers who wish to offer a preprinted menu, but still wish to personally plan each menu, a good alternative is to offer a menu which simply lists some of the most frequently served menu items, without prices, and then custom-create a personalized menu with the client's input. Since there are no preprinted prices, astute caterers can price the menus based upon the current market prices of the food and the current market conditions for off-premise catered events. They may charge more when food costs are high, and when there is greater demand for catering services such as during the Christmas holidays, and less during slower periods when food costs are less and demand for catering is less.

Printed off-premise catering menus should not appear crowded, nor should the type be too small. Many excellent menus leave 50 percent blank space, with wide borders and space between listings for better readability. Menus should also include descriptions for items that are likely to be unfamiliar to the reader. The menus should also reflect the image that the caterer wishes to project. Menus printed on inexpensive paper will convey a different image than ones printed on 24-weight bond paper with gold inlays.

Exhibits 3-1 and 3-2 are actual menus used by off-premise caterers in South Florida. Note that neither menu shows prices. Menus without prices can be printed in large quantities and used for years, using inserts to announce new, not-on-the-menu items.

PLANNING GUIDELINES

There are no strict, do-or-die rules for planning off-premise catering menus. There are always exceptions which result from regional preferences, the client's desire for something innovative, and the capabilities of the caterer and staff. For example, most caterers would not advise serving chocolate souffles to a group of 500 dignitaries at an off-premise location with no kitchen; however, there are caterers who have perfected this technique, and are able to serve 500 souffles at the peak of perfection.

As a rule, it is always better to keep off-premise catering menus as simple as possible. When planning menus with clients, off-premise caterers should strive to create menus with the following characteristics:

They have worked well for past events.
The staff has prepared them before for groups of approximately the same size.
They feature signature dishes for which the caterer is known.
They feature locally grown and raised foods. California caterers might feature abalone and artichokes, while those from Florida could feature stone crabs and key lime pie.

Some clients request that their guests be offered a choice of entrees at a seated, served meal. For example, they will ask that a caterer offer the guest a choice of fish, beef, and chicken dishes. These clients request that the caterer take orders from each guest on the night of the function. This procedure may seem impractical because it requires the caterer to have extra portions of each entree item and to have extra staff in order to take and serve the special orders. If the client's budget allows for the extra cost, most off-premise caterers should comply with the request. If the budget does not allow for the extra expense, it is far better to convince the client to offer a buffet meal, whereby the guests can choose from a variety of entrees. Another option is to offer a multiple entree with smaller portions of two of more entrees on each plate. However, if the client

HORS D'OEUVRES MENU

CHILLED SEAFOOD

Jumbo Shrimp with Cocktail Sauce
Shrimp wrapped in Snowpeas with Honey Mustard Sauce
Lobster Medallions with Mustard Sauce
Mediterranean Swordfish in Endive
Smoked Trout Mousse English Cucumber Golden Caviar
Smoked Salmon and Avocado Sushi Rolls
Smoked Salmon Pate
Chilled Poached Scallops with Blueberry Mayonnaise
Grilled Swordfish, Tuna or Halibut Skewers Ginger Garlic
Salmon Mousse in Cherry Tomatoes, Belgian Endive,
    Cucumber Rounds and Peapods
Skewered Tortellini and Mussels Marinara
Cherry Tomatoes with Sour Cream and Red Cavair
Pasta Shells Stuffed with Scallop Seviche
Cherry Tomatoes with Smoked Oysters and Clams
Mussels in Red Pepper Sauce
Smoked Salmon with Capers, Onions and Cream Cheese
Fresh Florida Stone Crabs with Mustard Sauce

HOT SEAFOOD

Honey Coconut Shrimp
Scallops Wrapped in Bacon
Poached Scallops in White Wine with Dill Sauce
Fresh Fried Scallops with Shallot Sauce
Crabmeat and Conch Fritters Pineapple Piquant Sauce
Fresh Grouper Fingers with Cocktail Sauce
Mushrooms Filled with Crabmeat
Maryland Crabcakes with Orange Tarragon Mayonnaise
Grilled Shrimp Kebabs with Orange, Plum, Lemon or Chile-
    Apricot Sauce
Skewered Shrimp Wrapped in Bacon
Grouper Fingers in Beer Batter or Tempura Style
Mushroom Stuffed with Minced Clams
Cajun Seafood in Pastry
Crabmeat Imperial Barquettes
Seafood Stuffed Mushrooms
Shrimp in Almond Batter with Orange Mustard Sauce
Shrimp Tempura

COLD ASSORTED

Assorted Figs, Melons and Pears Wrapped in Proscuitto and
    Smoked Turkey
Rolled Smoked Ham with Cashews and Cream Cheese
New Potatoes Filled with Sour Cream and Caviar
Blue Corn Tortillas with Jalapeno Jelly and Cream Cheese
Fresh Fruit Skewers with Poppyseed Dip
Snow Peas with St. Andre Cheese
Skewered Ham with Papaya
Grilled Chicken Fingers with Honey Mustard Sauce
Pate on Apple Slices with Cornichons

HOT ASSORTED

Chicken Fingers with Raspberry Sauce
Curried Chicken Spring Rolls with Apricot Dip
Beef Sirloin and Onion Kebabs
Beef Sirloin on Pita with Basil Sauce
Hearts of Artichoke Tempura with Bearnaise

Date and Almond Rumaki
Bacon Wrapped Chutney Bananas
Mushrooms Filled with Sweet Italian Sausage
Mushrooms Filled with Brie and Pistachios
Miniature Quiches-Lorraine, Spinach and Broccoli
Spring Lamb Kebabs with Fresh Mint Sauce
Veal Picadillo in Baby Pattypan Squash
Mushrooms and Zuchinni with Herbed Dipping Sauce
Pineapple Cubes and Waterchestnuts Wrapped in Bacon
Wild Mushroom Pate in Mushroom Caps
Miniature Lamb Chops with Candied Mint Garlic Sauce
Skewered Veal Nuggets with Salsa Verde
Pecan Stuffed Mushrooms
Mushrooms Stuffed with Walnuts and Cheese
Mexican Chicken Fingers with Guacamole Sauce
Skewed Peanut Chicken
Miniature Cuban Sandwiches
Appetizer Pizza Squares
Cheese Mushroom Fingers
Mushrooms Florentine
Curried Chicken, Papaya and Pineapple Kebabs
Veal and Prune Kebabs
Philippine Lumpia with Sweet and Sour Dressing
Chicken Tempura
Vegetable Tempura

STATIONS AND DISPLAYS

Bills' display of cut and whole fresh fruits, crudites and assorted dips, pates, cut and whole imported cheeses, crackers, custom baked breads with your logo or special design and deluxe mixed nuts.

Carving Stations - tenderloin or sirloin of beef, honey baked hams, smoked or regular breast of turkey with assorted sauces to include basil horseradish, bearnaise, honey mustard and cranberry orange - mini rolls.

Pasta Stations - choose from our famous moroccan (spinach, pinenuts, chicken breast, raisins, linguine, lemon and white wine), fettucine alfredo. seafood, tortellini with shallot butter sauce, primavera shells with gorgonzola cheese sauce and ziti marinara.

Raw Bar in Dinghy Boat - our twelve foot dinghy boat filled with your choice of shrimp, lobster tails, stone crabs, oysters, clams, conch salad and special sauces.

Other Stations include fajitas, shrimp scampi, veal scallopine and for the casual affair, potato skins, tacos and fritters.

EXHIBIT 3-1 Catering Menu

MAIN MENUS

FIRST COURSES

HOT SOUPS - Lobster Bisque, Bisque of Bay Scallops, She Crab, Seafood Chowder, Cream of Watercress and Cream of Avocado
CHILLED SOUPS - Vichysoisse, Gazpacho, Cream of Watercress, Lemon-Orange Broth and Chilled Cucumber
Shrimp William
Shrimp Scampi
Fresh Florida Stone Crabs with Mustard Sauce
Fresh Florida Lobster Tail
Poached Fresh Salmon with Dill Sauce
Smoked Trout with Onions and Capers
Seafood Gazpacho with Shrimp and Crabmeat
Mushrooms with Escargot
Scallop Seviche
Pasta with Lobster and Tarragon
Antipasto Plate
Tomato Fettucine with Snowpeas Alfredo
Marinated Scallops with Coconut and Sour Cream
Pasta Shells Stuffed with Scallop Seviche
Angel Hair Pasta with Gold, Red and Black Caviar
Tortellini with Vegetables in Green Mexican Salsa
Breast of Duck with Angel Hair Pasta in Hazelnut-Raspberry Dressing
Angel Hair Pasta with Chevre
Fettucine Alfredo
Pasta with Lobster and Shrimp
Ratatouille
Angel Hair Pasta with Roquefort Sauce
Fettucine with Smoked Salmon

SALADS

Caesar with Pumpernickle Croutons
Spinach with Sweet and Sour Dressing
Marinated Mushrooms with Red Wine and Fennel
Three Green Salad with Brie
Mixed Greens with Shredded Gruyere
Snowpeas with Walnut Vinaigrette
Everglades - a Mixture of Greens, Watercress, Hearts of Palm and Artichoke, Mandarin Oranges, Radiccio and Vinaigrette
Mandarin Duck Salad
Bouche Salad - Heart of Palm, Asparagus, Cherry Tomato, Fresh Sliced Mushroom, Greens, Kiwi and Vinaigrette
Chicken, Avocado and Papaya Salad
Persian Fruit Salad
Greek Salad
Bibb Lettuce and Hearts of Palm Vinaigrette
Iceberg Roquefort Wedges
Layered Mozzarella and Beefsteak Tomato Salad
Minted Fruit Salad
Papaya and Avocado Salad
Pesto and Farfalle (Bowtie) Pasta Salad
Creamy Ziti Salad
Hearts of Romaine with Tomato, Artichoke Hearts and Stilton
Boston Bibb Lettuce with Oranges and Scallions Vinaigrette
Three Pasta Salad with Smoked Salmon

Spinach Salad with Enoki Mushrooms and Pinenuts Vinaigrette
Florida Palm Salad with Pineapple, Dates, Ginger and Peanut Butter Dressing
Tortellini with Dijon Mustard Vinaigrette
Royal Palm Chicken Salad with Pasta, Shrimp, Pineapple and Peaches
Lobster Salad
Swordfish, Pasta and Pecan Salad
Conch Salad
Crabmeat Salad
French Potato Salad with Bacon
Salad Nicoise
Tarragon Chicken Salad
Hearts of Palm Vinaigrette
Shrimp and Green Bean Salad
Potato and Sausage Salad
Jamaican Fruit Salad
Kiwi Salad
Apple Salad with Rum Raisin Dressing

BEEF

Roast Tenderloin of Beef - choose from Three Peppercorn Sauce, Bearnaise Sauce or Wild Mushroom Sauce
Sauteed Medallions of Beef with Three Mustard Sauce
Roast Prime Ribs of Beef Au Jus
London Broil with Mushroom Sauce
Broiled Center Cut New York Strip Steak with Mustard Cream
Broiled Filet Mignon with Mushroom Caps and Shallots
Beef Wellington

SEAFOOD AND FISH

Broiled Fresh Florida Lobster Tails with Lemon Butter
Fresh Florida Stone Crabs with Mustard Sauce
Broiled or Baked Red Snapper, Grouper or Dolphin - choose from Walnut Sauce, Butter Shallot Sauce, Fromage, Mango Peach, Tomato Cream or Blackened
Poached Salmon with Basil Cream Sauce
Scallops in Cream and Mustard Sauce
Shrimp Creole with Steaming White Rice
Grilled Swordfish Steak on Mesquite
Shrimp Dijon
Shrimp Scampi
Scallops Singapore with Ginger, Sherry and Scallions

EXHIBIT 3-1 (continued)

POULTRY

Boneless Breast of Chicken - choose from Indonesian Spiced, Veronique with Grapes, Raspberry, Lemon, Champagne, Apricot-Currant, Blueberry Glazed, Dijon, Apricot Fantastic, Shrimp with Tomato Sauce, Barbequed with Ginger, Artichoke, Blue Cheese, Sausage Stuffed, Applejack Sauce, Bourbon Sauce, Curried Cream, Sesame Coated, Stuffed with Spinach and Ricotta, Thai Peanut Sauce with Angel Hair, Apples and Cream, Mango Chutney, Fig Sauce, Italiano, Tarragon Cream, Cream Cheese-Scallions-Lemons, Sesame with Apricot, Coconut with Fresh Fruit, Carmelized Apples, Sesame with Orange Currant, and Marbella

Broiled Duckling with Orange or Raspberry Sauce

Fruit or Cranberry Stuffed Rock Cornish Game Hens

Rock Cornish Game Hen with Tarragon Cream Sauce

Quails Baked in Pear Halves

Roast Pheasant with Sour Cream Sauce

VEAL

Veal Scallops - choose from Marsala, Ginger Lime, Basil, Mustard Cream, Francese or Plum

Veal Medallions with Three Peppercorn Sauce

Roast Veal with Spring Vegetables

Veal Breast Stuffed with Baked Ham and Smoked Provolone

Veal Chop with our Special Mustard Cream Sauce

OTHER ENTREES

Rack of Lamb with Fresh Mint Sauce

Grilled Lamb Medallions with Candied Garlic

Mesquite Grilled Boneless Leg of Lamb with Mint Chutney Sauce

Roast Loin of Pork with Carmelized Apples or Black Currants

Broiled Filet Mignon with your choice of Shrimp

Medallions of Pork

POTATOES, PASTA AND SUCH

Potatoes Fontecchio-Roast New Potatoes with Garlic, Mint, Oil and Freshly Ground Black Pepper

Dilled New Potatoes, Twice-Baked Potatoes with Cheddar Cheese and Chiles

Duchess Sweet Potatoes with Bananas

Sweet Potatoes with Cider and Brown Sugar

Potatoes with Cheese and Onions

Duchess Potatoes

New Potatoes with Black Caviar

Baked Stuffed Potatoes with Bacon

Thanksgiving Mashed Potatoes

Praline Sweet Potatoes

Potato Puffs

Fettucine Alfredo

Angel Hair with Fine Herbs

Tortellini with Shallot Butter Sauce

Linguine with Red Cream Sauce

Linguine with Tomatoes and Basil

Linguine with Zucchini, Broccoli and Tomatoes

Pasta with Gorgonzola Cheese Sauce

Pasta with Mushrooms and Port

Pasta with Green Peppercorn Butter

Pasta Shells with Fontina Pesto Cream

Nutted Wild Rice

Brown Rice with Herbs

Wild Rice with Almonds and Raisins

Curried Rice

Special Rice with Lemon Grass and Coconut

Brown Rice Risotto

Oriental Fried Rice

Yellow Rice with Raisins

FRESH VEGETABLES

Stir Fried Broccoli with Ginger and Garlic

Broccoli with Lemon Butter and Pinenuts

Stir Fried Vegetable Medley

Green Beans with Hazelnuts, Sesame Seeds or Cashews

Tomato Stuffed with Vermecelli Pesto

Tomato Stuffed with Spinach and Riccota Cheese

Tomato Florentine

Sauteed Asparagus with Sesame Seeds

Fresh Jumbo Asparagus in Season with Shallot Butter

Sauteed Cherry Tomatoes

Ginger Candied Carrots

Hunter Style Carrots with Prosciutto and Madeira

Zucchini Parmesan with Basil and Pinenuts

Zucchini with Linguine, Broccoli and Tomatoes

Zucchini with Carrot Rounds and Fresh Mint

Zucchini Baked with Parmesan Cheese

Zucchini with Lemon

Sugar Snap Peas with Mint

DESSERTS

Strawberries Saboyan

Apple or Cheese Strudel

White Chocolate Mousse in a Chocolate Shell

Pears Stuffed with Gorgonzola

Poached Pears with Grand Marnier or Kirsch Saboyan

Cannoli with Raspberry Sauce and Shaved Chocolate

Caramel Custard

Pecan Tarts

Fresh Fruit Tarts

Raspberry Cream

Banana Rum Mousse

Kiwi and Strawberry Tartlets

Chocolate Pecan Tartlets

Candy Apple Walnut Pie

Peanut Butter Cream Fudge Pie

24 karat Cake

Black Forest Cake

Cheesecake with Fresh Fruit

Marble Fudge Cheesecake

Amaretto Cheesecake

Chocolate Banana Twin Ganache Cake

Key Lime Mousse Pie

Swiss Chocolate Mousse Pie

Ganache of Banana, Chocolate, Strawberry, Cappuccino or Amaretto

EXHIBIT 3-1 *(continued)*

EXHIBIT 3-2
Catering Menu Contemporary Caters, Inc.

CONTEMPORARY CATERERS, INC.
275 S.W. 14th AVENUE
POMPANO BEACH, FLORIDA 33069
Broward/Boca Raton 942-2617
305 942-2617
MENU

BEVERAGE SERVICE
Client will provide all Alcoholic Beverage, Caterer will provide complete Bar
Set-Ups to include: Ice, Beverage Napkins, Stirrers, Coke, Diet Coke, 7-UP,
Tonic Water, Club Soda, Ginger Ale, Orange Juice, Grapefruit Juice, Cran-
berry Juice, Bloody Mary Mix, Lemons, Limes, Cherries, Olives and Onions.

BUFFET
Crudite of Garden Vegetables with Dip

Imported and Domestic Fancy Cheese Display to Include:
Imported Saga Blue Cheese and French Delice Camembert with Herbs
Baked French Brie with Amaretto and Almonds
Diced Cheddar, Munster, and Swiss Cheeses served with
Imported Gourmet Crackers and French Bread Slices

Eggplant Capanata with Pita Points

A Uniformed Chef Will Hand Carve at the Buffet:
Please Select (2)
Sirloin of Beef with Beârnaise Sauce and Horseradish Remoulade
Roast Breast of Maryland Turkey with Cranberry Pecan Relish
Whole Legs of Smoked Baked Ham with Dijon Sauce
Served on assorted Mini-Rolls

Our Pasta Chef will Saute Fresh Garden Vegetables and Serve as a
Pasta Topping or a Great Additional Low Calorie Side Dish
with
Penne Pasta with Fresh Tomato, Garlic and Basil Sauce
Fettuccine Alfredo

Italian Bread Display with Butter

insists on a seated, served meal with a choice of the entree, the client should take
orders in advance and provide them to the caterer a few days prior to the event
along with a list of seat assignments for each guest.

Well-planned menus should consider the appropriateness of food flavors,
colors, textures, and shapes. Too much of any one of these components is not

good. Flavors should be interesting with some highlights, but not too tart or pungent. Natural colors such as red, red-orange, peach, pink, tan, brown, butter-yellow, and light green are good. Contrasting textures such as crispy croutons in a salad add interest and excitement to the menu. Interesting shapes are always welcome, as long as they are not all the same. For example, a plate with round sliced tomatoes, round sliced beef tenderloin and round scoops of potato salad and cole slaw are not as visually appealing as when these items are presented differently, perhaps by layering the tenderloin slices on a bed of radicchio, cutting the tomatoes into wedges, and serving the cole slaw and potato salad in cut-out vegetables.

Here are some additional guidelines for menu planning:

1. Serve foods that are popular. For example, prime ribs of beef will be better received by more guests than fillet of shark. *Restaurants and Institutions* magazine publishes an annual list of those food items that are the most popular. This list can be very helpful when developing catering menus.

2. Butlered (passed) hors d'oeuvres should be one or two bites, and not messy to eat. Passing hors d'oeuvres makes it much easier to control consumption, rather than holding them in chafing dishes where a few guests may overindulge and leave only scraps for the rest of the group. The quality of cooked-to-order, hot, passed hors d'oeuvres is usually superior to those that are cooked in advance and held in chafing dishes.

3. Use caution not to duplicate items on the menu, such as serving stuffed pea pods as an appetizer, and then again as the vegetable; or lobster bisque as the first course, and lobster tails as the entree.

4. Be aware of the capabilities of the kitchen staff, and develop menus that are compatible with the capabilities of the staff. A caterer who specializes in chicken and ribs does not need a five-star chef. A caterer who specializes in gourmet dinners will not be successful with a short-order cook as head chef.

5. Astute caterers consult with their chefs when planning menus with clients. Off-premise caterers need to know "when to say no" to unusual client demands. There are two sides to this situation. If caterers say "no" they may lose the client, or at least appear as being uncooperative. If the caterer says "yes," the kitchen may have difficulty producing the food. Unusual requests should be honored when possible, particularly during slower seasons, and for smaller-size groups. The busy holiday season is not a time to experiment.

6. There are no hard-and-fast rules for the number of items on a buffet, or the number of courses in a seated, served meal. The foods and courses can range from a few to several. Smart caterers always remember the "big picture" when planning courses. What is the purpose of the event, and what will satisfy the majority of the guests?

7. No menu is complete without including the appropriate beverages with the meal, whether it be a wine to accompany a particular course, coffee with dessert, or perhaps imported vodka with caviar.

8. Garnishing food is an art that is frequently overlooked. When planning menus, garnishes should be considered along with the main dish. Many

caterers garnish plates with herbs and ingredients used in preparing the dish. Others may wish to garnish with items that add color and/or enhance the appearance of the plate.

9. According to Judy Lieberman, off-premise caterer and author of *The Complete Off-Premise Caterer:*[4]

[a] seated meal must be planned so that each course pleases the palate in such a way that, while each one is enjoyed, the next can be anticipated and savored in its turn. A well-prepared formal meal builds to a crescendo with the main course, then tapers gently off to a sweet finish at the end of the meal. Guests should feel beautifully fed, not overstuffed or glutted with too many rich courses. Neither should they feel bored by repetition or confused by a series of intense and conflicting tastes.[4]

FOOD TRENDS

Off-premise catering is affected by food trends. Some off-premise caterers refuse to acknowledge the trends, and continue to operate successfully while serving the same food from decades past. Other caterers offer menus that are on the "cutting edge of food trendiness." There is room in most markets for caterers from both of these extremes, as well as those who offer some of both styles.

Most clients are budget conscious. In this decade, and into the next century, there certainly will be a strong demand for value. Clients will look for less expensive alternatives to the high-flying foods of the 1980s. Perhaps top round in lieu of tenderloin or chicken instead of steak will please the client. These same clients are very conscious of diet and nutrition, asking for dishes that meet their criteria for fitness to be low in fat, high in fiber and include fresh foods. (Many of today's clients are alternivores, who eat meat in very limited quantities.) Some of these items include:

Sausages made with veal, chicken, or turkey

Club sandwiches with fresh salmon fillet

Vegetarian meals encrusted in puff pastry

International foods such as sushi, Thai food, and other oriental dishes that are low in fat

Food free from harmful pesticides

Fusion dishes that combine foods from two or more countries or regions, such as burritos filled with sweet and sour pork

Less red meat and more starches (pasta, potatoes, and rice), fresh vegetables, and fresh fruits

Exotics such as buffalo meat, which are expensive, but very low in fat; rabbit, which is low in cholesterol and calories; and even ostrich, which is fast-becoming a very profitable bird to raise

In spite of the desire for healthy foods, many clients and guests wish to reward themselves after watching their food intake for a week. This reward can be in the form of a rich, calorie-laden dessert. Cookies and cheesecake are very popular. Others may wish to enjoy a thick porterhouse steak at the end of a week of eating every imaginable chicken dish. On Monday, it's back to chicken and yogurt, but at a weekend dinner, for many, it's time to indulge.

People planning catered events are looking for food they cannot prepare at home. They look for foods that are casual, convenient, comfortable, and creative. They want simple elegance without the frills.

The 1990s and beyond will see more of these items on off-premise catering menus:

Farm-raised fish and shellfish (aquaculture)
Foods irradiated to kill bacteria
Foods that have been genetically engineered to improve them, such as strawberries infused with halibut genes to keep them from freezing
Tofu
Eggplant and mushrooms as meat substitutes
Black beans, lentils, and other beans
Purple potatoes
Organic produce
Pitahaya—a sweet and mild fruit of an exotic cactus
A new fuzzless kiwi the size of a grape that is entirely edible
Cherimoya—a large, green, cone-shaped fruit with a delicious custardlike interior
Kiwano—a golden-yellow horned melon with the flavor combination of banana, cucumber, and lime
Miniature iceberg lettuce
Saigon red pineapple—great for centerpieces, but not sweet enough to eat
Foods containing fake fats such as "olestra" and "trailblazer"; they taste similar to fat but contain no fat

---

STARTER COURSE

Lemon Vermicelli with enokie mushrooms and julienne snow peas in a coriander, ginger and basil pesto

ENTREE

Pan-Fried Polenta with roasted corn and avocado salsa
Baked Phyllo Purse with red chard, feta and pine
nuts on a roasted orange bell pepper sauce
Grilled Eggplant, Fennel, Red Pepper, Asparagus and Shiitake Mushrooms
brushed with balsamic vinaigrette

DESSERT

Pecan Shortcake with caramel-pumpkin ice cream and poached red Indian peaches

---

The preceding is a vegetarian menu developed by a vegetarian chef, and printed in the August 1990 issue of *Special Event*:[5]

This type of menu is becoming increasingly popular, and may be standard fare in the next century. Off-premise caterers in the 1990s should begin to learn about vegetarian foods, since currently over 7 percent of the U.S. population is vegetarian, and this percentage is certain to grow as Americans age and continue to become more health conscious. Caterers should develop some outstanding vegetarian dishes that can be offered to clients along with the standard non-vegetarian menu. It is important to note that vegetarian food can taste good. There are numerous vegetarian cookbooks available in libraries and bookstores throughout the country.

COMPUTING FOOD QUANTITIES

After planning a proposed menu with a client, the next step for the off-premise caterer is to determine the various quantities and portion sizes for the menu items. This is necessary not only in order to be able to calculate the cost of the menu, but also to determine food quantities that are needed for purchasing, preparation, and production purposes.

Computing how much people will eat is to some degree guesswork, but after caterers have catered a number of events they begin to develop certain standards for consumption. Astute caterers will keep food production and consumption records of prior events, and by coupling these past histories with current requirements they can begin to better determine food quantities for future off-premise events.

Too much food is always better than too little. Caterers should never run out. Extra food is necessary for a number of reasons:

Staff make mistakes—spills, overcooking, miscounting food items.

A few extra guests may attend.

Guests may be unusually hungry.

There may be special, unforeseen requests. It may be necessary to feed other people at the last minute at the client's request, such as the musicians. Also, most off-premise caterers, at their own expense, feed their catering staff party food.

There should be a general comfort level for the caterer and staff. There are few worse feelings than worrying whether or not there will be enough food to feed the guests. Every caterer at one time or another has had to reduce portion sizes during the dishup period to insure that there is enough for everyone. This is no fun!

There is one main rule for computing food quantities: Don't guess who is coming to dinner—*know* who is coming to dinner!

There are many true stories about caterers who were expecting one type of group, and were horrified when another type arrived. The off-premise caterer who says to the client, "Don't worry, I know what your group will like!", may be asking for trouble, particularly if the caterer plans a meal high in cholesterol for a group whose members are all on the Pritikin diet.

Some major criteria for planning food quantities include the following:

What will be the average age of guests?
Are they male or female?
Where were they before, and where are they going after the event?
Are they from out-of-town on holiday, or local?
Are they sophisticated partygoers or occasional partygoers?

The local, sophisticated partygoers will eat less than the person from out-of-town who infrequently goes out. Those guests that have eaten little all day, and who have been active will be much hungrier at dinnertime than those who have been inactive after a heavy lunch. Guests will eat more if food is served buffet style. They will eat less if the room is crowded since it will be difficult for them to reach the food tables.

Recordkeeping after each catered event will assist the off-premise caterer with future food quantities. A report that includes the following information will be very helpful:

Number of guests guaranteed and number of guests who attended
Quantities prepared of each menu item
Leftovers for each menu item
Any unusual factors that may have affected consumption
Recommended future changes to food quantities

Off-premise caterers armed with accurate records and a knowledge of the group will be able to more accurately determine food quantities.

So how much is enough? Experience generally shows that off-premise caterers as a rule should provide between 5 and 20 percent extra for each menu item. This percentage will vary based upon the group's guaranteed number and the potential for extra guests. The smaller the group the larger the percentage overage, and the larger the group, the smaller the percentage overage. An example follows:

NUMBER OF GUESTS GUARANTEED	PERCENT OVERAGE	ORDER FOOD FOR
20	20	24
50	15	58
100	10	110
200	7.5	215
400	5	420

Please note that this is a general guideline, and may vary from caterer to caterer and region to region.

Who pays for this extra food? The client does, since it is imperative that the caterer include this extra food in the cost calculation for the particular event. Specific techniques for costing will be discussed later in this text.

Rules of Thumb for Computing Food Quantities

Some general guidelines follow regarding suggested food quantities per person for various food items. Please be advised that these are only guidelines, and that food portions may vary from region to region, and from caterer to caterer.

ITEM	PORTION PER PERSON
Assorted hors d'oeuvres	4–8 pieces if before dinner
	8–12 pieces if served with food stations
	18–24 pieces if all evening with no dinner
Shrimp–large	1–2 pieces if passed as hors d'oeuvres
	4–12 pieces if on buffet
Soup (first course)	6–8 ounces
Salads	1–4 ounces
Meat, chicken, or fish (entree)	4–8 edible ounces
Starch, vegetables (entree)	2–4 ounces
Desserts	Varies—the richer the dessert, the smaller the portion

For the uninitiated, determining food quantities can be stressful and difficult. Inevitably, novice caterers will, at least once, err on the side of too little food, and they can only hope that there is a store or some backup plan available to fill the void before the guests notice.

Determining How Much Food to Order

After determining the portion sizes, the next step is to determine how much food to order. Most recipes are not written for the exact number of guests at an off-premise event. A knowledge of basic math is necessary in order to convert the recipe to serve the group size. A simple example of this would be as follows:

An off-premise caterer has booked a party for 100 guests. Allowing for a 10 percent overage, it will be necessary to prepare food for 110 guests. The caterer plans on serving four items, and the recipes for each one of these items are written to serve various numbers of guests. The off-premise caterer needs to convert these to feed 110. The recipes are written for 8, 12, 25 and 50 guests respectively. The conversion formula is to divide the number of required servings by the number of servings in the recipe to determine a factor as follows:

$$\frac{110}{8} = 13.75 \qquad \frac{110}{12} = 9.2 \qquad \frac{110}{25} = 4.4 \qquad \frac{110}{50} = 2.2$$

The next step is to multiply the factor times the various items in the recipe to determine the quantities of each recipe ingredient. If the recipe for 50 calls for 2 gallons of milk, for 110 guests multiply 2 gallons of milk times 2.2 to get 4.4 gallons of milk. For some ingredients, such as baking powder, baking soda, yeast, and some seasonings, the factor method will not always work since these and similar ingredients are increased or decreased proportionately. Caterers need knowledge in quantity food preparation techniques. Otherwise, experimentation before the event occurs is mandatory.

Determining Yields   Food quantities become more complicated when dealing with food items that need to be trimmed, cut, and processed before preparing. One example might be freshly cut fruit. How many strawberries, grapes, melons, and kiwis will it take to produce 10 pounds of freshly cut fruit. The best way to compute this is by trial and error, since yields vary tremendously from season to season. Each off-premise caterer develops formulas based on how much of each fruit type is used, the size of the fruit, and how much yield is expected on the average. Caterers who have few events and are close to a food store are better off ordering less, when yields are uncertain, and then going to the store if they run short during the production as long as there is ample time prior to the party. Busier caterers will more than likely have use for any extra products at future events. The formula for computing an amount to order is:

Serving Size Divided by the Yield Equals the
Raw Portion Size

or

$$\frac{\text{Serving Size}}{\text{Yield}} = \text{Raw Portion Size}$$

An example of this would be a caterer who wishes to serve an eight-ounce sirloin steak, which will be cut by the chef from top sirloin butts. The caterer knows that 50 percent of the top sirloin butt can be used for steaks after the fat is trimmed off. How much top sirloin butt is needed to prepare 110 steaks?

$$\frac{\text{Serving Size (8 ounces)}}{\text{Yield (50\%)}} = 16 \text{ ounces per Steak Before Trimming}$$

$$\text{For 110 Steaks 16 oz. each} = \frac{1760 \text{ ounces}}{16 \text{ oz/lb}} = 110 \text{ pounds of Top Sirloin Butt}$$

Sirloin butts average 15 pounds each, so if the caterer is only ordering sirloin butt for this event, he will need to compute the total number of pieces by dividing 110 pounds by 15 pounds average each, which equals 7.33 sirloin butts, which should be rounded up to 8 pieces, totaling approximately 120 pounds.

CALCULATING FOOD COST

The food cost for each menu item can be determined by multiplying the amount of each ingredient times the cost per unit for the ingredient. In the top sirloin example, if the top sirloin butt costs $2.50 per pound, the total cost for the top sirloin butt is:

$$120 \text{ pounds} \times \$2.50 = \$300.00$$

To determine the cost per steak, simply divide $300.00 by 110 steaks ($2.73 per steak).

The cost of the meal can be determined by simply adding the cost of each menu item to be served, including:

Hors d'oeuvres
Appetizer(s)
Soup(s)
Salad(s)
Intermezzo course
Entree(s)
Starch(es)
Vegetable(s)
Garnish(es)
Rolls/bread/butter
Dessert(s)
Coffee/decaf/tea/cream/sugar/low-calorie sweetener
Any other food costs (i.e., frying oil for cooking)

Later chapters will deal with the ramifications of food cost, as well as various methods for pricing menus.

LEFTOVERS

Obviously, there are no leftover foods if the caterer runs out of food. Good caterers do not run out of food. There may be an exceptional situation where extra guests are fed; however, normally there are leftovers. Buffets and food stations normally generate more leftovers than seated, served events since the buffet and station food tables need to look full when the last guests are served.

The majority of leftovers result from guests not showing up and the minority of leftovers result from the extra food that the caterer brings to serve extra guests over the guaranteed amount.

The disposition of leftovers can be a major problem for off-premise caterers. Do they leave them with the client, do they reuse them, do they throw them out, or do they donate them to charity? Most off-premise caterers have established policies for disposition of leftovers. Their policies may be to follow one or more of the following rules:

Throw Out   "When in doubt, throw it out." This rule should apply to any foods that have not been stored at temperatures below 40 F and above 140 F. There is no need to risk food poisoning. Foods that have been left out on buffets and foods that do not appear fresh should be discarded.

Foods that have been exposed to contamination should never be used again. Individual unwrapped portions of food that have been served to customers may not be used again.

It is important to note that it is not always possible to identify food spoilage by appearance, smell, or taste. Food may appear to be safe even when it contains large numbers of harmful microorganisms, or toxins.

Give to Client Normally, clients for home parties and small business parties ask for the leftovers. Some caterers comply with these requests, while others refuse. These caterers who refuse to leave leftovers take the position that they have no control over how the food will be handled after they leave. Perhaps the client may leave the potato salad for hours out in the heat, refrigerate it, eat it the next day, and become violently ill. Of course, the caterer gets the blame. Some caterers advise the client that the local health department prohibits them from leaving food behind. This makes the health department the villain, not the caterer.

Also, many caterers bring display foods such as large cheeses that are used for display purposes at a number of parties. These are not the client's property since the cost of these cheeses is normally not charged in total to any particular client, but prorated over a number of parties.

On the other hand, many off-premise caterers who cater wedding receptions frequently prepare a "goody basket" for the bride and groom to take to their hotel. Corporate clients for upscale events are usually not interested in keeping the leftovers; however, one exception may be company picnics, where most clients ask that their employees take home the extra food. (Bring plenty of aluminum foil and carryout containers to these events. One word of caution is never give food for take-home if there is any doubt as to its freshness, or how it will be handled.) There are caterers who ask that their clients sign disclaimers in case anyone becomes ill from leftover food. An attorney should be consulted prior to preparing a disclaimer form.

Reuse This can be very risky for those who are unfamiliar with various foods. For example, some caterers may reuse large blocks of cheese that have been on display, or meats that have been braised and kept cool, but they know not to reuse mayonnaise-based salad that has been left out, or other foods that spoil quickly.

If leftovers are to be reused, the staff should do the following:

1. Store them in well-covered, well-sealed containers. Shallow containers are best to facilitate quick cooling of foods.
2. Store cooked and processed foods above and away from raw foods to minimize the dangers of cross-contamination.
3. Cool hot food to 45 degrees Fahrenheit, then cover.
4. Clearly label containers to indicate their contents and when prepared.

Give to Homeless of Local Charity [The Good Samaritan Laws Passed in 1991] . . . makes it easier for [off-premise caterers] to give food to the needy without fear of liability. This law allows anyone in the food service industry to give food away to those less fortunate, such as "street people" and to churches and agencies that have meal programs for the homeless and poor, without fear of liability in the event of food poisoning.[6]

Many of these agencies will pick up food either at the party site, or at the caterer's commissary the day after the event. For large events, some caterers will schedule a food pickup at the party site, knowing that more than likely there will be leftovers. This can reduce the extra work of taking the food back to the commissary for storage until disposition.

Some caterers erroneously think that food given to charity can be written off as a charitable contribution. This is not the case, since the food originally was charged to the caterer's operation as an expense when it was purchased. Deducting it again would be a violation of federal tax law. The same holds true for corporate clients who are deducting the caterer's bill as a business expense. They cannot double-deduct it again as a contribution. Those clients who are not deducting the cost of the party may perhaps receive some tax credit when the food is donated to charity; however, they should first contact their accountant. Additional deductibility questions should be referred to a trained accountant.

Serve at Staff Meals   Many caterers allow their staff to eat the leftovers before they leave the party. Others bring special food for their employees, particularly if their staff eats prior to the start of the party. Most off-premise caterers do not permit their staff to take home the extra food because this may encourage staff to take home things other than legitimate leftovers.

Use at Other Facilities   Some off-premise caterers operate other facilities where leftovers may be reused. For example, a caterer who operates a restaurant may resell the leftover roast beef as a barbecued beef sandwich the next day. Extreme caution must be used when doing this to insure that the food has been properly handled. One way a caterer may do this is to keep any extra food packed under refrigeration, or in coolers. This food is usually the "extra" that is brought for those unusual situations. Some caterers call this "food insurance" for emergency use only. This food is kept out-of-view of the client, since many times the cost of this food has not been added into the cost of the party, and is only there for emergencies if extra guests arrive. Since this food is truly the caterer's property, it can very well be reused as long as it is properly handled.

Reward Helpful People   Those who are behind the scenes at the site and who assist the caterer are good candidates to receive food. The helpful security guard, the loading dock attendant who assists the caterer in entering and leaving the building, or the building engineer who helps out when a fuse blows should be rewarded. Food is always a wonderful reward, and is less expensive to the caterer than giving money.

In closing this section, it is imperative that each off-premise caterer establish a leftover policy in advance of the party and advise the client about this policy. By doing so, there should be no misunderstandings about leftovers after the party. There have been instances where off-premise caterers have catered parties to perfection and then have been blamed the next day for not leaving the leftover food.

NOTES

1. Jerry Edwards, *NACE News*, National Association of Catering Executives, p. 8.
2. Joyce Piotrowski, *Catering Business*, May 1990, p. 1.
3. Excerpted with the permission of *Restaurants & Institutions* magazine, November 12, 1992 © 1992 by Cahners Publishing Company.
4. Judy Lieberman, *The Complete Off-Premise Caterer* (New York: Van Nostrand Reinhold, 1991), p. 133, 134.
5. *Special Events* Magazine, August 1990, p. 35.
6. Reprinted with permission of the author, Miles Theurich, and the CommuniCATER, official publication of the National Caterers Association, February 1992, p. 1.

Chapter 4

Beverage Service

Off-premise caterers need to be knowledgeable about alcoholic beverages and the laws that affect their sale and service. Most full-service off-premise caterers serve alcoholic beverages, and in some states, sell alcoholic beverages at various off-premise locations. These caterers generate additional profits through the sale of mixers and ice, as well as by providing bar service personnel. Those that are licensed to sell off-premise also earn profits from the sale of alcoholic beverages.

Off-premise caterers are frequently asked by clients for advice on brands and quantities of alcoholic beverages. The caterer who has no clue in this area will certainly not inspire much confidence in the client, particularly when the proposal is being compared with another's in which the caterer recommends how much and what kind of wines, liquors, and beers. Expertise in this area can mean the difference between being selected or rejected.

Off-premise caterers are frequently asked to provide bartenders to serve alcoholic beverages, and this can result in certain legal implications under the laws in each state. Additionally, when providing bartenders, it is imperative that these personnel be knowledgeable in proper bar service techniques. Untrained bar staff reflect poorly on the off-premise caterer's reputation. Some off-premise caterers even go so far as to turn down business if clients provide their own bartenders, since they may not perform up to the caterer's standards, which would reflect poorly on the caterer. There have been instances where bar staff hired directly by clients at off-premise events have smoked cigarettes behind a bar, and the guests have assumed that they were part of the caterer's staff. This certainly does not enhance the off-premise caterer's reputation.

Astute off-premise caterers will learn as much as possible about beverage service, recognizing it as a possible source of additional income, as well as a function that, when not operated in accordance with state laws, can result in legal problems.

STATE LIQUOR LAWS

Each state has its own laws for the sale of alcoholic beverages. These laws do not always make sense, but they must be followed by off-premise caterers in each state. One law that applies in every state is that if an alcoholic beverage is sold, the vendor must have a license to sell it. The definition of the word "sold" means that money must change hands as a required condition of accessibility to the alcohol.

Students at Florida International University enrolled at the graduate level of the Catering Management course I taught recently requested information from each state regarding their laws for the sale and service of alcoholic beverages. Thirty-eight of the fifty states responded. There are basically three scenarios for the sale and dispensing of alcoholic beverages:

1. Off-premise caterers are permitted to serve, but not sell alcoholic beverages. They may charge for mixers, ice, glassware, and other necessities. These caterers may pick up the beverage from the retail liquor vendor, but they may not pay for it with their cash, checks, or credit cards. They must provide payment with the client's check made payable to the liquor vendor for the exact amount of the purchase.
2. Off-premise caterers or their clients may obtain a special or temporary license which allows them to sell liquor at a specific event, at a specific time, in a specific place. This license is most always sold for charitable events, as opposed to regular corporate and social functions.
3. In a few states, such as California, off-premise caterers can obtain a license to sell and serve alcoholic beverages off-premises on a regular basis. The off-premise caterer must already possess a license to sell alcoholic beverages at an on-premise location. For example, a California restaurant owner who is licensed to sell alcoholic beverages at the restaurant and who wishes to cater off-premise may apply for a license to sell alcoholic beverages at off-premise events.

Anyone who wishes to serve and/or sell alcoholic beverage off-premise should contact the appropriate state authority that controls the sale of alcoholic beverages. In many states, off-premise caterers who do not follow the laws are subject to criminal charges.

LIQUOR LIABILITY

What if 100 jumbo jets crashed and there were no survivors? The casualties of these 100 jet crashes equal the number of people who were killed by drunk drivers in a recent year.

> In 1990, drunk driving killed more than 22,000 people in the United States. . . . Alcohol-related crashes injured an additional 355,000 people. A recent telephone survey conducted by the Gallup Organization found 42 percent of respondents personally knew someone who was killed or injured by a drunk driver. Mothers Against Drunk Driving (MADD) reports half of all traffic fatalities involve alcohol.[1]

In most states that follow the common law, the responsibility for the intoxication rests with the consumer, rather than the seller or server of the alcoholic beverages, when someone who is intoxicated injures or kills another. However, as part of society's increasing awareness of the devastating toll that alcohol abuse is taking on innocent victims, the majority of states have passed liquor liability laws, or "dramshop acts," which modify the common law rule by imposing liability on *sellers* of alcohol for injuries that an intoxicated person inflicts on himself or herself or a third party. Typically, these acts only impose such liability if the sale involves a minor, an obviously intoxicated person, or a known alcoholic. Please note that dramshop laws do not apply to those who *serve* alcoholic beverages such as catering staff who are dispensing the client's alcohol.

However, a growing minority of states, including Pennsylvania, New Jersey, and Massachusetts, take the law a step further and impose a "social host" liability on those who merely serve alcoholic beverages. In these and other social host states, when an off-premise catering staffperson serves a party guest, and that guest injures or kills himself or herself or a third party, and if that guest is deemed intoxicated under the state law (in most states either .08 or .10 blood alcohol level), the off-premise caterer, the staffperson, and the party host could be named in lawsuits and could be liable for a portion of the damages.

It is the responsibility of off-premise caterers in each state to know the laws in the state and follow them. Off-premise caterers should remember that there are legal costs involved to prove noninvolvement, even when there is no liability on the part of the off-premise caterer or staff. They also need to understand the relationship between the number of drinks consumed, the amount of alcohol in the drinks, the drinker's weight, and the period of time over which the drinks are consumed. For the average-size person, three one-ounce drinks consumed within a one-hour period can raise the drinker's blood-alcohol level to .08 or above.

SENSIBLE ALCOHOL SERVICE

There are a number of steps and procedures that off-premise caterers should follow in order to serve alcoholic beverages sensibly and thereby reduce the chances for legal problems due to intoxicated party guests:

1. Encourage shorter cocktail hours. For example, rather than having a one-hour cocktail hour, serve cocktails only for a half hour and then immediately serve the meal.
2. Be sure to serve plenty of attractive hors d'oeuvres during cocktail receptions. Cheeses, fried foods, and other hors d'oeuvres that are high in fat content are excellent choices since they help reduce the amount of alcohol that is absorbed into the system.
3. Have plenty of delicious, attractive nonalcoholic beverages available such as soft drinks, fresh juices, still and sparkling waters, a tropical punch, and/or nonalcoholic wines, beers, and champagnes.
4. Pour dinner wines rather than placing them on the table. This helps the off-premise caterer control the rate of consumption.

5. Close the bars before the event is over. This can be anywhere from an hour to a half hour before the party stop time. At most sporting events and concerts, the bars are closed at least an hour before the event is finished.

6. Serve plenty of coffee, pastries, and cappuchino toward the end of the event. This may slow down the consumption of alcohol, but keep in mind that coffee will not sober up a person who is already intoxicated.

7. Off-premise caterers should include in their catering contract a clause stating that they will refuse to serve minors, as well as those guests who are becoming intoxicated.

8. Carry liquor liability insurance.

9. Instruct bar staff to never give bottles of wine or liquor to guests who wish to pour drinks themselves and to never pour double-shot drinks.

10. When serving beer from kegs, station an attendant to serve the guests.

11. Certain managerial actions will limit off-premise caterers' liability:
    - ❑ Be visible in the area where guests are being served.
    - ❑ Train beverage and food service staff in sensible alcohol service techniques.
    - ❑ Insist that staff sign written statements that they have received training in sensible alcohol service.
    - ❑ Schedule sufficient staff so that there is plenty of time to check I.D. cards, as well as observe the behavior of guests.
    - ❑ Back up staff members who advise that someone appears to be intoxicated, or close to it, and should not be served additional alcoholic beverages.
    - ❑ Maintain a diary of any alcohol-related incidents, noting all of the significant details of the problem such as time of occurrence, action taken by management, witnesses to the occurrence, and any other significant details that might be supportive if you are required to appear in court at a later time.

12. Training for off-premise catering staff should include ways to identify intoxication and ways to deal with it. Some of the signs of intoxication may be seen in guests who:
    - ❑ Drink alone
    - ❑ Go from being loud to very quiet
    - ❑ Go from being quiet to very loud
    - ❑ Complain about drinks being weak
    - ❑ Change their rate of consumption
    - ❑ Order several drinks at a time
    - ❑ Light wrong end of a cigarette
    - ❑ Light more than one cigarette at a time
    - ❑ Have glassy eyes
    - ❑ Slur words
    - ❑ Lose coordination
    - ❑ Order double-strength drinks
    - ❑ Spill drinks
    - ❑ Are unsteady when they stand up

❑ Have mental lapses, such as forgetting they already ordered drinks
❑ Use foul, hostile, or sexually oriented language
❑ Gulp drinks
❑ Become overly friendly or animated
❑ Become drowsy

13. Have all beverage service employees acknowledge in writing that they will not serve alcoholic beverages to any person under legal drinking age, will not come to work after drinking alcoholic beverages, and will not serve alcoholic beverages to an adult who is suspected of giving these beverages to underage individuals.

The Beverage Law Institute in Tallahassee, Florida, provides training and consulting services for those who dispense alcoholic beverages. Some of their procedures for beverage servers include the following:

> Count drinks, but also be aware that . . . [guests] . . . may have been drinking elsewhere.
> Chat briefly with people ordering drinks.
> Slow down the speed of service when . . . [guests] . . . are drinking and ordering rapidly.
> Deter serving rounds—or at least delay service when there is more than one drink per person on the table.
> Beware of [guests] ordering multiple drinks, especially in the latter part of the evening or just before the bar closes.
> Respect wishes of individuals who indicate they do not want another drink. Suggest [nonalcoholic] alternatives.
> Be aware of food/snack items which are available and suggest them when appropriate.[2]

Alcoholic beverage servers should be aware of how alcohol impacts people differently due to age, sex, physical size, health, drinking experience, size of drink, type of drink, time of day, food consumption, medication, number of drinks and psychological frame of mind. Individuals at greater risk include:

> Those under 25 years of age
> Those ordering a third drink in less than an hour
> Ordering shooter or slammers
> Drinking alone
> Ordering rounds on top of rounds
> Drinking in large groups . . .
> Groups of all one sex
> Those who drink for more than 2 1/2 hours
> Those who are emotionally upset.[3]

Beverage servers should be trained to recognize the three stages of beverage consumption by guests. The first stage is the "acceptable stage," where a guest is pacing drinks and congenially behaves. The second stage is the "beware stage," where a guest appears to be becoming intoxicated. The third stage is the "cut-off stage," where a guest is intoxicated.

Servers may continued to serve drinks to those guests in the "acceptable stage." Servers should slow down the rate of consumption for those guests in the "beware stage" by serving them food or coffee, as well as becoming less available for drink reorders. Guests in the "cut-off" stage should not be served any more alcoholic beverages and should be asked to leave.

The off-premise catering owner, manager, or supervisor should generally handle the cutoff procedure, if possible with the support of the party host. When cutting someone off, caterers should be diplomatic, avoid an audience, make direct eye contact and be sure to have the support of security or other staff members in case of an altercation. An unruly guest should be asked to leave. It may be advisable to make the necessary transportation arrangements such as a cab or a ride with another party guest. A guest cannot be legally detained: In the event that the intoxicated guest drives away, it is imperative that the police be notified as soon as possible. The police should be advised of the make and model of the car, the license number, and the direction of travel.

TYPES OF BEVERAGES

Off-premise caterers frequently assist with the service of alcoholic beverages. Although it is not necessary for off-premise caterers to be as knowledgeable about beverages as a hotel bar manager, some knowledge is necessary. There are no recipes for Long Island Iced Teas, a popular seven-liquor drink, but a caterer should know the ingredients in a martini, and what should be stocked on a typical off-premise catering bar.

Basic Vocabulary   To better understand alcoholic beverages, it is best to have a basic knowledge of the associated vocabulary. This vocabulary is summarized from *Total Bar and Beverage Management*.[4]

After Dinner Drink—A dessert drink, often creamy with a liqueur base. A liqueur by itself or with coffee is often ordered after dinner.

Blended Whiskey—A straight whiskey in combination with either another whiskey, neutral spirit, or a combination of both. Seagram's 7 Crown is an example.

Bourbon—Whiskey distilled at not more that 160 proof, from a fermented mash of at least 51 percent corn and aged at least two years in new charred-oak barrels. Jack Daniels and Jim Beam are two examples.

Brandy—Any spirit distilled from fruit.

Brandy Snifter—A short-stemmed glass, large and rounded at the bottom and tapering to a small opening at the top to concentrate the aroma. Always used to serve brandy and cognac.

Canadian Whisky—Whiskey imported from Canada. Generally blended, and very smooth and mellow in nature. Examples are Canadian Club and Seagram's VO.

Chablis—A dry white wine originating in the Burgundy region of France. When most guests order chablis, they mean white wine.

Cognac—A brandy produced in the Cognac region of France. An example is Courvoisier.

Cordial Glass—A small, narrow, stemmed glass used exclusively to serve cordials or liqueurs.

Dry—A term that varies with the cocktail. A Dry Martini would mean one using very little dry vermouth, while a Dry Manhattan or Rob Roy would mean using dry vermouth instead of sweet vermouth.

Free Pour—A method of preparing cocktails without the use of a measuring glass. For most drinks one ounce of distilled spirits is enough.

Gin—A very strong, aromatic liquor distilled from rye and other grains and flavored with juniper berries. Gordon's, Beefeater, and Tanqueray are examples.

Jigger—A measuring glass used to measure liquor. The size varies, but 7/8 ounce is the most popular. This size allows the bartender to pour a little extra, yet still keep the alcohol at one ounce.

Liqueur—A distinctively flavored, very strong, sweet, syrupy liquor.

On the Rocks—Over cubed ice.

Port—Sweet Portuguese wine fortified with brandy.

Pouring Spout—For the convenience of the bartender, each opened bottle of liquor is usually capped with a pouring spout.

Rum—A liquor distilled from the fermented juice of sugar cane, sugar cane syrup, sugar cane molasses, or other sugar cane product. Bacardi and Ron Rico are two examples.

Rye—Whiskey distilled at not more than 160 proof from a fermented mash of at least 51 percent rye and aged at least two years in new charred-oak barrels. Old Overholt is an example.

Scotch—A very distinctively flavored, usually blended, whiskey imported from Scotland. Cutty Sark, Dewar's White Label, Chivas Regal, and Johnnie Walker Black Label are examples.

Sherry—A rich amber wine served often as an aperitif. True sherrys are always imported from Spain.

Splash—A unit of measure equal to about a quarter ounce.

Squeeze—Refers to a lime, which, when served as a garnish, is squeezed and then dropped into the drink.

Sweet—Most cocktails are sweetened by simply adding either sugar or simple syrup. Manhattans and Rob Roys are sweetened by adding more sweet vermouth.

Twist—A garnish made from a slice of lemon peel. The peel is twisted over the top of the drink before being dropped in.

Vodka—A neutral spirit that has been filtered through activated carbon to assure that any taste is removed. Vodka has no color, aroma, or taste, and is not aged. Examples are Smirnoff, Stolichnaya, and Absolut.

Distilled Spirits and Common Liquor Brands

Off-premise caterers are frequently asked to recommend to clients those items which should be provided on bars. Preferences vary locally. Bourbon is more popular in Kentucky than in South Florida, and wines will be more popular in California than in West Virginia. One should keep in mind that the following suggestions tend to be generic for the entire United States, and that regional difference will play a major role in final recommendations to clients. The following six liquors are basic selections for most bars in the United States: Vodka, Scotch Whiskey, Bourbon, Rum, Gin, and Canadian Whisky.

There are basically three categories of these items. The first is referred to in bars as "well" stock. This is usually one of the more inexpensive brands. Next is "call brands," which are medium-priced, such as Smirnoff vodka, Dewar's White Label scotch, Bacardi rum, Gordon's gin, and Canadian Club. The third and most expensive category is "top shelf" or "premium call." This selection could include brands such as Absolut or Stolichnaya vodka, Tanqueray or Beefeater gin, Crown Royal Canadian, Maker's Mark bourbon, and Johnnie Walker Black Label or Chivas Regal scotch. The client's preference will vary depending on budget and the invited guests.

Cognacs, Liqueurs, and Cordials

Some clients wish to provide after-dinner drinks for their guests, and off-premise caterers should be in a position to recommend some popular choices. Cognacs are served in brandy snifters, while liqueurs and cordials are served alone in cordial glasses or over ice. Some choices include:

Cognac—Imported brandy from the Cognac region of France (frequently ordered brands are Courvoisier, Hennessy, Martell and Remy Martin)
Amaretto—Italian almond-flavored liqueur
Benedictine—Made from herbs and brandy
B&B—Benedictine and brandy

Cointreau—French orange-flavored liqueur
Drambuie—Scotch-whiskey-based liqueur
Galliano—Golden-colored Italian liqueur
Grand Marnier—Cognac-based, orange liqueur from France
Kahlua—Mexican coffee liqueur
Sambuca—Italian liqueur made from the Sambuca plant
Tia Maria—Coffee-flavored liqueur from Jamaica
Cordials—Anisette, Creme de Cacao (light and dark), Creme de Menthe (green and white), Creme de Cassis, Creme de Banana, Creme de Noyaux (almond), Curacao (orange and blue), peppermint Schnapps, Rock and Rye, Sloe gin, Triple sec, peach liqueur, blackberry liqueur, and apricot liqueur

Wines   Wine knowledge can be a tremendous help in satisfying clients' needs. Off-premise caterers should learn all they can about wines, as well as how to pair wines with food selections. There are numerous wine groups around the country that meet to taste and talk about wines. Newspapers and periodicals frequently include articles about wine.

Caterers who lack wine knowledge or who are just beginning to learn should be wise enough to ask for their clients' preferences. Recently, a California caterer, who knew little about wine, told his client, who was a wine connoisseur, "Don't worry, I'll pick some wonderful wines for your ten-course dinner!" The outcome, of course, was that the guests were displeased with the caterer's suggestions, and after the third course went out and purchased wines suitable for their affair. The moral of this story is that caterers should ask clients for their wine preferences, rather than assume that they know what clients want.

The following are a few terms that off-premise caterers should know in order to discuss wines knowledgeably with clients:[5]

Aging—All wine ages or grows older in the bottle. Generally, wines will improve with aging, up to a certain point.

Appellation Controllee or **Appellation d'Origine Controllee**—The French government guarantees by law the contents of the bottle according to precise standards. These standards define the geographical origin of a named wine, as well as the grape species permitted to be grown, the maximum quantity of wine which can be produced, the minimum quality, and the minimum alcohol content.

Aroma—The perfume or odor of the wine.

Body—The substance of wine, usually referred to as light-bodied, medium-bodied, and full-bodied.

Bordeaux—A region in France producing red, white, and rosé wines. Red Bordeaux wines are sometimes referred to as Clarets.

Bouquet—Similar to aroma, but more complex, combining all of the different and interesting odors of the wine.

Breathing—Wines breathe or oxidize when they are in contact with the air.

Brut—French term indicating the driest of champagnes.

Carafe—Generally a clear glass container for serving wines. Available in several sizes, the most popular being the liter and half-liter sizes.

Chablis—A famous white wine from the French Burgundy region. In California, many white wines are generically labeled chablis.

Claret—English word for light red Bordeaux wine.

Cru—French word meaning "growth." Generally, it implies that the wine is of high quality. *Grand cru, premier cru, superieur cru,* and *premier grand cru classë* are all French terms indicating wines of superior quality.

Decant—A process of pouring wine from a bottle containing sediment into a container so as to leave the sediment in the bottle.

Dry—Term meaning the opposite of sweet. This does not mean sour.

Flinty—Term used to describe the taste of a dry, hard wine such as a chablis.

Flowery—Term used to describe the aroma of some wines, particularly the light, white German wines.

Fortified—Refers to wines to which alcohol has been added.

Fruity—Term applied to the bouquet of some wines, particularly young wines.

Light (bodied)—Term referring to the body, or consistency, of some wines.

Maderized—Term applied primarily to white and rosë wines which have oxidized, or passed their prime, and are turning a brownish tinge.

Magnum—A size equal to twice the amount of a full bottle of wine.

Pinto—A family of wine grapes and one of the most famous. Used in making many of the Burgundy and Champagne wines.

Punt—The pushed-up indentation in the bottom of the wine bottle.

Rhine Wines—Wines grown in the German Rhine region.

Rosë—A pink or rose-colored wine.

Sangria—A wine drink concocted of wine, fruit juice, sugar water or soda water, served chilled.

Sauternes—Sweet white wines from the Bordeaux region of France.

Sec—French word meaning dry. Can also mean medium-sweet when used to describe champagne.

Sediment—The natural deposit which forms in the bottle of wine, particularly older wines. It is harmless, but unsightly.

Sherry—A fortified wine, ranging in color from pale straw to deep amber and in flavor from very dry to very sweet.

Sour—An expression referring to a wine which has lost its flavor and is turning to vinegar. It indicates a spoiled wine which should not be served to a guest.

Tannin—The component in wine which gives an astringent taste, without which the wine would lack character.

Vin—The French word meaning wine.

Vintage—The year in which the grapes are picked (from which the wine is made).

Wine Primer for Off-Premise Caterers

The following primer has been excerpted from *Windows of the World Complete Wine Course* by Kevin Zraly.[6] In this section we will discuss the following wines, and how they are best served:

The White Wines of France
The White Wines of California
The White Wines of Germany
The Red Wines of Burgundy and the Rhone Valley
The Red Wines of Bordeaux
The Red Wines of California
The Red Wines of Italy and Spain
Champagne and Sparkling Wines

The White Wines of France

The four major white-wine-producing regions of France are Alsace, Loire Valley, Bordeaux, and Burgundy.

1. *Alsace*—Riesling, Gewurtztraminer, and Pinot Blanc are the three main wine white grapes grown in Alsace. Alsacian wine producers recommend the following food with these wines:

- ❑ Riesling—fish in a white or butter sauce
- ❑ Gerwërtztraminer—smoked salmon, turkey, Chinese food or a strong cheese
- ❑ Pinot Blanc—Pate, hamburgers

2. *Loire Valley*—The two main grapes grown in the Loire Valley are the Sauvignon Blanc and the Chenin Blanc. Loire Valley wines are chosen by style and vintage. The main ones follow, along with suggested foods:
   - ❑ Pouilly-Fume—smoked salmon, white meat chicken and veal with cream sauce
   - ❑ Muscadet—shellfish, clams, and oysters
   - ❑ Sancerre—shellfish
   - ❑ Vouvray—fruit and cheese

3. *Bordeaux*—The two major white wines produced in Bordeaux are Graves and Sauternes. They are produced mainly from Sauvignon Blanc and Semillon grapes, and they are most generally served with the following foods:
   - ❑ Graves—salmon or striped bass in a rich sauce, oysters, cheese, nuts, and lobster
   - ❑ Sauternes—desserts, strong cheeses, foie gras (goose liver)

4. *Burgundy*—All great Burgundy wines are produced from the Chardonnay grape in the following regions: Chablis, Côte de Beaune, and Maconnais. All white burgundies are dry and are best matched with foods such as fish with no cream sauces, escargot, and seafood.

The White Wines of California

The major grape varieties grown in California are Chardonnay, Sauvignon Blanc (sometimes labeled Fume Blanc), Johannesberg Riesling, Chenin Blanc and Gewurtztraminer. Some food suggestions are:

- ❑ Chardonnay—pasta with butter sauce, fowl, ham, seafood in sauces, salmon, veal, seviche, shellfish, pesto, linguini
- ❑ Sauvignon Blanc—chilled shellfish, turkey, poultry, salmon with a spicy mustard sauce
- ❑ Johannesberg Riesling—chicken breasts poached with raspberry vinaigrette, sauteed bay scallops with julienne vegetables

The White Wines of Germany

The three most important grape varieties in Germany are Riesling, Silvaner, and Muller-Thurgau. German wines are classified as either table or quality wine. The top three quality levels from the top are Auslese, Spatlese, and Kabinett. Riesling wines are the best. Some of the less sweet varieties go well with chicken, cold lobster, cold meats, and mild cheeses. The sweeter varieties are better consumed alone.

The Red Wines of Burgundy

The two major grape varieties are Pinot Noir and Gamay. All red Burgundies, except Beaujolais, must be made from the Pinot Noir grape. Beaujolais is produced from the Gamay grape variety. The major wine-producing regions of Burgundy are Beaujolais, Côte Chalonnaise, Côte de Beaune, and Côte de Nuit. Light Burgundies go well with chicken, duck, and veal while the heavier ones go well with lamb, game, goat cheese, and steak.

The Red Wines of the Rhône Valley　　A Rhône wine is a bigger, fuller wine than one from Burgundy. They are produced mainly from the Grenache, Syrah, and Cinsault grape varieties. The main Rhône Valley wines and their food pairings are:

- ❑ Tavel Rose—cold chicken, meat and poultry
- ❑ Côte du Rhône—chicken in a light sauce, white meats and small game
- ❑ Crozes-Hermitage—beef, game, and full-flavored cheeses
- ❑ Chateauneuf-du-Pape—ripe cheese, steaks, venison, wild boar
- ❑ Hermitage—beef, game, and full-flavored cheeses

The Red Wines of Bordeaux　　Red Bordeaux wines are produced in Medoc, Pomerol, Graves and St-Emilion. The major grape varieties are Cabernet Sauvignon, Merlot, and Cabernet Franc. They may be served as follows:

- ❑ Medoc—white meat
- ❑ Pomerol—roast beef or grilled beef with sauce
- ❑ Graves—duck, fresh salmon
- ❑ St-Emilion—roast beef or grilled beef without sauce

The Red Wines of California　　The major grape varieties grown in California are Cabernet Sauvignon, Pinot Noir, Gamay Beaujolais, Zinfandel, Gamay, Petite Sirah, and Merlot. They are excellent paired with the following foods:

- ❑ Cabernet Sauvignon—lamb, goat cheese, steak with pepper, Camembert cheese, charcoal broiled steak, veal with a light sauce, or Caesar salad
- ❑ Pinot Noir—pork loin, domestic pheasant, coq au vin, veal with a red wine or tomato sauce, roast beef, beef stew, roasted stuffed quail, or pork tenderloin with a fruity sauce

The Red Wines of Italy and Spain　　Among the favorite Italian wines are Chianti, Barolo and Barbaresco; suggested foods are as follows:

- ❑ Chianti—meat, chicken, pasta, pizza
- ❑ Barolo—meat cooked with wine, pheasant, duck, rabbit
- ❑ Barbaresco—meat, veal and mature cheeses

Spanish wines and suggested foods are:

- ❑ Light Rioja—chicken and veal
- ❑ Full-bodied Rioja—pork, lamb, steak

Sparkling Wines and Champagne　　Champagne is the most famous of all French wines. Invented by the Monk Dom Perignon at the end of the seventeenth century, it has grown in popularity over the centuries. Off-premise caterers most frequently serve it as a toast for festive occasions such as weddings, christenings, corporate celebrations, and ship launchings. Wines may be called champagne only if produced in the Champagne region of France. If not produced in Champagne, they can only be called sparkling wines. Brut is the driest, extra-dry is less dry than brut, and sec is medium-dry, which can be very sweet.

California sparkling wines are mostly produced in the northern growing regions of California. The better ones are fermented in the bottle (*methode champenoise*), and primarily produced from Chardonnay and Pinot Chardonnay grapes. Among the most popular brands are Korbel, Mumm's, and Domaine Chandon.

Champagnes and sparkling wines are sold in various bottle sizes as follows:

Split	187 ML
Half-Bottle	375 ML
Bottle	750 ML
Magnum	1.5 L (2 Bottles)
Jeroboam	3.0 L (4 Bottles)
Rehoboam	4.5 L (6 Bottles)
Methusalem	6.0 L (8 Bottles)
Salmanazar	9.0 L (12 Bottles)
Balthazar	12 L (16 Bottles)
Nebuchadnezzar	15 L (20 Bottles)

Beer   According to *Southern Beverage Journal*, "Americans spend over $45 billion a year on beer, and that's more than we spend on milk, juice, coffee and wine put together!"[7] Major brands such as Budweiser, Miller, and Coors account for the major share of the market, but there is a growing demand for brands from the microbreweries, particularly by those drinkers with sophisticated palates.

Coors recently produced an overview of the American beer market, portions of which are excerpted below as printed in *Southern Beverage Journal*, May 1992.[8]

Super premium—Winterfest, Michelob and Lowenbrau
Premium—Coors, Budweiser, Miller Genuine Draft
Low-calorie, premium—Coors Light, Miller Lite, Bud Light
Popular—Keystone, Old Milwaukee, Busch, Schlitz
Low-calorie popular—Natural Light, Keystone Light, Hamm's Light
Economy—Schaefer, Carling Black Label, Lone Star
Dry Beer (developed in Japan, has little aftertaste, and some have a little more alcohol)—Coors Dry, Michelob Dry and Bud Dry
Malt Liquor (higher alcohol content than standard beers)—Colt 45, Schlitz Malt Liquor
Imports—Heineken, Molson, Corona, Becks

Ice beer is new on the market and is gaining popularity, particularly among younger drinkers. It is less bitter, and some ice beers contain a higher alcohol percentage than regular beer, but less than malt liquor.

Most off-premise catering bars offer at least two choices from the above categories, such as one premium and one low-calorie, either domestic or imported. Beer from the keg is less expensive, but more difficult to handle due to its weight.

One problem with keg beer is that if it is not cold, or if it has been shaken up when transported to the party site, it will come from the tap too foamy. Under no circumstances should party guests be allowed to draw their own beer, not only due to liquor liability problems, but also because many people do not know how to properly draw beer by fully opening the spigot and tilting the glass so that the beer flows down the side of the glass to avoid a large head (foam).

For upscale catered events, beer from the can or bottle should be poured into a glass to avoid the unsightliness of beer containers around the room. Some brides are adamant about this since they do not wish to look at beer bottles and cans in their wedding pictures. One way to avoid this, without denying beer drinkers the pleasure or their brew, or serving from kegs, is to serve beer from quarts, which should insure that no guests leave the bar with a bottle or can.

Nonalcoholic Beers   There is an increasing popularity of nonalcoholic beers. More and more beer drinkers are opting for the nonalcoholic variety for health as well as safety reasons. Off-premise caterers who have suggested nonalcoholic beers to clients report an enthusiastic response. Most nonalcoholic brews contain small amounts of alcohol, usually between .25 and .4 percent. Federal regulations call for less than .5% alcohol in no-alcohol beer. Some of the most popular domestic brands are O'Doul's, Sharp's, and Cutter. Buckler, Kaliber, and Haake Beck are the leading European imports.

Waters   Nondrinkers like to have something stylish in their glasses, and for many, bottled waters are just the answer. Bottled-water drinkers are among the one-third of the adult population in the U.S. that does not drink alcohol. Other water drinkers are those who periodically abstain from drinking alcohol for a variety of reasons, or those who drink bottled water along with their wine. According to a prominent catering newsletter, "Today there are nearly 600 domestic and 75 imported brands of bottled water! . . . In the past five years, bottled water sales in the United States have doubled."[9]

There are various types of bottled waters with which off-premise caterers should be familiar:

> SPARKLING WATER has carbonation, which can be natural or added; carbonation levels, in turn, affect the degree of effervescence.
> STILL WATER is usually selected as an alternative to tap water.
> CLUB SODA is filtered and artificially carbonated still water, fortified with mineral salts.
> SELTZER WATER is filtered and artificially carbonated still water, usually salt-free, and without added mineral salts.
> SPRING WATER comes from a deep underground source and flows naturally to the surface. It is labeled "natural spring water" if it receives no further processing.
> NATURAL WATER is obtained, without processing, from a protected underground source such as a well, or a spring.
> FLAVORED WATER has natural or artificial flavoring added to it.

MINERAL WATER can occur in nature or be artificially created by adding minerals. Europeans classify mineral waters as light (500 milligrams or less per liter), moderate (500 to 1,500 milligrams per liter), or highly mineralized (more than 1,500 milligrams of dissolved minerals per liter).[10]

Some of the more popular domestic water brands include Artesia from Texas, Crystal Geyser from Napa Valley, Poland Spring from Maine, Quibell from Virginia, and LaCroix from Wisconsin. Sundance Juice Sparklers are fruit juices with flavorings that can double as mixers. Sophisticated palates appreciate waters that include blends of fruit essences and herbal extracts such as Sorelle and Aqua Libra.

Nonalcoholic Wines   In the early 1980s, nonalcoholic wine was called "wimp wine." Now, it is the drink of choice for the many nondrinkers who wish to celebrate, dine, and enjoy social occasions without stigma. Nonalcoholic wines gained credibility in 1986 when one of them won a gold medal in a Los Angeles County Fair. The trick to nonalcoholic wine is to keep the same "mouth feel" when the alcohol is removed. Among the producers that have been able to do this are Ariel, St. Regis and Sutter Home.

Ariel and St. Regis both use reverse osmosis, a process like the one used in household water softeners. The wine is put through a filter so fine that it filters out the alcohol molecules. . . . Sutter Home uses a process called the spinning cone . . . where regular wine is put onto the spinning cone, where the essences are removed and collected for later reintroduction. Then heat is applied to the cone to evaporate the alcohol.[11]

Nonalcoholic wines are available in the following types: Chardonnay, Cabernet Sauvignon, Blanc de Blanc, Blanc de Noir, Sparkling Wine, White Zinfandel, and Johannesberg Riesling. The bottles of these look like real wine bottles with corks and real foil capsules. The price of the nonalcoholic product is close to that of the "real McCoy." The only difference is that there are no government health warning labels, and some include nutritional information. Off-premise caterers should be knowledgeable about these products, as they continue to serve their clientele into the twenty-first century.

Soft Drinks   Soft drink consumption is increasing significantly in the United States. Off-premise caterers should look toward providing a wider variety of soft drinks, in order to better meet the needs of nondrinkers. In addition to colas, diet colas, club soda, tonic, lemon-lime, and ginger ale, off-premise caterers should be providing a diet lemon-lime as well as caffeine-free colas and diet colas.

For large, informal events, most soft drink distributors will provide beverage service stations using five-gallon tanks of syrup mixed with carbon dioxide and waters, and dispensed from spigots. This is the most economical way to serve soft drinks to large gatherings. Liter and two-liter bottles are more economical than the 12-ounce cans and assorted smaller bottle sizes, but the smaller bottles and cans present a more upscale image in that the guests perceive a fresher product.

LIQUOR, WINE, AND BEER QUANTITIES

Off-premise caterers are frequently asked by clients to recommend the necessary amounts of liquor, wine, and beer for catered events. Knowing how much the client needs is an indication of the caterer's professionalism.

Many alcoholic beverage outlets will take back for credit any unopened, unchilled, and undamaged bottles of liquor and wine. Even bottled and canned beer can be returned if it has not been chilled and is still in its original packaging. When suggesting quantities, it is always better to recommend too much, rather than too little, to be sure there is enough for the event, knowing that any excess can be returned or consumed later. Everyone is aware that it may be very difficult to find an alcoholic beverage outlet that is open late on a Saturday night. Why not have the client order more than enough, and avoid potential problems?

When determining quantities, much has to do with local customs. In south Florida, for example, the major alcoholic beverages served are scotch, vodka, white wine, and beer. Bourbon, Canadian whisky and gin are not nearly as popular. Rum is popular with younger crowds and those from out-of-town. The next factors to consider are the length of the party, the type of event, the time of day, the temperature if it is an outdoor event, and the purpose of the event. Consumption will always be greater at a Saturday night wedding reception lasting five hours, than at a one-hour weeknight corporate reception held at 5 P.M.

People are drinking less alcoholic beverages in the 1990s due to health, religious, and safety reasons. It is no longer considered "cool" to drink a lot. Today, drinking a lot means that the person has a drinking problem. As a general rule of thumb, guests will drink beverages on the average as follows:

LENGTH OF PARTY	NUMBER OF DRINKS
One Hour	Two
Two Hours	Three
Three Hours	Three to Four
Four Hours	Four to Five

It is important to note that from a one-liter bottle of liquor, which is 33.8 fluid ounces, one can pour approximately 33 one-ounce drinks, 27 one-and-one-quarter-ounce drinks and 22 one-and-one-half-ounce drinks.

In a .75 ml bottle of wine there are 25.3 ounces, or approximately five 5-ounce glasses of wine. Most bottled and canned beer come in 12-ounce portions, which is considered one serving. A liter of a soft drink will provide between five and seven glasses, depending on the size of the glass and the amount of ice used.

Exhibit 4-1 attempts to provide some very general recommendations regarding liquor, wine, beer, and mixer quantities. Local customs and other extenuating circumstances will certainly modify these recommendations. This is simply to provide some guidelines, from which novice caterers can begin to develop their own standards for their own operations. Suggested quantities are very liberal, knowing that mixers can be reused, and that unopened, unchilled wine, liquor, and beer, can be returned if desired.

Exhibit 4-1 does not take into account dinner wine served at the table. Off-premise caterers who provide table wine service can expect to serve another one or two glasses of wine at the table per person. Consumption will be greater if there was no preceding cocktail party. Therefore, off-premise caterers can estimate an additional one-quarter to one-half bottle of wine per guest. Caterers should insist that wine bottles only be opened at the direction of the host or caterer to avoid having excessive amounts of opened wine left at the end of the event.

When determining the amount of ice needed for an event, off-premise caterers need to consider the length of the party, the need for chilling wines, beers, and champagne, the necessity to fill water glasses and the temperature at the party site. A five-hour outdoor wedding reception with temperatures in the eighties, with wine, champagne, and water poured at the tables will require as much as five pounds of ice per person. A one-hour cocktail party on a weeknight in a downtown office building will need at most one pound per person. It is always best to be on the safe side by having too much ice, rather than too little. Extra ice can always be used to ice down leftover food.

BASIC DRINK RECIPES

Most off-premise caterers do not serve frozen drinks, those that are shaken, or those that combine more than two ingredients. Most drink orders are self-explanatory, such as scotch and water. To prepare this drink, one must simply put ice in a highball glass, pour the prescribed portion size of scotch, and then add water. The following is a summary of recipes for the most popular drinks served at an off-premise catering bar.

DRINK NAME	GLASS	INGREDIENTS	GARNISH
Manhattan	Rocks/Cocktail	1 1/4 oz. bourbon or blend, 3/4 oz. sweet vermouth	Stem cherry
Dry Manhattan	Rocks/Cocktail	1 1/4 oz. bourbon or blend, 3/4 oz. dry vermouth	Olive
Perfect Manhattan		Same as regular except use 3/8 oz. each of sweet and dry vermouth, and garnish with a lemon twist.	
Presbyterian	Highball	1 1/4 oz. bourbon equal amount of soda and ginger ale	Lemon twist
Martini	Rocks/Cocktail	1 1/4 oz. gin Dash dry vermouth	Olive
Rob Roy		Same as Manhattan, except use scotch instead of bourbon.	
Vodka Martini		Same as regular Martini, except use vodka instead of gin.	
Bloody Mary	Highball	1 1/4 oz. vodka Bloody Mary mix	Lime wedge/celerystick
Screwdriver	Highball	1 1/4 oz. vodka Orange juice	None

EXHIBIT 4-1
Liquor, Wine, Beer, and Mixer Quantities

LIQUOR—LITERS

	50 GUESTS				100 GUESTS			
	1 HR	2 HR	3 HR	4 HR	1 HR	2 HR	3 HR	4 HR
SCOTCH	2	3	3	4	4	5	5	6
VODKA	2	3	3	4	4	5	5	6
GIN	1	2	2	2	2	3	3	3
BLEND	1	2	2	2	2	3	3	3
BOURBON	1	2	2	2	2	3	3	3
RUM	1	2	2	2	3	3	4	4
BEER, CASE	1/2	3/4	1	1	1	1 1/2	2	2
LITE BEER, CASE	1/2	3/4	1	1	1	1 1/2	2	2
WHITE WINE, 5TH	6	9	12	12	12	18	24	24
RED WINE, 5TH	2	3	4	4	4	6	8	8

SOFT DRINKS—LITERS

	50 GUESTS				100 GUESTS			
	1 HR	2 HR	3 HR	4 HR	1 HR	2 HR	3 HR	4 HR
COLA	4	6	7	8	8	10	12	14
DIET COLA	4	5	6	7	8	9	10	11
DIET LEMON-LIME	2	2	3	4	4	5	6	7
LEMON-LIME	2	2	3	4	4	5	6	7
GINGER ALE	2	2	3	4	4	5	6	7
CLUB SODA	3	4	5	6	6	7	8	9
TONIC	3	4	5	6	6	7	8	9
SPARKLING WATER	3	4	5	6	6	7	8	9

FRESH JUICES—ORANGE, GRAPEFRUIT, AND CRANBERRY JUICES—QUARTS

	50 GUESTS				100 GUESTS			
	1 HR	2 HR	3 HR	4 HR	1 HR	2 HR	3 HR	4HR
	2	3	3	4	4	5	6	7

LIMES (165 COUNT)—CUT INTO 16 WEDGES

	50 GUESTS				100 GUESTS			
	1 HR	2 HR	3 HR	4 HR	1 HR	2 HR	3 HR	4 HR
	3	4	5	5	5	8	9	9

LEMON TWISTS—ONE LEMON PER FIFTY GUESTS—REGARDLESS OF LENGTH OF THE EVENT. FIVE ONION SKEWERS AND FIVE OLIVE SKEWERS PER EACH FIFTY GUESTS IS ADEQUATE. EACH BARTENDER SHOULD HAVE ONE BOTTLE OF SWEET VERMOUTH AND ONE BOTTLE OF DRY VERMOUTH. THIS WILL SUFFICE FOR MOST PARTIES OF ANY LENGTH.

BLOODY MARY MIX IS NEEDED FOR MOST BARS. FOR DAYTIME EVENTS, SIX QUARTS PER ONE HUNDRED GUESTS SHOULD BE ADEQUATE. FOR EVENING EVENTS, TWO QUARTS PER ONE HUNDRED GUESTS IS AMPLE.

BEVERAGE STATIONS (BARS)

Off-premise caterers frequently provide service bars for clients, along with mixers, ice, and glasses. Portable service bars take much physical abuse while moved from event to event, and they also only provide limited storage space. Many off-premise caterers prefer to use skirted banquet tables for beverage service. They provide more working space, there is plenty or storage space for backup supplies underneath the tables, and they generally look better than service bars.

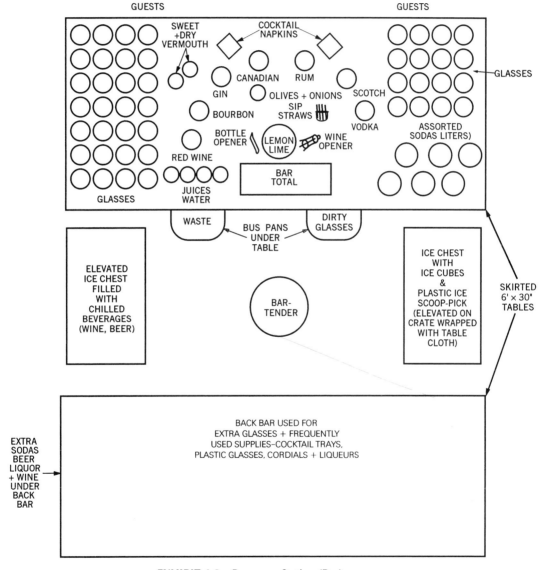

EXHIBIT 4-2 Beverage Station (Bar)

Exhibit 4-2 is a diagram of a service bar for a single bartender, using a 6-foot-long and 30-inch-wide table. Exhibit 4-3 is a listing of all equipment, supplies, and liquor necessary to set up and equip this single-service bar. Exhibit 4-4 shows various styles and shapes of bar glassware. The 13-ounce grand ballon is an excellent all-purpose glass.

Eight-foot banquet tables may be used to set up beverage stations for two bartenders. It is best that each bartender have his or her own supply of liquor, soda, and glasses to eliminate reaching. They generally can share ice and cold beers and wines provided the chests are strategically placed between them.

EXHIBIT 4-3

Beverage Station Setup—Equipment and Supplies

Two 6-foot by 30-inch tables
One 13-foot skirt for front bar (leave a four-foot opening at rear of bar for easy access underneath by bartender)
One 17-foot skirt for back bar
Two banquet cloths, or two 90-inch by 90-inch cloths (the color of the cloths and skirts should tie in with the color scheme of the event)
Clips to attach the skirts to the tables
Bowls for cut fruits, garnish, olives, onions, cherries, etc.
Stir straws
Sword picks (for onions and olives)
Ice chest for chilled beverages such as beers, wines, bottled waters, champagne, etc.
Ice chest filled with ice for drinks
Plastic ice scoops
Wine openers
Bottle openers
Bus boxes for trash and dirty glasses
Matches
Cocktail napkins
Cocktail trays
Plastic glasses
Basic bar glasses (balloon wine glasses are good all-purpose glasses)—please refer to Exhibit 4-4 for typical glasses used in off-premise catering
Specialty glasses such as brandy snifters/cordial glasses
Plastic pourers for liquor
Ice pick
Bar towels
Empty plastic crates (to elevate ice chests)
Small tablecloths to wrap around plastic crates
Liquor—basic

A selection of basic liquors such as vodka, scotch, gin, blended whiskey, rum, bourbon, and other requested brands

Wines and beers

At least one regular and one light beer, plus a white wine and a red wine. Please note that in some locations, blush, or rose wine is a must, and that some facilities prohibit red wine due to the possibility of staining carpeting and furniture.

After-dinner drinks (optional)

Kahlua

B&B

Bailey's Irish Cream

Cointreau

Drambuie

Tia Maria

Courvoisier

White Crême de Menthe

Green Crême de menthe

Other local favorites

Soft drinks, juices, and miscellaneous

Cola

Lemon-lime

Diet-cola

Diet lemon-lime

Ginger ale

Club soda

Tonic

Sparkling water

Orange juice

Grapefruit juice

Cranberry juice

Water

Sweet vermouth

Dry vermouth

Bloody Mary mix

Lemon twists

Lime wedges

Cocktail olives

Cocktail onions

GENERAL SERVICE PROCEDURES

Professional off-premise caterers who are serving alcohol should check with the client regarding whether to serve alcoholic beverages to band members, photog-

CATERING GLASSWARE

Goblet
$10\frac{1}{2}$ oz

Tall Wine
$8\frac{1}{2}$ oz

Tall Wine
$6\frac{1}{2}$ oz

Flute
$5\frac{3}{4}$ oz

Grand Ballon
13 oz Wine

BallonWine
$8\frac{1}{2}$ oz

Pilsner
12 oz

All Purpose Globet
11 oz

Banquet Goblet
$10\frac{1}{2}$ oz

Brandy
12 oz

Champagne
$8\frac{1}{2}$ oz

Champagne
$4\frac{1}{2}$ oz

Exhibit 4-4   Catering Glassware
Courtesy of Cardinal International, Wayne, NJ.

CATERING GLASSWARE

Footed Hi Ball
10 oz

Footed Hi Ball
8 oz

Footed Rocks
7 oz

Footed Rocks
$6^1/_2$ oz

Goblet
$10^1/_2$ oz

Wine
$8^1/_2$ oz

Wine
$5^1/_2$ oz

Sherry
$3^3/_4$ oz

Cordial
$1^1/_2$ oz

Champagne
$6^1/_2$ oz

Flute
$5^1/_2$ oz

Exhibit 4-4 (*continued*)

raphers, floral designers, and others engaged to work the event. As a general rule, serving alcoholic beverages to people working the party is not advisable. Under no circumstance should the caterer permit any staff member to consume alcoholic beverages while working a catered event.

Caterers should establish a clear policy with staff members as to how much wine and liquor to open prior to the event. Opening too little will result in wasted time during the event, and opening too much will result in wine that cannot be returned for credit. A good policy is for the caterer to prohibit any staff member from opening wine and liquor without first checking with a supervisor or manager.

Near the conclusion of parties where glassware is used, it is always good policy to station a catering staffperson near the exit to insure that guests do not leave with glassware. In most states it is illegal for persons to have open containers of alcoholic beverages in vehicles, so giving a plastic glass to those who have not yet finished their alcoholic beverages is not proper. Of course, it is permissible to give plastic glasses for unconsumed nonalcoholic beverages.

INTO THE TWENTY-FIRST CENTURY

According to an industry review conducted by House of Seagram, consumption of alcoholic beverages is expected to be down moderately over the next several years. New products that feature upscale images, light and more flavorful tastes, and unique selling propositions make significant gains. People are drinking less, but better-quality beverages. Wine consumption is expected to decline over the next decade, while "coolers" and lighter drinks are expected to continue to grow in popularity.

Nonalcoholic beers and wines are expected to grow dramatically in popularity. Some hotels, such as the Chicago Hilton Towers, offer nonalcoholic bars which include French sparkling cider; frozen alcohol-free Margaritas, Daiquiris, and Pina Coladas; and mineral waters, assorted fruit-flavored seltzers, and Sundance natural fruit sparklers.

NOTES

1. *Aide*, United States Automobile Association, April 1992.
2. *The Beverage Law Institute*, Responsible Vendor Program, p. 136.
3. *The Beverage Law Institute*, Responsible Vendor Program, p. 135.
4. *Total Bar and Beverage Management*, Lebhar Friedman, 1984, pp. 112–119.
5. *Wine Service Procedures*, Cahners Books 1976 Glossary. Excerpted with permission of Restaurants & Institutions magazine, (date of issue), © 1976 by Cahners Publishing Company.
6. Used with permission of Sterling Publishing Co., Inc., 387 Park Ave. S., NY, NY 10016 from *Windows on the World Complete Wine Course* by Kevin Zraly, © 1995 by Inhilco, Inc.
7. Duncan H. Cameron, *Southern Beverage Journal*, May 1992, p. 6.
8. Duncan H. Cameron, *Southern Beverage Journal*, May 1992, p. 68.
9. *National Caterers Association, CommuniCATER*, June 1992, p. 5. Reprinted with permission from the CommuniCATER, official publication of the National Caterers Association.
10. Gail Bellamy, *Restaurant Hospitality*, © 1992, Penton Publishing, April 1992, p. 142.
11. Mike Stepanovich, *The Wine News*, April/May 1993, p. 37.

Chapter 5

Equipment

This chapter discusses the equipment that is necessary to operate an off-premise catering business, including commissary equipment, transportation equipment, and off-premise catering equipment for food preparation and food service. It addresses techniques for determining equipment needs, and whether it is better to buy or rent equipment. Of equal importance is a discussion of the relationship between the off-premise caterer and the rental equipment company.

An understanding of commissary and transportation equipment is essential for success in this field. Caterers need to know the various types of cooking equipment, as well as the best ways to procure this equipment. Millions of dollars are wasted annually when inexperienced food service operators buy unnecessary equipment. Successful off-premise caterers from all parts of the United States report that it is not necessary to spend fortunes on commissary equipment. This chapter will examine how to buy equipment economically.

Caterers who are knowledgeable about equipment are better prepared to deal with clients who choose not to become involved in the rental of equipment for their private party. Rental equipment is an excellent way to generate additional profits for off-premise caterers when they rent or provide equipment for catered events.

DETERMINING EQUIPMENT NEEDS

The type of required off-premise catering equipment is determined by analyzing a number of factors:

Menu. The types of foods to be served will greatly influence the equipment selection. For example, a caterer who plans to serve a variety of deep-fried hors d'oeuvres will require more fryolator capacity than one who plans to simply offer an assortment of cold canapes. The caterer who serves cold canapes will in turn require rolling racks and refrigerated storage, whereas the caterer serving deep-fried hors d'oeuvres could store the raw product in plastic containers that could be keep cold in ice chests at the party site, if in accordance with local health department regulations.

Beverage Service. Will the caterer provide for service of alcoholic and nonalcoholic beverages? If so, glassware, bar utensils, and beverage stations (bars) will be necessary.

Style of Service. A caterer specializing in barbecues will more than likely require only plasticware for food service, whereas an upscale caterer will need silver-plated flatware, crystal stemware, fine linens, and other first-class equipment.

Existing Equipment. This encompasses equipment at the commissary as well as equipment at the party site. For example, an off-premise caterer who leases a fully equipped commissary will have little need for additional commissary equipment. Off-premise caterers who work frequently at party sites where there are existing bars will not need to be concerned with purchasing or renting bars for their events.

Number of Guests. What is the maximum number of guests that the caterer will realistically serve? Off-premise caterers who specialize in home parties for thirty or less guests, will require substantially less equipment than those who cater mega-events with thousands of guests.

Other Known Factors. This could include regional influences such as clambake equipment in New England, or elaborate barbecue equipment in the South or Midwest. There are specific equipment needs for each party which can best be determined by analyzing the party contract and preparing a layout of the event including the guest seating area, the cocktail area, the food preparation area, and all buffets tables and/or food stations. Diagrams require detailed thought, which will help the caterer think of everything necessary for an event, from major things like tables and chairs to the small details such as toothpicks, cutting boards, and buffet spoons.

PLANNING AND EQUIPPING A CATERING COMMISSARY

Chapter 2 discusses various methods for finding a commissary location. In this section, we will cover key factors in planning a catering commissary, as well as the types of necessary equipment.

Hire a professional planner. This will save money in the long run. Professionals know how to efficiently layout kitchens, and they know which questions to ask. Planners who work for restaurant supply companies are trained to sell as much equipment as possible, so it is best to a hire an independent planner who will have only the best interest of the off-premise caterer. Exhibit 5-1 is a generic off-premise catering commissary layout for a 1500-square-foot commissary provided by Hugh Cunningham of Ft. Lauderdale, Florida, who is a professional independent designer.

A professional planner will properly layout an off-premise catering commissary, ensuring that the following major areas are arranged for maximum efficiency:

Receiving and loading area
Storerooms
Refrigeration and freezer space

Preparation area
Main cooking area
Bakeshop
Potwashing, dishwashing, and sanitation area

Know The Menu. The menu will dictate the necessary equipment and its layout. Most commissaries will require ovens, broilers, steamers, but may not require deep-fat fryers, particularly if frying is to be done at the event site. Most fried foods, other than fried chicken, do not hold up well, and are best cooked and served immediately.

Involve Kitchen Staff. Solicit opinions from those who will be working in the commissary. These staff members normally possess years of experience working in other operations, dealing with good and bad equipment and designs. Tap their experience.

Know Projected Sales Volume. Hopefully, before caterers start planning a commissary, they have a general idea of projected sales volume. A caterer content with sales of $250,000 per year definitely will not need a commissary capable of producing $5,000,000 per year in sales. It is usually better to err on the smaller side, with the option of expanding, because a facility that is overly large will require extra maintenance. It is also simply not as efficient as a more compact facility where distances between work and storage areas are less.

Other Miscellaneous Points. Equipment should be placed so that excessive walking is reduced and so it is close to major utility connections; multipurpose equipment should be accessible to all staff; and the most-often-used equipment should be close at hand. It is always advisable to put equipment on wheels for cleaning purposes, as well as for future flexibility if the layout needs changing.

Caterers should also think twice before automating. Frequently, the purchase of highly automated equipment to decrease labor and minimize work tasks requires more labor to maintain and to keep clean than the amount of labor saved. For example, a caterer serving two buffets for 20 guests every weekday does not need a computerized slicing machine.

BASIC COMMISSARY EQUIPMENT

A listing of all basic commissary equipment follows, as well as discussion on criteria for purchase. Off-premise caterers should be aware that each catering operation will require a different mix and layout of equipment due to operational differences such as menu and unique facility requirements and constraints. The following listing and discussion should suffice as a checklist and guide to equipment selection. (An excellent reference book for foodservice equipment is *A Modern Guide to Foodservice Equipment* by Arthur Avery, published by Van Nostrand Reinhold Co., Inc., New York 1985.

GENERIC CATERING COMMISSARY DESIGN
1500 SQ. FT.

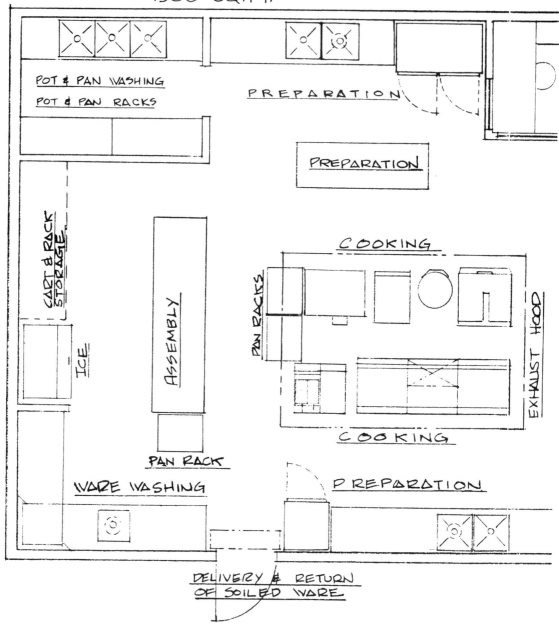

EXHIBIT 5-1 Generic Catering Commissary Design

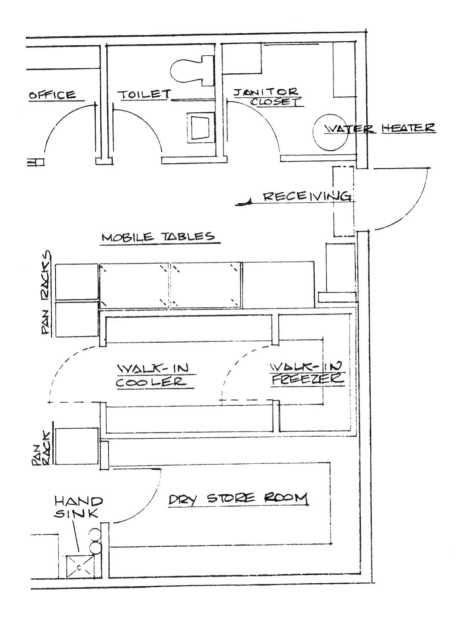

OFFICE

TOILET

JANITOR CLOSET

WATER HEATER

RECEIVING

MOBILE TABLES

PAN RACKS

WALK-IN COOLER

WALK-IN FREEZER

PAN RACK

HAND SINK

DRY STORE ROOM

EXHIBIT 5-1 (*continued*)

Conventional ovens
Convection ovens
Range tops
Microwave ovens
Deep-fat fryers
Tilting fry pans
Griddles
Broilers
Steam-jacketed kettles
Steamers and pressure cookers
Dish machines
Coffee makers
Food mixers
Food processors
Ventilation equipment
Reach-in and walk-in refrigerators and freezers
Ice machines
Slicers
Three-compartment sinks
Garbage disposals
Receiving scale
Hand and cooks sinks
Automatic fire system
Security system
Stainless steel preparation tables
Rolling baker's racks
Shelving

Conventional and Convection Ovens. A main concern is power source. Based on the specific location of the commissary, the designer can determine the best power source: gas, electricity or both. Up to three conventional deck ovens can be stacked on top of one another. It is important to specify the number of baking decks in each oven. Some newer models even have steam injection for crusting breads and rolls.

A convection oven operates with internal fans that blow away the cool air that surrounds the food as it cooks. These ovens cook in 25 percent less time, with 20 percent lower temperature, and require a shorter warmup period. They do tend to dry food out, so many caterers are choosing the new convection steam ovens that operate as pressureless steamers, a convection oven, and a high humidity convection oven. Many of the newest models are computerized so that, for example, in the case of cooking duck they can first steam the duck to seal the pores, then roast it, and finally at the end of the cooking cycle circulate hot air to brown the bird.

Range Tops. These come in flat-top configuration and open-top with burners. Gas ranges provide for better temperature control. Flat-top ranges will accommodate various sizes of pots and pans, but they take more time to heat up and cool down than open-top ranges. Many ranges can be purchased with single or double ovens below, or as freestanding or countertop models.

Microwave Ovens. These work well when thawing or reheating small amounts of food quickly. They do not brown unless they are purchased with a special attachment.

Deep-Fat Fryers. They come in countertop and floor models with capacities of 15 to 130 pounds. A rule of thumb for calculating fryer size is that it will take six times as much deep fat by the pound to the item to be fried. For example, a 15-pound fryer will fry 2.5 pounds of food product at one time (15 divided by 6). Obviously, a caterer specializing in fried chicken will need a larger-capacity fryer than a caterer who does little frying.

Tilting Fry/Braising Pans. These flat-bottomed pans can be used as kettles, griddles, fry pans, and grills. They can reduce preparation time by as much as 25 percent, since they tilt to save time removing the cooked foods.

Griddles. A griddle can be purchased as a separate piece of equipment, and is used for frying or scrambling eggs, for grilling sandwiches, and sautéing.

Broilers. Broilers use radiant heat to rapidly cook foods from either below or above. They are operated either by gas or electricity, and are great for searing meat.

Steam-Jacketed Kettles. These range in size from 20 quarts to 300 gallons and come in table-mounted and floor models. They cook foods quickly and the smaller models tilt to ease the removal of food. They are excellent for preparing soups, stocks, and sauces.

Steamers and Pressure Cookers. High-pressure steamers will cook small quantities of food very quickly, while low-pressure steamers will cook larger amounts of food, but not as quickly. One key consideration is to determine if there is an existing steam source in the commissary, or if the steamer will need a self-contained steam generator. Vegetables cook quickly in these steamers.

Dish Machines. The basic machines are those where dishes are washed on or in a rack. Flight machines are larger, and dishes are placed on a conveyor belt. Most dishwashers require a booster heater to bring the water temperature to 180 degrees for sanitation purposes, but some of the newer models are equipped with low-temperature, chemical sanitizing units. Several national chemical companies provide detergent for the machines, as well as preventative maintenance services, and even wholesale parts.

Coffee Makers. Most coffee companies provide coffee makers in exchange for using their coffee products. These units are installed in catering commissaries, where coffee is prepared, transferred to insulating containers and delivered to the party site. Normally, off-premise electric coffee makers are plug-in models that are purchased from restaurant suppliers.

Food Mixers. These are used for mixing, blending, kneading, whipping, and emulsifying. Stainless steel attachments such as whips, beater blades, dough hooks, and pastry knives are more expensive than aluminum, but will last longer and not react with food products that result in discoloration. Bench-model mixers come in capacities of 5 to 20 quarts, while floor models range from 20 to 80 quarts and more. For example, a 20-quart mixer can handle most mixing jobs for small-to-medium-size off-premise caterers. Mixers can be purchased with attachments to cut and chop foods.

Food Processors. Standard food processors are equipped with a bowl and blades or plates that operate on a horizontal plane. Commercial processors have a minimum horsepower requirement of 1/2 horsepower. A five-quart capacity bowl is minimum for a commercial unit. Some models come with larger bowls and more horsepower. Processors are sold with a variety of options including slicing disks for cutting vegetables and fruits, shredding disks for julienning vegetables and grating hard cheeses, and continuous-feed chutes. Vertical cutter mixers are good for large operations. Buffalo choppers are also used in off-premise catering operations. These operate as a bowl turns and a blade cuts soft food such as vegetables.

Ventilation Equipment. Local health and fire departments require the exhaust hoods and grease filter be placed above all cooking equipment in order to remove the heat from the commissary, as well as to filter out the grease which becomes a fire hazard. Exhaust systems and filters must be cleaned regularly to reduce the chance of fire.

Reach-in and Walk-in Refrigerators and Freezers. Walk-ins are used for bulk storage, while reach-ins are installed near the work areas. Walk-in refrigerators and freezers should be installed flush with the floor, should have doors with handles that also open from the inside, and should have a safety light or buzzer if the temperature is too high. Reach-ins come with one to three sections with single or double doors. Some are equipped with shelving, and some are designed to accommodate roll-in carts. Desirable features include adjustable legs, automatic defrost timers for the freezer, exterior-mounted thermostats, and locking doors.

Ice Machines. Icemaking equipment is rated by pounds produced in 24 hours. This rating is based on a water temperature of 60º F. and an air temperature of 70º F. A 10-degree increase in air temperature will reduce capacity by as much as 10 percent. Water-cooled ice machines are good inside since they reduce the amount of heat generated into the kitchen. Ice machines and bins are stackable. To determine the best capacity for an icemaker, estimate the amount of ice needed for the busiest week, multiply that amount times 1.2 and divide by 7. This is the correct size for the ice machine. The bin should normally hold twice as much ice as the machine makes in 24 hours. Off-premise caterers with heavy weekend demands may wish to obtain bins even larger than twice the machine capacity.

Slicers. These come in manual and automatic models which move the carriage carrying the food back and forth across a revolving blade. They are excellent for slicing meats, cheeses, onions, and firm tomatoes.

Three-Compartment Sinks. These are used for pot washing and are almost always required by local health departments.

Garbage Disposals. These should be durable and heavy duty. They are normally installed at the dirty-dish end of the dish machine.

Receiving Scale. This is a must for all off-premise caterers. Unweighed shipments can result in large losses due to shortweights.

Hand and Cook's Sinks. These are not only health department requirements, but are also necessary from the standpoint of efficiency and sanitation.

Fire and Security Systems. Fire-retardant systems are required in new commissaries, while security systems will help keep insurance rates lower and deter criminal activity. Local police departments can provide excellent advice regarding security systems.

Stainless Steel Preparation Tables. These should be conveniently located throughout the commissary and include adequate storage space underneath and above the tables.

Rolling Baker's Racks. These are aluminum-framed racks on wheels that hold sheet pans. Food and supplies are held on the sheet pans. Baker's racks may be wheeled directly into walk-in and some reach-in refrigerators.

Shelving. The width of the shelves should be determined by the items to be stored. For number 10 cans, 18- or 24-inch shelves are good, while 21-inch shelves are good for steam table pans. The best shelving lengths are 4 or 5 feet. Shelving is often purchased in four-tier units, but a fifth tier is optional and can expand capacity by an additional 25 percent.

FOOD HOLDING EQUIPMENT

Hot-Food Holding Equipment. This equipment should hold food at a desired temperature, should not cook it further, and should keep food at the proper consistency. Infrared heat is excellent for holding food for less than 15 minutes. For up to one hour, medium-term holding equipment, such as steam tables and insulated cabinets, is fine. For over one hour, cook-and-hold ovens are excellent.

Numerous manufacturers offer warming cabinets that keep preplated foods and bulk food hot. Some models control humidity, which keeps food from drying out.

The past ten years have brought the development of the portable and insulated pizza, food, and catering bags, many of which come with adjustable shelves to fit various-size pans, and handles that can be separated for two people to carry.

Cold-Food Holding Equipment. Cold foods can be held in refrigeration or in freezers. When transporting, refrigerated trucks are excellent, since baker's racks of food can be stored in the truck with little or no repacking. Another method for transporting cold food is to pack it in sealed plastic containers and chill in ice chests, if approved by local health departments. It is important that the food be sealed, and that food does not come into direct contact with the ice or water.

Criteria for Selecting Food Holding Equipment. The best food transportation equipment is lightweight, rugged, can be secured, has wheels or can be easily transported on dollies, and is leakproof.

OFF-PREMISE CATERING VEHICLES

Most caterers will need at least one vehicle for transporting food and supplies to the party sites. Some smaller off-premise caterers can transport everything required in a station wagon, while larger operators require a fleet of regular and refrigerated trucks. Before investing in a vehicle, most caterers should rent various sizes of vehicles in order to determine which size is best. Will a van be sufficient, or will it be necessary to invest in a larger truck? Some caterers have installed propane cooking equipment in vehicles. Others have invested tens of thousands of dollars in elaborate "kitchens on wheels."

Vans   Vans are very practical and quite economical for small-to-medium-size caterers who generally rent tables and chairs for events, rather than supply them themselves. It is recommended to always purchase, rent, or lease vans with heavy-duty suspensions. For example, in the Ford line of vans, the 350 model is superior to the 150 since it will carry the weight better. Caterers who have purchased the 150, or other lightweight models and who wish to carry heavier loads with more stability should look into such upgrades as heavy-duty shock absorbers, larger tires, and additional leaves in the springs.

Trucks   Trucks are not cheap. New refrigerated trucks cost upwards of $25,000 depending upon size and features. Many caterers find it more cost effective to rent trucks on an as-needed basis, while others believe in owning due to guaranteed access during busy periods. Caterers agree that reliability and flexibility are key elements in purchasing a catering truck.

Here are some criteria for selecting a truck for purchase, lease or rental:

1. Is the model reliable and easy to maintain?
2. The size should normally be no longer than 22 feet for driving ease and ability to turn corners in residential neighborhoods. Will the height of the truck allow it to enter areas where overhead clearances are limited?
3. Are there dual wheels in the back to offer more stability and to carry a heavier payload?
4. Avoid trucks with wheel wells that cut into the cubic space available.
5. Side doors are handy for loading and unloading items packed in the front first.
6. Lift gates are desirable for caterers who are transporting very heavy items such as ovens, dollies filled with chairs, and baker's racks and wheelers filled with food.
7. Is there adequate lighting in the carrying compartment?
8. Is there insulation to protect the contents from extreme heat and cold?
9. Are there guard rails inside on the walls?
10. Is there a drain for easy cleaning?
11. Are there safety and body protection options?
12. Is there an audible backup alarm that sounds when the truck is in reverse gear?

After selecting a truck chassis, off-premise caterers may choose to work with a local customized refrigeration or fabrication company to refrigerate the vehicle. The best option is a self-contained refrigeration unit with a built-in generator. Another option is a refrigeration unit which can be plugged into an outside power source.

OTHER TRANSPORTATION EQUIPMENT

Enclosed metal warming cabinets on wheels come in various sizes and heights and are excellent for packing items upright. Sheet pans filled with food slip right into these cabinets, which can be wheeled directly into refrigerated trucks.

No off-premise caterer should be without a two-wheel handtruck which can easily transport full ice chests, cases of sodas, and other heavy items that are easily stacked. Dollies have four wheels and are good for transporting heavy loads over level surfaces, but are impractical in areas where there are steps.

Some equipment, such as coffee makers, is best transported in custom-made plywood boxes, which offer more protection than the original cardboard box packaging. Plastic crates and containers are a must for transporting items of various sizes. Breakable items can be wrapped in old linens or plastic bubblewrap, and packed in plastic crates. Bus boxes with lids are also good for packing smaller items. Off-premise caterers should notice how local rental companies pack items, and use their proven techniques as appropriate.

EXHIBIT 5-2
Back-of-the-House Equipment and Smallwares

Work tables with folding legs (4, 6, 8 and 10 feet)
Portable propane ovens
Portable fryers
Portable grill
Propane gas tanks
Electric coffee makers
Electric tabletop convection ovens
Heat lamps
Electric counter top grill
Table top cassette au feu stoves
Electric hot plates
Rolling baker's racks
Warming cabinets
Chafing dishes for keeping food hot in kitchen
Stock pots (3, 6 and 10 gallon)
Woks
Sautee pans (8, 10, 12 and 14 inch)
Sauce pans, straight and slope-sided, nonstick (1.5, 2.75, 3.75, 5.5, 7 and 10
    quart)
Sauce pots (14 and 26 quarts)
Steam table pans (full and half size)
Sheet pans (full and half size)
Smaller baking pans to fit in convection and home ovens
Roasting pans with locking lids
Baking pans for pies, cakes, cookies, muffins and spring pans
Bread pans
Double boiler (8 and 12 quart)
Brazier pots
Egg poacher
Blender
Stainless steel bowls (assorted sizes)
Cutting boards, composition plastic (assorted sizes)
Skimmers
Fry baskets
Ice cream scoops (assorted sizes)
Wire whips (assorted sizes)
Piping bags with assorted tips
Ladles (assorted sizes)
Tongs (assorted sizes)

Knives (French, carving, cheese, bread, paring, boning, cleaver, etc.)
Knife sharpener
Steels
Cooks forks
Funnels (assorted sizes)
Serving spoons (regular, slotted, perforated)
Spatulas (assorted sizes)
Rubber spatulas (assorted sizes)
Spaghetti servers
Pie servers
Pie markers
Egg beater
Rolling pin
Can openers
Vegetable peelers
Melon ballers
Garnishing tools (zesters, strippers)
Pastry brushes
Garlic press
Parmesan cheese grater
Paddles (30 and 49 inch)
Juice extractor
Box grater
Broiler scraper
Fruit corers
Poultry shears
Clam and oyster knives
Colanders
China caps
Sieves
Food mills
Thermometers (meat, candy and deep fat)
Bus boxes with lids
Portion scales
Plastic food containers with lids (assorted sizes)
Beverage urns for holding cold and hot beverages
Ice chests
Garbage cans
Dollies
Hand trucks
Mop, bucket, and wringer
Brooms

Dust pans
Floor squeegee
Carton opener
Ingredient bins
Rubber floor matting
Oven and freezer mittens
First aid kits
Fire extinguishers
Extension cords
Hoses
Large funnel and metal containers for used cooking oil
Nonslip rubber floor mats

BACK-OF-THE-HOUSE EQUIPMENT

Exhibit 5-2 is a listing of the miscellaneous equipment and small wares necessary for most off-premise catering operations. This list should be used as a guideline or checklist for those caterers who are getting started in business. Readers should keep in mind that this list is not all inclusive, and that each catering operation will have some equipment and smallwares that are unique to that operation.

FRONT-OF-THE-HOUSE EQUIPMENT

Front-of-the-house areas are those where guests are. Front-of-the-house equipment can be classified as follows:

Tables
Chairs
Linens
China
Glassware
Flatware
Miscellaneous and other equipment
Tenting

Tables   Tables for off-premise catering generally can be described as banquet tables, round tables, conference tables, and special tables. Banquet tables are used for dining seating, buffets, food stations, and bars. Round tables are also used for dining, food stations, and buffets. Conference tables are narrower than regular banquet tables (18 inches wide versus 30 inches) and are effectively used when space is limited. For example, when working in a narrow hallway, a conference table may fit where a banquet table will be too wide. They also can be set up parallel to a banquet table to create an executive (wider) table. Special tables are used primarily for buffets and food stations to create various shapes other than simply straight.

Banquet tables. The three most frequently used sizes of banquet tables are:

8 feet by 30 inches	seats 8–10
6 feet by 30 inches	seats 6–8
4 feet by 30 inches	seats 4–6

Of course, longer banquet tables can be created by placing banquet tables end-to-end.

Round tables. Round tables are generally used for dining at catered events, and are considered to be more upscale than dining at banquet tables. Sizes are identified by diameter in inches, as follows:

72 inches	seats 10–12
66 or 60 inches	seats 8–10
48 inches	seats 6–8
36 inches	seats 4 (cocktail parties)
30, 24, or 18 inches	seats 2–4 (cocktail parties)

Conference tables. These are generally 18 inches wide, rather than the 30 inch width of regular banquet tables. The most common lengths are 6 and 8 feet.

Special tables. These include the following:

One-half round section	5 feet in diameter
Quarter-round section	8 and 10 feet in diameter
One-quarter pie	30 inch diameter
Rolling cake table	36 and 48 inch diameter table on wheels

Chairs The type of chairs used at off-premise catering events varies with the event. Brown wooden folding chairs are the least expensive, and are used where cost is a major concern. Folding Samsonite chairs are available in various colors, and are good when a nicer look is required. The white wood chair with the padded seat is a very popular chair at many events. The most expensive chair used at off-premise events is the ballroom chair, which has a thickly padded, upholstered seat. The chair frames and seats are available in assorted colors.

Chair covers are available for most chairs, and add an elegant look to the catered affair. Covers are available in various colors, fabrics, and sizes. Off-premise caterers should be sure when renting chair covers that they fit the chair to be used at the event, since many covers are made exclusively for stackable chairs used in hotels, restaurants, and banquet halls.

Linens Linens are an integral part of most parties; They are noticed by the guests as soon as they enter the dining area. They should blend with the atmosphere, have no wrinkles, and be placed evenly on the table so that the bottom edges are parallel to the floor (except, of course, on the corners of rectangular tables topped with rectangular cloths). For upscale events, linens should reach the floor, and for others, should fall at least 12 inches from the top of the table on all sides.

When purchasing linens, off-premise caterers should look for the following things:

Are stains easily removed during washing?
Will colors fade?
Do they easily resist mildew damage?
Are they fire retardant?
Do they require pressing?
What is the useful lifespan?
Can the napkins accommodate fancy folds?
How absorbent is the fabric?
Will they shrink?

Most linens are either cotton, cotton and polyester (Visa), or all polyester. Cotton linens are more elegant, but easily fade, shrink, and require pressing. Polyester linens do not easily fade, and many do not require pressing if properly washed and dried. The main disadvantage to polyester linens is that they are nonabsorbent, which is very undesirable, particularly in napkins. Blends of polyester and cotton combine the advantages and disadvantages of both.

Round tablecloths, like round tables, are classified by inches in diameter. When ordering round tablecloths to cover round tables, add 60 inches to the diameter of the table if you wish the cloth to reach the floor. For example, a 120-inch cloth will reach the floor on a 60-inch round table. A 90-inch round cloth will cover a 60-inch round table; it will not reach the floor but will fall approximately 15 inches all around. Frequently requested round tablecloth sizes are 90, 108, 120 and 132 inches.

Cloths for rectangular tables are available in assorted sizes such as:

60 by 120 inches	covers 8 foot by 30 inch table
60 by 90 inches	covers 6 foot by 30 inch table

Other sizes are dictated by local preference.

Table skirting is available in virtually every color imaginable. Most are made from polyester fabrics for long life and resistance to wrinkling. Common sizes are 8, 13, 17 and 21 feet. Skirting should be used for all buffet tables, food stations, and head tables where guests are seated on one side. To determine the amount of necessary skirting, measure the lineal feet to be skirted. For example, to completely skirt an 8-foot-by-30-inch table would require a 21-foot table skirt. This is computed by adding the dimensions of all four sides of the table as follows:

$$8 \text{ feet} + 8 \text{ feet} + 2\ 1/2 \text{ feet (30 inches)} + 2\ 1/2 \text{ feet} = 21 \text{ feet}$$

China The best china for use at off-premise catered events is durable and lightweight. The china should be in keeping with the caterer's image, the menu, and the caliber of the event. Plain white china is the most popular, followed by china with silver or gold trim, and black china can be very distinctive at many events. Some foods, such as smoked salmon, can be very elegantly presented on black plates. Coffee cups should have sufficiently large handles to avoid burning one's fingers.

When ordering china, it is imperative to consider menus and styles. Some basic china items include:

Platters
Show plates
Dinner plates
Salad plates
Bread and butter plates
Dessert plates
Soup and cereal bowls
Bouillon cup and underliner
Vegetable dishes (monkey dishes)
Coffee cups and saucers
Coffee mugs
Demitasse cup and saucers (for espresso)
Sugar and cream sets
Gravy or sauce boats
Salt and pepper shakers

Glassware   The quality of the glassware must be commensurate to the event. Plastic glassware is normally adequate for picnics and barbecues. For parties around swimming pools, and in certain public places, it is a necessity. Stemware is used for more upscale and elegant affairs, while tumblers suffice for many midscale events.

Annealed glassware is the least expensive, while tempered glassware possesses more strength. Leaded glassware is manufactured by adding lead oxide to the molten glass, which results in a very clear, crystal glass that produces a distinctive ring when tapped lightly.

When selecting glassware, keep in mind a few things:

Thicker glass is more durable.
A straight-sided glass has less strength than one with curves and bulges.
A flared glass has a greater tendency to chip, crack, and break.
Crystal carries the highest price tag, has the least durability, but has the finest
    and most delicate appearance.
Will the style be available when it is time to reorder?

Several caterers use a 13-ounce balloon wine glass as an all-purpose glass for water, wine, and most bar drinks except champagne, brandy, and cordials served straight up. Tulip and flute champagne glasses are used for upscale events, while the saucer champagne glass appears regularly at budget and midscale events. Please refer to Chapter 4 for diagrams of the various glassware types and sizes.

Flatware Flatware reflects the caterer's image, and when the table is set, tells the guests the number of courses to be served. The weight of the flatware is its most important characteristic. The heavier the flatware, the higher the perceived value. Flatware should be comfortable to touch, hold, and use. Balance is essential. Basic flatware is either silver-plated, stainless steel, or chrome. Gold-plated flatware is also available and used for those elegant bashes. However, gold-plated flatware is very difficult to maintain since it chips easily. Silver plate is more expensive, more formal, and harder to maintain than stainless steel since it needs to be burnished regularly. Stainless comes in a broader range of prices and is generally more casual. Chrome is the least expensive.

> Silver plate is a base metal electro-plated with silver to cover. The least expensive is silver over stainless. More durable, however, is an alloy of nickel, copper and zinc known as 70/30 brass or nickel silver. Since there is no standard for the amount of silver coating, the reputation of the manufacturer is important. Some manufacturers even add an extra coating to points of wear. Stainless steel varies in quality and price with the metals used in the mix. At the top of the line is 18/10. This is 18 percent chrome and 10 percent nickel. Nickel adds a warm silverlike luster. Chrome helps resist corrosion. Slightly below 18/10 is the popular grade, 18/8, which is 18 percent chrome and 8 percent nickel. What is known as chrome is really stainless steel without nickel and either 18 or 13 percent chrome.[1]

Basic flatware selections include:

Dinner knife
Butter knife
Dinner fork
Dessert or salad fork
Oyster fork
Teaspoon
Soup spoon
Bouillon spoon
Serving spoon
Demi teaspoon
Dessert spoon

Miscellaneous Other Equipment and Supplies

Exhibit 5-3 lists the major front-of-the-house items used at off-premise catered events. This listing should provide readers with some guidelines for selecting items to be used in an off-premise catering business.

Exhibit 5-4 includes those supply items frequently used at off-premise catered events. These items differ from equipment items in that they are disposable, that is, once used, cannot be re-used.

No current discussion of disposable products would be complete without addressing the topic of recycling. "Recycling within the special events industry can and should become an integral part of an industry that by nature produces an abundance of waste."[2] According to Tara Rosier, Operations Manager, Ambrosia

---

EXHIBIT 5-3
Miscellaneous Front-of-the-House Equipment

Chafing dishes (stainless steel, silver-plated, one and two gallon)
Serving trays and platters
Serving bowls
Serving spoons, forks, knives, ladles and tongs
Cake and pie servers
Assorted baskets for buffet items
Assorted buffet decor items (shells, nets, blocks, mirrors, etc.)
Water pitchers
Samovars (Urn for holding hot beverages)
Coffee pots
Water pitchers
Champagne fountains
Champagne and wine buckets
Candelabras
Bread baskets
Carving boards with warming lights
Carving knives, carving forks and sharpening steels
Cassette au feu stoves for warming and cooking
Punch bowls
Ashtrays
Plate covers
Votive candles (small candles in glass cups)
Glo-ice trays (used for raw bars, ice carvings and cold food displays)
Ice chests for ice for water glasses and dinner wine
Oval waiter trays
Tray stands
Cocktail trays
Bus boxes and lids
Trash cans
Staple gun
Fire extinguishers
Machines for popcorn, sno-kones, cotton candy and hot dogs
Wedding props (please refer to wedding section of text)

Production in Santa Monica, California, off-premise events generate hugh amounts of waste, and she suggests some tips for recycling.

1. For bars, place empty beverage containers back into their original boxes, which naturally separates glass by color and separates glass from plastic.

2. Aluminum cans should be placed in clear trash bags.
3. For casual events, trash containers should be placed around the event, with signs denoting the type of trash to be collected therein.
4. In the off-premise kitchen and commissary, cardboard boxes, wood produce crates, glass bottles, plastic containers, steel and aluminum cans all can be

---

EXHIBIT 5-4
Catering Supplies

Cold cups (cold drinks, wine, champagne)
Hot cups
Lids for cold and hot cups
Plastic plates (assorted sizes)
Plastic knives, forks and teaspoons
Paper dinner napkins
Paper cocktail napkins
Doilies for trays and underliner plates for soups, etc.
Beverage stir sticks
Coffee stirrers
Swordpicks and skewers for skewering foods
Drinking straws
Film wrap
Aluminum foil
Heavy duty tape such as duct tape
Plastic baggies
Wet-naps
Fuel for cassette an feu stoves
Sterno
Plastic gloves
Bug spray for flying insects and crawling insects (outdoor events)
Charcoal and charcoal lighter fluid
Business cards
Dish soap, silver polish, sponges and scrubbing pads
Plastic for covering tables
Heavy duty plastic for covering floors and carpets (like that used in homes and offices upon which equipment is placed)
Paper liners for sheet pans
Disposable bowls, platters and utensils
Garbage can liners
Disposable portion cups in various sizes
Disposable chef's caps
Wooden corn-on-the-cob skewers

recycled. Training staff and labeling waste receptacles will help promote recycling and reduce trash collection bills.

Paper products made from recycled materials are available, but are not generally suited for off-premise events. All paper products that are used at off-premise catered events go directly into landfill since they cannot be recycled due to clinging food. There is some recycling of polystyrene plastics if they are rinsed and sorted by type, which is impractical most of the time. From the standpoint of the environment, it is always better to use china dishes.

TENTING AND TENT ACCESSORIES

The main purpose of tenting at an off-premise event is to protect the guests from rain and other elements. Other purposes include augmentation of an existing structure, such as placing a tent alongside a building so that there is adequate room for the guests. Sometimes, tenting is provided to create a festive air, as for instance, erecting one inside an airplane hangar.

According to *Catering Today*,[3] there are eight basic types of tents and canopies on the market today. A description of each follows.

Rope and Pole Tent. This is a commercial grade of pole-supported tent that is pulled tight using guy ropes attached to stakes. These tents have center poles and range in sizes from 20 to 150 feet wide with expandable lengths. They must be installed by professionals.

Frame-Supported Tent. These tents are supported by aluminum frames, with the tent fabric being strapped or buckled to the frame. Sizes range from 10 to 40 feet wide, with expandable lengths. These tents have no center poles.

Marquees or Walkways. These are long, narrow tent structures used mainly for sheltering walkways, or defining an entry into a tent. Widths are from 6 to 10 feet, with expandable lengths.

Canopy Tents. These are residential grade, pole-supported tents that are pulled tight using guy ropes attached to stakes. Sizes range from 10 feet by 10 feet to 30 feet by 40 feet.

Tension Structures. These are commercial grades of pole-supported tents that utilize the strength of the vinyl-laminated fabric instead of the web or rope superstructure. Sizes range from widths of 30 to 80 feet with expandable lengths.

Free Span Structures. These are aluminum I-Beam structures with fabric panels between beams. Sizes range from 30 to 100 feet in width, with expandable lengths.

Quick-Up Framed Canopy. These are accordionlike canopies with collapsible legs that assemble quickly. Sizes range from 8 feet by 8 feet to 10 feet by 15 feet.

Economy Canopy. These are inexpensive frame-supported canopies which are usually 10 feet by 10 feet.

Off-premise caterers should be knowledgeable in these types of tents, as well as the various options available. Many rental companies do not provide tent sides unless sides are specifically requested. When ordering sides, it is important to specify whether they are to be clear, opaque, or opaque with windows. For events held after dark, or where opaque sides are used, lighting is essential. Theatrical-style lights are popular as are elegant chandelier lamps that hang from the tent frame.

Underneath the tent, off-premise caterers may wish to install astroturf, wooden floors (for dancing or to provide firm, even footing), or a combination of both. Frequently, flooring is installed over swimming pools to provide additional party space.

Off-premise caterers should insist that those installing floors over pools be fully insured and extremely experienced. An installation mistake could result in disaster.

Platforms are used to elevate musicians, those who speak, head tables, and bridal tables. These risers usually are available in 4-by-8-foot sections, and can be installed at heights of either 12 or 24 inches. Railings and steps are excellent safety precautions, while skirting can be attached to the platforms to improve their appearance.

To disguise tent poles, off-premise caterers may wish to place trees or shrubs next to the poles, or use canvas pole covers. For very elegant affairs, fire-retardant tent liners are used to completely cover the interior framework and poles.

Temperature control within the tent is critical, particularly in very warm or cold climates, or when it is necessary for all tent sides to be closed. Overhead or floor fans create a movement of air to help cool the area under the tent, but to truly create a comfortable atmosphere in hot, humid climates, air conditioning is necessary. Costs for this are very high, unlike the cost for portable heaters, which are fairly economical.

Formulas for determining total square footages necessary for tents are included in Chapter 6.

Finally, off-premise caterers must be knowledgeable regarding local regulations concerning tents. Many municipalities require that a tenting permit be issued prior to erecting a tent. Tent rental companies are frequently of assistance in this area, but it is the astute caterer who sees that this technicality is met prior to the party day. There are few worse situations than the sight of an inspector, on the day or night of the party, who asks to see the tent permit that was never obtained.

DO YOU RENT OR PURCHASE?

One of the questions most frequently asked by students of catering management, as well as those just starting in this business, is: "Is it better to rent or buy equipment?" The answer is: "It depends." It depends on a variety of factors which influence this decision. Nearly all off-premise caterers both own and rent equipment. Most off-premise caterers will purchase back-of-the-house equipment first, as part of their building process. Many say that the basic rule for deciding is to ask themselves whether they will use a piece of equipment six or more times per year. If the answer is yes, they buy; if not, they rent.

Let's examine the advantages of renting equipment as opposed to purchasing equipment:

1. There is no capital investment or need for cash.
2. There is no need to maintain this equipment.
3. As long as off-premise caterers satisfy the "minimum order for delivery requirements" of the rental company, they are not responsible for delivering renting equipment to the catered event. This responsibility falls upon the rental company; however, the caterer is responsible to see that the rental company does deliver.
4. There is no requirement for storage of rental equipment, since it is delivered and picked up at the party site.
5. Many rental companies require only that dishes and equipment be "rinsed free of food" at the conclusion of the event. They wash the dishes and equipment.
6. Off-premise caterers who rent equipment usually can select from a much wider variety of items, since rental companies have a wide assortment, and caterers are free to select from more than one rental company.
7. Rental companies have a much larger inventory, and many will even sub-rent from a competitor in order to provide off-premise caterers with the proper quantity. It seems that off-premise caterers who own their own equipment never have quite enough. For example, if they have place settings for 200 guests, the next party will be for 250 guests.
8. It is easier to pass on the costs of rental equipment than owned equipment to clients. There is no question that there will be a charge for the equipment, since caterers certainly are not going to pay the bill from their profits. With owned equipment, the actual cost of ownership such as wear and tear and losses is not as apparent as receiving an invoice after each event, so for some caterers there is a temptation to charge less, or not to charge for owned equipment.

What are the advantages to owning equipment?

1. Off-premise caterers who own equipment have greater control over the time of delivery. They are not dependent upon the rental company schedule.
2. Rental companies can be short on or out of stock of items and be unable to fill the order. There may be no rental equipment available in the area, such as in isolated rural communities.
3. Rented equipment may not be maintained up to the standards of the off-premise caterer.

4. Rental companies are not always accurate when counting equipment rented to caterers back into their inventories after the event. A few companies have been known to miscount in the rental company's favor, resulting in a large replacement bill for the caterers.
5. When rental companies invoice clients for lost or damaged equipment they bill at a replacement cost, which is normally higher than the actual cost. Their reason for this is that it takes their time to reorder, and while the item is not in service it cannot be rented, therefore resulting in lost revenue.
6. When in a competitive bidding situation, off-premise caterers who own equipment can discount its cost, or even not charge for it, in order to underbid the competition. This certainly is not a good business practice on a routine basis, but there may be particular events when this is appropriate.
7. Is there a market for renting equipment to other caterers, or to clients who only need equipment, but not the food?
8. Off-premise caterers can create a distinctive signature or stylistic identity with their own equipment.

In a case study prepared by Teri Woodard, Polster for off-premise catering seminars conducted by the National Restaurant Association, certain assumptions were made in order to compare the cost of owning versus renting equipment. In this study, it was assumed that a caterer would purchase or rent equipment sufficient to serve two dinners and two cocktail receptions per week for 100 guests. In addition to the actual cost of the equipment, she computed theoretical costs for:

Renting warehouse space
Utilities
Truck lease
Rental warehouse manager
Truck driver
Utility staff
Necessary packing containers
Repair and maintenance
Shipping containers
Replacement of broken and missing equipment
Cleaning supplies
Laundry equipment
Insurance
Payroll benefits
Advertising
Bad debt expense
Security
Depreciation
Other miscellaneous expenses related to owning equipment

In this example, the rental expense for the year was double the cost to purchase and maintain. This example will in no way directly apply to every off-premise cater, but it does identify the indirect costs of owning, as well as the high cost of renting.

In conclusion, off-premise caterers should determine the best solutions for their own particular circumstances. There is no one "right way." One Washington, D.C. caterer started in business as a rental company, and owns a huge equipment inventory that contributes greatly to the firm's bottom line. Another caterer rents all equipment for the front-of-the-house, and charges the client a price slightly higher than list. For this off-premise caterer, the income from rental equipment adds 5 percent or more additional profit to the bottom line.

DEALING WITH RENTAL DEALERS

Rental Company Terms   The relationships between rental equipment dealers and off-premise caterers can range from those which result in a "win–win" for both parties, to those characterized by mistrust, tension, aggravation, and dislike. The key to working with rental dealers is to understand dealers' terms, such as those of a prominent south Florida firm:

1. List prices are for one day's use only, and they apply to all rented equipment, even if some is not used. If equipment is returned late there is an additional charge; however, there are special rates for rentals in excess of one day. For example:

One Day	Pay One Day Rate
Two Days	Pay for One-and-One-Half Days
Three Days	Pay for Two Days
Four–Seven Days	Pay for Three Days

2. Most rental dealers provide special containers for china, glassware, flatware, and other equipment to ensure that all equipment is received sterilized, undamaged and table-ready.

   It is imperative that all rented equipment be counted and inspected upon receipt. Shortages and damaged equipment should be reported to the rental company immediately. If this is not done, the caterer will more than likely be billed for replacement costs for equipment not received, or for that which was damaged upon receipt. Rental companies also charge for missing shipping containers, and other items such as hangers for table linens.

3. Rental companies do not set up tables and chairs, and they expect them to be taken down and stacked upon conclusion of the event. Some companies will set up and break down at an additional charge. Care should be taken not to leave equipment where it may get wet from lawn sprinklers or rain.

4. It is policy that all china, glassware, and flatware must be rinsed free of food particles, and packed back into the shipping containers. Some companies

require that all equipment be washed, or a ware washing charge is added to the invoice.

5. Table linens should be free from refuse and dried to prevent staining and mildew. If linens are wet, it is best to spread them out to dry after the party is complete.

6. Most rental companies charge additional fees for deliveries above the street level, for locations outside their normal delivery area, and to any other unusual locations where extra labor or time is necessary.

7. The responsibility for rental equipment remains with the off-premise caterer from the time of delivery to the time of return. Rental company insurance does not cover equipment that is on rental. Off-premise caterers must insure that rental equipment is secure and protected from the weather. They should count all equipment at the conclusion of the party, and look for missing items at that time. Generally, a complete inspection of the party site will result in finding some of the missing items in unusual areas.

   Off-premise caterers may secure insurance for the loss of major items while at a party site. One off-premise caterer was billed $900 for the replacement cost of a 400-pound oven that was left overnight and stolen from a party site. Insurance is available to cover this type of loss, but not for smaller losses such as pieces of flatware or china.

   Another way to limit losses is to ask that the equipment be picked up at the end of the party. If late at night, this will usually result in an additional charge. Some off-premise caterers do not leave the highly pilferable items at the party site, but take them back to their commissaries for pickup by the rental company. These types of items include silver, flatware, samovars, and linens.

8. Rental companies generally do not require advance deposits from established off-premise caterers, and many extend credit and offer discounts. First-time renters can expect to pay COD, plus a security deposit. Some rental companies charge a cancellation fee to those who order equipment in advance, and then cancel the orders so close to the party date that the rental company is unable to rerent the equipment. Most rental companies have minimum order amounts for delivery of equipment.

Loss-Prevention Techniques

Off-premise caterers should train their staff to properly handle equipment. For example, use caution when handling candles so as not to drip the hot wax on the linens. Provide plenty of ashtrays for smokers. When working in very windy conditions, stemware should be cleared into bus pans and transported to the kitchen area.

An organized and efficiently operated dish return area can greatly contribute to reduction in losses. Everyone in the food service business has seen the chaotic dish room where dishes are stacked from floor to ceiling and breakage is inevitable. Off-premise caterers should set up tables for the efficient return and handling of the soiled dishes. There should be sufficient space for trays and bus boxes, and soiled dishes should be immediately rinsed and packed.

Trends in Rental Equipment   In the 1990s, rental companies are reporting trends toward better, more upscale linens; smooth, rather than cut glassware; china that is virtually unbreakable; and increased use of chair covers, gold-plated flatware, and crystal stemware.

Conclusion   The relationship between off-premise caterers and rental dealers can be excellent as long as there is mutual respect. Caterers should follow rental companies' rules, and they should ask their rental dealers how they can make their relationship work better. In turn, rental companies should recognize that off-premise caterers work under extreme pressure, and that rental merchandise must be delivered on time, every time, and that the equipment must be usable, with no shortages.

EFFECTIVE PURCHASING

If after carefully considering the pros and cons for purchasing equipment, off-premise caterers choose to buy all or some of their catering equipment, they need to consider various factors affecting the purchase decision. Before buying any equipment they should thoroughly consider the following:

Purchase price
Cost to operate
Cost to install
Depreciation
Obsolescence
Cost of insurance
Safety (approved by Underwriters Laboratory for electrical or American Gas Association for gas)
Design (easy to use, does what it's designed to do)
Cost to maintain
Proper size for operation
Stock or custom (stock is usually better and less expensive)

Leasing equipment is generally very expensive, but some dealers will finance 40 or 50 percent of the purchase price.

An often-overlooked factor is the impact of the investment tax credit which allows businesses to write off for tax purposes the first $10,000 (under current law) of equipment purchased, with the exception of vehicles. For some, the tax savings can mean the difference between renting and buying equipment.

As a general rule, it is best to buy what is needed to meet the current business demands, as opposed to buying more equipment than necessary to meet projected demands in future years. All one has to do is survey the large restaurants that have gone bankrupt, while the small ones with 40 or so seats continue to thrive. The same concept should apply to off-premise caterers. Less equipment in a smaller space is *usually* better than more equipment in a larger space.

When purchasing china, flatware, glassware, and other tabletop items, off-premise caterers should be able to negotiate with the seller to arrive at a price somewhere between the list price and 50 percent of the list price, which is generally the dealer's costs before shipping. When considering quantities, off-premise caterers should plan on sufficient supply to handle most events, but have the flexibility to buy additional items that are available on short notice for a particular event, *or* rent a similar pattern or style from a rental dealer.

Used equipment is readily available in most areas for significantly less money than new equipment. When shopping for used equipment, review the Sunday classified advertisements, visit the used-equipment districts in larger cities, and even contact new equipment dealers who may have used equipment taken on trade in.

According to Larry Levy, an equipment-savvy Maryland caterer, prior to going to look at used equipment, call and obtain the following information:

Name of the equipment, model, voltage, amp, and energy source
Length of ownership and whether equipment was purchased new or used
Why the equipment is for sale
Whether it has ever been repaired (By whom? when?)
Whether the price is flexible

Levy also advises that when considering equipment for sale at an auction you should obtain a list of the items to be sold, then preinspect the equipment and list those that may be worthy of a bid. Conduct further research by checking service labels, learn the original cost when purchased new, determine the installation cost, and then determine the maximum bid price and *do not exceed it.* For equipment that is sold in lots, you may choose to organize a group of buyers to purchase the complete lot, or buy the desired item(s) from the successful bidder of the complete lot.

Finally, off-premise caterers should not overlook the need for office equipment. Used desks, filing cabinets, and bookshelves are readily available. Chapter 14 addresses the purchase of a computer for word processing and accounting.

Telephones are essential communication tools. Before leasing or purchasing a phone system, caterers should know the number of people who will be on the phone at the same time. Each of these people should have their own phone, and there should be a sufficient number of lines for all phone users to simultaneously use the phone, while at least one line is free for an incoming call. Many caterers use pre-recorded messages for their clients who are put on hold. Imagine a caller hearing another caterer's ad while on hold listening to a radio station.

Phone systems should be expandable to meet the needs of growing businesses. One expandable system is the AT&T Partner's system. The best warranties are those that guarantee overnight replacement of any inoperative equipment.

No catering office is complete without a fax machine, which can be used to quickly forward proposals to clients, as well as make quick copies. Fax machine costs are dropping quickly, and this cost can quickly be recouped through time savings, overnight delivery cost savings, and copy cost savings.

NOTES

1. Lois Bloom and Patricia Boyer, *Food Arts*, September 1993, pp. 55–57.
2. Tara Rosier, "Recycling for the Special Events Industry," *Insight from ISES*, May/June 1992.
3. *Catering Today*, July/August 1990.

Chapter 6

The Logistics of Off-Premise Catering

This chapter deals with the planning and execution of the off-premise catered event. Off-premise catering creates unique challenges not found when working in one's own facilities. In effect, this chapter deals with many issues that are unique to off-premise catering, and some that are far more complicated when working away from a restaurant, club, or hotel, such as planning and designing the event. We will discuss in detail:

Discovering unique and exciting party locations
Site inspection
Planning and designing the event
The party packing list
Pulling, assembling, packing, and loading the party
Delivering and unloading food, supplies, and equipment
The show (the party itself)
Reloading, returning, and reviewing the event

In her book, *Entertaining for Business*,[1] Nancy Kahan provides her list of "Secrets for a Great Party." Some of her ideas apply to off-premise catering, and are excerpted here:

"Plan Ahead"—The great locations and the best orchestras are booked years in advance.

"Aim to delight, aim to please, do not aim to impress"—The most expensive is not always the right choice. The purpose of the party is to delight and please guests, not to impress them with the importance or wealth of the host or hostess. For example, a troupe of waiters who suddenly break into a dance routine between courses would be delightful, and considerably less expensive than a professional dance group that would cost thousands of dollars more.

"Don't settle for the ordinary—Find an undiscovered place"—The choices are unlimited. Two examples are under a bridge or on an unoccupied top floor of an office building.

"Don't be afraid to take calculated risks"—One example is a summer dinner under the stars, with an alternate plan in case of rain. Another is a progressive dinner party where guests enjoy different courses of a meal at different locations within a geographical area.

"Never assume anything"—All details must be checked and double checked. Astute off-premise caterers will review all details with the client, including all other arrangements that the client has made with decorators, musicians, photographers, entertainers, valet parking services and all providers of services for the event. For example, at some locations, electricity is limited. If the limited supply is to be shared with the musicians, the videographer, the entertainers and the lighting technician, a disaster could occur on the night of the event when fuses and circuit breakers blow.

"Know your clients' entertaining goals"—Caterers need to understand both the entertaining goals of the client and the client's entertaining style. When a party fails to meet the entertainment objective, it is considered a failure. For example, if the purpose of an event is for corporate employees to relax and have fun, and the menu is formal and the corporate executives give long, boring speeches, the event did not meet its goal.

DISCOVERING PARTY LOCATIONS

Astute off-premise caterers have developed lists of unique and exciting party locations. They have gone beyond the obvious locations such as private homes and places of business. They have conducted extensive research to locate unusual spots. Here are some of their secrets.

1. Review the Yellow Pages looking for the obvious, as well as facilities that might not be obvious, such as the interior of a shopping mall.
2. Look for theaters, museums, historical locations, and movie houses.
3. Contact local convention and visitors' bureaus and local chambers of commerce.
4. Read local *Key* magazine, and society and social columns.
5. Advertise in local publications for party locations.
6. Speak to real estate agents about private estates available for parties.
7. Speak and network with local caterers, rental companies, and other suppliers to the off-premise catering industry.
8. Contact local colleges, high schools, and auditoriums.
9. State and city film location services know of numerous interesting locations.

Off-premise events have been held virtually everywhere imaginable, including rooftops, parking garages, office building atriums, bus and train stations, historic schoolhouses, parking lots, and construction sites.

SITE INSPECTIONS

Prior to each catered event, off-premise caterers must visit the site to ensure that certain criteria are met. This visit is mandatory, and caterers should never rely on the clients' description of the location. A first-hand look is necessary to determine the available utilities, develop the proposed layout, meet key people at the party site, and check other details. Most off-premise caterers bring all or most of these things to a site inspection:

Sample menus, brochures, business cards
Notes or contracts from prior discussions with clients
Paper, pen, pencil, and a clipboard
Camera to photograph the party site
·Oven thermometer (if using on-site oven)
Preprinted site inspection checklist

A detailed discussion of each element of the site inspection follows.

Electricity   It would be an anomaly to find an off-premise caterer who has not blown a fuse with an electric coffee maker. Every caterer quickly learns that two electric coffee makers cannot be plugged into the same 20 amp circuit since with most makers each requires approximately 16 amps. Since electricity is becoming more popular as more and more fire marshals are becoming concerned with the dangers of propane, butane, and sterno, off-premise caterers should understand some of the technical aspects of electricity. Chris Coe, of Event Technical Services, Los Angeles, California in an article appearing in *Special Event* magazine,[2] gives some practical advice, which is summarized below.

To determine the total amount of electricity needed, it is necessary to compute wattage requirements for all electrical needs such as lighting, appliances, musicians, and videographers. Wattage is the total energy required and is computed by multiplying voltage (speed of electricity, usually 120 or 240) times amperage (the strength of the electricity). Some rules of thumb are:

Kitchen lighting = one watt per square foot.
Tent lighting where guests will be = 2.5 watts per square foot (this does
   not include heavy stage lighting or electricity for musicians).
Equipment wattage is stated on the equipment.
Ask musicians, lighting personnel, and others for their needs.

Once the total wattage is determined, divide it by 100 (usually 120, but this number provides for a safety factor), and this will determine the total amps required. For example, if 28,000 watts are needed, when this amount is divided by 100 it will reveal that 280 amps are needed, which would be fourteen 20-amp circuits. To provide the necessary power, be sure to order a generator with this as a minimum capacity. It is imperative to remember to put only one coffee maker on a 20-amp circuit to avoid blowing a fuse or a circuit breaker.

Most buildings only use 60 percent of their available electrical power. Licensed electricians can tap directly into that power surplus using a circuit panel board, or what is frequently called a gray box. If the event is near or in an existing building, this procedure may be less expensive and more efficient than renting a generator. The smallest quiet generators usually produce 50 amps.

Water   Water is needed for drinks, coffee, cooking and cleaning. During the site inspection identify the water sources, ensure that they are potable, and note if a hose or carrying containers are required. Obviously, if there is no water available, such as at an isolated site in the center of a field about to be developed, then it will be necessary to bring enough water. Many caterers bring five-gallon containers of bottled water. Others have insulating containers.

Garbage   Determine where all garbage will be left upon conclusion of the event. In some areas, off-premise caterers must take all garbage with them. At other locations, there are garbage cans available, and even staff to remove them. If there will be deep-frying at the party site, off-premise caterers should check to see if there is a container for used cooking oil. Otherwise, it will be necessary to bring containers for the used oil. Never dispose of oil or food on the ground or down a drain at the party site.

Off-Premise Kitchen and Staging Area   This is the area where the caterer will complete on-site preparation, and arrange everything for the service of the event. Some locations, such as churches, synagogues, and community centers are equipped with commercial kitchens. If so, the job will generally be much easier; however, during the site inspection it will still be necessary to check for things such as exhaust systems, trash containers, drainage, hot and cold running water, doorway size leading into and out of the kitchen, refrigeration, freezers, and fire extinguishers.

In those frequent instances where there is no commercial kitchen, caterers must evaluate various locations in and around the party site, using the following criteria:

Is the area covered?
Is it out of the guests' view?
Is it well-lit?
How close is it to where the guests are?
How close is it to the loading area?
Is it easy and safe for service staff to enter and exit this area?

Let us examine the typical locations used by off-premise caterers for cooking and staging catered events. This examination reveals some of their advantages and disadvantages.

Existing Home Kitchens. These are fine for small parties, but for larger at-home events they pose many obstacles such as ovens that are too small for full sheet pans and steam table pans, little storage space, inadequate refrigeration, and poor layout. When it is the only alternative, then caterers must remember to bring smaller baking pans, check the oven for accurate temperature controls, leave as much as possible in a back room or in the garage during the party to avoid cluttering the kitchen, bring adequate cold-food holding equipment, and be sure that there is adequate ventilation to remove cooking odors and heat from the home.

Garages and Carports. These are excellent in warmer climates, since the off-premise caterer has more open space, and is able to lay out the kitchen based on the needs of the specific party. Six- and eight-foot banquet tables can be placed strategically around the area. In most areas, it is fine to cook inside garages with butane, electricity, and sterno, but if propane gas is to be used for cooking, it and the applicable cooking equipment may be placed close to the garage, but must not be inside the garage.

Cook Tents. In those areas where there is no suitable, covered space for a kitchen, off-premise caterers will frequently rent or provide cook tents. They are available in various sizes, with the smallest being 10 feet by 10 feet. They are used frequently in such areas as parking lots, or outside commercial or public buildings with no interior cooking facilities. Cook tents may or may not need side panels and lighting, depending upon the weather and the time of the event. If all sides are closed, ventilation is limited, so it is best to close only the sides from where the inclement weather is coming.

Other Cooking and Staging Areas. The options are endless, but most experienced off-premise caterers have at one time or another worked on loading docks, in alleyways covered by overhangs, in empty rooms or offices, and in vacant storefronts. Where there is a will to have a party, the ingenious off-premise caterer will find a place to prepare the food in safe conditions.

Kitchens on Wheels. Buses, semitrailers, trucks, vans, trailers, and motor homes are all candidates for conversion to movable kitchens. Caterers to the film industry are fully equipped to prepare a gourmet meal from custom-designed kitchens on wheels. Off-premise caterers considering one of these units should fully investigate all of the options available and talk to those caterers with experience working with them, since they represent a major investment of time and money.

Rain Plan
While conducting the site inspection, it is absolutely imperative for the off-premise caterer and client to agree upon a plan of action in case of rain or inclement weather. Weather can ruin a fabulous outdoor event. Sometimes a tent will provide the solution. Other times, it may be necessary to move the party indoors. The solution should be agreed upon in advance of the event and the client and caterer should agree upon the time that the decision will be made. The time may be the morning of the day of the event, so that there is enough time to arrange for a last-minute tent installation, or to move the party to another location.

For major catered events with huge investments at stake, weather insurance is available to insure the sponsors from losses due to rain, wind, snow, and temperature. Worldwide Weather, of Great Neck, New York is one firm that insures such events. They recently paid $300,000 to organizers of a rib festival in Cleveland when foul weather ruined their event.

Existing Equipment
Many locations already have some features necessary for the catered event such as a bar, some tables and chairs, an outdoor barbecue grill, or some other equip-

ment that might facilitate the party, and reduce the amount of equipment that the caterers need to bring. Experienced caterers note these features and discuss them with clients to decide if they will be used at the party.

Delivery and Pickup of Food, Equipment, and Supplies

Where will off-premise caterers and rental equipment companies unload at the site? This can be very complicated, particularly in high-rise buildings where there are crowded loading docks and at least two different sets of elevators to reach the party site. While inspecting the site, caterers should decide where they will unload their equipment, food, and supplies, as well as where the rental company will unload their equipment. Most of the time, the rental company will deliver their equipment long before the off-premise caterer arrives on-site. There must be a place for secure storage of this equipment, as well as someone to receive and sign for it. Also, where will the rental equipment be kept until it can be picked up? If there is no secured place, then the rental company may need to pick up immediately upon conclusion of the event (usually at an extra charge); or the caterers will need to provide security for it, or take the equipment with them.

Proposed Party Layout

At this time the off-premise caterer, usually with the client, will begin to discuss where everything will take place during the event. Some public locations have floor plans drawn to scale, while most residences do not. Techniques for laying out and designing catered events will be discussed later in this chapter. Suffice it to say that during the site inspection caterers must at least prepare a "rough" diagram of the event, noting those significant features that will affect the layout.

Meeting the VIPs

At many public party sites there are those behind-the-scenes people who can be of supreme assistance prior to and during the event. Experience teaches off-premise caterers to find these people during the site inspection and advise them of the requirements for the event. These helpful people are loading dock personnel who can make delivery and leaving more efficient, building engineers who know the location of utilities and circuit breakers, and security staff who can assist with various security measures. For home parties, many clients employ cleaning and maintenance personnel who know where things are and can help solve minor problems before and during the event.

Details to Address During the Site Inspection

It is suggested that topics such as rental fees for the space, rules and regulations, insurance requirements, policies regarding liquor service, security, and parking for guests be confirmed prior to the site inspection. Minor questions regarding these and other special circumstances should be asked during the site inspection. Many off-premise caterers have been surprised by changes in the rules by the facility. For example, a caterer prepares to set up a bar in a particular spot. Someone from the facility informs him or her that this cannot be done because the rules were just changed and no one told the caterer. Some off-premise caterers require that someone from the facility signs the rules to avoid these last-minute hassles or frustrations.

Zoning, fire, and other permits can be an immense problem. Rental companies usually can help in these areas. Some caterers have found that it can be less expensive to hire off-duty fire-fighters than meet particular flame-retardant codes for tenting. If guests are traveling by motor coach to a private mansion in a private neighborhood, neighbors may complain about the noise from the motor coaches. Noise restrictions in some neighborhoods can ruin an outstanding party when the police arrive to shut down the event.

The timing for party setup and teardown is critical. Many museums and historical locations are open until late in the day, leaving off-premise caterers limited time to set up. At the end of the evening, most of these facilities require removal of all party equipment. Some have special fees for loading in and out, some require use of union labor, and many restrict rolling tables over valuable flooring.

If there are elevators, know how they work and where they go. Be sure that the clients have arranged for their use. Off-premise caterers should allow additional time for setting up and breaking down parties that are not on the ground floor. One major problem in high-rise office buildings is that cleaning personnel usually have exclusive use of some or all of the elevators, making it impossible for caterers to enter and exit. If this is the case, it is imperative that clients make the necessary arrangements.

Planning for the staff who will work the party should address things such as obtaining the exact directions to the party site, finding out where the staff will park, and determining where the staff will change after setting up and prior to the event.

Other details include obtaining an emergency phone number at the site that will be answered afterhours. This can be a problem in offices, where the switchboards close as the party begins. It is imperative to know the name and phone number of the person in charge of the facility during the party.

Site inspections should include an inspection of rest room facilities, as well as handicap access. Problems in these areas should be resolved in advance, so as to avoid problems during the event.

Finally, caterers should be aware that some restrictive rules are subject to negotiation, particularly if they will prohibit a party from being held at a facility. Such things as early setup can be discussed with the facility manager, and can sometimes be resolved by paying an additional fee. Off-premise caterers who frequently work at unique, public off-premise locations have learned to advise the client that there may be additional costs involved in the catering event due to unforeseen circumstances, and a contingency clause should be included in the catering contract. For example, if the site is not made available to the caterer on time, and the caterer needs to hire extra staff to have the party set up on time, then this would be a situation where the caterer would be able to charge for the extra staff.

PLANNING AND DESIGNING THE EVENT

Introduction   The results of the site inspection, coupled with the menu and other information, are the input for the party layout. For simple parties, the layout can be roughly sketched during the site inspection, but for large, complicated events, the rough diagrams and notes from the site inspection should be incorporated into a scale diagram of the event. This diagram should include:

Registrations tables and check-in areas
Gift, cake, and place card tables (for weddings)
Bars, buffets, and food stations
Seating for guests during cocktails and dinner
Service stations for staff
Dance floors, stages, and space for entertainers
Off-premise catering kitchen and staging area

The diagram should be to scale to ensure that things will fit where planned. Disasters have occurred when off-premise caterers "assumed" that a certain number of tables would fit into a specific room, and they did not. Off-premise caterers may contact Meeting Professionals International in Dallas, Texas for special templates used for diagramming parties to scale. Graph paper is also helpful.

LAYOUT AND DESIGN CRITERIA

The Front-of the-House Unlike hotel ballrooms and catering halls, off-premise locations used for catering have specific primary uses unrelated to food service, which can create unique challenges. The size, shape, and flow of the location influence the layout and design. Questions to ask while determining an overall layout include:

How many guests will be attending?
Where will they be arriving?
What are the menu and beverage arrangements?
What are the other planned activities, such as dancing, etc.?
Are there existing features such as bars and seating?
Where is the off-premise kitchen in relation to the party?
What is the theme of the party?

Prior to discussing each element of the layout, it is important that readers understand some generally accepted square-footage requirements.

TYPE OF PARTY OR REQUIREMENTS	SQUARE FEET REQUIRED PER PERSON
Standup Cocktail Party	5 to 6
Cocktail Party—Some Seating	8
Dinner—Rectangular Tables	8
Dinner—60" Rounds for 10	10
Dinner—48" Rounds for 6	12
60" Rounds for 8	12
72" Rounds for 10	12
Theater-Style Seating (Weddings)	6

| Dance Floor | 2 to 4 |
| Speakers' Platform | 10 |

For bands, allow 10 square feet per musician, 20 square feet for the drummer, 30 square feet for a spinet piano/keyboard, and 100 square feet for a grand piano. If the musicians are on risers or platforms, steps and railings should be provided for safety reasons.

For theater-style seating, allow three feet from the front of one chair and the back of the next one. Suggested spacing is five feet between guest tables at seated events. For large events in the hundreds of guests, the seating area should be divided into groups of tables, with six-foot-wide main aisles between sections. For example, a party with 40 tables could be divided into 4 groups of 10 tables each, with a 6-foot aisle in between.

Head tables where guests are seated only on one side are usually impractical at off-premise events where space is at a premium, since they take twice as much space as regular guest seating at round tables.

Coat checks and registration tables should be placed near the entrance for security and other reasons. Off-premise caterers should advise clients to provide adequate registration personnel to prevent long lines, which may extend outside the party site. Bars, buffets, and food stations should be placed strategically around the room. They should never all be clustered in one area. Bars should be set up so that guests may see them on arrival, but not so close to the entrance as to block guest traffic flow into the party. Bars generally require 100 to 150 square feet of space. One bar with one or two bartenders is generally adequate for efficient guest service for a party of 100, depending on the type of drinks offered and the skill of the bartender.

Buffets, food stations, and bars should act as magnets, drawing guests into the room, but never be placed close to the dance floor or music. Allow plenty of space between stations for guests to circulate, and adequate surfaces for guests to place empty drink glasses. Dramatic buffets and food stations create excitement, interest, and intrigue. Straight, long tables are boring. Exhibit 6-1 depicts various creative designs. Some basic rules for buffet setup are the following:

- ❑ Attempt to locate the buffets and food stations as close as possible to the off-premise kitchens to reduce distances traveled during initial setup and replenishment.
- ❑ Place low-cost items first.
- ❑ Expensive items such as caviar and beef tenderloin should be portioned by servers and carvers.
- ❑ Preportion appropriate items into smaller portions, since people prefer small amounts of many things.
- ❑ Guests take less food from small containers.
- ❑ The more attractive the buffet, the less people eat since they do not want to ruin its appearance.

If all guests are eating at the same time, 50 to 75 people can eat from each line. Since two-sided, self-service lines take less space, 100 to 150 guests can be served from one table instead of two single-sided buffet tables. Carvers or servers can stand at the end of each line, portioning or carving one or two expensive items. Exhibit 6-2 diagrams a simple buffet with food servers and one carver.

Buffets longer than 16 feet should be two tables wide (60 inches). This will make the buffet wider, more in proportion and less like a cafeteria line.

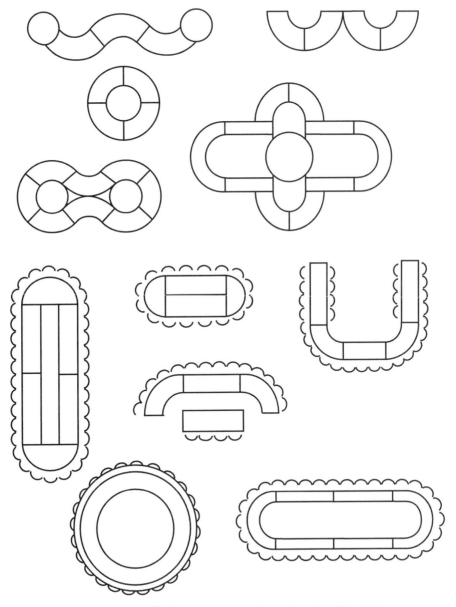

EXHIBIT 6-1　Buffet Layouts Courtesy of American Rental Association.

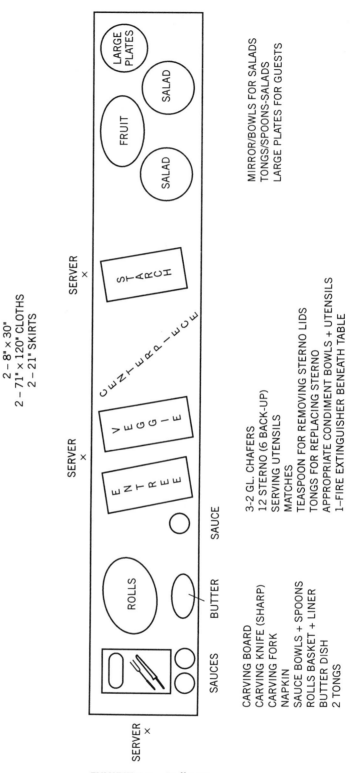

BUFFET DIAGRAM

2 – 8" × 30"
2 – 71" × 120" CLOTHS
2 – 21" SKIRTS

SERVER ✕

SERVER ✕

SERVER ✕

LARGE PLATES

SALAD

FRUIT

SALAD

STARCH

CENTERPIECE

VEGGIE

ENTREE

SAUCE

ROLLS

BUTTER

SAUCES

MIRROR/BOWLS FOR SALADS
TONGS/SPOONS-SALADS
LARGE PLATES FOR GUESTS

3-2 GL. CHAFERS
12 STERNO (6 BACK-UP)
SERVING UTENSILS
MATCHES
TEASPOON FOR REMOVING STERNO LIDS
TONGS FOR REPLACING STERNO
APPROPRIATE CONDIMENT BOWLS + UTENSILS
1–FIRE EXTINGUISHER BENEATH TABLE

CARVING BOARD
CARVING KNIFE (SHARP)
CARVING FORK
NAPKIN
SAUCE BOWLS + SPOONS
ROLLS BASKET + LINER
BUTTER DISH
2 TONGS

EXHIBIT 6-2 Buffet Diagram

120

Place trays and chafing dishes at an angle to the table to avoid a squared-off look. Raise the back corners of trays several inches with plates so that the trays slant toward the guests. Tier foods to interesting, yet reachable levels.

According to Irvin Kanode, in an article in *Catering Today*, "Buffets can be an ideal method of service for catered events. They provide an opportunity to be creative, using food presentations and unique decorations. Buffets give you a chance to show you are different than your competition."[3] His suggestions for buffet decor include:

Large, elevated floral centerpieces
Candelabras
Wicker or bread cornucopias filled with fruit and vegetables
Statues that match the theme of the party
Large pottery, clay, or wicker vases with silk flowers
Models of hot-air balloons
Ceramic kitchen tiles
Glass and other building blocks
Cast-iron pots and glass or stoneware casseroles
Hollowed-out pumpkins and other vegetables and fruits filled with food
Hand-made and clay pottery to hold decorations

Off-premise caterers frequently elevate buffet dishes and decor with the use of empty crates and boxes covered with linens and fabric. Many table linen rental companies will give caterers damaged linens, which can be rumpled up and placed between items on buffets.

Joyce Piotrowski, of Epicurean Events in Alexandria, Virginia, in her article in *Catering Business*,[4] offers her advice on designing food stations and buffets. She stresses the importance of preparing an exact diagram of the food station (buffet), along with a list of the items necessary for setup. This allows staff to set up without constant supervision.

Ms. Piotrowski also suggests looking for serving equipment at the wholesale giftware and tabletop shows. For decor, she has had wonderful results with large fans to decorate oriental stations and bleached cattle skulls for Mexican or Southwestern stations.

Lighting is one of the most frequently overlooked aspects of party design. Thousands of fabulously decorated and designed buffets and food stations have been lost in the dark because the off-premise caterer forgot to plan for proper illumination. A supply of spotlights, floodlights and lampstands is an important part of the caterer's arsenal of buffet props and decor.

The Kitchen and Staging Area   For smaller events in homes and offices, off-premise caterers generally use existing facilities, making the best of some very difficult situations. Of course, the menu must be compatible with the facility. Ask questions such as:

Where is there storage for backup supplies?
Where will items be cooked and kept warm?

Where can cold foods be prepared and kept cold?

Where will the hot- and cold-food dishup take place?

Where will the food servers pick up food and return dirty dishes?

Where can the coffee be brewed?

The answers to these questions will help an inexperienced off-premise caterer organize an off-premise catering kitchen within the confines of an existing kitchen or area.

For larger events where hundreds are to be served, and where there is no adequate facility, cooking tents are generally erected. Exhibit 6-3 depicts one way to lay out and design a large, off-premise catering kitchen. Some design criteria include the following:

❑ Design the kitchen so that the food servers can easily pick up food and return soiled dishes without going through the kitchen.

❑ It is good safety procedure to keep everyone who is not part of the kitchen staff out of the cooking area.

❑ The bussing area for dirty dishes should contain garbage cans, water for rinsing dishes, and room for empty dish and glass crates. This area ideally is distanced from the cooking area, especially on larger events.

❑ Four-, six-, and eight-foot banquet tables are excellent for use as kitchen work tables. Caterers should be sure to allow enough work tables for the type of food service to be provided.

❑ The coffee and dessert should be kept to the rear of the tent until ready to be served and should have space for all items pertaining to coffee and/or dessert service.

❑ Equipment and supplies necessary for hors d'oeuvres should be gathered and set aside prior to the main course. The same applies to all equipment and supplies for all courses.

❑ Arrangements should always be made to warm plates for hot food courses.

❑ Tables are necessary next to the ovens for space for the cooks to set down hot foods from the oven.

❑ The same area used to plate-up salads can be used to plate-up desserts.

❑ Place portable liquid-fuel warming ovens at the edge of the tent for ventilation. A large sign on an easel for the event's menu, which also lists ingredients of each item, should be placed near the food pickup area.

Finally, experience is one of the best teachers in determining the best ways to lay out catered events. These are only guidelines. Remember that a well-designed party will go a long way toward satisfying the client's needs, and will make everyone's job easier during the party.

THE PARTY PACKING LIST AND RENTAL ORDER FORM

Once the layout and design is complete for the catered event, the party packing list (pull sheet), and the final rental order form can be prepared. Most off-

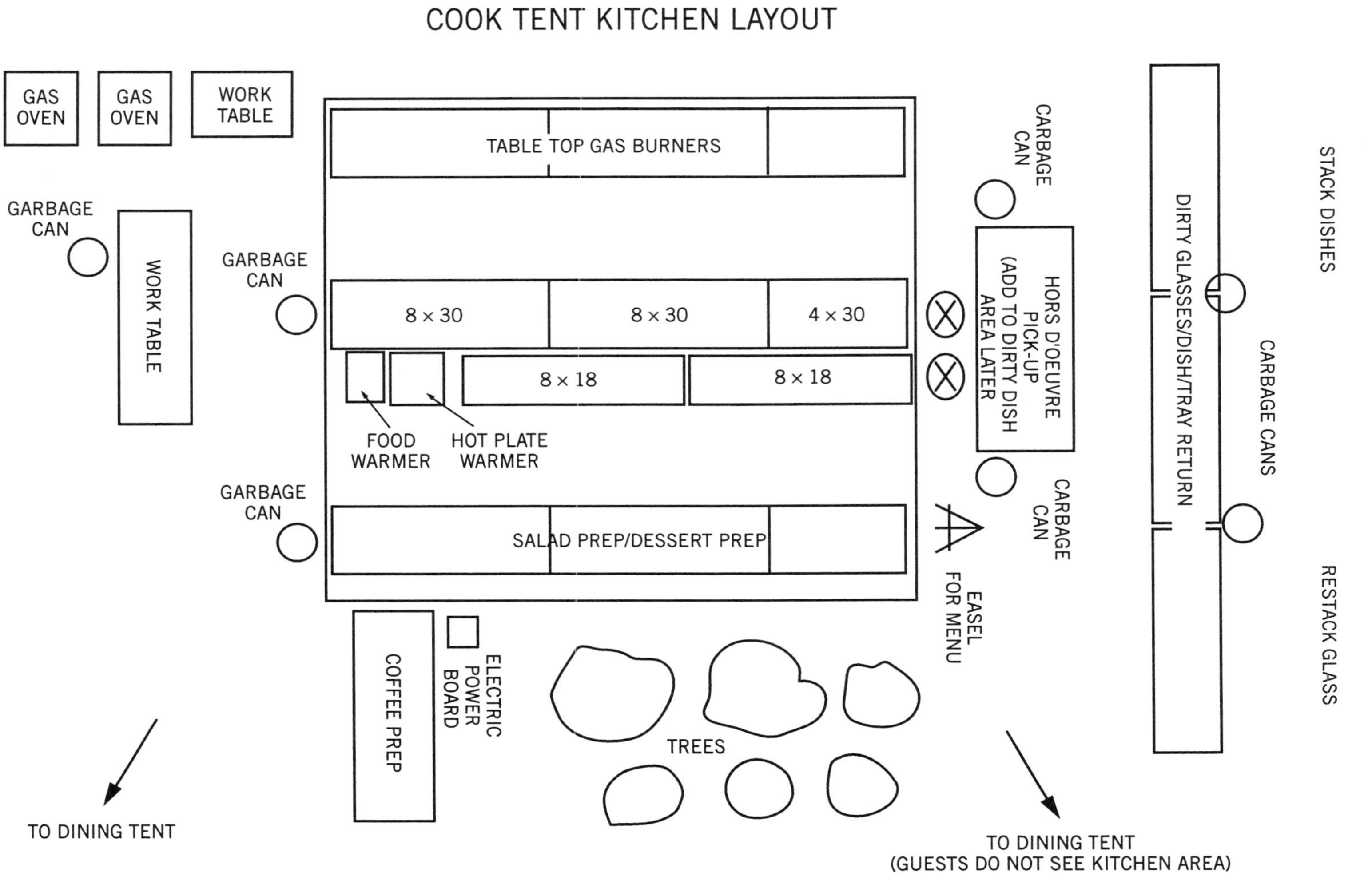

COOK TENT KITCHEN LAYOUT

STACK DISHES

RESTACK GLASS

CARBAGE CANS

DIRTY GLASSES/DISH/TRAY RETURN

TO DINING TENT
(GUESTS DO NOT SEE KITCHEN AREA)

CARBAGE CAN

HORS D'OEUVRE PICK-UP (ADD TO DIRTY DISH AREA LATER

CARBAGE CAN

EASEL FOR MENU

TABLE TOP GAS BURNERS

4 × 30

8 × 18

8 × 30

8 × 18

8 × 30

HOT PLATE WARMER

FOOD WARMER

SALAD PREP/DESSERT PREP

TREES

ELECTRIC POWER BOARD

COFFEE PREP

WORK TABLE

GAS OVEN

GAS OVEN

GARBAGE CAN

GARBAGE CAN

GARBAGE CAN

WORK TABLE

GARBAGE CAN

TO DINING TENT

EXHIBIT 6-3 Cook Tent Kitchen Layout

premise caterers have forms that make this task easier and reduce the likelihood of an error. Exhibits 6-4 and 6-5 are examples of a rental order form and a packing list form. The basic premise is to ensure that all necessary food, supplies, and equipment are delivered on time to the party. Items that are provided from the off-premise catering commissary are included on the pull sheet, and items to be rented are included on the rental equipment order form. One exception to this rule occurs when off-premise caterers obtain a small equipment order received directly at their commissary from the rental companies. In this case, the rental equipment should be included on the packing list so that the off-premise caterers are reminded to bring it to the event.

EXHIBIT 6-4
Rental Equipment Order Form

NAME OF CLIENT _____

DELIVERY ADDRESS _____

DELIVERY DATE _____   TIME TO DELIVER _____
DATE TO PICK UP _____   ORDER PLACED WITH _____ (NAME)
DATE ORDER PLACED _____

QTY ORD	QTY REC'D	QTY RET'D	ITEM AND DESCRIPTION	PRICE
____	____	____	CHAIRS	____
____	____	____	SAMSONITE	____
____	____	____	WHITE WOOD WITH PADDED SEAT	____
____	____	____	BALLROOM	____
____	____	____	OTHER _____	____
____	____	____	TABLES	____
____	____	____	8 FOOT BY 30" BANQUET TABLES	____
____	____	____	8 FOOT BY 18" BANQUET TABLES	____
____	____	____	6 FOOT BY 30" BANQUET TABLES	____
____	____	____	6 FOOT BY 18" BANQUET TABLES	____
____	____	____	4 FOOT BY 30" BANQUET TABLES	____
____	____	____	72" ROUND TABLES	____
____	____	____	60" ROUND TABLES	____
____	____	____	48" ROUND TABLES	____
____	____	____	36" ROUND TABLES	____
____	____	____	30" ROUND TABLES	____
____	____	____	QUARTER ROUND TABLES	____

EXHIBIT 6-4 (*continued*)

_____	_____	_____	QUARTER ROUND PIE TABLES	_____
_____	_____	_____	HALF ROUND TABLES	_____
_____	_____	_____	OTHER SPECIAL TABLES _____	_____
_____	_____	_____	UMBRELLA TABLES AND CHAIR SETS	_____
			TENTING AND ACCESSORIES	_____
_____	_____	_____	DINING TENT SIZE _____ WITH SIDES? _____	_____
_____	_____	_____	COOKS TENT SIZE ____ WITH SIDES? _____	_____
_____	_____	_____	CEILING FANS _____	_____
_____	_____	_____	TENT LINER _____	_____
_____	_____	_____	POLE COVERS _____	_____
_____	_____	_____	ASTROTURF _____	_____
_____	_____	_____	FLOORING _____	_____
_____	_____	_____	OVENS, RANGES AND FOOD WARMING CABINETS	_____
_____	_____	_____	SIX-BURNER RANGE WITH OVEN	_____
_____	_____	_____	FOUR-BURNER RANGE WITH OVEN	_____
_____	_____	_____	SIX-BURNER RANGE ONLY	_____
_____	_____	_____	OVEN ONLY	_____
_____	_____	_____	FOOD-WARMING CABINETS	_____
_____	_____	_____	LINENS, CHAIR COVERS, AND TABLE SKIRTING	_____
_____	_____	_____	132″ ROUND CLOTH COLOR _____	_____
_____	_____	_____	120″ ROUND CLOTH COLOR _____	_____
_____	_____	_____	108″ ROUND CLOTH COLOR _____	_____
_____	_____	_____	90″ ROUND CLOTH COLOR _____	_____
_____	_____	_____	NAPKINS TYPE _____ COLOR _____	_____
_____	_____	_____	60″ BY 120″ BANQUET CLOTH COLOR _____	_____
_____	_____	_____	90″ BY 90″ BANQUET CLOTH COLOR _____	_____
_____	_____	_____	62″ BY 62″ CLOTH COLOR _____	_____
_____	_____	_____	CHAIR COVERS COLOR _____	_____
_____	_____	_____	CHAIR COVER SASHES COLOR _____	_____
_____	_____	_____	SKIRTING COLOR _____ SIZE _____	_____
_____	_____	_____	SKIRTING COLOR _____ SIZE _____	_____
_____	_____	_____	CHINA—SELECT PATTERN AND COLOR _____	_____
_____	_____	_____	SERVICE PLATE (SHOW PLATE)	_____
_____	_____	_____	DINNER PLATE	_____
_____	_____	_____	DESSERT/SALAD PLATE	_____
_____	_____	_____	BREAD AND BUTTER PLATE	_____
_____	_____	_____	SOUP CUP UNDERLINER	_____
_____	_____	_____	SOUP CUP	_____
_____	_____	_____	COFFEE CUP AND SAUCER	_____
_____	_____	_____	DEMITASSE CUP AND SAUCER	_____
_____	_____	_____	CREAMERS	_____

EXHIBIT 6-4 (*continued*)

___	___	___	SUGARS	___
___	___	___	GRAVY BOATS	___
___	___	___	SALT AND PEPPER SETS	___
___	___	___	OTHER _____	___
___	___	___	FLATWARE—SELECT TYPE _____	___
___	___	___	DINNER KNIFE	___
___	___	___	BUTTER SPREADER	___
___	___	___	FISH KNIFE	___
___	___	___	TEA KNIFE	___
___	___	___	DINNER FORK	___
___	___	___	SALAD/CAKE FORK	___
___	___	___	COCKTAIL FORK	___
___	___	___	TEASPOON	___
___	___	___	SOUP SPOON	___
___	___	___	DESSERT SPOON	___
___	___	___	ICED TEASPOON	___
___	___	___	DEMITASSE SPOON	___
___	___	___	PASTA SPOON	___
___	___	___	SERVING PIECES AND EQUIPMENT	___
___	___	___	LARGE SERVING SPOON	___
___	___	___	SMALL SERVING SPOON	___
___	___	___	SERVING FORK	___
___	___	___	LADLE	___
___	___	___	CAKE/PIE SERVER	___
___	___	___	CAKE KNIFE	___
___	___	___	ONE GALLON ROUND CHAFER	___
___	___	___	TWO GALLON OBLONG CHAFER	___
___	___	___	EXTRA PANS HALF _____ FULL _____	___
___	___	___	50 CUP SAMOVAR	___
___	___	___	100 CUP SAMOVAR	___
___	___	___	COFFEE POURER	___
___	___	___	WATER PITCHERS	___
___	___	___	OVAL TRAYS	___
___	___	___	ROUND TRAYS	___
___	___	___	GLOW ICE DISPLAY	___
___	___	___	GLASSWARE	___
___	___	___	TULIP CHAMPAGNE	___
___	___	___	BUBBLE WINE GLASS 12 OZ	___
___	___	___	BUBBLE WINE GLASS 9 OZ	___
___	___	___	IRISH COFFEE MUGS	___
___	___	___	CRYSTAL CHAMPAGNE FLUTE	___

EXHIBIT 6-4 (*continued*)

____	____	____	CRYSTAL WINE GOBLET	____
____	____	____	CRYSTAL WATER GOBLET	____
____	____	____	BRANDY SNIFTER	____
____	____	____	CORDIAL GLASS	____
____	____	____	OTHER RENTAL EQUIPMENT	____
____	____	____	GENERATOR	____
____	____	____	PLATFORMS FOR MUSIC AND SPEAKERS SIZE ____	
____	____	____	STEPS FOR PLATFORMS	____
____	____	____	RAILING FOR PLATFORMS	____
____	____	____	SKIRTING FOR PLATFORM COLOR ____ SIZE ____	
____	____	____	DANCE FLOOR SIZE _____ TYPE _____	____
____	____	____	CHAMPAGNE FOUNTAIN	____
____	____	____	BRIDAL KNEELING BENCH	____
____	____	____	BRIDAL ARCH	____
____	____	____	GUEST BOOK STAND	____
____	____	____	FLOWER BASKET STAND	____
____	____	____	WHITE LATTICE GAZEBO	____
____	____	____	WHITE LATTICE CHUPPAH	____
____	____	____	OTHER MISCELLANEOUS EQUIPMENT	____
____	____	____	_____	____
____	____	____	_____	____
____	____	____	_____	____
____	____	____	SUBTOTAL OF ORDER	____
____	____	____	EXTRA FEE FOR NIGHT PICKUP	____
____	____	____	ABOVE-GROUND DELIVERY FEE	____
____	____	____	TOTAL PRICE OF ORDER	____
			NOTES FROM RENTAL CHECK-IN, I.E., DAMAGED	
			OR MISSING EQUIPMENT, OTHER PROBLEMS	
____	____	____	CREDIT DUE FOR THE ABOVE	____
____	____	____	BALANCE DUE RENTAL COMPANY	____

Rental equipment order forms can simply be copies of rental order forms supplied by the party rental firms with whom caterers do business. This practice may cause confusion if caterers deal with more than one firm. These forms may be inconsistent with each other and time consuming.

A rental equipment order form can be developed by listing these main categories:

EXHIBIT 6-5
Party Packing List

NAME OF PARTY _____

DATE OF PARTY _____

LOADED BY _____

VEHICLE TO BE LOADED _____

DEPART BY _____

NAME AND PHONE NUMBER OF CLIENT _____

LIST ALL FOOD TO BE LOADED FOR THE PARTY:

_____   _____
_____   _____
_____   _____
_____   _____
_____   _____
_____   _____
_____   _____
_____   _____
_____   _____
_____   _____
_____   _____
_____   _____
_____   _____
_____   _____
_____   _____
_____   _____
_____   _____
_____   _____
_____   _____
_____   _____
_____   _____
_____   _____
_____   _____
_____   _____

EXHIBIT 6-5 (*continued*)

Display Fruit	Leaf Lettuce
	Romaine
Display Vegetables	Watercress
	Hydroponic
Cheese:	Bibb Lettuce
Parmesan	Radicchio
Cheddar	
Swiss	
Brie	Fresh Basil
Blue	Fresh Dill
Saga Blue	Fresh Tarragon
Gruyere	
	Lemons
Half & Half	Limes
Whipped Cream	
Indiv. Creamers	Hearts of Palm
	Hearts of Artichoke
Butter Solids – Uns.	French Bread
Butter Solids – Salt.	Italian Bread
Butter Molds	Specialty Bread
	Hot Dog Buns
	Hamburger Buns
	Crackers
	Nuts
	Croutons

EXHIBIT 6-5 (*continued*)
Indicate Quantitites for all non-food items and equipment:

Pantry Items

_____ Salt
_____ Pepper
_____ Spices
_____ Sugar packets
_____ No-cal sweetener
_____ Individual packets
_____ Individual packets
_____ Salt
_____ Pepper
_____ Mayo
_____ Ketchup
_____ Relish
_____ Mustard
_____ Pam
_____ Frying oil
_____ Vegetable oil
_____ Bread crumbs
_____ Flour
_____ Olives
_____ Onions
_____ Cherries

_____ Coffee
_____ Decaf
_____ Ice tea bags
_____ Regular tea bags
_____ Pastry shells
_____ Sherry
_____ Cooking wine

_____ Cola
_____ Diet cola
_____ Ginger ale
_____ Lemon-lime
_____ Tonic
_____ Club soda
_____ Flavored waters
_____ Bloody Mary mix
_____ Orange juice

EXHIBIT 6-5 (*continued*)

_____ Cranberry juice

_____ Grapefruit juice

Linens

_____ Napkins (Color)

_____ 62 by 62 (Color)

_____   (Color)

_____   (Color)

_____ Banquets (Color)

_____   (Color)

_____   (Color)

_____ 132″ Round (Color)

_____   (Color)

_____   (Color)

_____ 120″ Round (Color)

_____   (Color)

_____   (Color)

_____ 108″ Round (Color)

_____   (Color)

_____   (Color)

_____ 90″ Round (Color)

_____   (Color)

_____   (Color)

_____ Towel mop

_____ Bib aprons

_____ 13-foot skirt

_____ Black waiter jackets

_____ White chef coats

_____ Logo tee shirts

_____ Theme uniforms

_____ _____

_____ _____

_____ _____

_____ _____

Pots and Pans

_____ Bus pans

_____ Bus pan lids

_____ Full sheet pans

_____ Half sheet pans

_____ Full food pans

EXHIBIT 6-5 (*continued*)

_____ Half food pans
_____ Full deep pans
_____ Medium sauté pans
_____ Large sauté pans
_____ Omelette pans
_____ Fry pans
_____ Medium sauce pans
_____ Small sauce pans
_____ Large cast iron fry pan
_____ 32 quart stock pot
_____ 15 quart stock pot
_____ Braziers
_____ Fry baskets
_____ Large colanders
_____ Medium colanders
_____ Skimmers
_____ Strainers
_____ Large steel funnel
_____ Extra large stainless steel bowls
_____ Medium stainless steel bowls
_____ Utility bowls
_____ 2 Quart measuring container
_____ 1 Quart plastic containers
_____ 2 Gallon chafing dishes
_____ Plate covers
_____ Full shallow aluminum food pans
_____ Full deep aluminum food pans
_____ Half shallow aluminum food pans
_____ Half deep aluminum food pans
_____ Oval waiter trays
_____ Round cocktail trays

_____ _____
_____ _____
_____ _____
_____ _____

China, Glassware, Flatware, and Tabletop Items
_____ Dinner knives
_____ Dinner forks
_____ Salad forks
_____ Teaspoons
_____ Bouillon spoons

EXHIBIT 6-5 (*continued*)

_____ Cocktail forks

_____ Salt and pepper shakers

_____ Ashtrays

_____ Water pitchers

_____ Coffee pourers

_____ Large rectangular silver trays

_____ Medium round silver trays

_____ Small oval silver trays

_____ Silver bread baskets

_____ 12-inch silver bowls

_____ 7-inch silver bowls

_____ 5-inch silver bowls

_____ Large rectangular aluminum trays

_____ Medium round aluminum trays

_____ 4-inch Acoroc bowls

_____ 5-inch Acoroc bowls

_____ 7-inch Acoroc bowls

_____ 12-inch glass bowls

_____ Special bowls _____

_____

_____

_____ Black lacquer trays

_____ Oval mirrors

_____ Round mirrors

_____ Glass carafes

_____ Large punch bowls

_____ 12-ounce bubble wine glasses

_____ Tulip Champagne glasses

_____ Brandy snifters

_____ Cordial glasses

_____ Martini glasses

_____ Coffee mugs

_____ 9 1/2-inch plates

_____ 7 1/2-inch plates

_____ 6-inch plates

_____ Coffee cups

_____ Saucers

_____ Creamers

_____ Sugars

_____ Votive candle holders

EXHIBIT 6-5 (*continued*)
Plasticware and Paper Goods

_____ 8-ounce styro cups
_____ 6-ounce styro cups
_____ 10-ounce hard plastic glasses
_____ Plastic forks
_____ Plastic knives
_____ Plastic spoons
_____ 10-inch plastic divided plates
_____ 10-inch plastic plates
_____ 7-inch plastic plates
_____ 6-inch plastic plates
_____ Plastic Champagne flutes
_____ 7-inch plastic bowls
_____ 12-inch plastic bowls
_____ Plastic gloves
_____ Cocktail napkins
_____ Dinner napkins
_____ Large doilies
_____ Small doilies
_____ Mini baking cups
_____ Swordpicks
_____ Wet-naps
_____ Wood stir sticks
_____ Sip straws
_____ Toothpicks
_____ Plastic storage bages
_____ Duct tape
_____ Film wrap
_____ Aluminum foil
_____ Bar kits
_____ Pourer spouts

Buffet and Food Station Decor

_____ Shells
_____ Glass pebbles
_____ Vases: type _____
_____ Hurricane lamps
_____ Glass blocks
_____ Fans
_____ Stapler gun and staples

EXHIBIT 6-5 (*continued*)

_____ Ribbon: colors _____

_____ Scissors

_____ Floral wire

_____ Floral tape

_____ Large carving boards

_____ Oval carving boards

_____ Small baskets: color _____ For _____

_____ Medium baskets: color _____ For _____

_____ Large baskets: color _____ For _____

_____ Extra large baskets: color _____ For _____

_____ Stick candles

_____ Votive candles

_____ Candelabras

_____ Wooden crates

_____ Plastic crates

_____ Fresh flowers and ferns

_____

_____

_____

_____

_____

Heavy and Bulky Equipment

_____ Convection ovens

_____ Gas grill

_____ Hibachi

_____ Table-top gas burners

_____ Empty coolers

_____ Coolers with ice

_____ Charcoal

_____ Garden hose and nozzle

_____ Five-gallon insulating containers

_____ Plastic tarp

_____ 100-cup coffee makers

_____ 50-cup coffee makers

_____ Garbage cans

_____ 6-foot tables

_____ Handtrucks

_____ Dollies

_____ Tall warming cabinets

_____ Short warming cabinets

EXHIBIT 6-5 (*continued*)

_____ Rolling racks with covers

_____ Wire frame chafers

_____ Dust pan

_____ Broom

_____ Butane fuel

_____ Propane fuel

_____ Large sterno

_____ Small sterno

_____ Fire extinguishers

_____ Matches (place with utensils)

_____ Liquid smoke

_____ Lighter fluid

_____ Ant spray

_____ Insect repellant

_____ Extension cords

_____ Spotlights

_____ First-aid kits (check supplies inside)

_____ Tray stands

_____ Table cassette au feu stoves

_____ Lava rock

_____ Rented equipment delivered to commissary

Utensils

_____ Plain cook's spoons

_____ Slotted cook's spoons

_____ 2-ounce ladles

_____ 4-ounce ladles

_____ 6-ounce ladles

_____ 8-ounce ladles

_____ Extra large ladles

_____ Wire whips

_____ Piping bags and tips

_____ Pastry brushes

_____ Plastic ice scoops

_____ Can openers

_____ Bottle openers

_____ Plastic funnels

_____ 9 1/2-inch utility tongs

_____ 6-inch tongs

_____ Silver serving tongs

_____ BBQ tongs

EXHIBIT 6-5 (*continued*)
_____ BBQ knives
_____ BBQ forks
_____ Ice cream dishers
_____   Size _____
_____   Size _____
_____ Wooden spoons
_____ Aluminum serving spoons
_____ Sauce spoons
_____ Carving knives
_____ Carving forks
_____ Kitchen forks
_____ Cooks spatula
_____ Rubber spatula
_____ Hamburger spatula
_____ Pie server
_____ Pie cutter
_____ Cake knife
_____ Cake server
_____ Sharpening steel

Chairs
Tables
Tenting and accessories
Kitchen equipment
Linens
China
Flatware
Serving pieces and equipment
Glassware
Rental equipment necessary at certain times, such as generators, gazebos, etc.

The rental list should detail the size, type, and color of the item. It is a good idea to leave space within the form for the caterer's notes when completing the form. For instance, there may be four 8-by-30 tables needed for the buffets, eight 8-by-30 tables needed for the kitchen staff, one 8-by-30 for the gift table, and two 8-by-30 tables for bar service. A total of fifteen 8-by-30 tables will need to be rented. It helps when completing this order form to have room to "place one's thoughts," which saves time in the long run. The top of the form or cover page should indicate:

Name of client
Date of event

Delivery address
Delivery date
Time of delivery
Date of pickup
Rental company name
Name of salesperson who took order
Date the order is placed

When developing a rental order form, consider printing it in multiple copies since this same form can be used to check in the order before the event and inventory the order after the event. Equipment damaged on delivery should be noted and replaced. Inventory after the event will verify to the caterer any losses charged by the rental company.

The objective of completing the rental order form is to list everything needed for the event that cannot be provided by the off-premise caterer. Caterers' current equipment inventories and the proposal or contract will determine the items required to be rented. When completing this form, go through the menu, necessary kitchen equipment, and other services provided and ask questions like these:

❏ Is there another event taking place at the same time at which owned equipment will be utilized, such as grills, trays, china, and glassware?
❏ How will each menu item be presented? For example, salad-size plates, bread-and-butter-size plates, and dinner plates may also be used as underliners when serving desserts or sorbet.
❏ What utensils will be needed for the guests and/or the servers? Does the contract specify providing platforms, dance floors, audio/visual equipment, or special lighting?
❏ On station parties: Is there seating for all guests? Will the dining tables be set with placesettings? If they are, then more glassware and fewer napkins need to be ordered.
❏ Will 60-inch rounds or 72-inch rounds be used for dining? If using 72s on an upscale event, three creamers and three sets of salt and pepper shakers per table are necessary.
❏ What other services are being contracted? The minister may need a sound system. The bride and groom may request kneeling benches. The harpist may need a small platform. The musicians may need chairs.

In closing, it is important to read the contract thoroughly and know the inventory for owned equipment to ensure that all necessary items are ordered in advance. A Sunday afternoon is usually not a good time to be trying to contact a rental company because something wasn't ordered. Also, a few additional chairs, napkins, and place settings should be ordered in the event unexpected party guests arrive.

A party packing list can be developed by listing these main categories necessary for the event:

All prepared and uncooked foods
China, glassware, flatware
Tables and chairs
Ovens and other pieces of major cooking equipment
Necessary pots, pans, and kitchen utensils
Coffee makers and samovars
Sodas, juices, ice, and bar supplies
Coolers with ice
Buffet and food station equipment and decor
Essentials used at every event, such as:

- ❑ Aluminum foil and film wrap
- ❑ Napkins
- ❑ Toolkit
- ❑ Broom, dust pan, and mop
- ❑ Fire extinguishers
- ❑ First-aid kits

Each catering operation's packing list will include basic items as well as those that are unique to the particular caterer. It is highly unlikely that two caterers will have exactly the same packing list. There are two common characteristics that all caterers' packing lists should share. One is that the lists should be very specific and include everything that the caterer may bring to the event. For example, "pots or pans" is not specific enough. What size and how many of each type are needed is mandatory. Second, the order of the list should coincide with the various storage areas within the caterer's operation and be in the same order as the shelving if possible. If, for example, an off-premise caterer has a front storeroom and a back storeroom, items in the front storeroom should be listed together in one section of the packing list, and those in the back storeroom should be listed in a separate section of the packing list.

Pull sheets should include a cover page that gives the following information:

Name of the party
Day and date of the party
Name and phone number of the client
Exact location of the party including directions
Deadline for completion of loading of the truck(s)
Specific truck(s) to be loaded
Time to leave for the party
Names of those responsible for packing and loading

Before completing a party packing list, keep in mind the objective is to list everything needed for the event that will be provided by the off-premise caterer; however, you must know that what you need is indeed in inventory. This will prevent lost time when actually pulling for the party.

The best way to start completing a sheet is to refer to the party contract, which lists all foods, beverages, equipment, and services to be provided by the caterer, and the completed rental form. Successful off-premise caterers ask themselves a series of questions about each menu item:

❑ What raw ingredients will be necessary to produce the food item at the party site? For example, for a Caesar salad caterers will need to bring romaine lettuce, croutons, parmesan cheese, and caesar dressing (if prepared in advance).

❑ How will this item be prepared? Continuing with the caesar salad, the caterer will need to bring a large mixing bowl, a grater for the parmesan cheese, a ladle for the dressing, and plastic gloves for mixing and dishup personnel.

❑ How will this item be served? For a buffet, caesar salad can be served from a variety of bowls; if a served meal, salad plates will be necessary. And do not forget the salad fork, trays, and tray stands. The details seem endless.

❑ Where in the kitchen will the salad be mixed and dished up? Be sure there are sufficient work tables. In the case of a salad that will be assembled, laid out, and designed, allow more tables for this purpose. If the salad is pre-plated, where can it be stored and kept cold?

❑ What other items are necessary, such as buffet decor pieces, buffet tables, and skirting?

❑ What other services have been contracted with the caterer? For instance, before a company picnic event some of the guests will have a softball game, and want sodas, waters, and ice handy.

This process is, of course, more involved and complicated for those caterers who deal in larger events, where everything is prepared-to-order on-site. Experience is the best teacher. Memorable are those stories about off-premise caterers who forgot an important item.

To conclude this section, it is suggested that quality time be allocated for preparation of pull sheets and rental order forms. This type of work requires total concentration. Those responsible for preparing these forms should find a time and place where they can work uninterrupted. These lists should be prepared long before the party date in order to determine if the caterer and the rental dealer have the necessary items. If not, this gives ample time to order additional equipment and supplies.

FOOD PRODUCTION SHEETS

Food production sheets provide commissary personnel with a list of things to prepare for each party. In the aforementioned caesar salad example, the production list would indicate the following:

Wash and trim 24 heads of romaine lettuce
Prepare one gallon of caesar dressing
Cut and toast two loaves of Italian bread for croutons
(Please note that there is no production required for the parmesan cheese.)

These lists detail all menu items and the time they need to be ready. Some include budgeted costs, as well as total food cost budgeted for the event, to provide the culinary staff with better insight.

GETTING THE GOODS TO THE PARTY

These are critical steps in the execution of the event. A sufficient amount of time should be allocated so that everything arrives on time at the party site. For smaller events that are close to the commissary, these steps take little time, but for larger, more detailed events, pulling, assembling, packing, and loading can be accomplished one or more days in advance.

Pulling and Packing the Off-Premise Event

In most off-premise catering facilities, party items are not all in one location, but are spread throughout the commissary. Carts, dollies, handtrucks and even shopping-carts will help move the items to the vehicle, or to a central assembly location, prior to loading.

Prior to pulling the party, the person responsible for purchasing must review the party needs, and ensure that all goods are in stock. This type of teamwork will lead to a smooth operation.

Persons pulling the party find items listed on the pull sheet. The larger, bulkier items should be taken to the delivery vehicle, while the smaller items that are loose should be assembled in a specified area and packed in containers such as plastic carrying crates. Fragile items should be wrapped in bubblewrap, linens, or wadded-up paper to prevent breakage. Bowls will not stick together if paper or bubblewrap is placed between each bowl. All equipment should be checked when pulled to ensure that it is in working order and not broken, cracked, or chipped. A few suggested packing methods follow:

- ❑ Use old briefcases for carrying knives and serving utensils, and plastic crates for plates (plates will be wrapped in film after drying).
- ❑ Use wrapped racks for cups, glasses, creamers, and sugars.
- ❑ Custom-made plywood boxes are good for coffee makers, samovars, and chafing dishes.
- ❑ Flatware film-wrapped in groups of ten can be packed in plastic crates (most discount and larger drug stores carry an assortment of plastic packing crates).
- ❑ Empty ice chests to be used later at the party site for chilling beer and wine can be packed with small unbreakable equipment.
- ❑ Whenever possible, pack food in the same container that it will be cooked in at the party site. For example, place stuffed mushroom caps on half sheet pans, covered with film wrap, and placed last in ice chests.
- ❑ Used plastic containers such as five-pound honey containers are good for packing bar utensil items such as pourers, stir sticks, wine and bottle openers, swordpicks, and ice picks.
- ❑ Plywood boxes with a sliding top can be custom-made to store doilies.
- ❑ Slim Jim–type garbage cans are excellent for packing tray stands.
- ❑ Use empty bus boxes with lids for small utensils.

❑ Assorted sizes of Tupperware with lids for cold food should be delivered in a refrigerated truck or on ice in ice chests, based upon local health department regulations.
❑ Hot foods are best shipped in insulated plastic containers, warming cabinets, or insulated thermal bags.

This list is not intended to include all packing techniques, but should at least inspire creativity when it comes to the myriad ways to pack for off-premise catering events. Please note that parties that are packed neatly and carefully will not only be delivered intact, but will also make a positive impression on clients, as compared to that made by caterers who arrive at a party site with food and equipment virtually spilling out of the van in beat-up, old cardboard boxes and rattling loose with no packing at all.

Equipment and supplies designated for certain areas at the party site should be packed together and labeled to help the unloading and distribution process at the party site. This procedure is critical for larger parties, where food stations, buffets, bars, and off-premise kitchens are spread out over a large area, or on a number of floors such as in an office building or department store. Some caterers even color-code items so that staff know exactly where to take the items when unloaded.

Loading the Vehicle The loading process should not be taken lightly. It is physically demanding, and improperly packed items may break, spill, crack, or chip. Rare is the off-premise caterer who has not, at one time or another, arrived at a party site with food spilled inside the vehicle. There are ways of minimizing the chances of this or other mishaps occurring.

❑ Everything should be packed together tightly. Whenever possible, crates and racks should be nestled together to avoid shifting in transit.
❑ Large, heavy, square or rectangular-shaped items should be loaded first and kept in the bottom portion of the load. This category includes such things as ice chests, glass and china racks, soft drinks in cases, and square or rectangular plastic or plywood containers.
❑ Lightweight and unusually shaped items should be loaded last, and inserted in areas where they will fit snugly to help keep the load from shifting in transit.
❑ Cold foods should be transported in accordance with local health department regulations, which may require a refrigerated truck or that it be sealed and packed in ice chests.
❑ Hot foods should be kept at safe temperature (above 140 degrees Fahrenheit) in insulated carrying containers, thermal bags, or hot-food holding cabinets.
❑ Loading staff must be trained in proper lifting techniques to avoid injury. This will be addressed in Chapter 12.
❑ Hooks, eyelets, and bungee cords help secure items in the truck when it is not full. Items can be kept from slipping by placing them on nonslippery surfaces, such as old rugs, towels, linens, cardboard, or crumpled paper.

❑ As each item is packed in the vehicle, it should be marked off on the pull sheet. Once the pull sheet is complete, it is advisable to double-check, and sometimes triple-check that all items are loaded. The checking process should, of course, be thorough for all parties, but for parties that are far from the commissary, off-premise caterers cannot afford to forget even one item, since there is no time to return. Some caterers leave staff at the commissary for the purpose of bringing forgotten items to the party site.

Delivery   The delivery process involves physically moving the food, supplies, and equipment from the catering commissary to the party site. The types of delivery vehicles are discussed in Chapter 5. In this section, we will discuss delivery procedures and standards.

Catering vehicles should always be free from dents and scrapes and immaculately clean and waxed. The delivery vehicle is an important marketing tool and should reflect the caterer's image. United Parcel Service is known throughout the world for its immaculately clean and well-maintained vehicles. It sets the standard in this area.

Drivers for off-premise catering firms also should be immaculately attired, uniformed, impeccably groomed, and courteous. Drivers represent companies' images and usually provide the first impression for a catered event.

Most caterers display their company name, address, and phone number on their vehicles. This is good marketing since the more a name is seen, the more it is remembered. Off-premise caterers from all over the country report receiving business from people who have seen their trucks.

Following are some proven techniques to improve the quality and timing of deliveries:

1. Allow enough time to reach the destination. Many caterers allow twice the amount of time necessary. Some make practice runs when traveling to unfamiliar areas. Pay attention to weather reports, check road conditions and allow extra time if bad weather or heavy traffic is expected. It's usually better to arrive early than late.
2. Institute a preventative maintenance program for all vehicles. Preventative maintenance spots potential problems before they occur, whereas a repair service is needed after something breaks. Drivers should not be permitted to make their own repairs, but they should make daily checks for brakes, tires, lights, horns, wipers, steering, unusual noises, oil, battery, and wiper fluid. In trucks with propane ovens, they should check for gas leaks.
3. Drivers should be provided with petty cash, a road map, written directions, a highway emergency kit, a first-aid kit, rain gear, umbrella, and a beeper, radio, or cellular phone.
4. On hot, sunny days, vehicles must be parked in the shade.
5. For large events, many suppliers will deliver certain prepared products such as desserts or specialty ethnic items directly to the party site. For

mega-events of thousands, suppliers will often provide a truck filled with their products at the event site. Also, when circumstances dictate, caterers consider alternative methods of delivery such as cabs, UPS, or courier service.

Unloading at the Party Site
Off-premise caterers should have established policies for unloading catering vehicles at the party site. This section does not apply to simply dropping off platters. It concerns procedures for larger, more involved events.

The main procedure to follow when unloading is to separate items depending upon where they will be used. Some things can be taken directly to their final destination, such as items for the buffet, bar, food station, or kitchen. Where access is restricted, items may be stored together and moved later. This procedure does not work well when delivering large parties into high-rise buildings. In these instances, sorting cannot occur until the goods reach the proper floor.

Unloading is best accomplished with few staff, rather than the complete party crew. It is easier to keep things organized when fewer staff are present. Under ideal conditions, everything for each food station, buffet, bar, and off-premise kitchen should be delivered to the spot where it is needed. When the setup crew arrives, everything is where it belongs and the crew can start setting up. Off-premise caterers simply provide a diagram with an itemized list of the setup to the people responsible for setup, and tell them that everything that is needed should be there. This procedure will eliminate the major confusion, frustration, and wasted time when staff must frantically search for supplies and equipment.

Handtrucks, dollies, and carts save time and energy. Men should never lift items weighing over 50 pounds, and women, over 25 pounds. Off-premise caterers should strive to minimize the number of times things are moved. Move materials along the shortest and straightest route possible. Equipment, food, and supplies to be used on buffets, food stations, and bars should be stored as close as possible to the point of use. For example, on a pasta station, the extra pasta, sauces, and ingredients should be kept as close as possible to the station to minimize the steps required for replenishment. Furthermore, some tools, utensils, and equipment should be stored in the same area at every event. For example, scissors are always kept in a crate under a worktable in the off-premise kitchen, or backup soft drinks are always kept outside the cook's tent.

Once the necessary equipment is on-site, the setup and party execution begins. This topic is discussed in detail in Chapter 8. When the party is over, it is time to reload the vehicle and return to the catering commissary.

Reloading and Returning
Cleaning and repacking should be accomplished as the party progresses. Once the caterers' responsibilities are complete, they can leave the party site. Most caterers can complete cleaning, packing, and reloading within one hour of the conclusion of their responsibilities. It is best to wait to reload the vehicle until most things are packed and ready for loading, rather than to load things randomly. This will result in a well-loaded vehicle that will reduce the chances for spills and breakage on the return trip.

The Perfect Route

by Ginger Kramer
COAST - A Special Events & Catering Company
Santa Clara, CA

EVENT FILE ROUTING SCHEDULE

	By:	Date:
Sales & Front Office:		
Verbal Quote Only		
Written Proposal Faxed & Mailed	_____	_____
Event File:		
File Label & Folder		
Return to Sales (Tentative Status)	_____	_____
Acceptance Sheet Received from Client	_____	_____
Post to Board (Definite Status) & Master Book	_____	_____
Deposit Received from Client	_____	_____
Coordinating:		
Event Report Initiated		
Pre-Schedule Staff	_____	_____
Send Event File to Purchasing	_____	_____
Purchasing:		
Food Sheet to: Chef/Kitchen Production/Inventory Control		
Beverage Order (copy to Inventory Control) (Order Placed)	_____	_____
Regular Linen Order	_____	_____
Custom Linen Order	_____	_____
Floral Order (_____)	_____	_____
Decor Order	_____	_____
Guest Equipment Order (_____)	_____	_____
Site Rental Agreement (_____)	_____	_____
Ice Delivery	_____	_____
Entertainment Order (_____)	_____	_____
Serviceware Order (_____)	_____	_____
Special:_____ (_____)	_____	_____
All check requests issued	_____	_____
Coordinating:		
Complete Event Report:		
Load Sheet		
Attach map to location	_____	_____
Make copies for Event File	_____	_____
Reconfirm Staff	_____	_____
Buffet Design Completed:	_____	_____
Final Guest Count: (#pp___ by ___)	_____	_____
File Completion: (Sales & Front Office)		
Client Contacted for Verbal Review		
Invoice: Copies to Acct./Event File/Invoice File	_____	_____
Verbal Review forwarded to General Manager	_____	_____
Critique Letter	_____	_____
Thank You Card	_____	_____
Lost Business Report forwarded to General Manager	_____	_____
Add to Mail List	_____	_____

EXHIBIT 6-6   The Perfect Route—Routing Schedule Reprinted with permission of the author, Ginger Kramer, and the CommuniCATER, official publication of the National Caterers Association.

Upon returning to the commissary, most off-premise caterers unload the vehicles, and clean and return everything to its original place. Those who do not, unload and clean the following morning.

POST-PARTY REVIEW

A post-party review should be conducted after every catered event to pinpoint specific problems that require attention, and find better ways to do things in the future. (The largest room in the world is the room for improvement.) Off-premise caterers can look at the post-party review in the sense that, given an opportunity to cater the exact same event again, what would they do differently? Some caterers sit down with staff after the event, while others wait until the next day to assess the event. Some require their staff to complete a report, while others request written comments from clients. Whatever the procedures, the comments should be in writing, and things requiring improvement should be acted upon immediately. The following topics should be addressed:

Amount of time allotted for setup
Quality and quantity of staff
Quality and quantity of food and service
Quality and quantity of equipment and supplies
Adequacy of music, flowers, decor, parking, security as appropriate
Any other problems

In addition to the post-party review, the following procedures should be in place:

Submit payroll hours to bookkeeping.
Report discrepancies to rental equipment company.
Make sure all invoices for the party are submitted to bookkeeping.
Invoice client for any remaining balances.
Write and mail thank-you letter to client.
Establish follow-up date for contacting client for future events.

Exhibit 6-6 is one off-premise caterer's system for keeping track of the logistical details discussed in this chapter.

NOTES

1. Nancy Kahan with Eleanor Berman, *Entertaining For Business*, Clarkson Potter, New York 1990.
2. Chris Coe, *Special Event*, May 1991, p. 30.
3. Irvin Kanode, *Catering Today*, June 1986, pp. 18–19.
4. Joyce Piotrowski, *Catering Business*, May 1990.

Chapter 7

Personnel Management

This chapter discusses all aspects of off-premise catering personnel management such as federal laws relating to personnel; recruiting, hiring, orienting, training, paying, evaluating, motivating, disciplining and terminating catering staff; managing turnover; staff uniforms; guidelines for preparing an employee handbook and maintenance of personnel records.

Excellent personnel management begins with selecting those staff with whom off-premise caterers enjoy working, and those who enjoy working in off-premise catering. It involves employing those who meet the job requirements, and then training them and retraining them to meet company standards. It also involves providing a healthy working environment where managers:

Listen to and involve staff in operations
Are fair and consistent when dealing with staff
Give immediate discipline
Catch staff doing things right and tell them
Create an enthusiastic, upbeat, and positive environment
Are organized
Are on the floor, working with staff who are serving guests, rather than hiding in the office

Off-premise caterers know that happy workers are productive workers. They realize that work is *not* the most important thing in Americans' lives. A recent Roper survey reported:

> In order of importance, [it] found, these are the 10 things that most affect Americans' lives: (1) children's education; (2) family health; (3) own health; (4) quality of life; (5) friends and relatives; (6) love life; (7) income and standard of living; (8) occupation; (9) leisure activity; (10) current political situation.[1]

According to Fern Canter, Director of Human Resources, Turnberry Isle Resort Club in Aventura, Florida, "Trust and understanding are the foundation of a long-lasting relationship." She lists these "employment vows," similar to marriage vows, for improved employer-employee relationships:

EMPLOYER TO EMPLOYEE

> I will make sure that you understand the requirements of the job before I hire you.

I will listen more than I speak during our employment interview.
I will insure that you are given sufficient training.
I will not be afraid to admit when I've made a mistake.
I will praise you publicly, but criticize you in private.
I will not hide behind my office door.
I will discuss your performance with you on a regular basis.
I will try to set a good example.
I will be supportive.
I will treat you with respect.

EMPLOYEE TO EMPLOYER

I will arrive on time.
I will ask questions when I don't know, and never assume.
I understand that servicing our clients is our number one priority.
I will work safely to prevent accidents.
I will not leave telephone inquiries on hold until they expire.
I will thank every customer and client.
I will not talk unfavorably about the company.
I will learn from my mistakes.
I will treat everyone with respect.[2]

These vows, when followed in off-premise catering firms, would certainly help create an outstanding working environment. Posting these vows around the workplace, and at off-premise party sites, would be an excellent way to remind everyone of mutual responsibilities.

FEDERAL LAWS

Off-premise caterers are directly affected by certain federal laws regarding personnel:

Fair Labor Standards Act of 1938, Amended
Child labor laws
The Immigration Reform and Control Act of 1986
The Americans with Disabilities Act
Worker's Compensation requirements
The Family and Medical Leave Act

It is important to understand the basic requirement of each law to determine its applicability. For example, the Fair Labor Standards Act affects all off-premise caterers, whereas the Family and Medical Leave Act generally exempts businesses with less than 50 employees. As we review the major aspects of each of these laws, off-premise caterers should consult legal counsel regarding specific questions.

The Fair Labor Standards Act of 1938, as Amended

Established Minimum Wage. This law established that there would be a minimum hourly wage. Currently it is $4.25 per hour. Employees who receive tips as part of their compensation, at the present time, may be paid as little as $2.125 (50% of minimum wage), as long as the wages paid by their employer and their tips equal the minimum wage. Employees must report tips earned to their employers so that appropriate amounts for federal income tax and social security tax may be withheld from their paychecks. Employers must also pay their portion of social security tax on the tips reported by their employees.

Established Overtime Pay. Pay at the rate of no less than time and one half the regular hourly rate must be paid for hours worked in excess of 40 within the workweek. Each workweek stands alone, and averaging of hours from a series of weeks is not permitted. Additionally, the workweek itself must be established in advance, and not be changed from week to week to avoid paying overtime. For example, the workweek could begin at 12:01 A.M. on Monday, and end Sunday at midnight.

Established Child Labor Laws. This law affects those who employ young people to bus and wash dishes, set tables, and perform other tasks. Highlights of its impact on those who employ fourteen- and fifteen-year-olds follow:

- ❏ They may not work more than three hours on school days, and no more than 18 hours in school weeks.
- ❏ They may not work more than 8 hours on nonschool days, and no more than 40 hours in nonschool weeks.
- ❏ They cannot maintain or repair machines or equipment, cook (except in an area not separated by partition and in customers' view), bake, or operate power-driven food slicers, grinders, choppers, cutters, and bakery-type mixers. Nor can they work in freezers or meat coolers, or perform any work in preparation of meals for sale except wrapping, sealing, labeling, weighing, pricing, and stocking.

    Additionally, they cannot load or unload trucks or engage in occupations in warehouses except clerical or office work.
- ❏ They cannot work prior to 7 A.M. or after 7 P.M., except between June 1 and Labor Day, when they can work until 9 P.M.

    Highlights of restrictions on sixteen- and seventeen-year-olds follow:
- ❏ There are no time restrictions on these workers, but they cannot operate, clean, or repair power-driven meat-processing machines, including slicers, nor can they operate, clean, or repair most power-driven bakery equipment, including dough mixers, roll dividers, or rounders. Pizza dough rollers with a certain number of safety features are an exception.

    Recently, fast-food chains have come under close scrutiny regarding the hours worked by fourteen- and fifteen-year-olds. Many are now reluctant to hire these workers due to the penalties that can be incurred for violations. One example would be a fourteen-year-old who is scheduled to work until 7 P.M. during the school year, but the establishment is extremely busy and the supervisor asks the employee to work until 7:30 P.M. This is a violation, and is punishable by law.

    A major fast-food chain recently agreed to pay a landmark fine of $500,000 to settle a lawsuit filed for child-labor violations. They are charged with allowing fourteen- and fifteen-year-olds to handle hazardous cooking equipment and to work longer and later than permitted under the child labor laws. Fines can range from $10,000 for illegally employing a minor who suffers a fatal injury to $400 for having a fourteen- or fifteen-year-old who works too many hours or during prohibited times.

Some off-premise caterers reduce their payroll expenses by employing young people to perform simple tasks such as setting tables, which can save them money because they are not paying more experienced personnel to perform this function. Those who do must always be aware of the federal laws.

States are toughening child labor laws.

> Bills requiring parental permission slips, hiking up penalties for violations and setting hour restrictions are in the works in many states. On the federal level, members of Congress are trying to reform the child labor provisions of 1938 Fair Labor Standards Act. . . which would mandate a national work-permit program as well as update the provisions of the 1938 Standards Act.[3]

Equal Pay for Equal Work. This requires that there be equal pay for equal work, and that there be no sex discrimination.

Record Keeping. This requires that all payroll records including journals, timesheets, wage and rate sheets, and individual earnings records be kept for a minimum of three years and that they are available for inspection by authorized individuals.

Off-premise caterers must maintain accurate records. Some employers have allowed workers to arrive for work early, or stay late, but since it was the workers' idea, not the employers', they did not pay overtime. These employers asked the workers to punch the time clock to show an eight-hour day. This is falsification of records, and can cost employers hundred of thousands of dollars in overtime back pay and penalties.

Overtime Exemptions. This section establishes criteria for those bona fide executives, administrative staff, professional employees, and outside sales people who are exempt from receiving overtime. This is a very technical area, and readers are advised to contact an attorney before excluding someone from overtime payment.

For executives to be exempt from overtime they must meet all of the following criteria:

- ❑ Their primary duty must be management of the enterprise.
- ❑ They customarily and regularly direct the work of at least two or more other employees.
- ❑ They must have the authority to hire and fire, or recommend hiring and firing.
- ❑ They must customarily and regularly exercise discretionary powers.
- ❑ They must devote no more than 20 percent (40% if in retail or service establishments) of their hours worked to activities not directly and closely related

to managerial duties. Readers should note that these percentage tests on nonexempt work would not apply in the case of an employee who is in sole charge of an independent establishment or a physically separated branch establishment, or who owns at least a 20 percent interest in the enterprise where employed.

❑ They must be paid a minimum of $155 per week exclusive of board, lodging, and other activities.

There is a special proviso for executives who are paid at least $250 per week. They are exempt if they regularly direct the work of at least two or more employees and the primary duty is the management of the enterprise, or a recognized department or subdivision thereof.

Those who are employed in outside sales are exempt from overtime if they meet the following criteria:

❑ They are employed for the purpose of selling, and customarily and regularly work away from the employer's place of business.
❑ They sell tangible and intangible items such as goods or services.
❑ Hours worked in other than selling activities are less than 20 percent of the total hours worked in the workweek.

The Immigration Reform and Control Act of 1986 This piece of legislation restricts the hiring of illegal entrants and tourists into the United states. In effect since June 1, 1986, this act requires employers to obtain a completed Form I-9 from each employee within three days of hire, unless the employee is hired for less than three days. If hired for less than three days, the Form I-9 must be completed at the time of hire. Employers are required to see written proof that an individual is eligible to work. Employees hired prior to 1986 are exempt from this act. Exhibit 7-1 depicts the I-9 Form, shows the lists of acceptable documents, and gives instructions for completion.

The Immigration Control and Reform Act of 1986 also prohibits discrimination against any individual on the basis of national origin or citizenship status. This discrimination includes hiring, firing, and recruiting. Some examples follow:

❑ An off-premise caterer refuses to hire Mr. Fernandez because Mr. Fernandez is from Mexico.
❑ An off-premise caterer refuses to hire Ms. Gonzalez, who is a permanent resident alien, because she is not a U.S. citizen.
❑ An off-premise caterer refuses to hire Mr. Chin because he speaks with an accent, and although understands and speaks English, he usually speaks his native tongue.

Having a "U.S. citizen only" hiring policy, unless required by law, or having a "green card only" policy is illegal. Refusing to hire a qualified applicant who can perform the job tasks because of an accent or desire to only have employees speak English on the job is strictly forbidden.[4]

U.S. Department of Justice
Immigration and
Naturalization Service
OMB No. 1115-0136

Employment Eligibility Verification

I-9

Please read instructions carefully before completing this form. The instructions must be available during completion of this form. **ANTI-DISCRIMINATION NOTICE.** It is illegal to discriminate against work eligible individuals. Employers CANNOT specify which document(s) they will accept from an employee. The refusal to hire an individual because of a future expiration date may also constitute illegal discrimination.

Section 1. Employee Information and Verification. To be completed and signed by employee at the time employment begins.

| Print Name: | Last | First | | Middle Initial | Maiden Name | |

| Address (Street Name and Number) | | | Apt. # | Date of Birth (month/day/year) | |

| City | | State | Zip Code | Social Security # | |

I am aware that federal law provides for imprisonment and/or fines for false statements or use of
false documents in connection with the completion
of this form.

I attest, under penalty of perjury, that I am (check one of the following):
☐ A citizen or national of the United States
☐ A Lawful Permanent Resident (Alien # A _____
☐ An alien authorized to work until _____ /_____ /_____
(Alien # or Admission # _____

| Employee's Signature | Date (month/day/year) |

Preparer and/or Translator Certification. (To be completed and signed if Section 1 is prepared by a person other than the employee.) I attest, under penalty of perjury, that I have assisted in the completion of this form and that to the best of my knowledge the information is true and correct.

| Preparer's/Translator's Signature | Print Name |

| Address (Street Name and Number, City, State, Zip Code) | Date (month/day/year) |

Section 2. Employer Review and Verification. To be completed and signed by employer. **Examine one document from List A OR examine one document from List B and one from List C** as listed on the reverse of this form and record the title, number and expiration date, if any, of the document(s).

	List A	OR	List B	AND	List C
Document title:	_____		_____		_____
Issuing authority:	_____		_____		_____
Document #:	_____		_____		_____
Expiration Date (if any):	___ /___ /___		___ /___ /___		___ /___ /___
Document #:	_____				
Expiration Date (if any):	___ /___ /___				

CERTIFICATION - I attest, under penalty of perjury, that I have examined the document(s) presented by the above-named employee, that the above-listed document(s) appear to be genuine and to relate to the employee named, that the employee began employment on (month/day/year) ___ /___ /___ and that to the best of my knowledge the employee is eligible to work in the United States. (State employment agencies may omit the date the employee began employment).

| Signature of Employer or Authorized Representative | Print Name | Title |

| Business or Organization Name   Address (Street Name and Number, City, State, Zip Code) | Date (month/day/year) |

Section 3. Updating and Reverification. To be completed and signed by employer.

| A. New Name (if applicable) | B. Date of rehire (month/day/year) (if applicable) |

C. If employee's previous grant of work authorization has expired, provide the information below for the document that establishes current employment eligibility.

Document Title: _____ Document #: _____ Expiration Date (if any): ___ /___ /___

I attest, under penalty of perjury, that to the best of my knowledge, this employee is eligible to work in the United States, and if the employee presented document(s), the document(s) I have examined appear to be genuine and to relate to the individual.

| Signature of Employer or Authorized Representative | Date (month/day/year) |

Form I-9 (Rev. 11-21-91) N

EXHIBIT 7-1   Employment Eligibility Verification I-9 Form

Lists of Acceptable Documents

List A

Documents that Establish Both Identity and Employment Eligibility

OR

1. U.S. Passport (unexpired or expired)

2. Certificate of U.S. Citizenship (INS Form N-560 or N-561)

3. Certificate of Naturalization (INS Form N-550 or N-570)

4. Unexpired foreign passport, with I-551 stamp or attached INS Form I-94 indicating unexpired employment authorization

5. Alien Registration Receipt Card with photograph (INS Form I-151 or I-551)

6. Unexpired Temporary Resident Card (INS Form I-688)

7. Unexpired Employment Authorization Card (INS Form I-688A)

8. Unexpired Reentry Permit (INS Form I-327)

9. Unexpired Refugee Travel Document (INS Form I-571)

10. Unexpired Employment Authorization Document issued by the INS which contains a photograph (INS Form I-688B)

List B

Documents that Establish Identity

AND

1. Driver's license or ID card issued by a state or outlying possession of the United States provided it contains a photograph or information such as name, date of birth, sex, height, eye color, and address

2. ID card issued by federal, state, or local government agencies or entities provided it contains a photograph or information such as name, date of birth, sex, height, eye color, and address

3. School ID card with a photograph

4. Voter's registration card

5. U.S. Military card or draft record

6. Military dependent's ID card

7. U.S. Coast Guard Merchant Mariner Card

8. Native American tribal document

9. Driver's license issued by a Canadian government authority

For persons under age 18 who are unable to present a document listed above:

10. School record or report card

11. Clinic, doctor, or hospital record

12. Day-care or nursery school record

List C

Documents that Establish Employment Eligibility

1. U.S. social security card issued by the Social Security Administration (other than a card stating it is not valid for employment)

2. Certification of Birth Abroad issued by the Department of State (Form FS-545 or Form DS-1350)

3. Original or certified copy of a birth certificate issued by a state, county, municipal authority or outlying possession of the United States bearing an official seal

4. Native American tribal document

5. U.S. Citizen ID Card (INS Form I-197)

6. ID Card for use of Resident Citizen in the United States (INS Form I-179)

7. Unexpired employment authorization document issued by the INS (other than those listed under List A)

Illustrations of many of these documents appear in Part 8 of the Handbook for Employers (M-274)

Form I-9 (Rev. 11-21-91)N

EXHIBIT 7-1 *(continued)*

I-9 Instructions

U.S. Department of Justice
Immigration and Naturalization Service

OMB No. 1115-0136
Employment Eligibility Verification

PLEASE READ ALL INSTRUCTIONS CAREFULLY BEFORE COMPLETING THIS FORM.

Anti-Discrimination Notice. It is illegal to discriminate against any individual (other than an alien not authorized to work in the U.S.) in hiring, discharging, or recruiting or referring for a fee because of that individual's national origin or citizenship status. It is illegal to discriminate against work eligible individuals. Employers **CANNOT** specify which document(s) they will accept from an employee. The refusal to hire an individual because of a future expiration date may also constitute illegal discrimination.

Section 1 - Employee. All employees, citizens and noncitizens, hired after November 6, 1986, must complete Section 1 of this form at the time of hire, which is the actual beginning of employment. **The employer is responsible for ensuring that Section 1 is timely and properly completed.**

Preparer/Translator Certification. The Preparer/Translator Certification must be completed if Section 1 is prepared by a person other than the employee. A preparer/translator, may be used only when the employee is unable to complete Section 1 on his/her own. However, the employee must still sign Section 1 personally.

Section 2 - Employer. For the purpose of completing this form, the term "employer" includes those recruiters and referrers for a fee who are agricultural associations, agricultural employers, or farm labor contractors.

Employers must complete Section 2 by examining evidence of identity and employment eligibility within three (3) business days of the date employment begins. If employees are authorized to work, but are unable to present the required document(s) within three business days, they must present a receipt for the application of the document(s) within three business days and the actual document(s) within ninety (90) days. However, if employers hire individuals for a duration of less than three business days, Section 2 must be completed at the time employment begins. **Employers must record: 1)** document title; **2)** issuing authority; **3)** document number, **4)** expiration date, if any; **5)** the date employment begins. Employers must sign and date the certification. Employees must present original documents. Employers may, but are not required to, photocopy the document(s) presented. These photocopies may only be used for the verification process and must be retained with the I-9. **However, employers are still responsible for completing the I-9.**

Section 3 - Updating and Reverification. Employers must complete Section 3 when updating and/or reverifying the I-9. Employers must reverify employment eligibility of their employees on or before the expiration date recorded in Section 1. Employers **CANNOT** specify which document(s) they will accept from an employee.

- If an employee's name has changed at the time this form is being updated/reverified, complete Block A.

- If an employee is rehired within three (3) years of the date this form was originally completed and the employee is still eligible to be employed on the same basis as previously indicated on this form (updating), complete Block B and the signature block.

- If an employee is rehired within three (3) years of the date this form was originally completed and the employee's work authorization has expired **or** if a current employee's work authorization is about to expire (reverification), complete Block B and:
  - examine any document that reflects that the employee is authorized to work in the U.S. (see List A **or** C),
  - record the document title, document number and expiration date (if any) in Block C, and
  - complete the signature block.

Photocopying and Retaining Form I-9. A blank I-9 may be reproduced provided both sides are copied. The instructions must be available to all employees completing this form. Employers must retain completed I-9s for three (3) years after the date of hire or one (1) year after the date employment ends, whichever is later.

For more detailed information, you may refer to the INS <u>Handbook for Employers,</u> **(Form M-274). You may obtain the handbook at your local INS office.**

Privacy Act Notice. The authority for collecting this information is the Immigration Reform and Control Act of 1986, Pub. L. 99-603 (8 U.S.C. 1324a).

This information is for employers to verify the eligibility of individuals for employment to preclude the unlawful hiring, or recruiting or referring for a fee, of aliens who are not authorized to work in the United States.

This information will be used by employers as a record of their basis for determining eligibility of an employee to work in the United States. The form will be kept by the employer and made available for inspection by officials of the U.S. Immigration and Naturalization Service, the Department of Labor, and the Office of Special Counsel for Immigration Related Unfair Employment Practices.

Submission of the information required in this form is voluntary. However, an individual may not begin employment unless this form is completed since employers are subject to civil or criminal penalties if they do not comply with the Immigration Reform and Control Act of 1986.

Reporting Burden. We try to create forms and instructions that are accurate, can be easily understood, and which impose the least possible burden on you to provide us with information. Often this is difficult because some immigration laws are very complex. Accordingly, the reporting burden for this collection of information is computed as follows: 1) learning about this form, 5 minutes; 2) completing the form, 5 minutes; and 3) assembling and filing (recordkeeping) the form, 5 minutes, for an average of 15 minutes per response. If you have comments regarding the accuracy of this burden estimate, or suggestions for making this form simpler, you can write to both the Immigration and Naturalization Service, 425 I Street, N.W., Room 5304, Washington, D.C. 20536; and the Office of Management and Budget, Paperwork Reduction Project, OMB No. 1115-0136, Washington, D.C. 20503.

EMPLOYERS MUST RETAIN COMPLETED I-9
PLEASE DO NOT MAIL COMPLETED I-9 TO INS

EXHIBIT 7-1 *(continued)*

Penalties for violating these antidiscrimination provisions and for hiring illegal aliens are severe, and can range from $250 to $10,000. There are criminal penalties for those who engage in a pattern or practice of knowingly hiring or continuing to employ unauthorized aliens, or engage in frauds or false statements, or otherwise misuse visas, immigration permits, and identity documents. A West Coast off-premise caterer was recently fined $11,000 for violations of this immigration act.

Employers must retain Form I-9s for three years after termination of the employee. Another West Coast caterer was fined $17,500 for not retaining the required paperwork. Also, when identification expires, such as a driver's license, caterers must verify the new I.D., and make a copy of it for the file.

The Americans (ADA) with Disabilities Act
This act prohibits discrimination against a qualified person with a disability, who, with or without reasonable accommodation, can perform essential functions of a job. Discrimination applies to hiring, firing, paying, promoting, and other terms and conditions of employment.

Employers must reasonably accommodate the disabilities of qualified applicants or employees unless doing so would result in an undue hardship. An accommodation poses an undue hardship if it is unduly costly, or would fundamentally alter the nature or operation of the business. An undue hardship is one that requires significant difficulty or expense, taking into account such factors as cost and company resources.

Employers may not use employment tests to screen out people with disabilities unless they can show that the tests are job-related and consistent with business necessity. Employers also have the right to reject applicants or fire employees who pose a significant risk to the health or safety of other individuals in the workplace.

All employers with 15 or more employees must comply with this law. Employers with 15 or fewer employees are exempt.

Off-premise caterers should:

- ❑ Compile accurate written job descriptions before advertising or interviewing. Carefully list the essential functions of each job.
- ❑ Limit questions on the job-application form that concern the applicant's ability to do the job.
- ❑ Eliminate questions on disabilities, past health problems, use of prescription drugs, hospitalization history, and workers' compensation claims.
- ❑ Review the way they conduct interviews to make sure that questions focus on applicant's ability to do a specific job and that interviews are conducted at locations accessible to the handicapped.

It is interesting to note that half of all workers with disabilities can be reasonably accommodated for less than $50. Some suggested ways to accommodate workers are to restructure jobs, to modify schedules, and to allow for part-time positions.

The Family and   The purpose of this law is to protect the jobs of those who must take off work for
Medical Leave Act family or medical reasons. Effective in August 1993, this law states that employ-
                     ees may take up to 12 weeks of unpaid leave every year for family and medical
                     leave for the following reasons:

❑ The birth of a son or daughter of the employee
❑ The placement of a child with the employee for purposes of adoption or fos-
  ter care
❑ The need to care for the spouse, son, daughter or parent who is seriously ill
❑ A serious health condition of an employee that makes the employee unable
  to perform the functions of the position

Following is a summary of the major exemptions:

❑ An employee who has less than one year of employment
❑ Part-time employees who work less than 1,250 hours per year
❑ Off-premise caterers with less than 50 employees

The 50-employee requirement and the exemption of part-time staff indicate
that this law will affect only the largest off-premise caterers.

Conclusion It is important to fully comprehend these personnel laws. They must be followed
              in order to avoid severe penalties which could contribute to business failure.
              Readers should contact an attorney prior to making major personnel deci-
              sions.

STAFFING LEVELS

The key to staffing for off-premise caterers it to have the proper balance between
regular staff who handle the day-to-day operations and part-timers who are on
call to work off-premise events as necessary. As a general rule of thumb, payroll
costs as a percentage of sales should be between 20 and 30 percent. Smaller caterers only employ one or two regular staff members, and schedule the remaining
staff as needed, when there are parties.

When computing payroll costs it is very important to consider, in addition
to the hourly wages paid, the cost for other benefits such as:

Employers' share of social security benefits
Federal and state unemployment insurance
Worker's Compensation insurance
Holiday, vacation, and sick pay
Employee meals
Bonuses and other compensation
Health insurance paid by employer

These costs can add 15 to 20 percent or more to payroll costs, over and above the regular hourly wages paid. Astute caterers realize that for every $1,000 that they pay in wages, the true cost is actually $1,150, $1,200, or more.

Much has been written about staffing levels for various events. It is dangerous to state exactly the number of staff required for an event since there are many tangible and intangible elements involved in making this determination. Some of these are:

Number of guests expected
Level of service expected by the client
Price charged for staff
Type of menu
Competency of the staff
Arrival of guests (all at once or staggered)

Elegant dinners with multiple courses require as many as one server for every five guests, and one kitchen staff for every twenty guests. On the other hand, an informal barbecue using plastic, with self-service, can be staffed with a skeleton crew of one or two staff members for each one hundred guests. Obviously, the price paid for the elegant dinner will be far greater than for the barbecue.

Off-premise caterers are continually perfecting the art and science of properly staffing an event. For many events, the staff size scheduled is purely an estimate based upon the caterer's experience. As more experience is gained, caterers learn better and more efficient ways to schedule.

When determining the size of the *regular* day-to-day staff, it is always better to err on the low side. For most caterers, it is easier to bring in additional staff during busier times than keep a larger staff in anticipation of busy periods, while paying them when business does not warrant their presence.

RECRUITING STAFF

How do off-premise caterers build a staff of qualified and highly motivated people? This process begins with recruitment through a variety of sources. There are thousands of people who would love off-premise catering work. The hours can be flexible, the work is interesting, the pay is good, and there is definitely a change of routine and scenery from one party to the next.

One of the best recruitment sources is referral from existing employees. Most will only recommend those who they feel will work out. Those employees who recommend others feel that their own reputation is on the line, and they also want to work with others with whom they are compatible. However, off-premise caterers should use caution in not hiring too many staff that are close to one another, or who are friendly away from work, since a problem with one of them could result in a problem with all of them. It is always best to recruit from a variety of people with different backgrounds and interests. Some sources of potential staff include:

Local high schools, culinary schools, colleges and universities
Homemakers
Senior citizens
Private industry councils
Employment agencies
Government job training agencies
Day labor companies
Local restaurants' staff on their days off
Off-duty flight attendants
Unemployed actors, actresses, models, and writers
Firms that specialize in providing staff to caterers

Ads for staff in local and neighborhood newspapers can be effective. Many caterers advertise on bulletin boards in their locale. A great sample advertisement appeared in the *National Off-Premise Caterers' Roundtable Newsletter,*[5] courtesy of Wayne Lavis, of Lavis Catering, Bloomburg Pennsylvania. This ad appeared as follows:

WANTED!
PART-TIME HELP

Do you like people and wish to help make them happy?

THEN JOIN OUR TEAM
LAVIS CATERING TEACHES

That work can be fun	Communication skills
That we work in a clean and healthy environment	Interpersonal skills
	Responsibility
What it is like to serve others	Care and concern for others
	Self-esteem
The personal and social joy of working	Flexibility
The skills which open opportunities within the industry	CONTACT OUR PERSONNEL OFFICE FOR AN INTERVIEW!!

Other ads can simply state the need for part-time staff who are energetic, hardworking men and women who wish to work once, twice, or more a week. Applicants need not be experienced, but they must be willing to learn.

Ads should reflect no bias against individuals according to their race, color, religion, sex, national origin, or handicaps. Smaller companies are not immune from charges of hiring discrimination. As a general rule of thumb, off-premise caterers should ask their attorneys to review their help-wanted ads prior to printing.

Here are some of the qualities necessary for success as an off-premise catering staff member:

Shows initiative—looks for things to do, self-starter
Enthusiastic
High energy level
Assertive, yet tactful
Sound mind and body
Team player
Flexible—can do many different jobs
Likes being in the public eye—on-stage
Good under pressure
Enjoys serving others
Not afraid of getting hands dirty

Some of these traits can be determined in advance through testing and reference checking, but the best way to see if people will be successful in off-premise catering is to schedule them for a larger party, where there is need for many staff. By observing people at work, astute off-premise caterers can determine if they have the necessary traits to become regular staff members.

INTERVIEWING AND HIRING

For many off-premise caterers, hiring is basically a guessing game. They have little or no idea what to look for, or they are so desperate for staff that they will hire virtually anyone who is interested in work. Caterers who understand the hiring process realize that the interview is the key factor in making the hiring decision. Prior to the interview, they have screened out those who do not seem to possess the communication skills, enough experience, or work attitude.

Both John Mossman and Miles Theurich, leaders of the National Caterers Association, have found that one excellent way to hire staff is to leave a tape-recorded message on their tape machines for prospective staff members to call in response to an ad. On the taped message they record all the details about the job and then ask the candidates if they would like to be considered for the position. If so, they ask the candidates to leave their names and phone numbers on the tape, along with the reasons why they should be hired for the position, including past experience. It is far easier to review the messages, and call back candidates that sound promising, than to talk personally to each applicant.

The Interview Fern Canter, of Turnberry Isle Resort Club, offers these tips every off-premise caterer should follow regarding interviews:

BEFORE THE INTERVIEW

Establish the philosophy or personality of your organization. Is it a bureaucracy, or a flexible structure under which competence can flourish?

Write this down and communicate it to every applicant,. . . [then] seek out the individuals with the appropriate characteristics.

Prepare a job description prior to the interview. . . .

DURING THE INTERVIEW

Establish a cordial relationship. Even if the interview is squeezed into ten minuses of a hectic day, try to avoid interruptions. . . .

Ask only job-related questions. . . .

Maintain control. If the candidate is saying something you do not need to hear, bring the interview back on track.

Let the applicant do the talking. . . . Lead the interview, do not overwhelm it.

Concentrate. . . . Evaluate the answer to a question before you jump to another.

AFTER THE INTERVIEW

Close the interview with an explanation of the status of his/her application. . . .

Evaluate [the applicant] against the job. Remember we all tend to be trapped by "mirror-imaging," hiring those who most resemble ourselves. Liking the person is not enough; make sure he/she fills the requirements of the job.

Keep written records. Do not lose sight of good applicants because you cannot remember who they were or what they said.[6]

Jim Sullivan, President of Pencom, Incorporated, and owner of five high-volume theme restaurants and bars in Denver offers some other interview suggestions:

Treat the applicant like a guest. Smile, acknowledge the person right away, and do not keep them waiting. . . .

Offer a beverage. . . .

Keep your application forms clean and up to date. . . .

Vary your application times. . . operators make interview times convenient for management rather than for the potential employees. . . .

Hire the smile. Inject some humor into the interview, and judge whether the person has a quick, charming, and genuine smile. . . .

Ask yourself: "How would I feel if this person worked for the competition?" If your response is "I don't care," the interview is over.[7]

Ask Job-Related and Legal Questions. Federal law prohibits discrimination on the basis of race, age, color, religion, sex, national origin, and disability. State laws may be even more stringent concerning preemployment questions. Based on guidelines issued by the Equal Employment Opportunity Commission (EEOC), the following topics are to be avoided:

❑ Age or date of birth unless needed to show that a minor is of legal age to serve or dispense alcohol

- ❑ Country of origin, place of birth or citizenship
- ❑ Maiden name
- ❑ Relatives' names (except if applicant is a minor)
- ❑ Past residences
- ❑ Religious affiliation
- ❑ Organizational memberships (other than professional)
- ❑ Sex
- ❑ Marital status
- ❑ Pregnancy status or future childbearing plans
- ❑ Age and number of children
- ❑ Child care arrangements
- ❑ Diseases or major illnesses
- ❑ Credit rating
- ❑ Homeownership
- ❑ Arrest records involving no subsequent convictions
- ❑ Native language
- ❑ Employers may not photograph an applicant until hired.

Questions such as the following are legal:

- ❑ Can you meet specified work schedules? Do you have other activities, commitments, or responsibilities that may hinder this?
- ❑ What is the name and address of person (not relative) to be notified in case of an emergency?
- ❑ To what professional organizations do you belong?
- ❑ Who referred you? Whom may we contact for character references?
- ❑ What do you like most about off-premise catering? What did you like most about your last job? Where would you like to be in five years? Do you enjoy work that involves detail? If you could do anything in the world, what would that be? What do you feel are your strengths and weaknesses? If you could change anything about yourself, what would that be?

Employers may ask for proof of age if there is a minimum age requirement in order to perform the job, such as bartending.

Employers may ask about education and experience in military service as it relates to a particular job, but not about the type of discharge from the military service.

"Foolproof Foodservice Selection System."[8] According to Bill Marvin, his "Foolproof Foodservice Selection System" is an excellent way to screen prospective staff members. His screening test helps reveal applicants who are more likely to succeed than not. It is based on his actual experience when he needed to quickly create an organization of 150 people to feed athletes at the U.S. Olympic Training Center. These people would be needed for two weeks' work and then dismissed. Marvin needed a quick way to find the right people. Extroversion, pride, responsibility, and energy were measured by asking a quick series of questions. The test works best when ques-

tions are asked without lengthy conversation. Those that scored the highest were hired, and those that were the most successful on the job scored in the top third of the screening interview. This process could certainly be adapted to off-premise catering firms when large crews are needed for short periods of time. Marvin's questions and answers, adapted to off-premise catering, follow:

1. As a member of the catering staff, how would you help develop repeat business?
   Positive replies: Show personal action or interactions such as learn customers' names, ask questions, make suggestions, see that the food always looks and tastes good.
   Negative replies: Be friendly, give good service.

2. If I asked your best friend to describe you, what would he or she say?
   Positive replies: People-oriented answers such as outgoing, lots of fun, friendly, positive.
   Negative replies: Nice person, good worker.

3. If you saw someone you thought you recognized, but weren't quite sure, what would you do?
   Positive replies: Go up and ask, make an effort to talk to them.
   Negative replies: Just keep walking, wait until sure.

4. What qualities do you need to be a great staff member for an off-premise caterer?
   Positive replies: Like people, work hard, do more than expected, smiling, flexible, patient, lots of stamina, good work habits, attention to detail, good communicator.
   Negative reply: Be nice.

5. Is it difficult for you to carry on "small talk" with people?
   Positive reply: No, not at all.
   Negative replies: Sometimes, depends upon the situation.

6. What recent accomplishments do you take pride in?
   Positive replies: Specific advancement toward a goal, completed courses, finishing a difficult project, job advancement, family success.
   Negative reply: Has not found enjoyment or a sense of accomplishment in completing tasks, appears happy just to "go with the flow."

7. What are some reasons for your successes?
   Positive replies: My personality, my optimism, desire to succeed, positive self-image.
   Negative replies: Don't know; just lucky.

8. What would your previous employers say about your work?
   Positive replies: Hard worker, dependable, ideal employee, valuable, would rehire.
   Negative reply: Did a good job.

9. What would you do to make a negative situation positive?
   Positive reply: Find out the problem and fix it.
   Negative reply: Get a manager and stay calm.

10. What kind of people irritate you?
    Positive replies: Lazy, negative, complainers.
    Negative replies: I like everyone.

11. What do you do with your time off?
    Positive replies: Make lists, get organized, get right at things.
    Negative replies: Hang out with friends, take it easy.
12. What activities have you been involved in during the past two years?
    Positive replies: Participative activities, aerobics, sports, volunteer work, charities.
    Negative replies: Not many, I just work.
13. What motivates you to get your job done?
    Positive replies: Money, recognition, pride in my work.
    Negative replies: Making people happy, giving good service.
14. How do you feel about doing more than one activity at a time?
    Positive reply: It is a challenge.
    Negative reply: Can only do one thing at a time; it doesn't bother me.

When grading the exam, allow two points for positive answers, zero points for negative answers, and one point if too close to call answers. The highest possible score is 28, scores over 22 represent prime candidates, and those with scores of 18 to 22 are marginal candidates.

Exhibits 7-2 and 7-3 are English and Spanish applications for employment that meet current legal requirements. They were prepared by the Florida Restaurant Association in conjunction with the U.S. Justice Department. Exhibit 7-4 is a personnel record form that is very useful when scheduling staff. Off-premise caterers may wish to ask applicants to complete this form along with the application.

Checking Is it necessary for an off-premise caterer to check all references for every prospec-
References tive staff member? The answer to this question lies in the positions being filled. It would be suicidal not to check thoroughly the references for someone applying for a general manager position, but probably not for a last-minute requirement to add two more staff to a large catered event. As a general rule, the more responsible the position, the more thorough the reference-checking process.

In gathering other information about the applicant, state laws vary. Off-premise caterers should first speak with their attorneys prior to conducting reference checks.

Criminal records. Over 90 percent of the nation's counties will release criminal records by telephone or mail. A number of states will not release arrest records that did not result in a conviction.

Driving Records. For those positions that require employees to drive company vehicles, employers should check driving records.

Worker's Compensation Records. A number of states will provide this information. In some cases, however, requests for this information are covered by federal and some state laws.

Federal and State Court Records. All federal judicial districts can provide information about civil, criminal, and bankruptcy cases. In most states, employers can

APPLICATION FOR EMPLOYMENT

Instructions: PRINT IN BLACK INK OR TYPE. Fill out the application form completely; if questions are not applicable, enter "N/A". Do not leave questions blank. Resumes will be accepted as additional information but not in place of a completed application. Be sure to sign the application when it is completed.

EQUAL OPPORTUNITY EMPLOYER: It is our policy to abide by all Federal and State laws prohibiting employment discrimination solely on the basis of a person's race, color, creed, national origin, religion, age, sex, marital status, or physical handicap, except where a reasonable, bona fide occupational qualification exists.

NAME _____ Social Security No. _____ - _____ - _____
              (Last)   (First)   (Middle)
                                                                                              Work _____
ADDRESS   (Current) _____ Home _____
              (Street)   (City)   (State)   (Zip)   (Phone)
                                                                                              Work _____
         (Permanent) _____ Home _____
              (Street)   (City)   (State)   (Zip)   (Phone)

Type of position desired _____

Salary Expected $ _____   Full-Time ☐   Part-Time ☐   Date available for work _____

CAN YOU *AFTER EMPLOYMENT*, SUBMIT PROOF OF U.S. CITIZENSHIP OR VERIFICATION DOCUMENTS OF YOUR LEGAL RIGHT TO WORK IN THE UNITED STATES? Yes ☐   No ☐

WERE YOU PREVIOUSLY EMPLOYED BY THIS ORGANIZATION? No ☐   Yes ☐   If yes, date(s) _____

HAVE YOU EVER BEEN CONVICTED OF A FELONY, OR PLEADED NO CONTEST IN A FELONY, OR BEEN CONVICTED OF A MISDEMEANOR RESULTING IN IMPRISONMENT OR A FINE OVER $500 IN THE LAST TWO YEARS (Conviction will not necessarily disqualify an applicant)?   Yes ☐   No ☐

         If yes, explain _____

IS THERE ANY REASON YOU CANNOT PERFORM THE ESSENTIAL FUNCTIONS OF THE POSITION/POSITIONS FOR WHICH YOU ARE APPLYING? _____

         If yes, explain _____

EDUCATION: MILITARY: Active Duty Dates From _____ To _____

(NOTE: TRANSCRIPTS MAY BE REQUIRED FOR VERIFICATION OF EDUCATION)   Branch Served _____   _____
                                                                                              (Rank, Rate or Specialty)

Type of School	Name and Location of School	Number of Semester Hours Completed	Graduated?		Type of Diploma or Degree	Major Field of Study
			Yes	No		
HIGH SCHOOL OR G.E.D.						
COLLEGE, UNIVERSITY, TECHNICAL OR VOCATIONAL						

Current licenses/registrations (Indicate types and dates received): _____

Fill out only if applying for a position which requires a driver's license.

         Driver's License: No. _____ State _____

         LIST ANY MOVING VIOLATIONS IN THE PAST FIVE YEARS: _____

If applicable, are you of legal age to serve alcohol (18 yrs. or older)? Yes ☐   No ☐
Special Skills/Qualifications: List all special skills you possess and machines or office equipment you can use: _____

OTHER LANGUAGES (INCLUDE SIGN LANGUAGE)	SPEAK			READ			WRITE			SIGN		
	Fair	Good	Excellent	Fair	Good	Excellent	Fair	Good	Excellent	Fair	Good	Excellent
_____	☐	☐	☐	☐	☐	☐	☐	☐	☐	☐	☐	☐
	Fair	Good	Excellent	Fair	Good	Excellent	Fair	Good	Excellent	Fair	Good	Excellent
_____	☐	☐	☐	☐	☐	☐	☐	☐	☐	☐	☐	☐

6/93

EXHIBIT 7-2   Application for Employment (English)

EMPLOYMENT RECORD: Please indicate previous employment. Start with present or most recent position, including military service. Use additional sheets if necessary.

Employer: Mailing Address: City and State:						Type of Business		Full Time	☐
						Business Phone No.		Part Time	☐
								Seasonal	☐
Starting Date		Leaving Date		Starting Base Salary	Ending Base Salary	Starting Position Title	Present or Last Title		
Mo.	Yr.	Mo.	Yr.						
Immediate Supervisor's Name:					Briefly describe your duties and responsibilities:				
Explain reason for leaving:									

Employer: Mailing Address: City and State:						Type of Business		Full Time	☐
						Business Phone No.		Part Time	☐
								Seasonal	☐
Starting Date		Leaving Date		Starting Base Salary	Ending Base Salary	Starting Position Title	Present or Last Title		
Mo.	Yr.	Mo.	Yr.						
Immediate Supervisor's Name:					Briefly describe your duties and responsibilities:				
Explain reason for leaving:									

Employer: Mailing Address: City and State:						Type of Business		Full Time	☐
						Business Phone No.		Part Time	☐
								Seasonal	☐
Starting Date		Leaving Date		Starting Base Salary	Ending Base Salary	Starting Position Title	Present or Last Title		
Mo.	Yr.	Mo.	Yr.						
Immediate Supervisor's Name:					Briefly describe your duties and responsibilities:				
Explain reason for leaving:									

Employer: Mailing Address: City and State:						Type of Business		Full Time	☐
						Business Phone No.		Part Time	☐
								Seasonal	☐
Starting Date		Leaving Date		Starting Base Salary	Ending Base Salary	Starting Position Title	Present or Last Title		
Mo.	Yr.	Mo.	Yr.						
Immediate Supervisor's Name:					Briefly describe your duties and responsibilities:				
Explain reason for leaving:									

Do you have any relatives working for our company?   No ☐   Yes ☐   If yes, list names, relationships, and place employed. _____

Who were you referred by? _____

Please read carefully before signing. If you have any questions regarding the following statements, please ask for assistance.

I hereby certify that the following statements, as well as those on any attachment(s) to this form, to the best of my knowledge are true and correct and that they are all given of my own free will. I agree that any misstatement(s) or omission(s) as to material facts will constitute grounds for unfavorable consideration or dismissal from employment.

I authorize you to communicate with all my former employers, schools, officials, and persons named as references. I hereby release all employers, schools and individuals from any liability for any damage whatsoever resulting from giving such information.

I understand that, as this organization deems necessary, I may be required to work overtime hours or hours outside a normally defined work day or work week. If employed, I understand and agree that such employment may be terminated at any time and without any liability to me for continuation of salary, wages, or employment related benefits.

YOU MAY CONTACT:

Present Employer   Yes ☐   No ☐
Former Employer   Yes ☐   No ☐

_____   _____
Applicant's Signature   Date

EXHIBIT 7-2 (*continued*)

SOLICITUD DE EMPLEO

**Empleador afirmativo de
oportunidades iguales para todos**

Instrucciones: En letra de molde o en máquina de escribir. Llene la solicitud por completo; si la pregunta no aplica, indique "N/A". No deje las preguntas en blanco. Los resúmenes serán aceptados como información adicional pero no como substituto a la solicitud. Asegúrese firmar la solicitud cuando la complete.

Empleador de oportunidades iguales para todos: Es la norma de esta compañía de cumplir con las leyes Federales y estatales que prohíben la discriminación de empleo basado solamente en la raza, color, credo, origen nacional, religión, edad (mayor de 40), sexo, estado civil, o desabilidad física, amenos que exista una razonable cualificación del puesto.

NOMBRE _____ No. de Seguro Social _____ - _____ - _____
(apellido)   (nombre de pila)   (segundo nombre)

DOMICILIO (Actual) _____
(calle)   (ciudad)   (estado)   (zona postal)

Teléfono _____
(trabajo)   (casa)

(Permanente) _____
(calle)   (ciudad)   (estado)   (zona postal)

Teléfono _____
(trabajo)   (casa)

Clase de posición deseada_____

Sueldo esperado $ _____ tiempo completo ☐ tiempo parcial ☐   Fecha disponible para trabajar _____

¿Puede Ud., después de empleado, someter prueba de ciudadanía o de verificación de su derecho a trabajar permanentemente en los Estados Unidos Norteamericanos?

Sí ☐   No ☐

¿Ha sido empleado previamente por esta organización?   Sí ☐   No ☐   Si, de fecha _____

¿Ha sido Ud., en cualquier ocasión, convicto de un delito mayor, o ha declarado no contesto en un delito mayor, o ha sido convicto de un delito menor que resultó en su encarcelación o en multa de más de $500.00, durante los últimos 2 años (Convicción no necesariamente descalificará al solicitante) ?   SÍ ☐   No ☐

Si la respuesta es afirmativa, explique _____

¿Hay algún motivo por el cual no pueda desempeñar las funciones esenciales de la posición\posiciones por las cuales está solicitando? _____

Si la respuesta es afirmativa, explique _____

EDUCACIÓN

Servicio militar: Fechas de servicio de _____ Hasta _____

Ramo de Servicio _____ Especialidad _____

(NOTA: Documentos de educación podrán ser requeridos para su verificación)

(Título - Categoría o Especialidad)

Clase de escuela	Nombre y localidad	No. de horas creditos cumplidos	Graduación		Clase de tílulo/ grado	Campo de especialización
			Sí	No		
Escuela Secundaria o equivalente						
Universidad, Colegio o escuela técnica/vocacional						

Licencias/registraciones actuales (indique clases y fechas recibidas) _____

Complete solamente si solicita una posición la cual requiere licencia de conducir_____

Licencia de conducir automóvil: (número) _____ (estado)_____

Enumere infracciones de tránsito durante los últimos 5 años _____

¿Es Ud. de edad legal para servir alcohol (18 años o mayor)? _____

Cualificaciones: Enumere todas sus habilidades y maquinarias y equipo de oficina que puede operar: _____

Idiomas que habla (incluya lenguaje de señas para los sordos)

	Hablar			Leer			Escribir			Seña		
	regular; bien; excelente			regular; bien; excelente			regular; bien; excelente			regular; bien; excelente		
_____	☐	☐	☐	☐	☐	☐	☐	☐	☐	☐	☐	☐
_____	☐	☐	☐	☐	☐	☐	☐	☐	☐	☐	☐	☐

Forma 2
Junio 1993

EXHIBIT 7-3 Application for Employment (Spanish)

Enumere todo empleo pasado, empesando con el presente; incluya servicio militar.
Si es necesario, use páginas adicionales.

Empleador Domicilio Ciudad y estado				Tipo de negocio		Tiempo completo ☐
				No. de teléfono		Tiempo parcial ☐ Temporal ☐

Fecha al comenzar		Fecha al terminar		Sueldo al comenzar	Sueldo al terminar	Puesto al comenzar	Título actual
Mes	Año	Mes	Año				

Nombre del Supervisor	Brevemente describa sus obligaciones y responsabilidades

Explique el motivo por el cual dejó el trabajo:

Empleador Domicilio Ciudad y estado				Tipo de negocio		Tiempo completo ☐
				No. de teléfono		Tiempo parcial ☐ Temporal ☐

Fecha al comenzar		Fecha al terminar		Sueldo al comenzar	Sueldo al terminar	Puesto al comenzar	Título actual
Mes	Año	Mes	Año				

Nombre del Supervisor	Brevemente describa sus obligaciones y responsabilidades

Explique el motivo por el cual dejó el trabajo:

Empleador Domicilio Ciudad y estado				Tipo de negocio		Tiempo completo ☐
				No. de teléfono		Tiempo parcial ☐ Temporal ☐

Fecha al comenzar		Fecha al terminar		Sueldo al comenzar	Sueldo al terminar	Puesto al comenzar	Título actual
Mes	Año	Mes	Año				

Nombre del Supervisor	Brevemente describa sus obligaciones y responsabilidades

Explique el motivo por el cual dejó el trabajo:

Empleador Domicilio Ciudad y estado				Tipo de negocio		Tiempo completo ☐
				No. de teléfono		Tiempo parcial ☐ Temporal ☐

Fecha al comenzar		Fecha al terminar		Sueldo al comenzar	Sueldo al terminar	Puesto al comenzar	Título actual
Mes	Año	Mes	Año				

Nombre del Supervisor	Brevemente describa sus obligaciones y responsabilidades

Explique el motivo por el cual dejó el trabajo:

¿Tiene familiares empleados por nuestra compañía?   Sí ☐   No ☐   Si respuesta es afirmativa, de los nombres, relaciones y lugar de empleo. _____

¿Quien lo recomendó? _____

Favor de leer cuidadosamente antes de firmar. Si tiene preguntas sobre las siguientes declaraciones, favor de pedir asistencia.

Yo certifico que las siguientes declaraciones, junto con los anexos, son fieles, correctas y exactas dentro de lo mejor de mi conocimiento y que todos están redactados a mi voluntad. Estoy de acuerdo que cualquier misinformaciones o omiciones de hechos constituyen motivo para consideración no favorable o despedida de trabajo.

Autorizo que se pongan en comunicación con patrones anteriores, escuelas, oficiales y personas cuyos nombres se dieron de referencia. También descargo de toda culpa a todos empleadores, escuelas e individuos de cualquier responsabilidad-obligación por cualquier daño que resulte por facilitar dicha información.

Comprendo que, como sea necesario por esta organización, tal vez se me requiera que trabaje más de las horas normales o mas de la definición de un día o una semana de trabajo. Si empleado, comprendo y estoy de acuerdo de que tal empleo puede ser terminado en cualquier instante y sin ninguna responsabilidad a mí por la continuación de salario, pago, o beneficios relacionados con el trabajo.

Ud. puede comunicarse con:
Empleador presente: Sí ☐   No ☐
Empleador pasado: Sí ☐   No ☐

_____   _____
Firma del solicitante   Fecha

EXHIBIT 7-3   (*continued*)

EXHIBIT 7-4
Staff Personnel Record

NAME _____

ADDRESS _____

SOCIAL SECURITY NUMBER _____

LIST ALL PHONE NUMBERS _____

PHONE NUMBER WHERE THERE IS AN ANSWERING MACHINE _____

BEST TIMES TO CALL _____

DAYS AND TIMES AVAILABLE TO WORK _____

ARE YOU OF LEGAL AGE TO SERVE ALCOHOLIC BEVERAGES? _____

UNIFORM SIZE _____

IN CASE OF EMERGENCY NOTIFY (NAME, ADDRESS AND PHONE NUMBER)

_____

_____

SKILLS (CHECK THOSE THAT APPLY)

____ BARTENDING	____ BAR RUNNER
____ AMERICAN SERVICE	____ KITCHEN
____ RUSSIAN SERVICE	____ PASTA STATION COOKERY
____ CARVING STATION	____ (OTHER) _____

OTHER INFORMATION _____

_____

_____

find out whether one is or has been a plaintiff or a defendant in a lawsuit, and in some states, actually review the pleadings.

Verification of Educational Requirements. Virtually all colleges and universities will verify attendance and degrees for employers.

Credit Information. Private companies provide credit histories for a fee. As with Worker's Compensation records, this type of information may only be obtained in accordance with certain consumer credit protection laws. This often requires the applicant to sign a release at the time of application.

Previous Employers. Many employers will simply verify dates of employment, while others will offer more information. A key question to ask is, "Would you rehire the person?"

PAYING CATERING STAFF

Regular Pay   When caterers gather, one controversial topic for discussion is the issue of paying catering staff as independent contractors rather than employees. Of course, the advantage to paying staff as independent contractors is that off-premise caterers need not pay the employer's share of social security taxes, unemployment taxes, Worker's Compensation insurance, and other expenses directly related to payroll expenses. The amount of savings can be sizable, reaching as high as 20 percent of total payroll expenses for some caterers. Staff employed as independent contractors are responsible for paying their own taxes and do not receive unemployment benefits.

The Internal Revenue Service has developed a series of questions that are used in individual situations when trying to ascertain someone's status as an independent contractor. The following questions are asked of the employer. The more "yes" answers, the more unlikely that a person is an independent contractor, and the more likely the person is an employee.

1. Do you provide the worker with instructions on when, where, and how work is performed?
2. Did you train the worker?
3. Are the worker's services a vital part of your company's operations?
4. Is the person prevented from delegating work to others?
5. Is the worker prohibited from hiring, supervising, and paying assistants?
6. Does the worker perform services for you on a regular and continuous basis?
7. Do you set the hours of service for the worker?
8. Does the worker work full-time for your company?
9. Does the worker perform duties on your company's premises?
10. Do you control the order and sequence of the work performed?
11. Do you require the worker to submit oral and written reports?
12. Do you pay the worker by the hour, week, or month?
13. Do you pay the worker's business and travel expenses?
14. Do you furnish tools or equipment for the worker?
15. Does the worker lack a "significant investment" in tools, equipment, and facilities?
16. Is the worker insulated from suffering loss as a result of the activities performed for your company?
17. Does the worker perform duties solely for your firm?
18. Does the worker not make services available to the general public?
19. Do you have the right to discharge the worker at will?
20. Can the worker end the relationship without incurring any liability?

After reviewing these questions, it becomes quite apparent that more catering staff are classified as employees, and should be paid as employees. What about the caterer who contracts for a party, and arranges for the client to directly pay the staff? Is this legal? Off-premise caterers should consult their attorneys on this question. State laws vary. Part of the answer may lie in the actual catering contract between the caterers and the clients. Another significant factor is; Who is supervising the workers, the clients or the caterers?

In order to determine a fair hourly rate or salary, off-premise caterers should review the wage rates in the area, the cost of living in the area, the existing supply of qualified staff, and the caterers' ability to pay. As a general rule of thumb, wage rates in rural areas are less than in metropolitan areas. Off-premise caterers who pay at least average, or above-average wages for their geographical area will more than likely attract above-average staff. Paying less per hour usually results in below-average staff.

Premium Pay   When staff needs to travel long distances to party sites that are far from the catering commissary, compensation becomes an issue. For example, do off-premise caterers pay premium pay to staff who need to drive two or three hours to a party site? Many do. A formula that works and is fair to both the employer and employee is to pay for the hours spent traveling one way. If it takes two hours to travel to a distant party location, the off-premise caterer may choose to pay two hours extra for the time that the employee spends traveling to the party. This policy is at the discretion of the caterer, and is influenced by competitive factors.

Overtime Pay   Overtime deals with hours worked in excess of 40 in a workweek. Overtime hours should be distributed as fairly as possible among staff. If no one wishes to work overtime, management may require staff to work overtime in order to meet production deadlines. Whenever possible, overtime should be preplanned so that necessary arrangements can be made. However, before anyone can work overtime, it must be approved in advance by management. Under no circumstances can employees on their own decide to work extra hours. In accordance with federal law, employees must be paid at least time and one half their regular hourly rate for hours worked in excess of 40.

Sometimes the hours of catered events are extended beyond the planned stop time. In this situation, some caterers pay their staff extra hours pay for those extra hours worked. This is not to be confused with overtime pay, which is for hours worked in excess of 40 in a week.

Recording Hours   Recording employee hours worked at off-premise events can pose unique prob-
Worked at   lems, since few off-premise caterers use time clocks at party sites. Actual hours
Off-Premise Events   worked should be recorded by the party supervisor. No staff should be permitted to start work prior to their scheduled starting time unless approved in advance by management. Staff members who are late should be paid for the actual hours worked, not scheduled hours. Some off-premise caterers will send staff home if they are late, others give written or verbal warnings. Exhibit 7-5 is a sample payroll form that can be adapted for use by off-premise caterers.

Tipping Policies   Off-premise catering staff may receive a portion of their compensation in the form of tips provided by clients. Catering staff members must report tips given directly to them by clients on IRS Form 4070 (Employee's Report of Tips to

EXHIBIT 7-5
Payroll Record

NAME OF THE PARTY _____

DATE OF THE PARTY _____

NAME OF EMPLOYEE FIRST AND LAST	SCHEDULED START TIME	ACTUAL START TIME	STOP TIME	HOURS WORKED

NAME AND SIGNATURE OF PERSON PREPARING THIS REPORT

NAME _____

SIGNATURE _____

Employer), if they exceed $20 per month. Employers, in turn, must deduct the necessary federal income tax withholding and social security tax from the employee's paycheck on these reported tips, and, of course, pay the employer's share of the social security tax.

Tips collected by the employer and distributed to employees are subject to all payroll taxes.

EMPLOYEE BENEFITS

This section covers various employee benefits that may be offered by off-premise caterers. It is important to note that at this time none of these benefits are required by federal law, but most caterers provide at least some of these benefits as part of their benefits packages. Some of the more common benefits are:

Employee meals and breaks
Vacation pay
Sick pay
Holiday pay
Health insurance paid by employers
Pay for jury duty

Employee Meals and Breaks

For regular staff members, most caterers establish times for breaks and meals throughout the day. For staff working at off-premise events, the question of meals and breaks becomes more complex. Some caterers prefer to feed their staff prior to the start of the event. They bring special food for the staff to consume. Others feed staff after the guests have eaten, as long as there is leftover food. Other caterers do not feed their staff if shifts are shorter than five or six hours, but do for longer ones.

It is desirable to offer brief breaks to staff after the party is completely set, but before the guests arrive. After the party begins, there is no time for breaks until after food service is coming to a close. Most caterers allow staff who arrive first to go on break first, and those who came later to take their breaks later. As long as guests are present, some staff should be left on the floor for coffee and other service.

Vacation Pay

Who is entitled to vacation pay? When are employees entitled to it? And to how much are they entitled? Most caterers offer vacations to permanent, regular employees, but offer none to those staff who work on-call. The amount of vacation pay is usually computed based upon the average hours a person works per week, up to 40. For example, a person who averages 30 hours of work per week will be paid 30 hours for each week of vacation pay earned.

It is considered bad policy to pay employees vacation pay and allow them to "work the vacation" for regular pay. Vacations are necessary for relaxation and rest. Vacations should be scheduled at a time mutually convenient to both the employer and the employee. Most vacations should be scheduled during the slower seasons, and normally, no one should be allowed vacation during annual busy periods such as the Christmas holidays.

The majority of employers do not permit employees to take vacation until they have completed a minimum of one year's work. Those employees who take time off during their first year must do so with the employer's permission, and will not be paid. Common vacation polices are:

One-week paid vacation after completing one year of service
Two-week paid vacation after completing two to five years of service
Three-week paid vacation after completing five to fifteen years of service
Four-week paid vacation after completing fifteen years of service

At termination, employees are generally paid for any unused vacation pay, but caterers should use caution and not permit staff to build up large amounts of unused pay. A good policy adapted by many caterers is that employees must use the vacation each year, or lose it.

Sick Pay   Most companies offer somewhere between 5 and 10 sick days per year. These policies can encourage a use it or lose it mentality. Many progressive employers have no specific sick pay policy. They decide entitlement to sick pay on a case-by-case basis for their regular, permanent employees. As for staff who work off-premise, calling in sick at the last minute cannot be tolerated. Some caterers even require that staff who are unable to work find their own replacements.

Off-premise caterers who offer a written sick pay policy of so many days per year and who feel that the policy is being abused by employees may consider such actions as:

Buying back unused sick time when an employee leaves
Disciplining staff who abuse the benefit
Paying bonuses for good attendance
Paying only one-half the daily rate for days taken off due to illness

Holiday Pay   Major holidays are:
New Year's Day
Martin Luther King's Birthday
Presidents' Day
Easter
Memorial Day
Independence Day
Labor Day
Columbus Day
Veterans' Day
Thanksgiving Day
Christmas Day

Holiday pay poses some interesting situations for off-premise caterers, in as much as holidays are generally busy days for caterers. How do caterers pay staff who work or do not work on holidays? Policies vary from company to company. Some caterers choose not to work holidays. Those who cater on holidays may pay nothing extra, while others choose to pay double time, and pass the cost on to the clients. For regular staff members who are given holidays off, most caterers will pay these people their regular pay. Competitor's holiday pay practices should be noted. For example, in many catering markets, staff who work New Year's Eve are paid double pay, at minimum.

Health Insurance   The cost of health insurance continues to skyrocket, and more and more caterers are reevaluating the desirability of paying for it for staff. Many offer a health insurance plan, but require the employee to pay the full amount. Others pay for some or all of it. Ultimately, it is the competition for employees that contributes to the final decision. National Health Insurance is in the planning stages and may impact off-premise caterer payroll expenses considerably.

Pay for Jury Duty   From time to time, regular employees are required to perform jury duty. Most employers pay the employee at least the difference between their regular pay and that which they receive for jury duty as long as the employees present documentation.

Summary   Off-premise caterers should consider the true costs of all benefits before offering them to staff, and they should be aware of competitor's policies in order to attract the best possible staff. They also must provide benefits to employees in a consistent fashion, so that all workers feel that they are being treated fairly.

ORIENTATION

The first day on the job determines to a great extent how well things will go in the future. Proper orientation is not, "Go find Jim, and he'll show you what to do." For new employees, many caterers conduct orientation meetings at the beginning of each season. This procedure works well for the part-time staff who work the parties, but who are not involved on a daily basis. For regular, daily employees, orientation should include the following:

Personally welcome new employees.
Show employees how they fit into the overall scheme of the operation or the
    party.
Explain the purpose of the company.
Introduce the employee to co-workers.
Give the employee a tour of the party site or operation.
Review the main rules and regulations regarding the job.
Explain and demonstrate major job duties.

Show employee his/her designated work space and equipment to complete assigned tasks.

Assign the new employee to another employee to "trail," or follow.

Check back periodically with the new employee.

TRAINING

Training for off-premise catering staff includes regular training sessions, usually conducted in groups, and on-the-job-training, which is an ongoing process. Some caterers have formal training programs for staff, while others conduct training on an informal basis. Those with high employee turnover rates obviously have greater needs for ongoing training programs than caterers with low turnover. However, all caterers need continual training if they are to provide first-class service.

Key points to consider when developing a training program are:

What things do staff members need to know to be successful?

Who will help them learn these things?

How can training results be evaluated?

Group training sessions should last from 15 to 30 minutes and focus on one or two main points. They should always keep the needs of the guests and clients in mind, and staff involvement should be encouraged by allowing for discussion during the sessions.

Specific training topics for off-premise caterers could include such topics as:

Techniques for carrying trays

Cooking pasta at a pasta station

Carving meats at a carving station

Creating attractive displays

Serving wine properly

Creating and building attractive food displays

Recognizing and correcting hazardous conditions

Other sessions can be directed toward building enthusiasm and *esprit de corps* among staff. Successful caterers and restaurateurs constantly work with their employees to further their development. They are never content with the way things are and they are always striving to improve.

MOTIVATING

Motivating catering staff to perform to the best of their abilities, keeping the client's needs continually in the forefront, is a never-ending challenge for seasoned and novice off-premise caterers alike. Off-premise caterers each have their own style of motivating people. Most understand that all need to be challenged by their work, recognized for their good work, made to feel they are part of the company, and safe from danger. These underlying needs can be met in a variety of ways which include:

Pay commensurate with the work and commensurate with the competition
Adequate employee benefits
Organized workplace
Firm and fair leadership
Rewards for those who do things right
Discipline and subsequent termination for those who continuously do things wrong, or who are troublemakers
Empowering employees to solve customer service problems themselves, rather than taking time finding and consulting with management
Scheduling the best performers for the most and the best shifts
Allowing the best staff members to grow into supervisory and managerial positions
Scheduling breaks and meals for staff as appropriate
Providing hot and cold beverages at off-premise sites
Briefing staff prior to each event regarding the purpose and importance of the event
Frequent performance appraisals
Making the off-premise catering operation a truly hospitable place to work by projecting a lively image, conducting upbeat staff meetings, and including staff in future planning

Jerry Edwards, a prominent Baltimore, Maryland off-premise caterer recently wrote in the *National Association of Catering Executives Newsletter* about ways that he motivates his staff during those uncommonly busy periods:

> When in the depths of overtime, work side-by-side with them, or at least make your presence known. If they see you working as hard as they, it lessens the chance they'll resent you for not doing the same.
> Do some dirty work! Not all of it, rather just enough to remind them that you can. It lets them know that you have done it and will continue to do so whenever necessary.
> Listen to their problems. While it's likely you can't solve them, it shows that you are there for them to talk to and that you care enough about them to listen.
> And never forget to give recognition to your staff for all their hard work, especially during stressful and overbooked periods. Help them understand the "big picture" by letting them know that it can't happen without them.[9]

TURNOVER

Staff turnover is a method of measuring how long staff work for an employer. For some caterers, turnover is virtually nonexistent, while for others, there might be a completely new staff every two years. Fast-food chains, for example, completely turn over their staff two or three times every year. In catering, with the complexity of work, this would be suicidal. Some turnover has advantages in that it keeps employees from becoming too complacent, unmotivated, and lackadaisical in performance of their duties. On the other hand, catering an event with all new employees is not much fun either. Turnover created by people moving away, students who graduate, and other external reasons is unavoidable. Unfortunately, some caterers do not treat their staff properly and they defect to other employers. This type of turnover should be avoided at all costs through excellent hiring, training, motivation, pay, and benefits.

PERFORMANCE REVIEWS

Employees require feedback as to their performance. Excellent managers see that employees receive useful feedback on a timely basis. Performance reviews serve as a basis for encouraging more effective work performance and provide dates for decision making regarding future job assignments and compensation.

Permanent staff should be evaluated not less than annually, except in their first year, when evaluations should be performed no less than three times. It is advisable to establish probationary periods for all new employees, which can last from three to six months. During the probationary period, employees who are not meeting expectations may be terminated without warning. At the end of the probationary period, every employee should receive a performance review.

Progressive catering managers evaluate the performances of all staff after each catered event to identify problem areas and determine needs for further training. Many use these evaluations for future scheduling purposes. Excellent performers receive the best schedules and shifts. Those that are mediocre will be scheduled less frequently and those that performed poorly will not be rescheduled.

Exhibit 7-6 is a staff evaluation form which addresses performance areas such as quality of work, quantity of work, ability to follow directions, and other criteria. This form can be used for both regular staff and those that work as needed.

DISCIPLINING AND TERMINATING

Effective discipline must be consistent. It must be given as a result of specific behavior problems, rather than personality conflicts. Discipline normally follows these steps:

1. Verbal warning.
2. Written warning.
3. Suspension without pay.
4. Termination.

EXHIBIT 7-6
Staff Evaluation Form

NAME OF EMPLOYEE _____

EMPLOYEE'S POSITION _____

NAME OF PERSON(S) RATING _____
_____

DATE OF REVIEW _____

RATING SCALE OF 1 TO 5

1   UNSATISFACTORY

2   NEEDS IMPROVEMENT

3   SATISFACTORY

4   ABOVE AVERAGE

5   OUTSTANDING

QUALITY OF WORK   QUANTITY OF WORK

ACCURACY ____   AMOUNT COMPLETED ____

NEATNESS ____   COMPLETED ON TIME ____

ORGANIZATION ____   CONSISTENCY ____

ATTENTION TO DETAIL ____

FOLLOWING DIRECTIONS

COMPLY WITH INSTRUCTIONS ____

FOLLOWS RULES AND REGULATIONS ____

CARE AND USE OF EQUIPMENT ____

FOLLOWS SAFETY AND SANITARY RULES ____

OTHER CRITERIA

PUNCTUALITY AND ATTENDANCE ____

GETS ALONG WITH GUESTS ____

GETS ALONG WITH OTHER EMPLOYEES ____

PERSONAL APPEARANCE AND HYGIENE ____

OTHER BEHAVIOR ____

DATE REVIEWED WITH EMPLOYEE _____

EMPLOYEES COMMENTS AND REACTION _____
_____
_____
_____
_____

MUTUALLY AGREED UPON STEPS TO IMPROVE PERFORMANCE _____
_____
_____
_____

SIGNATURE OF EMPLOYEE _____

SIGNATURE OF PERSON REVIEWING PERFORMANCE WITH EMPLOYEE
_____

Employees who steal, who are insubordinate, or who use alcohol or drugs while working should be terminated immediately.

Documentation of unacceptable behavior is imperative. With staff who are frequently late, it is not enough for a manager to warn them by saying, "You are always late!" Documentation of exact times and dates is essential. Some efficient managers keep track of details such as these by making verbal notes on cassette tape recorders. Verbal and written warnings should include a clear statement of expectations, such as "You must be dressed and working at your workstation by 8 A.M. each day!" Finally, warnings should include the consequences for not doing what is necessary, such as suspension, transfer, demotion, or termination.

The two forms of termination are voluntary and involuntary. A voluntary separation occurs when an employee resigns. Smart managers always identify the reasons why employees leave, and obtain letters of resignation so that employees who quit cannot receive unemployment benefits which may directly contribute to an increase in their unemployment rates.

Involuntary separation, or firing, should be considered a last resort after trying all else. Dr. Elio Bellucci, J.D., Professor of Hospitality Management at Florida International University, offers these procedures:

> Include in staff manuals that the relationship between the employer and employee will continue to be that of an employee at will and that the employer shall have the right to terminate the relationship without just cause, or any cause at all.
>
> Discharge employees for only legitimate, nondiscriminatory reasons. Employees' race, color, age, sex, national origin or other protected characteristics must not play roles in decisions to dismiss.
>
> Document all personnel actions. Do not delay necessary actions, and when taking action, be specific.
>
> Consult legal counsel before terminating employees.
>
> Insure that all procedures and policies as outlined in employee handbooks have been fully complied with before terminating employees.
>
> Conduct exit interviews with terminated employees.
>
> Treat all employees alike, and be sure that terminations are consistent with past practices.[10]

Additional termination guidelines are provided by Paula Michal-Johnson, author of *Saying Good-Bye: A Manager's Guide to Employee Dismissal*, published by Scott, Foresman (1985):

> Anticipate an employee's reaction and how it might affect you. Your goal is to remain calm no matter what the other person does.
>
> If you feel that the employee could endanger you or your company through reprisal, request security support. You also might want a third person present during the termination interview.
>
> Never express how badly you might feel, as this will be interpreted as hypocrisy. Treat the person who is losing the job with dignity.
>
> Experts recommend dismissing an employee early in the week so he or she can begin looking for another job.

Don't try to make an example of the fired employee. Limiting the number of people who know the details of the firing will lessen the chance of the employee suing for defamation.[11]

STAFF HANDBOOK

All off-premise caterers, regardless of size, should have written procedures regarding employment. This handbook will not replace personal contacts, but it can assist in informing staff regarding vital information. As a rule of thumb, the larger the company, the more information should be included. Following is a checklist of topics that should be included in the handbook, along with an explanation of some topics that have yet to be discussed in this chapter.

Policy Statement   A sample policy statement could be as follows:

> *ABC Catering is known throughout this area as a reputable, service-oriented firm that provides excellent food and service to its corporate and social clientele.*
>
> *Our goal is to astonish the guest by delivering more than promised on a consistent basis. This can be accomplished through teamwork within our company. All staff are expected not only to perform their own jobs, but also to assist other staff members whenever needed.*
>
> *At ABC Catering we put our staff first. We realize that an outstanding staff will deliver and produce the types of events that will exceed the guests' expectations, creating wonderful word of mouth that will generate future business.*
>
> *Our staff is composed of friendly, caring, courteous, and concerned individuals who enjoy working for us. Our staff smiles, keeps promises, is always pleasant to our clients and guests, listens attentively to guest requests, and always exhibits a positive, can-do attitude. We endeavor to empower our staff to handle any special customer request quickly and courteously.*
>
> *We produce special events and parties that are user-friendly for the guests, and hassle-free for the clients. We treat our clients and guests the same way that we wish to be treated when we are out.*
>
> *Our staff members have self-pride, pride in our food and service, and pride in our organization.*
>
> *We are pleased to welcome you to our team.*

Handbook Topics   Alcohol and drugs—policy to prohibit use
Americans with Disabilities Act—Company compliance
Attendance—Policies
Automobiles—Where to park (the company is not responsible for personal vehicles or their contents)
Breaks—When and where
"Carry In" Bags
Compensation—Payroll deductions, signing in and out, minimum shift lengths
Equal Opportunity Employer—ABC Catering reaffirms its policy of treating all employees and applicants, whether or not they are members of minority groups, equally according to their individual qualifications, ability, experience,

and other employment standards. There is to be no discrimination due to race, religion, color, national origin, sex, age, or handicapped or veteran status.

Exit interviews—Conducted for all terminated staff prior to leaving

Family and Medical Leave Act—Company compliance

Gambling on the job—Prohibition

Grievance procedures

Grooming policies

Holidays and holiday pay policy

Hours of work—Hours normally open

Moonlighting—Working for other caterers

On-the-Job Injuries—All on-the-job injuries, regardless of the nature or severity, must be reported immediately to the supervisor. All employees are insured through Worker's Compensation Insurance. Those employees who do not report injuries are subject to disciplinary action.

Overtime policy

Pay policy-adjustments for error, advances, and lost paychecks

Pension plan—if any

Performance reviews

Personal phone calls and mail

Probationary period

Promotions and transfers

Property—Care of company property (not responsible for personal property)

Rules and regulations—Miscellaneous

Safety and sanitation rules

Security—Policy for checking employees bags and personal property, policy on employees taking-home leftovers, etc.

Sexual Harassment—Problems must be reported to management, and management will investigate by interviewing the alleged offender and others, ask for legal advise in those situations that are unclear and will take appropriate disciplinary action if there is, in fact, sexual harassment.

Sick pay policy

Smoking—Prohibited in all food production and service areas

Suggestions—Encouraged: how to submit them

Teamwork—Its importance

Telephone courtesy and calls—Policies and procedures for answering telephones and for placing phone calls

Terminations—Policies

Training programs

Uniforms—Professional off-premise caterers should have specific uniforms for all staff prior to and during the party. The policy should be extremely specific. For example, "white shirt" is not specific enough if caterers require a wing-tipped collar tuxedo shirt with black studs. The policy should address accessories that may or may not be worn, use of makeup, how the uniform will be worn (all buttons must be buttoned), and who will pay for the cost of the uniforms. Some employers provide the complete uniform, some pay for part of it, and others require the employee to pay for the complete uniform. Caterers and staff should consult their accountants regarding deductibility of uniforms for income tax purposes. A 1989 survey appearing in Catering Today reported that four out of five caterers require their staff to wear uniforms, 25 percent require that their employees pay for their uniforms, 61 percent paid for the uniforms, and 14 percent shared the cost. Two-thirds of the caterers surveyed required their staff to keep their uniforms clean and half required their staff to wear nametags. When considering uniforms, it is best to solicit staff opinions since they will be wearing them, as well as considering the look, wearability, purchase price, availability for reorders, and cost of cleaning.

Vacations—Company policy

CONCLUSION

To conclude this chapter, please keep in mind that off-premise catering is a people-oriented and a service-oriented business. Excellent food served by a poorly trained, indifferent staff never tastes as good and sometimes is as good as ruined by the bad service. However, well-trained, highly motivated staff can make even the best food seem even better, and ensure the success of catered events.

NOTES

1. Mike DeLuca, Penton Publishing *Restaurant Hospitality*, June 1993, p. 22.
2. Fern Canter, Director of Human Resources, Turnberry Isle Resort & Club.
3. Sarah Stirland, *Restaurants and Institutions*, August 15, 1993, p. 91.
4. *Anti-Discrimination Law: Employer Responsibilities*, The Florida Restaurant Association, Hollywood, Florida, 1993.
5. Reprinted with permission of the author, Wayne Lavis, and the CommuniCATER, official publication of the National Caterers Association, September 1989, p. 3.
6. Fern Canter, Turnberry Isle.
7. Jim Sullivan, *Top Shelf*, July/August 1992, p. 72.
8. Excerpted with permission of *Restaurants & Institutions* magazine, June 10, 1992, © 1992 by Cahners Publishing Company.
9. Jerry Edwards, *NACE NEWS*, June 1993, p. 1.
10. Dr. Elio Bellucci, Professor of Hospitality Management, Florida International University 1994.
11. Excerpted with permission of *Restaurants & Institutions* magazine, August 1, 1993, © 1993 by Cahners Publishing Company.

Chapter 8

The Show

In this chapter, we will discuss those elements that are key to the successful completion of off-premise catered events including the importance of client service, the role of the party supervisor, rules for setting tables, buffets, and food stations, proper service techniques, and the importance of the off-premise catering kitchen. The show is by far the most important time for off-premise caterers since this is the time when the clients and their guests receive the food and service that was promised. There is only one opportunity to perform, so it must be right the first time. Everyone who attends the event will in one way or another evaluate the food, the service, and the off-premise catering company. Good reviews will bring future business, while bad reviews will create bad word-of-mouth that will spread throughout the caterer's market, resulting in lost business.

Four out of five dissatisfied guests will not complain to the caterers or their staffs, but they will tell others. For every ten dissatisfied guests, seven of them will tell twenty others. It is apparent that caterers must focus all of their attention toward satisfying their clients and their guests if they are to continue to be successful and profitable. One sad commentary is that the average American company will spend six times more to get new customers than they will trying to retain old ones. Doesn't it make sense to go all-out in customer service, retaining those existing clients, rather than spending money advertising for new ones?

Customer service is a delicate, intangible product; it cannot be stored for future use. It is a direct function of customer expectation and perception. The perceived level of service equals how closely the guests' experiences match their expectations. If the service experience matches their expectations, then the service is generally unnoticed or taken for granted. The customer is neutral and the service is neutral. On either side of neutral is the memorable experience which may be good or bad.

To meet customer expectations, the service must be efficient, culturally attuned, caring, courteous, concerned, reliable, clean, safe, pleasant, and worth the investment. To exceed customer expectations the service must favorably astonish the guests.

Good service is a matter of opinion and a matter of perception. It is not what is said, but what is heard. This is the essence of miscommunication. An off-premise caterer says that roast beef will be served on the buffet, the customer is used to eating beef tenderloin, and assumes that beef tenderloin will be served. The caterer serves a steamship roast. The caterer never said tenderloin, but the client "heard" beef tenderloin. Some caterers will say, "this is not my fault, nor is it my problem," but it is! We are dependent on clients for future business, and we must at least meet their expectations, and many times exceed their expectations. In the preceding example, the caterer should have been specific as to what type of beef would be served. Of course, the client could have asked, but that is not the point. We are considered the experts, so we must be responsible.

The five most common service complaints are broken promises, rudeness, indifference, not listening, and negative attitudes. These all occur when there is contact with clients and guests. These are moments of truth, and they occur thousands of times during most off-premise events. The clients' and guests' perceptions of off-premise firms is a total of all of these moments of truth from the bartenders who serve the drinks to the servers who serve the meals to the person at the door who says "good night." The goal for caterers should be to design the entire experience so that guests float through the party, barely noticing the servers, having their needs anticipated. The experience should be user-friendly and hassle-free. Long waits for food and beverages, unpleasant servers, poor food, and unpleasant, dirty surroundings are examples of ways to antagonize guests, and ruin any chances for future business.

Everyone in all catering organizations must be motivated toward creating a wonderful experience for clients and guests. Everyone from the chef to the busperson must be geared toward guest satisfaction. Progressive off-premise caterers empower their staff to solve service problems on the spot, without involving a supervisor, which may take too much time. This could be anything from obtaining a special meal for a guest to helping a person who may have difficulty walking to a buffet.

Complacency regarding customer service will quickly result in clients taking their business to the competition. In most markets, there are other catering firms waiting for a competitor to "blink" by not delivering as promised.

Caterers who think that food quality is the most important aspect of their service are mistaken. Clients are equally concerned with such things as the caliber of the service staff, the table appointments and buffets, and even the accessory services such as the music. A band or deejay blaring loud music while guests are conversing and dining will ruin an event. For example, Disney perceives itself as providing a fantasy experience in their theme parks. It does not think of itself as an amusement park. Successful off-premise caterers realize that they provide a complete entertainment experience, rather than just food.

How do off-premise caterers build a successful customer service system? There are some basic rules:

❑ People before paperwork—do paperwork when there are no customers to be served. Without customers, there will be no paperwork to do.
❑ Always be courteous, even when you are extremely busy.
❑ Always say please, thank you, and you're welcome.

Before catered events, clients and prospective clients deal with the caterers' office staff. Basic things such as the following make it easy to do business with caterers, and greatly contribute to creating user-friendly, customer-oriented perceptions:

❑ Are phones answered within three rings?
❑ Are calls returned promptly (never more than 24 hours)?
❑ Are written proposals provided when promised?
❑ Are changes to plans made easily and efficiently?
❑ Does the caterer deliver what he or she promises?

During the event, there are certain times when service may break down, such as when all guests arrive at one time and the lines at the bars are seemingly unending, or when there are long delays between courses. In these instances, the guests' experiences fall short of their expectations.

Service should be at regular increments throughout the meal and should be directed toward anticipating the needs of guests or clients before they ask.

This chapter will address how off-premise caterers can establish service standards, and follow through to ensure that these standards are at least met, and hopefully exceeded.

SUPERVISING AND MANAGING

Prior to discussing specific techniques for providing outstanding service, it is advantageous to address the responsibilities and duties of the party supervisor or manager. In a prior chapter, we detailed the delivery of food, equipment, and supplies to the party site. At this point, we are assuming that the trucks have arrived, one of them perhaps, having been driven by the party supervisor, and it is time to start setting up the event.

The supervisor, with some assistance, first needs to make sure that the equipment is unloaded and organized where setup staff can find it. If there is rental equipment, this must also be organized, unwrapped, sorted, and counted. If there are problems with the equipment, the supervisor at this time should call the rental company to correct them. Next, setup staff should be assigned to the various setup duties and should be provided with diagrams for the various bars, buffets, stations, and the off-premise kitchen. For place-settings at the table, the supervisor should prepare a sample place-setting for staff to follow.

Also, the supervisor must be responsible for checking in staff, and assigning them setup duties as they arrive. Many caterers prefer to stagger staff, by scheduling a few staff early to help unload, organize the equipment, perhaps skirt the buffets, and for other duties. Once things are organized, other staff can perform the more routine functions such as setting tables, bars, buffets, and other areas.

As the crew sets up, the supervisor should meet with the client to make sure that the various accessory service providers are on schedule, and that the food service schedule is properly coordinated with the program and music. Also, the supervisor should oversee the setup process, solving problems as they arise.

The event supervisor must also be aware of the setup in the kitchen in order to direct service staff as to where food will be picked up and where dirty dishes, glasses, and so forth will be placed. Normally, there will be one person who is in charge of the kitchen. This person must see that the kitchen is setup as shown in a diagram and operates in a manner to meet the clients' needs. The kitchen supervisor must oversee the following:

❑ Is the kitchen set up properly, neatly, and safely for the particular function?
❑ Are all of the necessary equipment, food, supplies, utensils, and plastic gloves on hand?
❑ Have the scheduled staff checked in and been assigned duties?
❑ Are staff properly trained and briefed?
❑ Are there recipes available for on-site food preparation?
❑ Are there any last-minute changes in the menu or service that need to be discussed?

If all is on schedule, the party should be set up approximately one hour before the guests arrive. This will give the set up crew a chance to change and freshen up. During this time prior to the start of the event, the supervisor should conduct a detailed meeting going over everyone's responsibilities during the party. For large events, a large poster or flyers are very effective for informing the staff of their responsibilities. This briefing should cover the purpose of the party, the clients, the guests, and anything else that will assist the staff in properly serving the event. The following topics should be included in the briefing:

❑ Have a complete discussion of menu and beverage arrangements.
❑ Review the schedule of events.
❑ Brief staff on special information such as the location of rest rooms for guests.
❑ Review all procedures for serving, such as how to pass hors d'oeuvres, serve the meal, and bus dishes.
❑ Answer pertinent questions from staff.
❑ Give staff an upbeat send off for a great party.

Once the briefing is complete, the staff reports to their assigned stations, and the supervisor should start checking all stations, bars, the kitchen, the accessory service providers, and all other details. If the party is on target, the supervisor should have an opportunity to meet some of the guests, and even develop some contacts for future business. A supply of business cards for the staff is also very helpful for guests who ask about the catering. The supervisor should see that everything is kept on schedule, and may even help out at busy times such as early in the party at the bars, or in the kitchen when the main course is being dished up, and may assist with the dirty dishes at the end of the event. In other words, the party supervisor should be expected to do whatever is necessary to ensure the party's success.

Once the food service is complete, the supervisor should see that staff receives breaks and a meal if appropriate. Normally, by the time the staff has finished breaks, the guests are leaving, and break down can commence as soon as the guests leave. At this point the supervisor should do the following:

❑ Count all equipment and see that it is returned to a safe place or loaded into the catering vehicle.

❑ Make sure all trash is bagged and placed in the proper place.
❑ Deal with any leftovers.
❑ Check out staff and be sure they have left the party site.
❑ Collect for the party from the client, if not already paid.
❑ See that the catering vehicle is returned to the commissary and unloaded (if appropriate).

SETTING UP FOR SERVED MEALS

Most off-premise caterers allow two to three hours of setup time prior to the event. This will vary depending upon the size of the event, the complexity and location of the setup, and other factors. It is always better to allow too much time than too little, in the event there are unforeseen problems that may be encountered during the setup. The setup crew can be a skeleton crew composed of 25 to 50 percent of the total staff scheduled to serve the event. These staff should be attired in a setup uniform designated by the caterers. This preparty work involves heavy lifting, and workers will frequently perspire. The setup uniform could be a tee-shirt or golf shirt imprinted with the caterer's name, matching slacks or shorts, and comfortable shoes. A uniformly attired, efficient, and organized setup crew is a signal to the client that things will go well.

It is advisable to have all of the tables set at least one hour prior to the start of the event. This results in several things:

❑ The client is reassured that everything will go as planned; this gives the client also time for a break.
❑ It allows time for problem solving if something goes wrong.
❑ It gives staff time to refresh and change.
❑ It leaves time for a staff meeting.

Unlike hotels, where nonservice staff setup the tables, many off-premise caterers rely on their service staff to perform this function. A diagram of the room layout will show where tables are to be placed. A supervisor should check that each table leg is locked in place for safety reasons, and that there is at least five feet between each table to allow room for chairs and walking space. When rolling round tables, staff should keep the legs opposite their bodies and wear heavy gloves to protect hands from slivers and sharp metal edges. Tables must be carried, rather than rolled over certain floors that may scratch, and over dirty and muddy surfaces.

The menu for a seated, served meal determines the place-setting. Guided by the sample place-setting completed by the supervisor, staff may begin to set the tables once they are all in place. It is easier to set the tables without the chairs in place, since they get in the way as servers are moving around the tables. If this is the case, how does the staff know where to place the flatware? They can use the creases on the linens as guidelines as shown in Exhibit 8-1. Imagine that the table is the face of a clock, and place the knives at 12 and 6 o'clock, and then evenly place the remaining knives depending whether the table is to be set for

SETTING A ROUND TABLE
WITHOUT THE CHAIRS IN PLACE

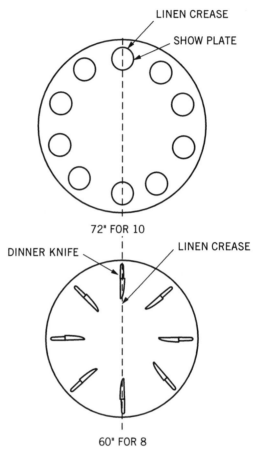

STEP 1   LINE UP KNIFE OR SHOW PLATE ON EACH END OF THE CREASE
STEP 2. FOR 10 SETTINGS, PLACE 4 KNIVES OR SHOW PLATES SPACED
         EVENLY BETWEEN THE 2 KNIVES ON THE CREASE
         FOR 8 SETTINGS, PLACE 3 KNIVES OR SHOW PLATES SPACED EVENLY
         BETWEEN THE TWO KNIVES OR SHOW PLATES ON THE CREASE

EXHIBIT 8-1   Setting a Round Table Without the Chairs in Place

eight, ten or twelve guests. When placing the linens on the tables servers should be trained not to drag clean linens on the floor or ground, to see that they hang evenly from all sides, and to make sure that the hem sides are down and that the creases all run in the same direction for uniformity. Servers' hands must be clean before handling linens.

Although not always possible, it is advisable to place the centerpieces on the tables as soon as the linens are on, but prior to setting the tables in order to avoid knocking over glasses. By doing this, the servers know how much room will be available for the place-settings. On occasion, very large floral arrangements may necessitate that the place-settings be compacted to make room. For a damp floral arrangement, a napkin should be folded and placed under the arrangement to protect the more expensive cloth. Wet cloths can mildew if not handled properly after the event.

The basic pieces of a place-setting are listed here:

Dinner knife	For main course
Butter knife	For butter
Salad knife	For salad course
Fish knife	For fish dishes
Dinner fork	For main course
Salad fork	For salad course and some deserts
Fish fork	For fish dishes
Oyster fork	For shellfish
Soup spoon	For soups in bowls
	For pasta
Teaspoon	For some dessert, sorbet,
	Coffee and hot tea
Iced tea spoon	For iced tea
Bread and butter plate	For bread and butter
Show plate	Left under courses served
	Prior to main course
Water goblet	For water
Wines glasses	For assorted wines
Champagne glass	For champagne
Napkin	

One of the most efficient ways to set a large number of tables is to assign one particular item per setup person. This eliminates presorting into sets of eight, ten, or twelve for each table and assigns responsibility for a particular item to one person: Jane sets the dinner knife, Joe sets the dinner fork, Sue sets the salad fork, and so on. When each of the staff is finished with the assigned item, they start a new item until the tables are set. It is very easy to misplace items when everyone is handling all of the items. For example, one server has extra teaspoons, and momentarily sets them down and forgets. Another server is short of teaspoons, and cannot find any more. Setting tables in an assigned fashion can save significant time, effort, and frustration. Once the place settings are on the tables, the chairs may be placed at each place-setting by just touching the front edge of the chair to the linen. The chairs should never be shoved under the table, or pushed into the table cloth.

Exhibit 8-2 is a sample place-setting for a multiple-course dinner. Note that the utensils are placed in order of service from outside in. The bottom edges of the flatware and show plate should be one inch from the edge of the table. Please note that the coffee cup and saucer are not preset, which is standard for a meal of this caliber. In circumstances where speed is important or for breakfasts and lunches, the coffee cup and saucer may be preset. Again, the saucer should be one inch from the edge of the table, and the cup handle should be angled at four

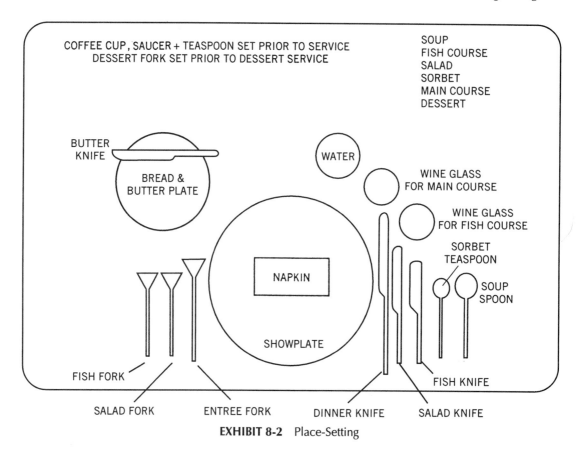

COFFEE CUP, SAUCER + TEASPOON SET PRIOR TO SERVICE
DESSERT FORK SET PRIOR TO DESSERT SERVICE

SOUP
FISH COURSE
SALAD
SORBET
MAIN COURSE
DESSERT

BUTTER KNIFE

BREAD & BUTTER PLATE

WATER

WINE GLASS FOR MAIN COURSE

WINE GLASS FOR FISH COURSE

SORBET TEASPOON

NAPKIN

SOUP SPOON

SHOWPLATE

FISH FORK

FISH KNIFE

SALAD FORK   ENTREE FORK   DINNER KNIFE   SALAD KNIFE

EXHIBIT 8-2   Place-Setting

o'clock. Since this place-setting is very full, the dessert fork and coffee teaspoon with be placed prior to the dessert and coffee service.

In addition to those items depicted in Exhibit 8-2, tables will also require salt and pepper shakers, sugar bowls, creamers, and ashtrays (if smoking is allowed). The salt and pepper shakers are preset but removed when clearing the main course. The sugars and creamers should be placed prior to the coffee service. Ashtrays remain out throughout the meal, and they must be kept clean.

Standards vary from caterer to caterer, but a general rule of thumb for numbers of these items per table is:

Tables of six   Two sets
Tables of eight   Two to three sets
Tables of ten/twelve   Three sets

Exhibit 8-3 shows a variety of napkin folds. For better results, use 100% cotton table linen. In some parts of the country, placing a folded napkin in a glass is considered unsanitary. Also, off-premise caterers should remember that if the first course is to be preset, the napkin cannot go in the center of the show plate.

Tuxedo

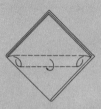

- Fold napkin in quarters.
- Roll the first layer of napkin toward you to the center.

- Fold the second layer toward you and under the first—DO NOT ROLL.
- Leave the same width of napkin as the rolled edge.
- Fold the next layer of napkin away from you and under the second leaving the same width as other two folds.
- Fold under the right and left side edges to center back.

Candle

- Fold napkin in half diagonally forming a triangle.
- Fold one-fourth of the base edge of napkin up forming a cuff.

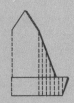

- Turn napkin over. Carefully roll left to right.
- Tuck the remaining corner inside the cuff to hold the Candle firm.

- Position the Candle with the highest point of the napkin facing you.

Crown

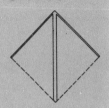

- Fold the napkin in half diagonally forming a triangle.
- Fold the left and right hand corners of the triangle to the top forming a square.

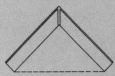

- Turn the napkin to form a diamond. Fold the bottom point 2/3 of the way to the top point and fold the bottom point back again to the base line.

- Turn napkin over and tuck the far corners into one another forming a round base.
- Stand a napkin upright and flair out the two top corners to form a Crown.

EXHIBIT 8-3 Napkin Folding Made Easy. Courtesy Artex International

In this instance, it must go above the show plate, or perhaps in a simple, flat fold underneath the forks.

When setting tables with small candles, supervisors must check that the candles are placed so as not to ignite a centerpiece or a napkin. At one event, a quick-thinking, observant waiter discovered that a centerpiece was on fire and simply doused the fire with the water from the water glass. This averted what could have been a major disaster if left unchecked. When removing candles with hot wax after the event, servers must be instructed to wait until the wax is hard to avoid dripping it on the linens or on themselves.

Exhibit 8-4 depicts a sample setup for a service table to be used by the service staff for storing items required during the meal. One table is required for approximately every one hundred guests. Most items are kept on top of the table, but some items such as chilled wines, bus boxes, dirty dishes, and racked wrapped cups and saucers (when not preset) are kept underneath the service table. Service tables may be used in conjunction not only with served dinners, but also with buffets and food station parties.

6' × 30"—BANQUET TABLE
17' SKIRT AND 72" × 120" CLOTH

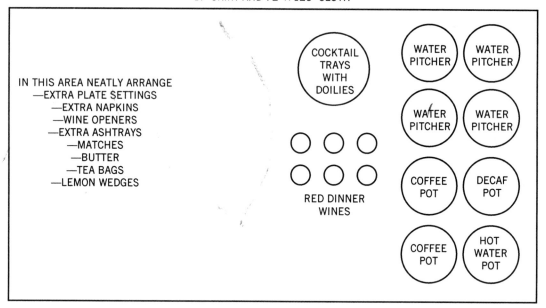

* STORE 6 DEEP BUS PANS UNDERNEATH (STACKED)
* STORE CHILLED WHITE WINE UNDERNEATH OR BEHIND IN ICE CHEST
* CAN BRING COFFEE MAKER DIRECTLY TO SERVICE TABLE AT TIME OF COFFEE SERVICE
* STORE COFFEE CUPS + SAUCERS, WRAPPED, IN DELIVERY CONTAINERS UNDERNEATH

EXHIBIT 8-4 Service Table

SERVICE PROCEDURES FOR SEATED, SERVED MEALS

Serving Butlered Hors D'Oeuvres Frequently, prior to served meals, off-premise caterers serve hors d'oeuvres that are passed butler-style. Although this is a relatively simple procedure to learn, there are a few rules that servers must follow to make this part of the evening most enjoyable for the guests:

- ❑ Know the name of the item and any accompanying sauce, along with the ingredients and method of preparation (fried, oven-baked, grilled, etc.).
- ❑ Warn guests if foods are very hot or spicy.
- ❑ Always smile and show courtesy toward the guests.
- ❑ Carry a supply of cocktail napkins in your free hand.
- ❑ Always return to the kitchen with dirty dishes and glassware.
- ❑ Keep the passing trays looking neat. If guests place dirty cocktail napkins or skewers on passing trays, remove them immediately, and carry them in your hand underneath the tray until you can dispose of them.
- ❑ When passing hot food during times that are not busy, return to the kitchen after approximately five minutes, since the food will be cold.
- ❑ Once a tray of hors d'oeuvres is depleted to the point that it does not look appetizing, return to the kitchen for a fresh one.
- ❑ Always pass to different guests during each trip by going different routes.

Serving the Meal When serving guests, there are a number of standard procedures that are in use throughout the country:

1. Serve food from the left, with your left hand, while walking forward in a counterclockwise direction.
2. Always serve female guests at each table, before serving male guests.
3. Clear from the right, using your right hand, except for such items as bread and butter plates, side dishes, and unused silver that are on the guests' left. These should be cleared from the left with your right hand.
4. Serve beverages from the right with your right hand, moving clockwise around the table. Some caterers consider soup a beverage.
5. Never reach across in front of guests, and if two guests are leaning toward each other talking, clear and serve from their outsides.
6. Servers should not make unnecessary noise, and should be as inconspicuous as possible.
7. When clearing a table, service staff should never place flatware on plates in front of guests, nor put their fingers in glasses.
8. Water glasses should be replenished throughout the meal, and ashtrays should be emptied frequently by placing a clean ashtray over the top of the dirty one, removing both from the table, and setting the clean one on the table.
9. Table numbers and unused place-settings should be removed once all of the guests are seated.
10. Dining tables, chairs, buffet tables, and bars should not be broken down and removed until the guests have left the event.

11. Food service personnel should make every move count. They avoid wasting motions, anticipate their next move by planning ahead, and are always accomplishing something. In short, they rarely stop.

The Service Staff Food servers are responsible for serving food and beverages to guests. Many off-premise caterers have found that each member of the service staff can be designated as either a server or a runner. The runners bring the food from the kitchen, assist serving the guests if necessary, and return to the kitchen with soiled dishes. The servers stay with the guests at all times. They serve and clear. The ratio of servers to runners depends upon the menu, the distance to the kitchen, and other unique factors. A ratio of one to one is a good place to start, then caterers may adjust. The total number in the service staff will vary depending on the level of service to be offered. Anywhere from one service staff per five guests, to one service staff per twenty guests is standard.

During the staff meeting prior to dinner, the supervisor must instruct the service staff as to the order in which tables will be served. One acceptable way is to divide the seating area into sections of five to ten tables, with a lead server in charge, who will not only serve but see to it that the tables within the section are served in the correct sequence. The lead server will make sure that each table has been completely served prior to starting the next table. For smaller events, the supervisor can direct the order of service. Of course, the head table is always served first, then the others in designated sequence.

Water, Roll, and Butter Service Icewater should be poured ten minutes prior to the guests being seated, and should be kept filled throughout the meal. Chilled bottled water is not served until after the guests are seated, since it is not served with ice to keep it chilled. Butter is placed on the bread and butter plate in a uniform fashion prior to the guests being seated. Warm rolls or bread can be placed in baskets on the table or individually on the bread and butter plate just after the guests are seated, or if not served hot can be preset in baskets on the table.

Servers should make sure that breads or rolls and butter are replenished frequently throughout the meal.

Seating the Guests and Starting Service Servers may assist the guests with seating, seeing that they are comfortable, placing the napkin across laps and serving a last minute drink from the bar. Next, hot rolls or bread should be served. If it was not preset, then the first course should be served. Some items such as chilled soups work well preset, while hot appetizers and mixed salads such as Caesar must be served once guests are seated.

As a general rule, each course should take about 15 to 20 minutes to serve, consume, and clear. Most guests at parties prefer to dine at a moderate rate, not rushed, nor waiting 15 to 30 minutes between courses.

As each course is served, it is essential before the servers start serving a table that the runners have supplied a sufficient number of orders to service the complete table. Never should servers begin a table and then have to wait for more meals. Also, the supervisor and lead servers must be sure that each table is completely served before starting the next table.

The Importance The key to excellent banquet service is the timing of the service of each course.
of Timing Guests in the same area of the room should receive their food at approximately
the same time. Aside from scheduling sufficient service staff, there must be sufficient kitchen staff as well as an organized way to dish up each course in the off-
premise kitchen. Some cold courses may be preplated, which eliminates the pressure of dishing up to order. Hot food that is preplated and held in warmers is
simply not as fresh or as good as hot food that is plated and served within a matter of minutes.

Off-premise caterers have developed their own systems for hot food dishup;
some, of course, are better than others. Exhibit 8-5 is a proven dishup system,
which when properly staffed will plate 200 fresh hot-food meals in 15 minutes or
less. Please note that this is a double-sided line, with plates being prepared on

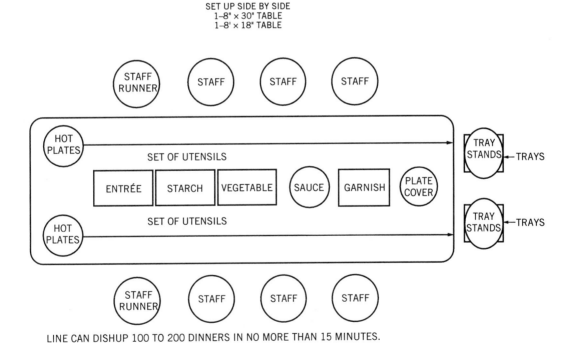

LINE CAN DISHUP 100 TO 200 DINNERS IN NO MORE THAN 15 MINUTES.
FOOD KEPT WARM IN CHAFING DISHES.
STAFF DISH ONTO PLATE, SLIDE PLATE ALONG.
TWO STAFF CAN ACT AS RUNNERS TO REPLENISH FOOD + PLATES.
SERVICE STAFF CAN GARNISH + COVER PLATES.
REMEMBER TO PROVIDE AMPLE NUMBERS OF DISH UTENSILS, HOT TOWELS, AND PLASTIC GLOVES.
INSIST FOOD SERVICE RUNNERS RETURN WITH EMPTY *TRAYS* + PLATE COVER.

EXHIBIT 8-5 Double-Sided Hot Food Dishup Line

each side. This system involves the use of hot plates, hot food, efficient dishup staff, and plate covers.

Another method is to serve the hot food from skirted buffets setup around the perimeter of the area where the guests are seated. The kitchen staff, which must be impeccably attired since they are in view of the guests, stand behind the buffet lines and portion food onto plates carried by the food servers. Each server carries one plate in each hand with a napkin, and walks through the line just as a guest would, but at a much quicker pace, and when the plate is complete, walks toward the supervisor, who directs which table is to receive the meal. The servers continue to return to the line until everyone is served.

When plating hot food, all plates should look the same. A sample plate should be prepared and shown as an example of how all plated dishes are to look.

Clearing Procedures   When everyone at a table is finished with a course the dishes with flatware for the course must be removed, including flatware designated for the course that guests did not use. If one or two people at a table have not finished a course, and are way behind the others, it is permissible to ask them if the course may be set to the side, so that the next course may be served. Clearing should be done from the right, with the right hand. The plate should be kept below eye level until in the aisle space. Then it may be transferred to the left hand. Generally, clearing starts with a woman, and goes clockwise around the table.

Clear glassware from the right side, with the right hand. Stemware should be taken by the stem or bottom of the glass. Glasses, plates, and flatware should be carried to the dirty-dish area on large waiter trays, or bus boxes, which should always be kept out of sight behind the service table. Bus boxes are excellent when there are long distances to walk, when it is very windy, and when the service staff is unable to carry heavy trays. Broken glass should never be placed in a bus box, but should be deposited in the trash. Glasses, china, and flatware should be placed in separate bus boxes to minimize breakage and losses.

When clearing the main course, clear the bread and butter plate and knife, as well as the salt and pepper shakers. Good service also dictates that the tables should be crumbed, preferably using a small metal table crumber.

Procedures for   Carrying fully-loaded waiter trays can be dangerous. Million-dollar lawsuits have
Carrying Trays   resulted from accidents involving dropped trays. Before lifting a tray, staff should see that it is properly loaded and balanced, and that there are not items that may tip over. Before loading a tray with dishes and glasses it should be clean, and either have a nonskid surface or a damp napkin to keep items from sliding. Heavier items should be loaded toward the center of the tray, and lighter items toward the exterior. Plate covers should be properly nested together. Servers should carry trays that they can comfortably handle. Trays should be lifted by squatting down. One hand goes under the tray, and the other supports the tray as the server stands up using his or her thigh muscles. Trays should be carried above the shoulder and steadied with the free hand if necessary. They should be carried with the

hand away from the door hinges (if any) at the party site to ease entry and exit. Try to carry trays around rather than through crowds, but if impossible, servers should use extreme caution. The tray should be lowered, using the squatting technique, onto a service table, kitchen table, or a tray stand that should be opened up with the free hand before lowering the tray. When unloading trays, servers should unload from the center out, or from opposite sides so that the tray does not become unbalanced and tip over. Tray stands should never be placed in the center of the room, other than just prior to serving or clearing. Otherwise, they should be kept around the perimeter of the room away from guests or out of sight.

Beverage Service   When serving cocktails and other drinks from the bar, servers should always use cocktail trays carried in their left hands, and they should serve beverages from the right with their right hands.

When pouring wines at the table, the glass should be filled one-third to one-half full, depending upon the glass size. The wine glass should never be lifted from the table when filling it. Normally, a four- to five-ounce portion is sufficient. There are an increasing number of nondrinkers, so servers should consider their needs also and offer a nonalcoholic beverage, perhaps a glass of nonalcoholic wine if available. When guests decline wine, their glass or glasses should be removed from the place setting, indicating to the other servers not to offer wine.

Wines may be served at the tables by the food service staff, or some of the bar staff who are not busy during dinner. Specific assignments should be made as to who is responsible for wine service for each table.

Prior to serving coffee, servers must place the creamers and sugars on each table, as well as the coffee cup, saucer and spoon if they were not preset. The cups and saucers should be placed to the right of the place-setting, with the edge of the saucer one inch from the table's edge and the handle of the coffee cup angled to four o'clock. The cup should be seeded in the center of the saucer. For some events, cognac, cordials, and after-dinner drinks are served at this time. In addition, dessert should be served.

Many guests prefer to have their coffee with their dessert and cordials, so caterers should try to coordinate these three activities so that guests receive their desserts and beverages at approximately the same time. This can be accomplished by assigning different servers different duties. For example, at a party for fifty guests with six servers, two servers can pour coffee for everyone, two can serve cordials, and two can run and serve dessert. Of course, all servers should start at the same table, and serve tables in the same order.

Coffee should be poured from the right, with the right hand. Servers should not remove the cup and saucer from the table when pouring coffee. Servers should use a clean napkin, held in their left hand next to the left of the coffee cup, to prevent coffee splashing the guests while they are pouring. Extreme caution should always be used when handling and serving hot beverages. Decaffeinated coffee must be identified by some method such as tying a ribbon around the handle. Be prepared to serve tea upon request, and know the location of hot water, tea bags, and lemon wedges. As coffee is served, replenish cream and sugar if needed.

Russian Service   This style involves the service of food from platters that are arranged in the kitchen. The food servers transfer the food from the platters to the guests' plates with a spoon and fork. Skilled personnel are required for this type of service. It is not used frequently at off-premise events because it is more difficult than plated service, and requires additional equipment and utensils. An excellent description of this service technique is contained in Food and Beverage Service, by Axler and Litrides (Wiley 1990).

PROCEDURES FOR BUFFETS AND FOOD STATIONS

Introduction   Buffets and food stations differ from served meals in that guests generally serve themselves. There are some exceptions to this such as perhaps a preset first course, followed by guests going to buffets, or dessert and coffee being served at the table. Place-settings may or may not be provided for buffets, and in most instances food station menus are designed so that foods may be eaten on small plates with forks only. There may not be seating for everyone. Guests are expected to eat standing up. When there are no place-settings or seats, the flatware and napkins must be provided on the buffets or food stations.

Setting up buffets and food stations can require additional time, because of the time-consuming process of designing the display of food and decor. If there is a theme for the event, there may be specific new items to be included in the displays. If these items are provided by clients or decorators, off-premise caterers must see that they are delivered on time for the setup. Ice carvings are the exception; however, the container for the carving may be preset.

Buffet and station diagrams are critical to smooth-running setups, so that staff may work without continually looking for the party supervisor. The diagram of the buffet or station should show:

The name and location
The number and size of the tables, cloths, and skirts
The name and amount of equipment, china, flatware, and utensils

To avoid confusion as to which food items are to go in which containers, small, removable labels may be placed on the containers during setup. These labels can be attached to the diagram until needed.

Before starting the setup process, everything necessary as shown on the diagram at the buffet or station should be placed next to the location for the buffet or food station. This makes the job setup much faster for the setup staff.

Staff must be instructed as to how much creativity is permitted in designing these tables. Some clients prefer a clean, simple look, while others appreciate creativity.

Following is a list of generic procedures regarding food stations and buffets.

PLANNING

1. The number of food stations and buffets may vary, but approximately one buffet or type of food station should be provided for every 75 to 100 guests.
2. In general, each main dish will require one-and-a-half to two lineal feet of space on the buffet table or station.
3. The backs of buffets and food stations should be skirted if guests will see them.
4. Bring extra bowls, display props, utensils, dishes, platters, cassette au feu stoves and fuel, chafing dishes and chafer fuel. These items will be essential if items are broken in transit, misplaced, or out of order.
5. Determine replenishing methods for foods, and provide the necessary containers and utensils. Some backup food items may be stored beneath the station or buffet, as long as they are kept at proper temperatures and covered.

SET-UP

1. Cassette au feu stoves should be tested as staff places them on food stations and buffets. Extra fuel should be stored beneath the station.
2. Chafers should be filled with water as soon as they are put in place. Chafer fuel tops should be loosened; but not removed, and the fuel installed under the chafer water pans. Most chafers have fuel holders; however, for those that do not, fuel should never be placed directly on the table. A small plate or ashtray should be used. It is a good idea to leave a pack of matches near the chafing dishes, and to store extra fuel beneath the table. The chafer food pans should be brought to the kitchen, where they will be filled later with hot food.
3. Fire extinguishers should be provided near buffets and food stations using open flames.
4. Plates for the guests' use never should be stacked more than nine inches high. Taller stacks take away from the appearance of the table.
5. Votive candles should never be placed next to napkins or any other flammable item.
6. Candelabras should be positioned so that hot wax will not drip on food, napkins, or serviceware.
7. Staff who use cassette au feu stoves for tabletop cooking should be thoroughly instructed on their proper use, and how to replace fuel safely and properly.
8. Chafer fuel should be lit 30 to 45 minutes before the hot food is brought out.
9. Food in chafing dishes must be kept hot. Food must be hot before being placed in the chafer. Chafers are not designed to warm food, only to keep it hot. In order to keep food hot:

❏ Place solid food items only one layer deep in the pans.
❏ Cook fried foods as needed.

❑ Keep lids on the chafers until the guests arrive. (One exception is fried foods, which will become soggy if covered.)
❑ Avoid setting chafers in drafts and in the wind.
❑ Use custom-made, lucite shields that stand up around the perimeter of the chafing dishes to protect the fuel from drafts.

SERVING

1. Instruct the staff as to proper portion sizes, particularly for high-cost items.
2. Servers should know what they are serving and the ingredients of the item in case a guest wishes to know.
3. Carvers should be instructed as to the number of orders they should obtain from each piece of meat.
4. Servers who are cooking foods to order must be trained as to ingredients and procedures.

REPLENISHING FUEL AND FOOD

1. Staff should be trained as to how long fuel burns and how to safely replace it. They must be trained to use extreme caution. When replacing fuel, it should be recapped with its own lid, or extinguished with the top of the chafing dish fuel holder. Used cans of fuel should never be touched barehanded, since they can be very hot, and many time flames are invisible. Staff should be instructed to use tongs that will grasp the can tightly and then place the can on a small china plate. Once this is accomplished, a new can of fuel should be properly placed beneath the chafing dish and lit.
2. Chafing dishes full of food and water are very hot and heavy. When removing a pan of food from the chafer, use extreme caution to keep hands, arms, and faces away from the rising steam.
3. Specific staff must be assigned to bring food from the kitchen to the food stations and buffets. Bowls, hot food pans, or platters should not be removed from buffets or stations until fresh replacements are ready to be setdown. In some cases, food may be simply added to the existing container. Once a container of food is half-depleted, it should be replenished.

BREAK DOWN

1. Staff should never break down food stations and buffets until specifically directed by the supervisor. This is a sensitive area, and staff should not be permitted to make this decision. When most guests have eaten, some duplicate food stations may be quietly brokendown, with foods consolidated to those that remain open. Where there is only one station or buffet, it is always best to leave this open until it is very evident that everyone has eaten, and then check with the client before breaking down. Dessert and coffee stations are normally kept open until the end of the event.

2. After extinguishing all chafing dish fuel, the food pans should be removed first from the chafing dishes and carried to the off-premise kitchen, along with other foods from the buffet. Extreme caution must be used when carrying chafing dishes containing hot water so as not to splash hot water on guests or staff.

3. The kitchen should be ready to receive the buffet items. Advise the kitchen supervisor in advance so space can be arranged for receiving chafers, bowls, baskets, and so on.

4. Skirting and other linens should never be removed from buffet tables and food stations until all of the guests have departed.

HANDLING COMPLAINTS

When events are executed properly, there should be few if any complaints. In those rare occurrences when complaints arise, there are some preferred ways to handle them:

1. Allow people to blow off steam. Let them say what is on their minds and never interrupt them unless you need them to clarify a certain point, or perhaps provide more details.

2. Try to identify the problem, and let them know you understand the problem by repeating what you heard them say.

3. Offer a brief apology, let them know the alternative solutions and resolutions, and tell them what you intend to do.

4. Follow up if necessary and always remember to be polite and courteous at all times, regardless of how you really feel.

SUMMARY

Properly supervised and executed, off-premise catered events are guaranteed to create positive word-of-mouth, which will generate future business. The *show* is the key time in every off-premise caterer's schedule. Nothing in the catering business is more important. There are no second chances to get it right!

Chapter 9

Marketing Off-Premise Catered Events

Marketing off-premise catering encompasses developing an image and a marketing plan, utilizing various marketing tools, which produce shoppers and buyers, qualifying shoppers and buyers, and selling to qualified buyers. The end result of these efforts is hopefully profit and satisfied clients. Exhibit 9-1 depicts this prototype. The importance of understanding this concept cannot be overestimated in today's business climate. Customers are becoming more demanding and selective when shopping for catering. It takes more than the ability to cook and serve excellent food to be successful in the catering profession. If clients do not know about off-premise caterers, they cannot buy from them.

Competition for off-premise business increases as more and more players enter the arena. Supermarket delis, national food service management chains, hotels, restaurants, private clubs, and others look to off-premise catering as one way to increase sales.

Smart caterers cannot accept excuses for poor sales performance. They must find ways to increase sales through better marketing. They must show prospective clients how their companies are different from the competition, and how clients can benefit from doing business with their firms.

In this chapter we will examine ways to develop a marketing plan, to utilize marketing tools and to sell catered parties that will hopefully result in profits and satisfied clients.

CATERING MARKETS

The two major off-premise catering markets are social and corporate. The social market includes personal parties at home, fundraisers, wedding receptions, reunions, bar and bat mitzvahs, baptisms, graduations, proms, birthday parties, and wedding anniversaries. Corporate catering involves catering for business events such as grand openings, groundbreakings, retirement parties, holiday parties, employee parties, parties to promote business, and sales-incentive parties, as well as catering for regular business meals.

Corporate catering is generally more profitable since corporate event planners generally have predetermined, large budgets with leeway for add-ons. They are more experienced in planning events, and know exactly what they need. Many have limited time to spend planning events, and prefer to work

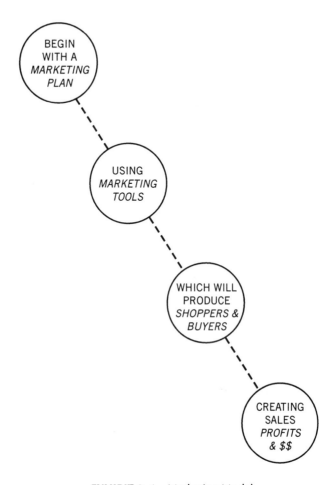

EXHIBIT 9–1 Marketing Model

with off-premise caterers who will handle all of the details. Most are willing to pay a premium price for this service. Social catering usually involves dealing with clients or committees who require more of the off-premise caterer's time, who watch pennies closely, and who want to become involved in every aspect of the event.

Within each of these markets there are several levels of catering:

Budget
Midscale
Upscale

A budget event for a corporation could be dropping off luncheon platters, while one for a social client might be a child's birthday party. Budget parties are low-priced and usually involve little service. Midscale events are those that involve more service and are more expensive than budget, but are not as expensive as upscale. A midscale event might be a retirement dinner for a middle-manager, or a modest wedding reception held at a community center. Upscale events are the most expensive, involve the most service, and, of course, are the most profitable. An upscale corporate event might be a grand opening for a fine jewelry store. For a social client it could be a bar mitzvah with seven food courses, three bands, the finest crystal and linens, and one food server for every five guests.

It is important to note at this juncture that there will be times when off-premise caterers are not marketing directly to actual clients, but to "intermediaries." These include independent meeting planners, who are frequently engaged by small and medium-size companies and government agencies; special event producers, who specialize in executing large special events; independent party planners, who work with noncorporate clients; ground transportation companies and destination management companies, who handle arrangements for convention groups while away from their hotel; and travel agents and representatives of convention and visitors' bureaus.

When marketing to these prospective clients it is important to note that they generally represent major pieces of business, that they may expect commissions, and that they generally are easier to deal with than many social clients. Off-premise caterers wishing to expand their businesses would do well to direct a major portion of their marketing toward these intermediaries. They can bring caterers major revenues.

DEVELOPING A MARKETING PLAN

Off-premise caterers frequently overlook the need for a marketing plan. They simply respond to clients' demands, and as long as there is a satisfactory profit, everything is fine. Startup caterers who need financing from a financial institution must develop a marketing plan for inclusion with their loan request.

Effective marketing plans begin with a financial goal. A business without financial goals is like a ship without a destination. It leaves its home port and flounders helplessly at sea with no destination. Successful off-premise caterers develop clearly defined financial goals. They determine their financial needs and aspirations and then create a plan to achieve these goals.

For example, some startup off-premise caterers wish to earn an annual profit of $100,000 per year after five years in business. This is certainly a lofty goal, but it can be reached in increments. For example, first-year profits could be $20,000; $40,000 the second year; $60,000 the third year; $80,000 the fourth year; and $100,000 the fifth year. Based on financial budgets, which will be discussed in Chapter 14, these caterers realize that they will earn 20 percent profit on their sales. This would result in projected sales and profits as follows:

YEAR	PROJECTED SALES	PROJECTED PROFITS	% PROFIT
1	$100,000	$20,000	20
2	200,000	40,000	20
3	300,000	60,000	20
4	400,000	80,000	20
5	500,000	100,000	20

The first step for these startup off-premise caterers is to conduct a marketing survey to determine a variety of things such as the area of their market, population spending patterns, and demand for their services. This type of information can be gleaned from the following sources:

County population density and distribution figures
Maps of major trading areas
Business profiles of area businesses from area newspapers and magazines
Yellow pages for competition
Local chambers' of commerce
United States Census of Business

Favorable signs for positive growth areas are the opening of chain stores and restaurants, a progressive chamber of commerce, good schools, good transportation, and good public services.

Armed with the data obtained from the survey, caterers should next examine those markets they wish to penetrate. This, of course, must be in concert with the caterer's image. New caterers who make fabulous barbecue could market their services to both social and corporate clients concerned with lower budgets. It would be difficult to market themselves as upscale caterers to the same clientele. Caterers' images reflect their reputation, style, and personality, and should be used to attract customers.

Coupling their images with the market survey data, off-premise caterers can easily determine their target markets. Knowing who they are and who they wish to reach will greatly assist them in selecting the best marketing tools to create their marketing plans.

The next step is to establish a marketing budget. How much do off-premise caterers spend marketing their businesses? Some spend very little while others may spend up to 5 percent of their gross sales. Startup caterers should ask themselves these questions:

❑ Is there available cash to spend on advertising?
❑ How quickly do we want business?
❑ Are we ready to handle the business?
❑ How much business can we handle?

Most caterers learn by trial and error which marketing tools produce the best results. As they gain experience they develop more effective marketing strategies. They always think in terms of the bottom line when evaluating their marketing plans. If one form of marketing does not bring the desired results, they discard it and look for better alternatives.

Your marketing plan should show prospective clients how your firm differs from the competition, and how you will provide specific benefits to clients. It should leave a positive impression:

❑ We are professional and easy to work with.
❑ Our parties are hassle-free and user-friendly.
❑ There are never long lines and there is always plenty of food.
❑ We guarantee you will be satisfied with our services, or your money back.
❑ We will assist you with other areas of your event such as music, flowers, photography, rental equipment, and valet service.
❑ You will receive the best in service from our caring, courteous, and friendly staff who are empowered to meet all your catering needs.
❑ You needn't worry; you can be a guest at your own party.

One underlying theme to all marketing plans is to utilize time and money to bring the greatest return on investment. For example, five visits to a major corporation prior to obtaining a contract for a large catered event will bring more bottom-line profits than five visits to a social client who is planning one house party for 30 guests.

An examination of the myriad marketing tools should lead not only startup caterers but also those experienced in the field to a better understanding of the best ways to develop and implement marketing plans.

MARKETING TOOLS

In this section, we will examine the various forms of advertising, publicity, promotions, and other actions that off-premise caterers may utilize as part of their marketing plans. These marketing tools include:

Positive word of mouth
Networking
Publicity
Brochures
Newsletters
Business Cards and stationery
Photo albums, letters of recommendation, plaques, and awards
Direct mail
Yellow page advertising
Preprinted menus
Cold calling
Signs, logos, and names

Radio and cable television ads
Billboards
Advertising in programs, magazines, newspapers, and other publications
Advertising specialties
Food tastings
Videos
Other marketing tools

Postive Word of Mouth

This is by far the best form of marketing, and many caterers' complete marketing plans are based on the good words of satisfied clients and guests. They realize that one successful party breeds more successful parties. They know that they are only as good as their last party; therefore, they dedicate all of their energies toward making their parties the best they can be.

The problem for startup firms is that with no business, they cannot generate positive word-of-mouth. Some new firms resort to catering parties at cost, or even at a loss in order to generate goodwill and positive word-of-mouth.

Networking

As we near the end of the twentieth century, *networking* has become a popular term. Basically, networking is meeting and talking with people. It could be the service station attendant, the lady in the produce section at the supermarket, or a person at an adjacent restaurant table. All of these people, at one time or another, will need catering. The more people off-premise caterers know, the more likely they will be called when these people need catering. However, it is not enough to just meet these people, it is also necessary to keep in touch with them.

One popular way to keep in touch with those who are potential buyers of off-premise catering is to join and be active in the following types of groups:

Chambers of commerce
Civic clubs such as Rotary, Kiwanis, Lions, and Elks
Church or synogogue groups
Special interest groups
National Caterers Association
National Association of Catering Executives
Meeting Professionals International
International Special Events Society
Convention and visitors' bureaus

One main advantage to networking is that it focuses on establishing relationships with people first. It is not going directly to these people, and on the first meeting asking them to buy catering. It is getting to know people, and keeping in touch with them. When they are ready to buy, they will contact the ones that they know. Networking is one of the best ways to do business.

Publicity   Publicity is free media exposure which directly and indirectly produces revenue. In most cases, publicity is an editorial recommendation, an unbiased opinion that says an off-premise caterer is good. Publicity can help establish off-premise caterers as leaders in their field.

The basic way to generate publicity is to write and submit press releases. Exhibit 9-2 is a press release created by the New York catering firm, Great Per-

---

EXHIBIT 9–2

Great
Performances

12
FOR IMMEDIATE RELEASE
WHY IS THIS WAITER DIFFERENT
FROM ALL OTHER WAITERS?

On April 2, 1985, a group of waiters and waitresses will have the unique opportunity to learn the basic principles of a Passover Seder _ _ its traditions, symbolic foods, and rituals.

"Conducting a 'Seder Workshop' is unprecedented in the catering industry!", says Janet Lee, co-owner of GREAT PERFORMANCES, a catering company with a specialized party staff agency. This workshop will familiarize 'Great Performers' with the distinctive style of service for this ancient traditional holiday. It will be held at 2:30 p.m. at 125 Crosby Street, New York City.

"Passover is the second biggest day for party bookings, surpassed only by Thanksgiving", says partner, Liz Neumark. "Since we teach 'How to Carve a Turkey', it seemed only natural to demonstrate 'What is a Seder'?"

Conducting this workshop is Mrs. Gilda Angel, the gourmet columnist for "Jewish Week", a metropolitan publication, and the author of the soon to be published book *Sephardic Holiday Cooking*. Mrs. Angel, a widely respected lecturer on Jewish tradition and ritual, is the wife of the Minister of the Spanish and Portuguese Synagogue, the oldest Orthodox temple in New York.

Lee and Neumark approach professional waitressing and bartending as an art and have set standards of excellence for their staff comprised of women and men in the arts. The trademark of a Great Performer includes outstanding service, confidence, and pride. Monthly workshops are held to improve party skills.

GREAT PERFORMANCES offers a range of party services including customized catering, entertainment and party planning. They are located in Soho at 125 Crosby Street.

For further information contact: Janet Lee - (212) 000-0000
                                      Liz Neumark - (212) 000-0000

3/19/85

formances. According to David F. Ramacitti, author of *Do-It-Yourself Publicity*, "Virtually any small business could legitimately send out a minimum of six press releases per year, and many could easily double that number. . . . In today's increasingly competitive marketplace, you should be taking advantage of every opportunity available to receive positive public exposure, especially if it doesn't cost anything."[1] Some events that are worthy of press releases for off-premise caterers are:

Grand opening of business
Major anniversaries of business
An exciting party or an unusual challenge
Staff changes within the firm
Expansion or renovation
When a key person within firm is appointed officer in an affiliate group such as
    the National Association of Catering Executives
Catering for a celebrity
Winning an award

One off-premise caterer gained publicity by announcing "Thanksgiving Dinner on the Mayflower." Some press showed up on Thanksgiving, there was dinner and it was on the Mayflower, a Mayflower moving van. It sounds corny, but it worked. The caterer gained free media exposure. Larger off-premise catering firms engage public relations firms to generate publicity, but this can be costly. Nils Johanson, of Bowman's Catering in Detroit, uses a public relations firm on an "as needed" basis, spending on the average of $400 per month. The public relations firm writes about things that may be interesting to the media, which create a greater public awareness but are not intended to generate direct phone calls for orders. They simply reinforce or help create an image in the public's eye.

Janet Lee and Liz Neumark of Great Performances in New York City, achieved response through their use of publicity. They and their staff appeared in *People* magazine, the *New York Times*, and numerous other publications. This is an excellent example of how off-premise caterers can do their own publicity by deciding on which media source to use, creating a media event or story, and writing and packaging a press release. There are numerous books on writing press releases available in bookstores and libraries.

Brochures Many off-premise caterers rely heavily on brochures. One caterer in Canada identified major businesses in his area that employed over 200, called each firm and obtained the name of the catering decision maker, produced a high quality sales brochure, and mailed it to 900 companies. This brochure generated over $100,000 in sales.

Successful brochures must not look like the typical piece of junk mail. A first-class brochure should include color photos and interesting text. It may include slots for a personalized letter and a proposal, as well as a business card and a Rolodex card. The following steps will help you produce an excellent brochure:

1. First establish credibility by telling readers about the number of years in business, prominent clients, awards received, memberships, and other significant facts.
2. Advise readers of foods and services, telling them how they will benefit from doing business with your firm.
3. Guarantee your work. Inform readers that you will not overlook any detail and that their event will be perfect.
4. Brochures should be easy to read, and messages should be delivered in as few words as possible. As with good teaching, good brochures should tell people what you are going to tell them, tell them, and then tell them what you told them.
5. Brochures and other pieces of direct mail should be addressed to a specific person. Personalized, handwritten envelopes are opened more frequently than computerized labels addressed to "Occupant" or "President." Hand-delivering brochures with tuxedo-clad servers will certainly gain attention.

Newsletters   Off-premise caterers around the country have discovered that publishing a newsletter is a very personal way to keep in touch with clients. With costs running as low as 25 cents each, newsletters represent excellent value.

The first step to producing a newsletter is to determine its contents, which should be presented in a personal manner. According to *Restaurants and Institutions*, restaurant newsletters from around the country include such topics as:[2]

Coming events
Coupons and promotions
Recipes
Food, menu trends
Owner or chef column
Celebrity news
Mailing-list signup
Trivia, puzzles, contests, and jokes
Maps, other locations
Business tips
Customer comments, testimonials
Employee profiles

Also cover current tax laws and how they affect the deductibility of expenses for off-premise catering. Under the new tax law there are some exceptions where employers may deduct 100 percent of the cost of certain entertaining expenses, rather than 50 percent. Off-premise caterers should contact their accountant for specific examples that could be promoted to their clients in the newsletter.

There are writers and newsletter companies that specialize in newsletter design, production, and mailing. If affordable, this is the recommended approach. If not, off-premise caterers produce their own with the help of their word processor/computer.

Newsletters should be written with the reader in mind, be published on a specific timetable (such as quarterly, monthly, annually), and should always result in increased awareness of the off-premise caterer.

Business Cards and Stationery

These two items are a definite necessity for all off-premise caterers. They should reflect the caterers' image. A caterer who markets budget events does not need stationery and business cards that are gold-inlaid. A simpler approach will be less costly, and definitely more effective.

Some experts recommend not to use unusually shaped business cards or those that fold over, since they are not easily stored in standard business card cases, while others use gimmicky ones with great success. All catering staff should be given cards to hand out, not only while working, but also to others whom they meet. (Cards at caterered events should be given out only upon request from a guest.)

Staff should carry business cards in their uniform shirt or jacket pocket for quick retrieval. It is very awkward to wait while one searches through a wallet. There are some good card- carrying cases available, and some caterers have given these cases with a supply of cards to their staff.

Photos, Albums, Letters of Recommendation, Plaques, and Awards

These are excellent marketing tools since they help to establish off-premise caterers' credibility with clients. They tell the client about the caterers' past successes. However, these past achievements will not close catering sales. Many off-premise firms display these items in the lobbies leading to their offices, or in their offices. Some make copies of letters and awards and include them in their direct mail pieces.

Direct Mail

Direct mail is mailing information to prospective clients. It includes such things as off-premise catering menus, brochures, newsletters, and other promotional literature. All direct mail pieces should attract attention, arouse interest, and stimulate a desire in readers to take action. All successful direct mail pieces are written with the readers' interest in mind.

A list of 35 ways to improve direct mail efforts appeared in *Celebrate*, a publication directed at caterers published by Korbel Champagne Cellars. They are reproduced here:

1. Make time for file maintenance. For every 1,000 people in your data base (mailing list), you can figure that your file will need one update per day.
2. An unattended data base will reach half-life value in approximately three years—in other words, only half the names and addresses will still be valid.
3. In a mail campaign, your customer list will generate 2 to 10 times the response of a rented list.
4. Don't retain what you can't maintain. Never include information in your data base that your company cannot or will not maintain—it will eventually undermine the integrity of the entire system.
5. On a business data base, always store both job titles (for addressing) and job function codes (for selecting).

6. A customer list used several times a year with no routine "cleaning" procedure will have approximately 5 percent inaccurate zip codes.

7. Unlimited one year use of a mailing list is usually only double the cost of one time use.

8. For better response rates, have the reply form go back to a specific individual, not just to the company or department.

9. Use first class postcard mailing as a low cost way to clean your in-house customer and prospect data base.

10. Knowing something about your customers is just as important as knowing everything about your product.

11. It takes an average of 10 days to deliver a piece of third class mail.

12. Dimensional mailing works. Six months after receiving an advertising specialty in the mail, almost 40 percent of the recipients could recall the name of the advertiser.

13. You should plan to mail to all names in your data base at least four times a year.

14. Ninety percent of all mail responses will be returned within two weeks of the first response.

15. Carefully consider the size of your mailing piece. Overly large or small sizes often cost more for preparation as well as postage.

16. Fulfillment of requests should be mailed out within 48 hours of the receipt of the request. This applies to requests for most catering proposals and requests for basic menu information.

17. Get full value for your postage by including additional enclosures. You can mail up to 3.4948 ounces under bulk rate at no additional cost.

18. A well-timed follow up will often yield response equal to or greater than the initial mailing.

19. For faster processing and delivery, drop your mail at a General Mail Facility (GMF) rather than a branch post office.

20. To increase your sales without increasing your budget in a direct mail campaign, mail to one half of your list, but mail two separate mailings to this half.

21. Personalized response forms make responding easy and increase results.

22. The most important parts of a direct mail letter are the first sentence and the P.S. Why? They are the most frequently read.

23. More than 50 percent of your future business will come from current customers. It costs five times as much to get a new customer as it does to maintain current ones.

24. Multiple mailings are more effective than single mailings on a cost per lead basis.

25. Ask for referrals (Do you know of anyone else who would be interested in this product or service?) on all response devices.

26. Offer prospects several ways to respond for information: mail (Business Reply), telephone (800 number), FAX.

27. To save money on oversized mailings, use booklet envelopes (opening on the long side) rather than end flap openings, so they can be machine inserted.

28. Reply devices should always restate the entire offer.
29. Write the reply device first, then the letter copy.
30. Rely on a full service direct mail firm for your next project. Experience counts more than it costs.
31. Self-mailers will not generate as high a response as a letter with typed envelope and separate business reply card.
32. In presenting your offer, use the word "you" and "your" often in your direct mail letters—they are personal and powerful communicators and will increase your response.
33. Include a reply-paid response card with a reward. Your fulfillment package should always have a business reply card, questionnaire or telephone "hotline" number to further qualify leads.
34. A separate reply device pulls better than one that needs to be detached.
35. Use only white, ivory, ecru or light gray paper for personalized direct mail letter packages. Using colored stock for reply cards, however, will usually yield a higher response.[3]

According to Judd Goldfedder, of the Customer Connection, Escondido, California:
80% of direct mail returns come from existing customers.
61% of third-class bulk mail is read when the recipient knows the sender and is a customer.
58% of third-class postcards are read.
There is no difference in response rate between first and third-class mailings.[4]

Yellow Pages Advertising
Most off-premise caterers advertise in the yellow pages. According to a recent poll of the members of the National Off-Premise Caterers Roundtable, caterers in smaller markets tend to rely more on word-of-mouth advertisements, while caterers in larger markets tend to use yellow pages advertising as their primary advertising vehicle.

A study conducted by Statistical Research, Incorporated, a Westfield, New Jersey company, revealed that nearly one-third of all customers referred to the yellow pages before obtaining a service. Off-premise caterers should also track the source of their business. Some have a special number just for yellow pages callers, and others ask, "How did you hear about us?"

Excellent yellow pages ads are clear, uncluttered, full of useful information, have strong headings, completely describe the products and services, give addresses, phone numbers, and business hours, and how long caterers have been in business. Photographs and graphics are fine as long as they reproduce clearly. Timing of ad placement is critical since missing a deadline can result in one full year with no yellow pages exposure.

An advantage of yellow pages advertisements is that they are available any time of the day or night. They are there when the client is ready to buy.

Preprinted Menus
A complete listing of menu choices is an excellent sales tool that can be mailed or given to prospective clients. These menus may or may not include prices. According to Nancy Loman Scanlon in her book *Catering Menu Management,*

"The presentation of catering menus in an effective marketing format can lead customers to purchase the most profitable menus and services."[5]

A popular size for menus is 9 inches by 12 inches, which fits easily into business mailing envelopes and is standard in the printing industry. The quality of the paper should match the quality of the catering company. Budget caterers should use less expensive paper, while upscale caterers should use textured 24-weight bond paper in pastel colors with a contrasting print color. Most professional printers can provide advice as to typeface and styles, illustrations, and artwork.

In conclusion, descriptive copy about menu items is helpful to readers, and helps to sell unusual and interesting items. Also, in today's nutrition-oriented environment, everyone wants to know ingredients and preparation techniques.

Cold Calling   Cold calling can be done in person or over the telephone. New off-premise caterers should definitely consider calling prospective clients within their market area. By inquiring in advance of the call or visit the name of the person responsible for planning catered events for businesses, caterers can frequently ask for that person by name when making the cold call. The purpose of the cold call is to make contact with a prospective client, and provide the prospect with information about the off-premise caterer. If the person in charge of catered events is not there, then off-premise caterers can leave or mail some information, and follow up at a later time.

Established off-premise caterers who resort to cold calling need to be aware of its negative effects. Clients may perceive these cold-calling caterers as having business problems. (Why is it necessary for them to call door-to-door?)

It is a rare individual who likes to make cold calls, and who can do them successfully. There can be much rejection in this marketing technique with very little tangible results in actual sales. But there is always the hope that the prospective client will call the caterer when there is a need for off-premise catering.

Signs, Logos,   The name will not make or break an off-premise catering firm but it can set the *and Names*   tone, attract attention, and help create the caterer's image in the public eye. A name that begins with the letter A, such as "A Touch of Class" or "An Elegant Affair," is generally a good choice since yellow pages listings, and lists of recommended caterers for specific locations, are in alphabetical order. It never hurts to be at the top of the list. A look through the yellow pages will provide some excellent guidance in selecting a name.

When designing signs and logos, it's always best to consult professionals. Be prepared to pay for signs and logos that are large enough and that are easily seen and are professional. This is not an area in which to cut corners. If signs look professional, prospective clients will think of the caterers as professional.

Signs and logos on catering commissaries, vehicles, uniforms, and even cocktail napkins and matches can lead to name recognition and ultimately more business. Miles Theurich of Theurich Catering has found that silkscreened signs purchased in quantity for present and future trucks are much more economical than handpainting the vehicles. He also suggests magnetic signs for sales vehicles and vans since they do not destroy the value of the vehicles for resale or trade-in.

Radio and Cable Television Ads

Off-premise caterers should be aware that these mediums are available and can be very expensive. Larger catering firms have used them successfully. Startup off-premise caterers could certainly spend their marketing money more effectively in other areas.

Billboards

These are used infrequently, but some caterers have experienced some success by bartering a portion of the cost of the catering services for billboard companies in exchange for billboard advertising space. Prime billboards located on major thoroughfares certainly can bring off-premise caterers significant name recognition.

Advertising in Programs, Magazines, Newpapers, and Other Publications

Many caterers advertise in programs created exclusively for fundraising events. This is certainly a charitable gesture, but it is unlikely that much business will result from these ads since people do not consult fundraising programs when selecting a caterer. Unless an off-premise caterer is catering for the fundraiser, and wishes to contribute to the cause, these should be avoided.

Many cities have city magazines that caterers report as being good advertising vehicles. Some have classified sections in the back which offer reduced rates.

Caterers in small to medium-size communities may find that newspaper advertising can generate substantial revenue. In larger markets, some papers have special advertising sections for smaller firms and special sections and editions. Prices are charged by the inch, with the larger ads having lower per-inch prices.

According to many advertising experts, it is far better to place smaller ads on a regular basis in a few publications that produce results than larger ads in a helter-skelter fashion in a number of publications. Consistency is the key to effective advertising.

Advertising Specialties

Advertising specialties are useful items bearing the name, address, phone number, and message of the advertiser, such as key chains, calendars, and pens. There are some 15,000 articles of merchandise classified as advertising specialties. This type of item is best used to reinforce a basic sales message that appears in another medium, or to serve as a continuous selling reminder when seen by itself.

Advertising specialties are well-suited for seeking new clients, thanking existing customers, promoting new facilities and products, and starting sales conversations. Should off-premise caterers use them? Yes, but their use will not determine the success or failure of the marketing program. They should be merely part of the marketing toolkit and they should be reminiscent of the trade. Advertising can be placed on plastic paperclips used for catering proposals, table crumbers for staff and clients, and wine openers.

Food Tastings

Whenever off-premise caterers gather to discuss common needs and problems, the topic of food tastings is one that generates much discussion. Some off-premise caterers allow their prospective clients to taste the food on the menu prior to the party, while others strictly refuse to do so. Their reputation speaks for itself. Some caterers report that they will do food tastings only for major events, or for clients who have requested an unusual item that the caterer has never prepared.

The disadvantage to tastings is they are expensive and take time. The advantage is that when caterers actually sit down with prospective clients and spend time discussing the menu and the clients' need, they significantly increase their chances of gaining the business.

When conducting food tastings there are a few rules to follow:

1. Catering chefs should be present for tastings, since they are usually more receptive to input directly received from clients.
2. Tastings should be limited to no more than three tasters. More than three creates a food happening, rather than a decision-making meeting.
3. Foods should be presented in exactly the way they will look for the event. Pictures should be taken of the foods.
4. Listen to the taster. Some may have a great knowledge of foods and will give advice as to exactly what needs to be done. Others will not, and simply say that "it needs something." In this case, off-premise caterers need to be prepared to offer suggestions.

Another form of food tasting is one designed to generate new business. Off-premise caterers may simply invite clients and prospective clients to their commissaries to taste their culinary specialties, and hopefully book future parties with those in attendance. Other off-premise caterers have coupled their food tasting with another business wishing to gain marketing exposure, such as an office building needing to lease space, or an automobile dealership. In conclusion, tastings can be very effective marketing tools if targeted at a large number of guests. They are generally part of most caterers' marketing arsenal.

Videos   Increasing numbers of caterers show prospective clients videos of their work. Current video technology makes it easy for even the novice to record and edit actual parties.

Other Marketing   To conclude this section on marketing tools, there are some other effective ways
Tools   to market:

- ❏ Speak to groups about off-premise catering.
- ❏ Offer special promotions and discounts during slow periods.
- ❏ Invite a well-known culinary author to a catering facility.
- ❏ Produce videos that show party styles and locations.
- ❏ Use customer comment cards to generate feedback and mailing-list information.
- ❏ Offer free seminars for those who plan special events such as fundraisers, employee picnics, and corporate client entertaining.

THE MARKETING PLAN

The marketing plan should be based on off-premise caterers' knowledge of local catering markets, competition, marketing budgets, and cash available for marketing-related expenses, and a thorough knowledge of all marketing tools at their disposal. Armed with this arsenal of knowledge, off-premise caterers should be able to effectively and profitably market their services. There is no universally accepted marketing plan. Each one is different based on market differences. Every caterer must develop a plan that is effective in that caterer's market.

A marketing plan must be based on a realistic budget, and should not exceed that budget. For example, if startup caterers plan to spend 5 percent of projected first-year annual sales of $100,000, then there would be $5,000 to spend on first-year marketing efforts. This could include:

Business cards and stationery
Preprinted menu
Food tasting at facility for prospective clients
Quarterly newsletter
Small yellow pages ad
Sign on building and truck
Special direct mailing piece for those who will be cold-called.

Plans for forthcoming years will be based on the successes and failures of each of these marketing tools. Ideally, the less spent on marketing, while still achieving desired sales results, the better off off-premise caterers will be. The art to effective marketing is balancing marketing expenditures with actual revenues.

SELLING TO SHOPPERS AND BUYERS

Up to this point, we have addressed marketing efforts that will produce shoppers and buyers for off-premise catering services. We are now at the stage where interested persons are ready to discuss catering and specific parties with a knowledgeable person. Enter the catering salespersonnel. These people are the ones who can put themselves in the shoes of the shopper. They are willing to serve before trying to collect. They always remember that the client's message is: "Can you help me? Can you fix it? Am I important?"

Successful catering salespeople always put the client first. They know that if they satisfy the needs and desires of the prospective client, they will ultimately gain the client's business. Successful sales staff stay in touch with their clients and show them appreciation for their support on a regular basis. A successful salesperson keeps things in perspective, remembering that there will be good days and bad days. They look at things on a long-term basis, rather than just day-to-day. They take their business seriously, but they also have fun, and never take themselves too seriously.

Salespeople who are successful have a sincere interest in their clients. They do their homework before meeting with clients, ensuring that they understand all there is to understand about a particular event. They know that when prospective clients interrupt, they mean that the point under discussion is a key point in their buying decision making.

To paraphrase Mike Roman, Director of Education for CaterSource, a Chicago-based consulting firm for caterers, catering can be very difficult to sell since it is not tangible; it cannot be taken from the shelf and examined; a catering contract is nothing but a piece of paper with a series of promises; most buyers of off-premise catering have never bought catering before; and catering is not needed on a regular basis like toothpaste. Smart salespeople are very aware of these disadvantages and know that there are various ways to turn them into advantages. For instance:

Show pictures and videos of previous parties.
Guarantee that the work will be executed to perfection.
Provide numerous reference letters to skeptical clients.
Give explicit details in all catering proposals.

The Catering Salesperson

Where are there people who can fulfill these lofty ideals? In many off-premise firms, it is the owner or manager who sells the majority of events. Many prospective clients prefer to deal with the person in charge. Off-premise caterers who do the selling themselves feel that they maximize their chances of gaining the business, which is the driving force behind the company. With no sales, there is no business. They also know that the business that they book will meet their standards. Additionally, they need not worry about salesperson turnover.

Before hiring someone to sell catering services, caterers should determine if perhaps hiring someone to answer the phone would be sufficient. Some owners and managers truly enjoy the selling process, and should never give that responsibility to others. Other caterers may wish to hire someone on a part-time basis and others may wish to involve a family member in the business. Hiring someone to a full-time position is a major step that must not be taken lightly. During busy periods, there is great need for help, but during slower times the need diminishes.

It is not an easy task to hire and train an effective salesperson. Those that come highly trained demand high salaries, and may not be loyal, while those with no experience require maximum training in food preparation, etiquette, food presentation, local traditions, entertaining locations and trends, staff relations, client relations, organizational skills, food and beverage service, and numerous other details. Off-premise catering owners and managers must personally train new sales staff. This is too important a job to delegate. They normally should not expect new sales staff to create new sales, but simply to respond to existing requests. One excellent way to start new sales staff is to break them in by having them answer the telephone and obtain such details as:

Basic customer information
Date, time, and location of the event
Number of expected guests and budget

Next, new staff may sit in on meetings between off-premise caterers and clients, and then begin to arrange small, simple parties themselves in accordance with prescribed company procedures.

How much business should a catering salesperson sell, and how much should a catering salesperson be paid? Much depends on the size of the catering firm, and the prices the firm charges. Some catering salespeople sell in excess of $500,000 per year, others much less.

Salespeople are paid by various methods such as a regular salary, an hourly rate, salary or hourly rate plus a commission on sales, or total commission. First, all pay plans must be in accordance with federal and state laws. Further information on legal ramifications is in the Chapter 7 of this book. Each method of payment has advantages and disadvantages.

- ❏ *Flat salary*. Easy to administer; no incentive for salespeople to produce.
- ❏ *Hourly rate*. Little incentive to produce sales; tendency to expand hours for overtime pay.
- ❏ *Partial commission*. Little security for salesperson; some incentive.
- ❏ *Total commission*. Little security for salesperson; complicated to administer; creates incentive for salesperson to produce.

There is no perfect answer to this question, and off-premise caterers must make pay decisions based upon their individual circumstances. Much of this decision will be determined by the payment practices of other caterers within the same marketplace. In essence, much will be decided by the supply and demand of talented salespeople within the area.

Qualifying Shoppers and Buyers   An effective marketing plan will produce numerous catering inquiries each day. Some callers are interested in planning a specific event, while others are shopping for general information. Experienced caterers will all attest to the countless hours that can be wasted if prospective callers are not properly screened. Some caterers have driven miles to meet with a client, spent half a day meeting with the client, only to learn that this event is unworkable for the caterers due to the size of the party, the budget, the date, or the location.

Most callers do not understand the costs of off-premise catering. They are not concerned about budgets until they discover the costs. They are nervous about the event, and feel that their reputation hinges on the party. Some callers know exactly what they want, while others haven't a clue.

Astute off-premise caterers have learned the secret of qualifying callers to determine if they are truly prospective clients. They know how to separate the "timewasters" from the revenue producers. The four key points to qualifying clients are:

Date of the party
Number of expected guests
Location, type of party and budget

A brief discussion of each follows:

Date of the Party. This will determine the off-premise caterer's availability, as well as whether the caller is inquiring about a specific party, or just shopping. The date also reveals the caller's sense of urgency. Is the party next week or next year? Acting quickly on a party for the following week will more than likely gain the contract. The date also may be on a holiday, when prices may be higher, or when the caterer does not work.

Number of Expected Guests. The answer to "How many guests are you expecting?" will reveal whether the party is possibly too small or too large to undertake. When callers have no idea, this could mean either that they are not serious shoppers, or that they are very early in the planning stage.

Location, Type of Party and Budget. This will help establish the caller's budget. A party at an exclusive private villa will more than likely have a larger budget than one at a city park. If the party is at a private home, the address will often reveal the caller's lifestyle, income level, and probable budget. The address of the business will many times indicate the type of business, as well as the economic resources available for the event. More than likely, an exclusive downtown law firm planning a grand opening will have a larger party budget than an inner-city manufacturing plant planning an employee picnic.

Approximate Budget. The budget can be very difficult to obtain, since many people do not have a clue early on in the party planning. Others do, but do not wish to reveal it. To them, it is like a poker player revealing a hole card in a game of stud poker. Answers to your budget questions, such as, "I really do not know, but I want the party perfect," or "Last year we spent $xxxx," or "I want it elegant, but I don't want to spend too much," will all provide more budget information. These answers reveal these clients already understand that it is going to take more money to produce "the perfect party" or to have "it elegant" than to produce one that is not.

The Next Step Once off-premise caterers have obtained answers to these and associated questions, which can be done in a matter of minutes, they can decide on the next step. This could be one of the following:

❑ Continue the dialogues, schedule appointments, or submit proposals.
❑ Offer to send callers some general written information.
❑ Thank callers for calling; explain that they will be unable to cater their parties.
❑ Establish calling follow-up dates for those callers with insufficient information.

The key point to remember here is that time is money. Caterers must use their limited time marketing and selling their services to the most qualified shoppers.

There are times when caterers should refuse a party. These include times when they are too busy or when the party will not generate an adequate profit. There are also times when the prospective client is too difficult, too indecisive, or overdemanding. It may be best to gracefully decline working with these people since the resulting frustrations and hassles are not worth the effort. Life is too short to spend time dealing with these types of clients.

The Sales Interview

After qualifying clients, the next step is a meeting to discuss the specific elements of the event, in order to prepare a written proposal. During this meeting, off-premise caterers must establish their credibility with prospective clients by discussing prior events, showing pictures and letters, and providing references. During this meeting, many clients are nervous about their forthcoming event, and professional caterers must dispel that nervousness. This can be done by showing clients that they will do an outstanding job, as well as guarantee the work.

Clients also want to see suggested menus. Some will ask to see actual parties, while others ask about food tastings. Smart clients will ask off-premise caterers about their licenses and their insurance. Most wish to know whether caterers will handle the other arrangements such as rental equipment, flowers, music, and decor. Others wish to know who in management will supervise their party, as well as how many parties caterers handle at one time. One of prospective clients' biggest fears is running out of food. Off-premise caterers can never stress enough that there will be more than adequate food for the guests.

Smart salespeople will ask key questions:

- ❑ "What type of party do you imagine?"
- ❑ "What message do you wish to give your guests?"
- ❑ "What is the overall goal of the event?"
- ❑ "Who will be making the decision regarding catering?"
- ❑ "Is there a theme?"
- ❑ "Was there a similar event last year? If so, what did you like and not like about it?"

Exhibit 9-3 is a sample format that can be used during the sales interview. Most main points are included, and salespeople can use this type of format as a guideline for the sales interview. Once these questions have been answered, salespeople have sufficient information to produce written proposals for their clients.

The Written Catering Proposal

As soon as possible after meeting clients, catering salespeople should prepare the written proposal. Many in sales are creative procrastinators due to their fear of rejection. These people must realize that they will not cater everyone's party, and all they can do is the best possible job to convince clients that they will do the

EXHIBIT 9-3
Special Event Information

(This form can be referred to during sales interviews to insure that all of the necessary details are addressed prior to preparing a catering proposal.)

Name and address of client(s): _____

_____

_____

Phone numbers: _____

Fax number (s): _____

Exact location of the event: _____

Day and date of the event: _____

Minimum number of expected guests: _____

Starting and ending times: _____

Proposed menu: _____

_____

_____

_____

_____

_____

_____

_____

_____

_____

_____

_____

_____

_____

_____

_____

_____

_____

_____

Type of beverages to be served (liquor, wine, beer, champagne, cordials): __

_____

Number and location of bars: _____

_____

Equipment

    Tables for guests (number and size): _____

    Type of chairs and chair covers: _____

    Napkins and linens (color, sizes, number): _____

    Banquet cloths and skirting: _____

China color and pattern: _____

Type of glassware: _____

Number of service tables: _____

Size and location of cook's tent: _____

Tenting for guests (size, location, lighting, plants, floor covering): ____

Size and location of dance floor: _____

Size and location of platforms and staging (skirting, railings and steps):

Audio visual equipment required: _____

Other Services

Staffing to set up, serve and clean up the event:_____

_____

Music and entertainment: _____

Floral requirements (for guest tables, buffets and food stations, passing

trays and other areas): _____

_____

Photographer and videographer: _____

_____

Wedding or other specialty occasion cake: _____

_____

Valet parking: _____

_____

Security: _____

_____

Uniforms for staff:_____

_____

Location Layout and Planning

For weddings and receptions

 Ceremony: _____

 Receiving line: _____

 Gift table: _____

 Guest book table:_____

 Escort table (for place cards): _____

 Wedding cake table: _____

Location of cocktail reception _____

_____

Locations of buffets and food stations _____

_____

Location of seating for guests _____

_____

Rain plan _____

best catering job. One way to quickly turn off clients is to delay providing proposals, or not to submit them on the dates promised. Aside from all of this, it is much easier to prepare a proposal when all of the details are fresh in one's mind. The longer one waits, the more difficult it is to remember the various details.

Catering proposals are basically unsigned contracts. Some off-premise caterers prepare proposals in letter format, while others have preprinted forms which are simply filled in. Proposals can be powerful sales producers. All proposals should include those elements discussed in Chapter 2, such as date, time, and number of guests, menu, beverage service, service staff, equipment, other services, methods of payment, and other legal details as appropriate.

To paraphrase Mike Roman of CaterSource, proposals should be very descriptive. Words such as fresh and imported are excellent if they are accurate. Clients should be informed of portion sizes, product origins, grades and cuts of meat and method of preparation and service. All words should be completely spelled out with correct spelling. Pricing should be accurate, with no surprises at a later time. In order to separate themselves from the competition off-premise caterers make their proposals unique by:

Personally delivering the proposal;
Delivering the proposal with an overnight service;
Using stamps, rather than a postage meter;
Putting the proposal in an elegant binder.
Creating a sense of urgency with clients by giving an expiration date for the proposal.

Catering proposals and sales presentations should address how the clients and their guests will benefit from the services that are offered with such statements as the following:

❑ "Your guests will love the food, and we guarantee there will be plenty of it."
❑ "Your guests will not wait in long lines for food."
❑ "You can be a guest at your own party."
❑ "All you need to do is just attend."
❑ "We will handle the worries for you."
❑ "Your guests will rave about the party for months."

Exhibit 9-4 is a sample proposal format that can be stored in a computer, then completed with the specifics for each catered event.

CLOSING THE SALE

Once the proposal is delivered, clients usually wish to review it prior to their decision. Often, others are involved in the decision-making process such as committees, bosses, fiancées, family members, and other interested parties. Some caterers give their clients a certain number of days to reply. They do this by guaranteeing the price. If clients go past the deadline, the price may increase.

EXHIBIT 9-4
Sample Proposal Form

Off-Premise Catering Company Letterhead
4000 DePaul Boulevard
Chicago, IL 60666

Phone number
Fax number

                                        Date of proposal

Client name
Address
City, State, Zip

Dear (name of client):
        Thank you for the opportunity to provide you this proposal for your
forthcoming (name of event). I enjoyed meeting with you (include here the
names of others at the meeting and any other specific things about the meeting such as time, location and any other things that will make the proposal
more personal). The specific details as I understand them are as follows:
                DAY AND DATE OF EVENT: (Fill in)
                MINIMUM NUMBER OF GUESTS: (Fill in)
                EXACT LOCATION OF THE EVENT: (Fill in)
                STARTING AND ENDING TIME OF THE EVENT: (Fill in)
                PURPOSE OF THE EVENT: (Fill in)
        You can be assured that we will do an outstanding job for you and
your guests. We solely rely on the word of mouth of satisfied clients and
guests for our future business. Unlike other caterers, you will find that
at least one owner of our firm will oversee each detail of your event
from set-up to break-down. We guarantee perfection in the execution of
each and every detail.
        We proudly submit the following proposal that has been created
exclusively for your event.

MENU (Include all menu items to be served)

BEVERAGE SERVICE (Include details of beverages to be served, number of
bartenders, and non-alcoholic items to be provided by caterer)

EQUIPMENT PROVIDED (Include a listing of all items such as tables, chairs,
linens, china, flatware, glassware and other equipment)

SERVICES (Include details regarding music, photographers, and other services to be provided by the off-premise caterer)

[Note: It is also advisable to include, in the equipment and services section of proposals, details of equipment and services that clients intend
to provide themselves]

```
PRICING Pricing for the food, equipment and services is as follows:
(Include all pricing details including policies regarding gratuities, ser-
vice charges, other charges and sales taxes).

     Other pertinent information regarding our polices is included on
the attached page.
     Please feel free to call me with any questions, comments or
changes. We are in the service business, and we wish to provide you with
the best of service and food.

Sincerely,



(Name and title of off-premise caterer)
```

Most catering sales closings occur automatically, without the salesperson directly asking for a decision. They basically occur as clients realize that the benefits offered by a particular caterer are those that are in the clients' best interests.

There are a number of powerful video and audio cassette sales tapes available, which teach proper sales and closing techniques. Off-premise caterers should develop a habit of listening to them, and providing them to sales staff. They are an outstanding marketing investment.

One particularly good program is presented by Joel Weldon, a prominent, nationally known corporate seminar leader. Mr. Weldon's cassette programs address all areas of management, but his selling program is one from which every off-premise caterer can benefit. He looks at selling from a building-block approach as follows: From his cassette program "Sell It with a Million Dollar Attitude" (1-800-852-8572)[6].

The Foundation is one of honesty, client interest, knowledge, positive attitude, and preparation on the part of the salesperson.

Building Block One is the "Preapproach," predominately consisting of the marketing tools that were presented earlier in this chapter.

Building Block Two is the "Approach." Most salespeople only have seven to fifteen seconds to make a first impression, and it better be good. The successful salesperson upon approaching a client should exude a positive attitude, confidence, sincerity, and a high level of expectancy. The salesperson's appearance should be professional, he or she should be well-prepared for the meeting, and, of course, should arrive at the meeting on time.

Building Block Three is "Attention." To capture a client's attention Weldon suggests that you may want to:

Tell about a benefit
Make a promise

Pay a compliment
Arouse curiosity
Exhibit something dramatic
Ask a question
Offer to be of service
Use a startling statement
Mention a referral

Building Block Four is "Qualifying," which is finding out the prospect's needs. At this stage, off-premise caterers should decide whether or not they are the best caterers to serve the client, and if so, pursue the party, and if not, walk away politely and quickly.

Building Block Five is "Interest," which involves the selling of benefits that will meet prospective clients' needs as a result of the qualifying questions. Excellent salespeople tell and show prospective clients how they will benefit from using their catering services. They sell benefits rather than features. A feature of a caterer might be good food, but this should be shown to buyers of catering in a benefit format such as, "Your guests will rave to you about the food if you choose our catering service."

Building Block Six is "Conviction." This is gained as salespeople ask prospective clients questions, asking them to agree or disagree with the salesperson's statement. For example, after the previous statement of "Your guests will rave to you about the food...," a professional salesperson might say, "Wouldn't that be great?" Most clients will respond favorably to this statement, creating a unit of conviction.

Building Block Seven is "Desire," which is created by involving prospects in the presentation, showing them the potential benefits, and gaining units of conviction. Once enough units of conviction are made, the sale can be closed.

Building Block Eight is "Resolve to Buy Now." This is done by creating a sense of urgency to act now, such as, others want our services on this date, but we will hold it

---

Catering Policies

1. Advance deposits are not refundable in case of cancellation.
2. Your price per person is based upon a minimum guaranteed number of guests. If your final guarantee is less than the minimum guarantee, we reserve the right to increase the per person price.
3. We do not serve alcoholic beverages to minors or to guests who appear to be intoxicated.
4. Clients are required to provide a final guaranteed number of guests no less than four working days prior to the party. This guarantee cannot be reduced.
5. We prepare for the number of guests that are guaranteed, and you will be billed for the guaranteed number, unless more than the guaranteed number attend the event.
6. Clients need to note the start and stop times of their event. Service that is provided prior to, or after these times is subject to an additional charge.
7. Increases in guarantees 48 hours or less prior to the event, may be subject to a surcharge.

for you for two days while you decide." Another example is, "we are about to institute a price increase, but we will guarantee you the lower price for one week."

Building Block Nine is the "Close." Weldon suggests the use of positive and expectant physical actions such as writing things down, handing a proposal to a client for signature, and assuming the sale has been made with a statement such as "We will arrive at your house next Friday night at 5 P.M. with the food."

Building Block Ten is the "Sale." This occurs when your prospect wins and becomes a customer. At this point successful salespeople ask clients for referrals and why they chose them. Also, at this point it is smart selling to give the buyer something extra after the sale is made. This could be something as simple as a picnic basket of food for the bride and groom to take to their hotel room after the wedding reception; or for a corporate event, perhaps a framed photo of the party taken by the caterer.

Listening to cassettes while in the car, exercising, or at other times when your mind is free is an outstanding way to learn. Smart caterers realize than an investment in knowledge always pays the best dividends. Those who have invested in cassette programs to improve their selling skills report increased sales, as well as increased job satisfaction.

CONCLUSION

Marketing is one of the major keys for success in off-premise catering. Caterers who understand how to develop and execute marketing plans are more likely to succeed than those who do not. Experienced off-premise caterers are always marketing their business. Marketing is second nature to them. They know when to emphasize marketing efforts, and when it is better to concentrate on executing those events already sold. They are always searching for better ways to sell their services, and to increase their share of the catering market in their area. Marketing for them is a never-ending pursuit of excellence.

NOTES

1. David F. Ramacitti, *Do-It-Yourself Publicity*, American Management Association, New York, 1990.
2. Excerpted with permission of *Restaurants & Institutions* magazine, June 1, 1993, © 1993 by Cahners Publishing Company.
3. Bob Brace, "Improving Your Direct Mail Efforts," *Celebrate*, Volume 1, No. 3, December 1992, a publication of Korbel Champagne Cellars.
4. Excerpted with permission of *Restaurants & Institutions* magazine, February 1, 1994, © 1994 by Cahners Publishing Company.
5. Nancy Loman Scanlon, *Catering Menu Management* (New York: Wiley, 1992).
6. Joel Weldon, *Sell It with A Million Dollar Attitude*, 1993.

Chapter 10

Pricing

Pricing off-premise catered events involves the accurate estimation of actual costs to produce the event, and knowing the amounts to mark up these costs in order to produce satisfactory profits. The computation of the actual costs is the "science" of pricing, and the amount of markup is often referred to as the "art" of pricing. Astute caterers not only accurately compute costs, they also know how much they can charge for their services.

How much do off-premise caterers charge for their services? Amounts vary depending up such factors as the supply of caterers within a market area, and the demand for their services. A greater supply of caterers when demand is constant can result in lower prices. Of course, caterers who are in a market where there is little competition may charge more for their services.

Supply and demand can be further identified by the levels of caterers within the market compared with the demand for various levels of service. For example, the few upscale caterers within markets where all other caterers are midscale or budget will have greater freedom in pricing events than those who have many competitors.

Prices vary significantly from one area to another. In order to better understand these variances, the following summary of restaurant prices for major metropolitan areas will reveal major differences. Readers need to understand that restaurant and off-premise catering prices are not the same; however, the following illustration will show how selling prices for meals vary from city to city around the United States, and how prices have declined in many major markets over the past three years.[1]

Restaurant Meal Prices: 1993

CITY	AVE. PRICE	AVE. OF 20 MOST EXPENSIVE	AVE. OF 20 BEST VALUE
New York	$30.20	$63.59	$11.46
San Francisco	27.31	51.16	13.09
Miami	25.13	42.43	12.05
Cleveland	22.68	34.44	15.31
Chicago	20.97	44.97	10.64
Seattle	18.62	33.74	9.00
Phoenix	17.58	31.04	10.85
Denver	17.06	29.04	10.15
New Orleans	16.68	34.60	7.38
Kansas City	12.64	25.23	8.91

Restaurant Meal Prices: 1991 vs. 1993

CITY	1991 AVE. PRICE	1993 AVE. PRICE	PERCENT DIFF.
Los Angeles	$27.91	$23.76	−15%
Philadelphia	26.59	23.38	−12%
Boston	22.29	19.23	−14%
Atlanta	18.89	18.49	−2%
Dallas	18.00	17.51	−3%

Although off-premise catering prices may vary significantly from restaurant prices, it is quite obvious that pricing varies significantly from city to city. Additionally, most caterers report that catering prices are less in most rural areas than in nearby cities. Another interesting trend is that prices have actually decreased in a number of metropolitan areas because people are more budget conscious in the 1990s than they were in the 1980s.

Caterers should carefully analyze clients and their needs. For example, a corporate client who, on a moment's notice, requires a very specialized service will not be very price sensitive, but a bride on a limited budget whose wedding is in two years has a year to shop. The bride has much less urgency than the corporate client, and most brides will shop for the best price.

Many caterers effectively use pricing as a sales tool, since properly priced parties will create sales. These prices are fair both from the caterers' and clients' perspective. Effective pricing creates a win–win situation. Clients achieve their budget objectives, and caterers make satisfactory profits. Pricing policies should take the long-term view. A greedy off-premise caterer who overcharges a desperate client will more than likely never again caterer for this client, *and* this client might tell many others that the caterer charges too much. Fair prices, producing winners for caterers and clients alike, will produce long-term profits and satisfied clients.

PRICING FOR PROFIT

The main goal of all pricing strategies is to maximize the bottom line. The art of pricing is learning the amounts to charge that will produce sales. Caterers whose prices are extremely high will earn large profits on those parties they cater, but the number of parties catered may not be enough to generate sufficient income to cover overhead expenses and required profits. Underpriced caterers may successfully sell virtually every client, but fail to produce sufficient revenues to cover overhead expenses and profits.

The art of pricing is to charge enough to earn an overall profit, but not so much that most proposals are lost. The middle ground is where most off-premise caterers are found. As a rule, somewhere between 50 and 75 percent of all proposals should result in contracts.

Frequently, clients ask caterers to reduce quoted prices. For example, a caterer quotes a price for an event that will generate a $1,000 profit for that particular event. The client says they will work with the caterer if the price can be lowered by $250, which will mean $250 less profit for the caterer. Should the caterer take the party? This depends on the caterer's philosophy. Some say, "75 percent of the pie is better than no pie at all." Others say, "clients either do business on my terms, or we do not do business." A good philosophy is not to reduce a price without reducing something in the party. In this example, the caterer might agree to cater at the reduced price, but serve top sirloin instead of beef tenderloin. Another might compromise, doing the party for $125 less, making one or two minor reductions in the menu.

What should off-premise caterers expect to earn for their efforts and what are some common percentages? These figures vary dramatically from one caterer to another depending on pricing structure, local market conditions, and other factors; however, some common ranges follow:

Food cost percentage	20 to 40% of Gross Sales
Payroll and benefits	20 to 30%
All other expenses	10 to 30%
Net profit percentage	
Before federal income tax	10 to 40%

Prime cost is a term used widely within the foodservice industry. It is the total of the food cost and the direct labor cost. Some operations may have low food costs, but high labor costs, and vice versa. For example, caterers serving steaks will more than likely have higher food costs and lower labor costs since little labor is needed to cut, season, and broil steaks. Conversely, caterers that serve upscale menu items that require significant labor to produce will have higher labor costs, and lower food costs. For caterers, prime cost will normally be less than 60 percent of sales. Therefore, caterers with high food costs of 40 percent of sales should have labor costs of no more than 20 percent of sales to stay within the range. Those with lower food costs will normally have higher labor costs.

"HOW MUCH WILL IT COST FOR A WEDDING?"

Too frequently, this is the first question from a nervous bride or her parents. There are numerous potential clients whose main concern is cost. Smart caterers do not directly answer the cost-related questions until they ask their own qualifying questions (as discussed in Chapter 9), such as date, number of guests, location, entertainment goals, and other questions that reveal the client's true conception of the event. Prices should not be given until these questions are answered to the satisfaction of the caterer, and the precost of the party has been computed. It is bad policy to quote erroneous prices, only to later advise clients that there are additional charges not originally estimated. Clients will question caterers' credibility, and some may even refuse to pay, leaving the caterer with the decision of whether to "absorb" or "eat" the difference, or decline the party.

PRECOSTING CATERED EVENTS

Precosting parties involves accurately estimating all expenses that are incurred in order to produce the event. These include:

Food costs
Commissary labor cost to produce the food
All costs to deliver, set up, serve, and clean up
Equipment costs (rental and owned)
Other costs (flowers, decor, music, misc.)

Computing Food Costs   The first step is to accurately estimate the actual cost of the food necessary to produce the event. Off-premise caterers should maintain accurate, up-to-date cost records for most menu items. Costs for major items such as meat and seafood are volatile and can change dramatically in a matter of days. Beef prices always increase prior to and during the Christmas holidays, and seafood prices change depending on the weather and fishing conditions.

Standard recipe cards must be maintained and updated frequently. Costs must be computed for each recipe ingredient. Exhibit 10-1 shows this procedure. Costs are obtained from recent invoices and supplier price quotes.

In the following example, the cost for each item on the menu was computed on the standard recipe card, and the total food cost is computed by adding the cost of each menu item as follows:

MENU ITEM	FOOD COST
Shrimp raw bar	$3.00
Caesar salad	.55
Beef tenderloin	4.00
Baked rice	.11

EXHIBIT 10-1
Costing a Recipe

Item: Baked Rice

Ingredient	Recipe Quantity	Price	Total Amount
Rice, long grain	8 lb	$0.70/lb	$5.60
Butter	1 1/2 lb	2.00/lb	3.00
Onions	2 1/2 lb	0.40/lb	1.00
Chicken stock	8 qt	0.25/qt	2.00
Salt	1/8 lb	0.20	.03
	Total cost		$11.63
	Number of portions		110
	Cost per portion		0.11

Stir fry vegetables	.45
Garnish and sauce	.50
Rolls and butter	.30
Coffee, decaffeinated, cream, sugar	.25
Chocolate pecan torte	.90
Total dinner price	$10.06

This total food cost per person is multiplied by the number of expected guests, plus a planned overage. This planned overage is generally a percentage of the total number of guests. The larger the number of guests, the smaller the percentage; and vice versa. In Chapter 3, 10 percent was used as a planned overage for a dinner party for 100 guests. Using this as a guideline, the total cost for this meal for 100 guests is:

$10.06 per Person × 110 Guests   (100 plus 10% extra) = $1,106.60

Many caterers prefer to round up to an even number, which in this case would be $1,110 food cost.

Computing Commissary Labor Costs   It is easy to overlook the cost of the commissary labor to prepare this party. In this example, many preparation tasks will be completed in the commissary, such as cooking and cleaning the shrimp, cleaning the salad greens, trimming the meat, and preparing the vegetables. The labor to perform these functions must be accounted for and included in the cost of producing the party. The ideal way to compute the labor costs is to actually time each process. For example, if it takes one cook, who is paid $10 per hour including payroll benefits, six hours to cook and clean the shrimp for the raw bar, this would equal $60. Labor costs should be computed for all items and totaled. In this case, let us assume the commissary labor costs to produce the remainder of the menu to be $240; the total is now $300.

Computing Other Labor Costs   After computing food and commissary labor costs, the next step is to compute the other labor costs necessary to produce the party, for instance:

Cost to pull, pack, deliver, return, clean, and store
Cost of commissary labor at the party site
Cost of service and beverage staff at the party site

Most caterers use estimated figures based on past parties to estimate the cost of pulling, packing, delivering, returning, cleaning, and storing. Smart caterers know better than to underestimate these costs. These costs are very real, and can amount to hundreds of dollars for each party. In our example, let us assume that it takes 20 hours to perform these functions, and that those staff are paid $7.00 per hour including payroll benefits. Twenty hours times $7.00 per hour equals $140.

Commissary labor at the party site is computed by estimating the actual hours necessary. This case, for example, is for six staff for seven hours at $8.00 per hour including payroll benefits:

$$6 \text{ Staff} \times 7 \text{ Hours Each} \times \$8.00 \text{ per Hour} = \$336$$

Finally, laborwise, the cost for service and bar staff must be computed. This is done, again, by simply multiplying the number of staff times their hourly rate times the number of hours worked. Let's assume that there will be ten servers and two bartenders for this event, each earning $12 per hour including payroll benefits. Six staff will work seven hours, and six staff will work five hours. The cost is computed as follows:

6 staff × 7 hours x $12 per hour	=	$504
6 staff × 5 hours × $12 per hour	=	360
Total service and bar staff	=	$864

We now know the total labor cost to produce this event.

Commissary labor to prepare the food	$300
Labor to pull, pack, deliver, etc.	140
On-site commissary labor	336
Service and bar labor	864
Total labor	$1,640

Computing Equipment Costs   Off-premise caterers frequently provide equipment such as china, glassware, flatware, table, chairs, and linens. In some cases, equipment is rented from party rental companies, in others it is owned by caterers, and sometimes it is a combination of both methods. How do caterers charge clients for equipment?

Rental Equipment. Most off-premise caterers add markups to their cost for rental equipment. Also, most rental companies offer discounts from list prices to caterers. This means that off-premise caterers produce profits from rental equipment. To compute the cost of the rental equipment, caterers simply add up the costs of all rental items. Once the rental orders are placed, these costs may be verified with rental companies.

For example, let us assume that the list price of all equipment necessary to produce this party is $2,000 and the rental dealer offers caterers a 10 percent discount. Therefore, the cost to the caterer of the rental equipment is $1,800.

How much do off-premise caterers mark up rental equipment? This varies from one caterer to another. All caterers must invest time to order, receive, handle, rinse or wash, and repack this equipment. On most large parties there will be some small losses of equipment due to breakage, burns, and theft by guests. Smart caterers prefer to absorb these costs in their markups, rather than pass them on to clients directly, which can result in disputes. Novice caterers have been known to sacrifice all of their profits from a party due to equipment losses. Of course, major losses that are due to clients' negligence must be charged directly to clients after the event.

Owned Equipment. Off-premise caterers also own equipment which they provide to clients for their events. Some do not directly charge for it, while others charge just as if it was equipment rented from a rental dealer.

Pricing Accessory Services

Many off-premise caterers assist clients by arranging for accessory services such as music, entertainment, flowers, valet parking, security, photography, and wedding and special occasion cakes not made in-house. Some caterers include these services in a package plan, some price them separately, some ask clients to pay these people directly, and some charge markup on some or all of these services. They reason that as the professional who recommends these other services they share some of the responsibility for the results. Additionally, they spend time arranging for these services (and supervise them on-site), and they feel that their expertise in knowing who to recommend is worth something. Therefore, they add a markup when billing clients for these services.

How much markup is proper? This, like rental equipment, varies from caterer to caterer, but is invariably less than markups applied to food costs. Markups in the range of 10 to 25 percent are fairly common. Sometimes, in an extremely competitive situation, caterers may simply provide these services at cost in order to gain a pricing edge.

Where the clients deal directly with the accessory service providers, is it ethical for off-premise caterers to receive commissions from those suppliers they recommend? This is a touchy subject which will spark debates from coast-to-coast. The main point is that commissions received from accessory service suppliers must be reported as income.

Pricing Beverage Services

Off-premise caterers frequently provide beverage mixers, ice, and other bar services, and certainly must pass these costs on to clients. Again, the amount varies from one caterer to the next, with an average between $1 and $2 per guest. Also, in this example, we will estimate that the cost of mixers and ice is $100.

Precost Summary

To summarize the costs involved in this sample event we have estimated the following costs:

Food costs	$1,110
Labor costs	1,640
Equipment rental costs	1,800
Beverage mixers and ice	100
Total cost	$4,650

A BASIC PRICING METHOD

Pricing Food

With the estimated costs computed, the next step is to determine the various markups and food cost percentages. There are various formulas which will bring the same results. With the goal of a food cost in the range of somewhere between

20 and 50 percent, let's examine two ways to obtain this with our sample menu with a $1,110 food cost. The first way is to divide the food cost by the desired food cost percentage. For example:

FOOD COST	DIVIDE BY FOOD COST PERCENTAGE	SELL PRICE	MARGIN
$1,110	25%	4,440	3,330
$1,110	30%	3,700	2,590
$1,110	35%	3,171	2,061
$1,110	40%	2,775	1,665
$1,110	45%	2,467	1,357
$1,110	50%	2,220	1,110

By subtracting the actual food cost from the selling price, one can determine the amount of gross margin produced from the food sales. For example, in the 25 percent food cost example, the gross margin from the food sale is $3,330 ($4,440 less $1,100).

Another way to price food is to multiply the food cost by a markup factor:

❑ A markup factor of 5 will produce a 20% food cost.
❑ A markup factor of 4 will produce a 25% food cost.
❑ A markup factor of 3 will produce a 33 1/3% food cost.
❑ A markup factor of 2.5 will produce a 40% food cost.
❑ A markup factor of 2 will produce a 50% food cost.

For example:

FOOD COST	MARKUP FACTOR	SELL PRICE	MARGIN
$1,110	4	4,440	3,330
$1,110	3	3,330	2,220
$1,110	2.5	2,775	1,665
$1,110	2	2,220	1,110

Again, the gross margin is computed by simply subtracting the estimated food cost from the selling price.

Labor Price   Some off-premise caterers add the labor cost to the food cost, and then apply a markup factor. In our example, the combined food and labor cost, or prime cost, is $2,750 ($1,110 + $1,640).

FOOD AND LABOR COST	MARKUP FACTOR	SELL PRICE	GROSS MARGIN
$2,750	1.5	$4,125	$1,375
$2,750	2	$5,500	$2,750
$2,750	2.5	$6,875	$4,125

Please notice in this prior example that the markup factors produce greater margins since we are not only marking up food cost, but also labor cost.

While some caterers mark up the food and labor, others simply mark up the food and charge for the labor at cost, or slightly above cost.

Equipment Pricing   Off-premise caterers who own their equipment charge anywhere from the same price as the local rental equipment dealers down to nothing. Most, on the average, charge somewhere in between these two extremes. For example, on a small home party they may charge the full local retail price; but when bidding on a large event they may choose to charge little or nothing for the equipment, content with profits from the food and other areas.

Off-premise caterers report a similar pricing strategy with rental equipment from dealers. Some may charge their discounted price, plus a small allowance for losses, while others may apply liberal increases to the prices charged them by the dealers. As with our example, please note the financial impact of various pricing strategies:

EQUIPMENT LIST PRICE	DISCOUNTED PRICE	SELL PRICE	MARGIN
$2,000	$1,800	$1,800	$ 0
2,000	1,800	2,000	200
2,000	1,800	2,200	400
2,000	1,800	2,400	600
2,000	1,800	2,600	800
2,000	1,800	2,800	1000

Please note that in these examples, the margins are prior to any losses due to missing items or damaged merchandise.

DETERMINING THE MARKUP

So far, we have discussed the math involved in pricing but not the art of determining the amounts of markup. There are no easy answers to these equations. Most caterers learn pricing by trial and error within their markets. They quote a price too high, they do not earn the work; they quote too low, they earn the work, but lose money. As these caterers progress through the learning curve, if they are to survive, they learn the art of pricing for profit.

Market Factors   Several factors influence pricing within various catering markets:

❏ What are competitors' prices for similar events?
❏ What are previous prices charged to clients?
❏ How many guests are expected?
❏ How badly is the business needed?
❏ Is this a bidding or nonbidding situation?
❏ Who else is bidding on the events?

❑ What is the customer's perceived value of the party?
❑ Once quoted, do clients expect to negotiate the price?
❑ Once quoted, do clients expect a discount?

Some Common Pricing Techniques

Mark up More for Smaller Parties. For example, a markup factor of 2 for a chicken dinner that costs $5 each for 20 guests will only produce a margin of $100 ($5 × 20 × 2 = $200 less $100 cost). Is this sufficient profit? It certainly is not for a full-service caterer who is cooking at the party site. In this instance, a larger markup factor would be appropriate.

Mark up More for Lower-Food-Cost Parties. In the above example, the food cost for chicken is low compared with a lobster dinner, where the food cost may be $15. A markup of 2 on the chicken produces a $5 margin, while a markup of 2 on the lobster produces a $15 margin ($15 × 2 less $15 = $15).

Number of Expected Guests. With more guests, smaller markup factors may be sufficient. The $5 food margin on the chicken dinner for a group of 1,000 will produce a food margin of $5,000. Many caterers charge less per person for larger events.

Number of Previous or Expected Bookings for Particular Day or Night. Special holidays and other major events such as New Year's Eve, the last Saturday before Christmas, or the Super Bowl are generally busy days for off-premise caterers. There is a large demand for work. Astute caterers realize that they can charge more on these days than during slow periods, such as a Tuesday night in July in Arizona. Also, since these days and nights are generally busy, when pricing, off-premise caterers should remember that there may be additional, unexpected expenses, such as renting extra vehicles and paying premium pay to staff on New Year's Eve.

Probability of Need to Negotiate or Discount. In some instances, it is better to price parties higher, anticipating the later need to reduce the price or offer other concessions. It is not advisable to reduce the price without deleting something from the party, or receiving a concession from the client. For example, a $2 per-person price reduction will result in the elimination of some food, or perhaps, the client agrees to pay for the complete party one month in advance.

Some caterers offer discounts for parties held during slow seasons and for those held during certain times of the day. Others offer discounts for those clients who sign contracts months or years in advance, or who agree to buy all parties from the caterer.

Inexpensive Parties Breed More Inexpensive Parties. When pricing parties, every off-premise caterer has learned not to give a low price to those clients who say there will be many people there who will buy in the future. There may be, but these people inevitably will expect the same low price. Beware!

Catering for Charities. Most charities are able to negotiate very low prices because there is always a novice caterer who is willing to work for nothing in order to obtain exposure. For newcomers to this field, this may be a great launching pad. Most experienced caterers have learned that they must charge a realistic price which will result in not only a profit, but also a sufficient budget to produce excellent food and provide excellent service. Charitable events are not ones to reduce quality or quantity, regardless of the input received from the event planners. Their main goal is to earn as much as possible which, unfortunately, does not work to many caterers' advantage.

Value of Time. Off-premise caterers reach a point in their careers when they ask themselves "What is my time worth?" For example, is it worth it to sacrifice a long-awaited day off to earn a meager profit? For a regular client, it might be worth it. In other situations, perhaps by quoting a higher price, the result will be earning a sufficient profit to make it worthwhile.

Looking Beyond the Price. There are clients who are looking beyond the price to things such as elegance, the "look and image," and other tangible and intangible factors. Some clients take pride in saying that "so-and-so is the caterer." Some, rare as they may be, enjoy telling others how much they paid for an elegant party.

PRICING A PARTY

With the combined knowledge of precosting techniques and various pricing philosophies, off-premise caterers are now prepared to price parties. Using the preceding example, *one way* to price this party would be as follows (Please note that this is not policy, but only one example.):

$1200 food cost times factor of 2.5 =	$3,000
Labor at cost	1,640
Equipment	2,200
Beverage mixers, ice, etc. at $2 PP	200
Total price	$7,040

Total Costs		
Food	$1,200	
Labor	1,640	
Equipment	1,800	
Mixers, etc.	100	
Total cost	$4,740	
Total projected profit from the party		$2,300

SERVICE CHARGES, GRATUITIES, AND SALES TAXES

Each state has specific laws regarding gratuities, service charges, and sales taxes. It is incumbent upon caterers in every state to learn and comply with those laws. Penalties are severe for violations.

Service charges are basically specified percentages added to all or a portion of the price. Caterers use different techniques, depending on their circumstances. In the previous example, if there was a 15 percent service charge on all invoice items, this would be computed on the $7,040, or an additional $1,056. Some caterers prefer to charge for service on food and labor only. Service charges are subject to sales taxes, since they are not voluntary.

Gratuities, on the other hand, are voluntary, and are paid purely at the discretion of clients. They are generally not subject to sales tax.

Reports from around the nation indicate that 50 percent of off-premise caterers do not impose a service charge, 25 percent do, and 25 percent sometimes do, depending on the situation. When considering whether to impose a service charge, off-premise caterers should review competitors' practices, and develop an acceptable strategy. One strategy, in a market where all caterers impose a service charge, may be *not* to impose one.

Many states provide sales tax exemptions to charitable organizations, churches, synagogues, and not-for-profit organizations. Off-premise caterers must obtain sales tax exemption certificates from these organizations with their tax-exempt number in order to avoid penalties. Some states have laws regarding charging sales tax on labor. One California floral designer was led to believe that labor at the party site was not taxable, and for eighteen months did not charge sales tax on this labor. He was audited, at which time he was told that it was in fact taxable, and that he owed the state $58,000 in back taxes.

DELIVERY AND OVERTIME CHARGES

Some off-premise caterers charge clients to cover the costs of delivering the food to the party. This is generally the case where there is no on-site preparation, and the caterer is simply preparing the food and delivering it to the party. Some clients pay the delivery charge without hesitation, while others refuse to buy from those caterers who charge for delivery. To avoid the latter situation, many off-premise caterers simply add the cost of delivery into the food cost, not showing it as a separate charge.

What happens when a party continues beyond the specified stop time? How should caterers charge for this type of overtime? Normally, overtime charges are specified in the catering contract, so that there are no surprises if the party goes longer than planned. These charges are usually based on the hourly rate paid to staff, the number of staff, extra food and beverages served, and some form of markup to these costs. The majority of overtime costs are usually for labor, since by the end of the event most guests have eaten and drunk their fill. In those circumstances where off-premise caterers are providing accessory services such as music and valet parking, overtime fees must be added to the final bill.

For example, let us assume that a party goes one hour overtime and there are three staff who are working the event who will stay. They are each paid $12 per hour including payroll benefits. No extra food or beverages are expected to be consumed. Three staff at $12 per hour equals $36 in extra payroll expenses. The caterer may wish to mark up the labor 2 or 3 times, to $72 or $108 to the client, thus generating an additional profit of $36 or $72.

Please note that if the overtime is caused by the caterers not fulfilling their responsibilities on schedule, it is considered unreasonable to charge clients.

OTHER PRICING METHODS

Off-premise caterers do not use one universal pricing method. Caterers have their own unique methods for pricing that fit their style and needs. However, all successful caterers have one thing in common. They charge prices that not only produce sufficient profits but generate repeat business. What are some other pricing techniques?

Budget Pricing Method

With this method the client gives the caterer an overall budget for the event. It may be just for food, staff, and equipment, or it may also include accessory services such as music and decor. For example, a client tells a caterer that the budget for a forthcoming event is $5,000 for 100 guests. This budget is for food, staff, and equipment only. Astute caterers first determine their desired profit for the event, and then budget for the expenses as follows. In this instance, let's assume that the off-premise caterer wishes to earn a profit of $1,500 from this event. When deducted from the total budget of $5,000 this leaves $3,500 for all expenses, which include food cost, labor, and equipment. At this point, the caterer simply computes the menu, staff, and equipment needs at cost, which should total $3,500. Please note that these are computed at cost, not at retail, since profit was budgeted first.

Cost-Plus Method

From time to time off-premise caterers may be requested to cater a special event where the client wishes to provide some or all of the food. An example is the grand opening of a supermarket, where the supermarket provides the food, but requires the off-premise caterer's expertise in executing the event. In this circumstance, the off-premise caterer may wish to charge a flat fee for time, expertise, and profit. This amount should be at least what the caterer would normally earn on an event of similar magnitude. Above the flat fee, the caterer would simply charge the client the cost of labor, equipment, and miscellaneous food expenses, and other specific costs for the event.

Range-Pricing Method

This method is used when off-premise caterers are quoting prices for an event in the distant future, where costs may be uncertain. For example, when quoting a price for a Florida stone crab dinner or Maine lobster dinner two years in advance, there is no sure way of knowing the cost of these fresh seafood items two years out. In these instances, caterers may wish to simply quote a price range, which would include both best-case and worse-case scenarios.

Package Price

This price includes all components necessary to produce an event including food, beverage setups, staffing, equipment, music, and flowers. Package prices should be designed for a minimum number of guests, since the price is per person.

If there are fewer people than the minimum, there will be insufficient revenue to cover costs and produce profits.

An example of a package price for 100 guests follows:

100 Dinners at $15 pp	$1,500
100 Beverage mixers, ice at $2 pp	200
Staffing	750
Equipment	1,000
Band	750
Flowers	300
Total before tax and other charges	$4,500

Here, the caterer may wish to price this package at $44.95 per person, for a minimum of 100 guests.

SUMMARY

In this chapter we have discussed a number of ways to cost and price parties. Successful and profitable off-premise caterers have developed pricing strategies that work within their markets. They are continually cognizant of changes within their marketplaces that affect their price strategies, and their pricing, in turn, reflects these changes.

NOTES

1. *Restaurant Hospitality*, © 1994 Penton Publishing January 1994, p. 46.

Chapter 11

Purchasing, Receiving, and Storing Foods

This chapter addresses techniques for purchasing, receiving and storing foods. Poor execution in these areas can mean the difference between financial success or failure. Thousands of dollars a year can easily be lost by purchasing mistakes, as well as failure to properly receive and store merchandise. This chapter will provide readers with the knowledge necessary for competence in these areas.

PURCHASING FOR OFF-PREMISE CATERERS

Introduction to Purchasing

Those who purchase foods for off-premise catered events need knowledge in computing yields. For example, how many Caesar salads can be produced from one case of romaine lettuce? How many heads of romaine are there in a case of romaine? Without knowledge in this area, how can they purchase a sufficient quantity of romaine for a dinner party of 50 guests who will be served Caesar salad as a first course?

Product specifications, such as prime and choice beef, define the various qualities and forms of products. For example, when preparing shrimp salad, shrimp pieces or broken shrimp will be less expensive than whole shrimp. For beef stew, stewing beef is more practical and less expensive than top sirloin butt.

The timing of purchases is another important element of the purchasing function. Purchasers should know the shelflives of products and understand how these products will be used by the culinary staff. A whole frozen turkey received on the day of the party will create turmoil in the kitchen. More lead time is needed so that the turkey may be thawed properly and safely prior to cooking. Fresh strawberries to be used with a saboyan sauce should not be received until the day of the party.

Off-premise caterers should realize that the goals of purchasing should be to order the proper product, of the correct quality and quantity, at an excellent price, to be delivered at the right time from a reputable supplier.

Ethics in Purchasing

Many off-premise caterers purchase food and other products themselves, since they realize the importance of savings in this area. Others concentrate on other areas of their businesses, and delegate this function to a staff member. In the latter case, the caterer should insist upon ethical purchasing practices such as the following:

❏ Prohibit the purchaser from accepting personal gifts of more than a specific dollar value. For example, during the holidays, a purchaser may accept a gift valued at no more than $50 from a supplier.

❏ Purchasers should show no one supplier favoritism and buy from the best qualified suppliers.

❏ Purchasers should not make personal purchases from suppliers for themselves or other catering company employees.

❏ In a bidding situation, the order should be awarded to the lowest bidder who meets the company specifications for the product.

Determining Purchasing Needs

Purchasing for off-premise catered events differs from purchasing for restaurants since caterers know the number of guests that are expected and their menu. Purchasing needs are determined by reviewing the catering menus for a certain period of time. Many off-premise caterers work on a week-to-week basis for major meat, poultry, seafood, and dry store items, and daily for breads, produce, fresh fish, and other perishables. For example, each Monday morning, purchasing agents will review the needs for the forthcoming week, starting with the following Wednesday, through the weekend and parties on Monday and Tuesday of the following week. All major needs for various parties are consolidated, and bids are received for these items. Produce and other perishable items should be ordered and received as closely as possible to the time of use.

One mistake made by many purchasers is failure to check the amount of products on hand in inventory before ordering. Frequently, purchasers order items that are not truly needed. It only takes a few minutes to check current inventories. Another mistake is ordering in too large of a quantity. If caterers need only six heads of romaine, there is no need to order a case of 24 heads. In these and other cases, off-premise caterers are frequently better off going to a local supermarket or wholesale club and picking up these products, rather than ordering from suppliers who deliver only in larger-than-needed quantities. Why should a caterer who needs only three dozen eggs for a two-week period order a 30-dozen case from a wholesaler? It is normally better to pay a few cents a dozen more at a supermarket, than pay a bit less per dozen but have 27 dozen extra eggs taking up refrigeration space and tying up money.

Astute off-premise caterers maintain very low inventory levels. They buy only products that they need. They realize that unneeded foods in inventory represent money that could be utilized elsewhere. They also realize that the more foods that are on hand, the more likely it is for theft to occur. It is much easier to control and inventory smaller supplies of foods.

Some large-volume caterers buy certain foods in bulk, but only when savings are significant, when they have available cash to pay for these items, and when they have sufficient secure storage for these products. For example, some large-volume caterers buy items such as mayonnaise, tuna, and frozen shrimp in large quantities, when they are able to save 20 percent or more on the regular price and use it within a three-month period.

Determining Purchasing specifications must be developed in writing for each menu item.
Purchasing Although time-consuming, the results will save off-premise caterers thousands of
Specifications dollars annually. Purchase specifications for products should include:

The intended use of the product

A general and detailed description of the product to be purchased

Other information such as origin, grade, size, portion size, brand name, container
size, and packaging

The key point to remember when developing purchasing specifications is
to buy sufficient quality to meet the menu needs, no more, or less. For example,
caterers who specialize in prime beef must buy USDA Prime beef, while caterers who specialize in deli-platters will not need to order prime beef. Caterers
who specialize in pasta will produce their own rather than buy prepared pasta
products.

Selecting Suppliers When selecting suppliers, off-premise caterers generally have a large number
from which to choose. In order to select the proper suppliers, caterers should
consider factors such as honesty, fairness, product knowledge, proper items
in stock, and fair pricing. Off-premise caterers should choose suppliers who
are known to sell clean, fresh, uncontaminated food products. Suppliers to
the catering professional must be "user-friendly," providing extra service
when unusual situations arise. For example, there are instances when clients
add extra guests at the last minute, and caterers need suppliers who are able
to respond to these needs quickly. Delivery reliability is crucial to off-
premise caterers who are always working with deadlines. Suppliers must be
able to deliver products at times convenient to caterers. A meat delivery
promised and expected at 9 A.M. will do no good at 2 P.M. Excuses regarding
traffic and mechanical problems cannot normally be tolerated. Timing is
everything!

Many successful off-premise caterers think of their suppliers as partners. As
partners, their relationships should be up-front and aboveboard. Each should
share and respect the policies of the other. When requesting quotations, off-
premise caterers should give reasonable purchase estimates. For example, an off-
premise caterer who expects to buy $20,000 per year in dry stores should give
this estimate to the supplier, rather than overestimate to receive a potentially
lower price. Suppliers and their drivers should be treated with respect and courtesy. They are partners in off-premise caterers' success.

How many suppliers are enough? The answer to this question will vary from
one caterer to the next. Some caterers deal with only a few suppliers, while most
buy from hundreds of sources every year, which gives them greater flexibility
and control over pricing and quality. Recently, a few major food service suppliers who originally sold dry goods, supplies and frozen foods have added meat,
fish, and fresh produce to their product lists, offering essentially one-stop shopping for off-premise caterers and other foodservice companies.

For meats, produce, fish, seafood, and dry goods it is advisable to select two or three suppliers that meet off-premise caterers' product standards, and request bids for the majority of purchases. Food product requirements for last minute items, or for those in very small quantities are normally picked up at a nearby supermarket or wholesale club.

Purchasing Meat   Off-premise caterers may purchase meat from three basic sources:

❑ Local retail markets are good for emergency purchases, but are very expensive.
❑ Local meat cutters buy meat by the case, break up the case lot, and butcher meat to satisfy caterers' requirements. They are responsive to caterers' needs, are less expensive than local retail markets, but more expensive than meat distributors.
❑ Meat distributors buy meat directly from the meat packer, and then sell it to off-premise caterers by the case. They do not break up case lots.

Every off-premise caterer should obtain a copy of the *Meat Buyer's Guide to Standardized Meat Cuts,* published by the National Association of Meat Purveyors, 1920 Association Drive, Suite 400, Reston, Virginia 22091-1547. By using this pictorial guide, caterers in all geographical areas of the United States are able to readily identify all cuts of beef, lamb, pork, and veal.

Purchasing Produce   Produce is available from a variety of produce distributors, who buy directly from the farming companies, produce packers, and local produce markets. These distributors deliver most orders that meet minimum standards and offer competitive prices. Most cities have at least one wholesale produce market where buyers may go and select fresh produce from a variety of wholesalers who display their products for viewing. Those who buy in this fashion can easily save 30 percent or more; however these caterers need time to shop and a vehicle in which to transport the produce. Also, off-premise caterers may buy from wagon-jobbers, who buy directly from the produce market based upon the orders that they have received from their clients, and then deliver these orders to their catering and other clients.

There are two publications that offer excellent information regarding specifications, shelflife, receiving, handling, and storing of produce:

Produce 101, Produce Marketing Association, P.O. Box 6036, Newark, Delaware 19714

Fresh Produce Foodservice Directory, The Packer, P.O. Box 293, Shawnee Mission, Kansas 66201

Purchasing Fish and Seafood   Frozen fish and seafood are available from the major national wholesalers, while fresh fish and seafood are sold by local firms who specialize almost exclusively in these products. Caterers located in cities bordering major oceans, gulfs, and rivers may buy fresh fish from local fishermen who sell their daily catches at the wharfs.

It is always more desirable to use fresh, rather than frozen fish when budgets permit. Prices for fresh fish vary, depending on the season, weather conditions, and demand. Some of the more popular fresh fish include salmon, swordfish, halibut, grouper, dolphin (the fish, not the mammal), haddock, snapper, trout (both freshwater and saltwater), bass (both freshwater and saltwater), tuna and scrod (young cod). The popularity of fish varies from region to region based on local preferences and availability.

Most off-premise caterers purchase some of their seafood in a frozen state, such as scallops, lobster tails, and shrimp. Whole Maine lobsters and stone crab claws are always purchased fresh. Sea scallops are sold by size, such as 20–30 count, which means there are 20 to 30 scallops on the average per pound. Lobster tails are sold by size such as 4- to 6-ounce tails and 6- to 8-ounce tails.

For most off-premise caterers, shrimp is the most frequently used seafood. Like scallops, shrimp are sold by size, called counts. For example, "16–20 count" means that there are 16 to 20 shrimp per pound. The range goes from "U-10," under 10 per pound, the largest shrimp, to 300–500, the smallest. The most common product form is green headless shrimp, which is raw, head off, and shell on. Off-premise caterers with limited facilities should investigate cooked shrimp for use as cold shrimp cocktails and hors d'oeuvres. There are some excellent products on the market that taste nearly as good as fresh cooked, cost no more, save labor, and are always consistent. (Every off-premise caterer has at one time or another overcooked shrimp). These shrimp are always cooked to perfection.

Purchase Orders Purchase orders are written order forms used by off-premise caterers to document and verify orders placed for food and supplies. They are most highly recommended as a means for control for large volume caterers. Smaller firms may wish to also use purchase orders to keep track of their orders and receipts. Most firms at least have an in-house form listing their purchasing needs by categories which can be used as an order form, but these forms do not replace purchase orders as a form of control.

How many copies of each purchase order are sufficient? This depends on the operational needs, but some successful food operators report that a four-part form works well. Copy distribution works as follows:

Original copy	Mailed or faxed to supplier
Second copy	Sent to accounting for control
Third copy	Sent to receiving department and kept until foods arrive; upon receipt of foods this copy is signed and forwarded to accounting with invoice
Fourth copy	Kept in purchasing

Purchase orders should be prenumbered in advance for control over the number of purchase orders issued by the company and to prevent employees from issuing unauthorized purchase orders, and should include the following information:

❑ Date of the placement of the order
❑ Payment terms
❑ Supplier's name, address, and fax number
❑ Off-premise caterer's name, address, and address for delivery
❑ Description, quantity, and quoted unit cost of each item ordered
❑ Blank column for the person receiving the merchandise to document the quantity of each item received
❑ All quoted prices extended and totaled on the purchase order after the merchandise has been received, and compared with the invoice; discrepancies reconciled with the supplier immediately
❑ Signature of the purchaser and that of the person receiving the merchandise

Exhibit 11-1 is a sample purchase order form.

EXHIBIT 11-1
SAMPLE PURCHASE ORDER FORM   PURCHASE ORDER NUMBER 0001

ORDERED BY: ORDERED FROM:
ABC OFF-PREMISE CATERING FIRM   BEST SUPPLIER
MAIN STREET   MAIN STREET
ANYWHERE, USA   ANYWHERE, USA
FAX NUMBER   FAX NUMBER

ORDER DATE _____ DELIVERY DATE _____ PAYMENT TERMS _____

QUANTITY ORDERED	DESCRIPTION	QUANTITY RECEIVED	UNIT COST	TOTAL COST

GRAND TOTAL

SIGNATURE OF AUTHORIZED PURCHASER _____

RECEIVED AS NOTED ABOVE _____
                                    (RECEIVING AGENT)

Purchase order forms are available from a variety of sources such as stationery stores. Another excellent source for information regarding purchase orders and other purchasing functions is *Purchasing, Receiving and Storage*, by Jack Ninemeier, CBI Publishing, 286 Congress Street, Boston, Massachusetts 02210, 1983.

Tips For Effective Purchasing

Generally speaking, the purchaser wants to pay as little as possible, the seller wants to receive as much as possible, and the agreed-upon price is somewhere between these two extremes. Market prices for food items are based upon what the market will bear, according to the supply and the demand for products. For example, as the Christmas holiday season approaches the demand for meats increases, while supplies remain constant or decrease, resulting in higher meat prices.

The following practices will result in lower food purchasing costs:

Edible Portion Cost. Off-premise caterers save thousands of dollars per year through effective purchasing techniques. They realize, for example, that the lowest price is not always the least expensive. Instead, they think in terms of cost per serving, or edible portion cost. For example, when purchasing meats, the least expensive cuts also contain more fat and bones and must be trimmed, which involves a labor expense to perform these butchering chores. Other inexpensive cuts may be too tough to eat. Caterers often are wiser to buy cuts that are trimmed of fat and bone and ready to cook, thus saving labor expenses, resulting in a lower edible portion cost.

The Make-or-Buy Decision. Off-premise caterers should carefully analyze their menus and determine which items to make in-house, and which items to buy from suppliers. Items such as pasta, breads, desserts, mayonnaise, certain sauces and other frequently used items fall into the latter category. For example, the cost of ingredients to make bread and pasta is a fraction of the price paid for prepared products; however, other factors enter into the make-or-buy decision. These factors must be weighed carefully each time before making a decision:

- ❑ Is the necessary equipment available to make the products?
- ❑ If equipment is not available, what is the cost to purchase it?
- ❑ Is there skilled labor available? What is the cost?
- ❑ What are the quality considerations? Will a product made in-house be of superior quality to that which can be purchased?
- ❑ Is this product so unique that the only alternative is to prepare it in-house since no supplier handles it?
- ❑ How does producing products in-house relate to the overall operation? What impact will it have on other functions?

Competitive Bidding. It is imperative to obtain competitive bids from at least three suppliers for most purchases, and buy from the lowest bidder who meets caterers' specifications for the product. Exhibit 11-2 is a sample competitive bidding form for produce. Many caterers become comfortable dealing with certain suppliers, and they soon stop obtaining bids. Once preferred suppliers realize that there is no bidding for business, they are free to increase their prices. Competitive bids will help keep food costs under control.

Can You Do Better? It never hurts in a purchasing situation to ask certain suppliers if they can do better. This practice gives suppliers an opportunity to offer an extra incentive, or give a discount. The worst case is that suppliers will say "no." However, it is surprising how frequently they will negotiate a better deal.

Less Service for a Lower Price. Certain suppliers will offer lower prices as long as deliveries are limited to certain days. Some paper goods suppliers offer lower prices, but only deliver once or twice per month. Frequently, supermarkets and wholesale clubs offer better prices than those suppliers who deliver. One example is soft drinks, which are invariably less expensive from supermarkets and clubs. Off-premise caterers must determine if the savings are worth the time spent shopping for and transporting these lower-price items.

Less Expensive with No Adverse Effect on Quality. Basically, purchasers should buy the least expensive product that will not reduce the food's quality. For example, broken shrimp pieces are less expensive than whole shrimp, and can be used in dishes such as shrimp salad. Random-packed boneless chicken breasts (which are not of uniform weight) can be used for many chicken dishes rather than those of uniform size, which are significantly more expensive. Ungraded tomatoes can be used for marinara sauce, rather than paying extra for those that are graded.

Seasonality. Caterers need knowledge as to the seasonality of particular items. For example, there are times during the year when it is less expensive to use limes than lemons. In the late fall fresh strawberries are expensive, and not good quality.

Pay for Purchases with Cash. Certain suppliers offer discounts for cash purchases.

Price Trend Speculation. Some off-premise caterers who use large quantities of certain items have experienced success by speculating on prices. For example, a caterer who expects to use 2,000 pounds of shrimp in the next three months may wish to buy all 2,000 pounds now if the price is expected to increase.

Purchase in Larger Units. Larger units of purchase are usually less expensive than smaller units. Flour sold in 100-pound bags is less expensive per pound than that in 10-pound bags. Care must be exercised to not overbuy, resulting in spoilage and high inventory levels.

Special Promotions. Frequently, suppliers offer special promotions which may result in significant savings.

EXHIBIT 11-2
QUOTE SHEET

PREPARED BY _____

DATE _____

PRICE QUOTES

ITEM & GRADE	UNIT OF PURCHASE	COMPANY A	COMPANY B	COMPANY C
APPLES, EXTRA FANCY, 88 COUNT	DOZEN/CASE			
AVOCADOS, HASS 48 COUNT	DOZEN/CASE			
BANANAS (40# PER CASE)	POUND/CASE			
BROCCOLI, CALIFORNIA 14 COUNT	POUND/CASE			
CABBAGE, RED, LARGE HEADS	POUND/50# BAG			
CABBAGE, WHITE, LARGE HEADS	POUND/50# BAG			
CARROTS, CALIFORNIA JUMBO	POUND/50#BAG			
CAULIFLOWER, CALIFORNIA, 12 PER CASE	POUND/CASE			
CELERY, CALIFORNIA 24 COUNT	STALK/CASE			
CUCUMBERS, SUPER SELECT	POUND/BUSHEL			
EGGPLANT, FANCY	POUND/BUSHEL			
GARLIC, JUMBO (30# PER CASE)	POUND/CASE			
GRAPEFRUIT, PINK, FLORIDA 18 COUNT	DOZEN/CASE			
GRAPES, RED, CALIFORNIA, EXFANCY	POUND/CASE			
GRAPES, WHITE, CALIFORNIA EXFANCY	POUND/CASE			
LETTUCE, LEAF, DOLE CALIFORNIA, FANCY	HEAD/CASE			
LETTUCE, ICEBERG, DOLE CALIFORNIA, FANCY	HEAD/CASE			
LETTUCE, ROMAINE, DOLE CALIFORNIA, FANCY	HEAD/CASE			
LEEKS, CALIFORNIA	BUNCH/CASE (24 BUNCHES/CASE)			
LEMONS, SUNKIST, US#1, 165/CASE	DOZEN/CASE			
LIMES, US#1, 150-160/CASE	DOZEN/CASE			
MELONS, CANTALOUPE, FANCY, 15/CASE	EACH/CASE			
MELONS, HONEYDEW, FANCY, 15/CASE	EACH/CASE			
MUSHROOMS, US#1, WASHED, 10# BASKET	POUND/BASKET			
ONIONS, JUMBO, SPANISH	POUND/50# BAG			
ORANGES, CALIFORNIA, 56/CASE	DOZEN/CASE			
PARSLEY, CALIFORNIA	BUNCH/DOZEN			
PEARS, ANJOU	POUND			
PEPPERS, GREEN BELL	POUND/CASE			
PEPPERS, RED	POUND/CASE			
PINEAPPLES, DOLE, 7/CASE	EACH/CASE			
POTATOES, IDAHO, 90/CASE	POUND/CASE			
POTATOES, BOILING	POUND/50# BAG			
RADISHES, POLY BAG	BAG/DOZEN			

EXHIBIT 11-2 (*continued*)

ITEM GRADE	UNIT OF PURCHASE	PRICE QUOTES COMPANY A	COMPANY B	COMPANY C
SCALLIONS, BUNCH	BUNCH/DOZEN			
SHALLOTS	POUND/5# BAG			
SPINACH, CALIFORNIA FLAT LEAF	POUND/10# CASE			
TOMATOES, VINE RIPENED, 5 X 6	POUND/18# BOX			
WATERCRESS	BUNCH/DOZEN			
WATERMELON, EXTRA LARGE, JUBILEE	EACH			

Go to the Market. Significant savings are available to those who shop at wholesale clubs and local volume-purchase markets. Caterers who do this need time and transportation, but many report purchase savings of 50 percent or more.

RECEIVING INCOMING MERCHANDISE

The cardinal rule in this section is that the person who orders merchandise should not be the one to receive it, unless he or she is the sole owner of the catering company. There are too many opportunities for collusion between the purchaser and the supplier if the purchaser is also the receiver. For example, a purchaser may indicate that certain goods were received when they were not, and then receive a kickback or other reward from the supplier. It is essential to have at least two people involved in these all-important functions.

Many off-premise caterers make the mistake of not employing a qualified receiving employee. This person may have other duties (not purchasing) but should be thoroughly trained in product knowledge. This knowledge can be gained through training by the chef, the off-premise caterer, the purchaser, and others who possess high quality standards. When in doubt about the quality of a product, they should consult with the chef, owner, or manager before signing for receipt of the merchandise. It is always easier to reconcile problems with the supplier's driver present. The driver can return with the inferior product, rather than leave it at the commissary where it must be stored, or could even be used in error.

Those who receive foods, supplies, and rental equipment should be extremely particular, checking and inspecting for quality and quantity. Successful caterers do not accept products that do not meet their standards. For example, when receiving rental equipment they check all items for quantity, and they inspect glassware and china for cleanliness, chips, and cracks, flatware for corrosion or tarnish, chairs for cleanliness and stability (any cracked wooden chair legs; missing screws, nuts, and bolts?), linens for snags and tears, and dance floors and stages for missing pieces, rough edges, and other unsafe conditions. They can never be too particular.

Deliveries should be scheduled during slow periods of business so that food products can be carefully examined, weighed, and quickly moved to their proper storage areas.

Foods received in refrigerated shipments should be checked for temperature. Chilled products should be at least 45°F, and frozen products below 0°F. Frozen seafood should be checked for excessive "glazing," (the ice on the exterior of products such as shrimp and lobster). Excessively glazed products should be returned since off-premise caterers cannot stay in business paying premium prices for frozen water.

When receiving produce they inspect for ripeness, color, and cleanliness, and bruises, spoilage, and other adverse factors. Counts of produce items such as lemons and limes are very important, and caterers should frequently count to ensure proper sizing. Items that do not meet or exceed quality standards are returned, and these caterers insist that their supplier deliver the proper quality in time for the event. Of course, the best indication of produce quality is taste.

Off-premise caterers always must first weigh in all meat, fish, seafood, poultry, and other products sold by weight. Oftentimes, short-weights can result in direct losses on the catered event, or perhaps running out of food. All packing ice should be removed before weighing poultry and fish, which are frequently packed with ice. Short-weights should be corrected by either a credit, or delivery of additional product. After weighing, meats should be inspected to insure that they comply with specifications as documented in the *Meat Buyers' Guide*.

All meats should be federally inspected and show that USDA stamp, or verification can be confirmed in writing from the supplier. Meats that arrive in dirty, torn, damaged, or broken wrapping and boxes may be contaminated and should not be accepted. Any that smell sour or rancid should be rejected. Meat texture should be firm and elastic. Any that feels slimy, sticky, or dry should be rejected.

Fresh poultry should be below 45°F, and should be packed in crushed ice. Poultry that is purple or greenish in color should not be accepted, nor should that which smells bad, has darkened wing tips or soft, flabby, sticky flesh.

Once fresh fish is weighed, it should be inspected for freshness, appearance, damaged flesh, and other signs. Fresh fish should always be packed in crushed ice, and be between 32 and 45°F. Signs of freshness include clear eyes, tight scales, bright red gills, firm elastic flesh, fresh odor, and bright skin.

Fresh and frozen seafood should be checked for quality, as well as proper sizing. Often, the labeled size is not the size in the container. For example, 5-pound boxes of raw frozen headless shrimp that are graded 16–20 count should contain between 80 and 100 shrimp per box, with an average of 90 per box. This number is obtained by multiplying 5 pounds (in the box) times the minimum, average, and maximum counts of shrimp per pound (16, 18, and 20 respectively). These counts are important since menu costs and selling prices for shrimp are determined by these counts. If there are too few shrimp in the box, this could mean the shrimp are larger than they should be, or when frozen, too much water was frozen along with the shrimp. In this instance, the caterer's actual cost per shrimp will be more than specified. If the shrimp are too small, the costs will be lower per shrimp, but the client will not receive the size of shrimp promised by the caterer.

The standard pack for green headless shrimp is a 5-pound net-weight block. With ice and packaging the gross weight generally is 6 to 7 pounds. Two-kilo blocks are also sold, and off-premise caterers should beware of paying for 5 pounds when they are only receiving 2 kilos (4.4 pounds). Cooked (IQF) shrimp are packed in plastic bags weighing from 1 to 30 pounds, and they should be checked for weight and proper sizing upon receipt.

Milk and dairy products should be checked for temperature (40°F), expiration dates, smell, and appearance. Cheese should be rejected if it is discolored, excessively moldy, or dried out. Cheese rinds should be undamaged.

Eggs should be checked for cracks and excessive dirt. Eggs' temperature (40°F) may be checked by breaking one and measuring the temperature of the yolk. Acceptable eggs will have firm yolks, no noticeable odor, and the white will cling to the yolk.

Frozen foods should be checked for signs of thawing and refreezing such as large ice crystals, ice at the bottom of the carton, and deformed containers. All frozen foods should be received at less than 0°F.

Canned foods should be checked for leakage, broken seals, dents along seams, rust, and missing labels, not only upon receipt but before using. Dry foods such as sugar, cereal, flour, and dried beans should be completely dry when received, and they should have no broken seals in their packaging.

One common discrepancy occurs when there is a difference between the invoiced amount and the amount received. For example, the invoice reports 70 pounds of choice beef tenderloin, but upon weighing there is only 68 pounds. This must be noted on the invoice, initialed by the receiving agent and the driver, and immediately reported to the supplier for proper credit. The receiver must be absolutely sure to note all discrepancies on all invoices so that the bookkeeper can pay the proper amount. Carelessness in this area is very costly and cannot be tolerated. (If two pounds of tenderloin at $6 per pound is $12, over $600 per year would be saved if this error were rectified once per week.)

Receiving personnel should be required to submit all invoices daily to the bookkeeping office. Discrepancies can be resolved more easily shortly after they occur. Trying to reconstruct what occurred on December 1, on January 10 of the following year, is virtually impossible.

STORAGE PROCEDURES

The following storage guidelines for food service operators are recommended by the National Assessment Institute. Off-premise caterers should comply with all of these guidelines in order to meet normal sanitation and food handling standards.

Refrigerated Foods "Refrigerator temperatures should be kept below 45°F. Place thermometers in several areas of the refrigerator where they can be easily read and checked often. Check the internal temperatures of refrigerated foods on a regular basis, to make sure the foods are kept at 45°F or less.

Always refrigerate fresh meat, poultry, and fish.

Cover stored foods to prevent contamination from other products or direct contact with refrigerator shelves.

Fresh fish should be stored in crushed ice and kept drained.

If possible, provide separate units for different types of foods. If different foods must be stored in the same unit, store meats, fish, and dairy foods in the coldest part.

To prevent cross-contamination, be sure that prepared foods are stored above raw foods.

Do not store packaged food and wrapped sandwiches where they can get wet.

Do not overload the refrigerator. Too much food in the unit can raise the temperature of the entire unit.

Do not store refrigerated foods on the floor of a walk-in refrigerator.

Food packages should be stored in a way that cold air can circulate around all surfaces of the container.

Frozen Foods Keep temperature range for frozen foods between 0 and –10°F.

Do not thaw and refreeze frozen foods.

Do not thaw foods at room temperature.

Keep frozen foods in moisture-proof packaging.

Use the "First In, First Out" rule.

Store frozen foods to allow for air circulation between packages.

Do not freeze large quantities of unfrozen foods. This can raise the temperature of the entire unit and damage stored foods.

Defrost freezers regularly.

Be sure that foods do not thaw during the defrost cycle of self-defrosting freezers.

Dry Foods Apply the "First In, First Out" rule.

Keep foods in dry storage tightly covered and protected from contamination.

Remember that cereals and pasta deteriorate rapidly, as do canned foods containing products that are high in acid such as tomatoes.

Keep these areas well ventilated and well lighted.

Store foods at least six inches off the floor in a way that allows adequate air circulation.

Store items on ventilated shelves.

Install window coverings or frosted glass to reduce heat and exposure to light.

Cover all interior surfaces with easy to clean, corrosion-resistant materials.

Do not allow smoking, eating, or drinking in dry storage areas. Check with local health department for specific rules.

Do not store garbage in dry storage areas.

Seal walls and baseboards to help keep out pests. Keeping the area clean and well-maintained will discourage pests."[1]

PAYMENT POLICIES

Invoices for purchases should be paid when they are due. There is generally no advantage to off-premise caterers who pay their bills early, unless a discount is offered by the supplier. Excess cash can, of course, be invested to earn interest. Caterers who regularly pay their bills past due dates will be faced with higher prices and poorer quality products, as well as late-payment fees and interest. Additionally, they will waste valuable time answering supplier phone calls regarding payments. Slow payers lose their negotiating edge since suppliers offer their best prices to those who will pay on time. A few companies offer 1 or 2 percent discounts for those who pay early. Obviously, these are attractive terms, and should be utilized.

Astute off-premise caterers know that when making large purchases for equipment and large food orders, it is advantageous to first negotiate the price, and then negotiate the terms for payment. Most suppliers, eager to conclude the sale, will offer better terms once the price is agreed upon since they wish to ensure that the sale is made.

Most off-premise caterers will, at one time or another, be faced with a cash shortage, and will be unable to pay certain invoices when due. Rather than ignore the problem, and wait for suppliers to call, it is far better to meet with the suppliers, inform them of the problems, and develop suitable payment plans. This technique will help maintain good supplier relationships and eliminate the unpleasant phone calls from suppliers demanding payment.

Whenever possible, purchases should be paid for by check. Frequently, off-premise caterers need cash to pay for emergency purchases, or to pay suppliers who only accept cash. Petty cash funds are the answer to those cash payment situations. Whenever petty cash is handled by employees other than the owner, certain rules should apply:

❑ Only one person should have access to the petty cash fund, which is kept secure at all times. This individual signs a receipt for the money upon receipt.
❑ The fund should be established for an amount commensurate with the off-premise caterer's cash needs. Usually, this amount ranges from $100 to $400, and no more than $1,000.
❑ The fund must be available at all times for an audit or spot-check, and it must contain cash and receipts equal to the designated amount of the fund. Shortages are the responsibility of the person in charge of the fund.
❑ The fund is replenished by turning in the receipts to the bookkeeping office for a check to replace the total amount of the receipts.

The advantage of this system is that it pinpoints control and responsibility for the money. One person is responsible and accountable.

CONCLUSION

In this chapter, we discussed the major elements of purchasing, receiving, storage, and payment. It is imperative that off-premise caterers understand product specification, proper receiving procedures, and effective storage procedures. Huge sums of money can be lost in these areas. Also, it is important that off-premise caterers understand and practice the various techniques for saving money in purchasing as discussed in this chapter in the section *Tips for Effective Purchasing*.

NOTE

1. National Assessment Institute, *Handbook of Safe Food Service Management*, Regents/Prentice Hall, p. 60, 61, 62. Englewood Cliffs, N.J., 1994.

Chapter 12

Sanitation and Safety Procedures

Sanitation and safety procedures are of paramount importance to off-premise caterers. The safety of customers and staff must always come first. The examples and procedures in this chapter will assist off-premise caterers in this endeavor.

SANITATION

Introduction According to an article in *Restaurant Business*, "Christmas in Denver wasn't so merry last year [1992]: Sixty local citizens came down with Hepatitis A, apparently transmitted by an infected worker at a catering company."[1] In another example, the emergency room at a Southern California university was overrun with vomiting students who ate improperly handled macaroni salad served by a caterer at a welcoming picnic for freshman students.

Food poisoning is every caterer's nightmare. It can ruin a business overnight. A western fast-food chain has yet to recover from the outbreak of food poisoning caused by the *E. coli* bacteria in its hamburgers. Before identifying procedures for preventing food poisoning, let us examine the various types of foodborne illnesses and how they occur.

Food can be contaminated biologically, chemically, and physically. Biological contamination is caused by harmful bacteria, viruses, and parasites. Chemical contamination is caused when substances such as cleaning compounds, additives, or pesticides get into food. Physical contamination is caused when hair, broken objects, metal shavings, dirt, etc. get into food.[2]

Bacteria are the main culprits of foodborne illnesses, and they are found in many potentially hazardous foods such as milk, milk products, eggs, meat, poultry, fish, shellfish, and edible crustacea. They grow best at temperatures between 45 and 140°F.

Viruses are spread by food handlers who do not wash their hands after using the rest rooms, and who sneeze, cough, and touch their mouths with their hands. Foods that are not heated after handling are those that are most likely to transmit viral illness.

Parasites live within animals and fish. They are killed when food is heated to a high temperature. An example is trichinosis in pork.

Chemical contamination is caused by certain food additives such as sulfites, pesticides on incoming produce, pesticides used in-house, toxic metals such as copper, brass, cadmium, lead, and zinc (used in galvanized food containers) coming in contact with certain acidic goods, and toxic housekeeping products contacting foods. An example of the latter occurred in a New England restaurant, when a careless cleaning employee tossed detergent on raw lobster tails stored on shelves underneath the steamtable.

Causes of Foodborne Illnesses

Salmonella. Salmonella microorganisms may be found in poultry, red meats, shellfish, and eggs, as well as prepared foods such as chicken, egg, and ham salads. Salmonellosis is the foodborne illness caused by salmonella and symptoms start twelve to thirty-six hours after eating the contaminated foods. These symptoms include nausea, vomiting, cramps, and fever. Poor personal hygiene by food workers and working with dirty, unsanitized equipment and utensils may cause salmonellosis.

E. coli. These bacteria are found in the intestines of cattle, with contamination taking place in the slaughterhouse. Hamburgers, roast beef, and unpasteurized milk are the primary source of human infection. Symptoms, which occur twelve to twenty-four hours after ingestion, include severe diarrhea, cramping, and dehydration. Cooking beef to an internal temperature of 155°F kills this bacteria.

Shigella, Yersinia, Lisertia, Campylobacter jejuni, and Vibrio parahaemolyticus. These are other forms of bacteria which may cause food poisoning through poor personal hygiene and unsanitary food handling.

Staphylococcus aureus (staph). Staphylococcal food intoxication is a common foodborne illness, and is caused by toxins in such foods as ham products, cold meats, salads, custards, milk products, and cream-filled desserts.

Food contaminated with staphylococcal microorganisms are usually those which require a lot of handling during preparation. Potentially hazardous food that is left too long in the danger zone is at risk because *once the food has been contaminated by the toxin, you cannot depend on heat or cold to destroy the toxin.* The growth of this bacteria can be inhibited by keeping potentially hazardous foods below 45 degrees F or above 140 degrees F, not allowing food to remain at room temperature, moving foods through the danger zone quickly, and cooling foods in shallow pans.

A large percentage of healthy people has been shown to carry harmful staphylococci. Staphylococcus aureus is usually found on hands and in the nose and throat. Wounds, cuts, burns and infections in the nose or sinuses, and pimples are common places where staphylococcal microorganisms thrive. Sneezing, coughing, or touching the skin can spread the staphylococcus bacteria. Food managers should watch for these problems in their employees. Employees with severe cuts, wounds, or burns must make certain their injuries are properly bandaged, and an effective barrier, such as a disposable glove, worn when handling food. Employees with infected cuts, burns, or boils should be excluded from food handling and warewashing (dishes, utensils, pans, etc.) duties.

Symptoms of this illness appear quickly, usually within two to four hours, and include nausea, severe vomiting, diarrhea, cramps, chills, sweating, headache, and severe fatigue. The effects of staphylococcal food poisoning last for one or two days.[3]

Clostridium botulinum. This is the organism which causes botulism, which can be found in canned foods. Food from cans with severe dents, and/or bulging tops, and those where the end of the can springs back when pushed in should not be used, even if it appears normal. This bacteria is deadly, unless quick medical attention is given.

Clostridium perfringens. This is very common causing between 10 and 15 percent of all foodborne illnesses in the United States. Contaminated meat and poultry, sauces, and casseroles are main sources, and contamination results when these items are improperly cooked, cooled and reheated. Symptoms are generally mild forms of nausea, cramps, and diarrhea.

Scombroid and *Ciguatera*. Scombroid poisoning occurs in fish such as tuna, mackerel, bluefish, mahi mahi, and amberjack when they begin to spoil. It cannot be killed by cooking. Symptoms include redness of the face, sweating, nausea, headache, rashes, hives, and diarrhea.

> Ciguatera is the most common type of seafood poisoning. It is found in fish caught in tropical waters such as snapper and grouper. There is no reliable test for ciguatera, but a high technology company is on the verge of introducing such a test. Nausea, vomiting, diarrhea, and cramps are the early signs of this problem. Other common symptoms include aches, chills and dizzy spells. Severe cases can produce an irregular heartbeat, and sometimes ciguatera can be fatal.[4]

Employee Hygiene   Poor personal hygiene could be a cause of sanitation problems within the catering profession. Off-premise caterers should insist that the following procedures be posted in catering commissaries and at off-premise sites. These procedures should be included in training manuals and in training programs. These procedures are critical to help prevent the spread of foodborne illnesses. Employees who fail to consistently follow these procedures should be disciplined and/or terminated. They are not negotiable. It only takes one mishap to ruin a successful off-premise catering company by the outbreak of a food poisoning incident.

1. Workers should wash their hands before starting work and after touching their hair, sneezing, coughing, using a handkerchief, smoking, visiting the rest room, and handling soiled or used tableware. Handwashing should be done with hot water and soap for at least 20 seconds using a nail brush. The arms below the elbow should be washed, and single-service towels should be used for drying purposes.
2. Kitchen workers should use disposable plastic gloves when handling foods, but they are not a panacea, since if workers' hands are not clean, they can contaminate the gloves. Gloves should never be worn when working around open flames or other heat sources, because they can melt or catch fire.
3. Jewelry should not be worn when working in the back-of-the-house since items such as rings can catch dirt, and other types of jewelry may fall into

the foods. Front-of-the-house staff may wear minimal jewelry in keeping with the caterer's image.

4. Hats or hair nets should be worn in all food preparation areas. Artificial nails should be banned since they may dislodge and fall into the food.
5. Kitchen garments should be light in color so as to reveal stains.
6. Catering staff should never touch the eating end of flatware, or the rims of glasses, bowls, plates, and cups.
7. Smoking, gum chewing, and eating should not be permitted in serving areas or in kitchens.
8. Food left on plates or that has dropped on the floor should never be served.
9. All dropped flatware, napkins, and tableware items should be replaced with clean items.
10. Food should not be touched with hands. Use disposable plastic gloves.
11. The tops and bottoms of serving trays should be kept clean at all times.
12. Food handlers should be careful not to drip sweat onto equipment or into food products.
13. Staff must be trained regarding food allergies. Many guests are allergic to certain foods and ingredients. Staff should always be certain when guests ask if certain foods contain specific ingredients. If staff members are uncertain, or cannot find out, they should advise the customer that they are not sure.

Preparing and Serving Food

Bacteria growth in food occurs when food temperatures are in the danger zone of between 45 and 140°F. This range may vary slightly in some jurisdictions. All catering personnel must be trained to thoroughly understand that foods must be brought through this zone from cold to hot and hot to cold as quickly as possible. The longer foods are in the danger zone, the more bacteria will grow.

Foods should never be thawed at room temperature, but as follows:

Gradually under refrigeration
By cooking frozen food immediately after removing from the freezer
In a microwave oven
Under potable running water for no more than two hours (water temperature should be between 70 and 75°F); however, local rules may vary.

Foods should be cooked to the following minimum temperatures (check internal temperatures in more than one point):

Poultry and stuffed meats	165
Pork and pork products	150 (170 in Microwave)
Beef	130
Ground beef	155
Reheating foods	165

Food should be held for short periods of time at no less than 140°F. Holding equipment such as chafing dishes should never be used to heat foods. Foods should be 140°F or more when placed in holding equipment.

Off-premise caterers should only use pasteurized milk and milk products that are kept below 45°F, and served from their original containers. Ice cream must be served with a scoop located in a dipper well with running water, clean and dry, or in the ice cream.

Raw eggs should not be used in Caesar salad or other dishes which require little or no cooking. Off-premise caterers should only use pasteurized eggs in these dishes.

Ice used to cool stored food cannot be served to guests. Ice for consumption should only be dispensed with scoops or tongs. Glasses, hands, or cups should never be used.

For buffets, sneeze guards are required by most health departments. Food temperature should be checked frequently by buffet attendants.

Food and drink that are prepared at a food establishment but served at some other place must be stored, transported, displayed and handled in a safe and sanitary manner at all times. When food is transported, the risk of contamination is great.

Carry all food, serving equipment, and utensils in tightly covered containers or securely wrapped packages to protect them from contamination.

Provide a supply of potable water at the remote site.

Keep all foods, whether chilled or cooked, at constant, controlled temperatures at all times.

Use insulated food carriers during transport or brief holding periods. Make sure correct temperatures are maintained.

Pre-chill foods that are to be served cold before you transport them. Keep them at a temperature of 45 degrees F or below for storage and for service.

Hold potentially hazardous food that is to be served hot at a temperature of 140 degrees F or above.

Clean and sanitize units used to transport food between uses.[5]

When cooling cooked foods, they must be chilled as quickly as possible to below 45°F. The following procedures should be followed:

Divide large quantities of food into smaller portions.

Place foods in shallow containers, of 2" deep or less, and stir to speed the cooling process. Use refrigerator units that are specially designed to chill food quickly,

OR

Use an ice water bath: place pans of food into larger containers filled with ice to pre-cool, if special refrigerator units are not available. Add ice periodically and stir the food in the pan to make sure the entire contents chill rapidly.

Move quick-chilled food to normal refrigeration within three to four hours.

Do not try to cool too much cooked food at one time; it will strain the capacity of a refrigerator. You could endanger other foods by raising temperatures in the refrigerator.[6]

Other important sanitation procedures include the following:

1. Refrigerator temperatures should range between 38 and 40°F. These may vary due to local regulations. They should be clean and sanitized inside and out. Condensation should never drip on foods, and fans should be kept clean.
2. Equipment and food surfaces should be washed, rinsed, and sanitized after each use, and as frequently as possible. Sanitizing may be accomplished by cleaning small utensils and equipment in an automatic dishwasher, or manually by washing in hot water, rinsing in clean and hot water, and sanitizing as follows:

   > . . . immerse [utensils] in an approved chemical and water solution at a temperature of at least 75°F for one minute or more. Follow the product instructions to get the correct amount and strength, equivalent to 50 ppm of quaternary ammonium. Use a test kit to monitor the proper strength of solutions. Sanitizing solution should not be used after the strength goes below minimum requirements.
   >
   > OR
   >
   > You could use a dish basket to immerse (dip) the utensils in clean, very hot (170 degree F) water for 30 seconds.
   >
   > Equipment too large for the sink compartment should first be washed and rinsed, then sprayed or wiped by hand, using chlorine, iodine, or quaternary ammonium solutions.
   >
   > Following the sanitizing process, air-dry utensils and table ware; never dry them with a towel.
   >
   > Use cleaned and sanitized drain boards or movable dish tables to stack and transport sanitized utensils."[7]

3. Dishmachines must operate with proper water temperatures as follows:
   ❏ Wash water temperature should be 140 to 180°F (120 for chemical machines).
   ❏ Final rinse water should be 180 to 200°F (165°F for stationary rack, single-temperature machines and 120°F for chemical machines).
4. All utensils and equipment must be stored at least six inches above the floor.
5. Off-premise catering facilities must be cleaned regularly, in accordance with established cleaning procedures. Spills should be wiped up immediately. When mopping floors, warning signs should be posted.
6. Facilities must be kept free of pests. The best way is to hire a professional, licensed pest control operator who will help develop an ongoing pest control program which includes prevention, repairs, chemicals, and traps.
7. Garbage should be deposited in garbage cans lined with heavy-duty plastic bags and removed frequently from the commissary. It should be deposited in containers or dumpsters outside. There should be enough covered containers to hold all garbage and refuse.
8. To reduce the chances for chemical contamination of foods, poisonous or toxic materials may not be stored near food preparation and serving areas, and must be clearly labeled. Detergents, sanitizers, polishes, chemicals used for maintenance, insecticides, and rodenticides are permitted near food service areas. They must be labeled, stored, and used only in ways that will not contaminate food.

Handling Customer   Off-premise caterers should know what to do if an outbreak of foodborne illness
       Complaints   occurs. Unlike à la carte restaurant meals where guests dine on a variety of
                       dishes, food poisoning for caterers usually involves many people eating the same
                       foods.

                       Samples of anything suspected should be kept. Involved employees should
                       be interviewed, and all supplier records kept. Some caterers may wish to conduct
                       an investigation using an independent laboratory.

                       Off-premise caterers should never immediately admit liability or offer to pay
                       medical bills. They should show concern by saying "I'm sorry that you are feeling
                       sick"; but never say "I'm sorry that our food made you sick." Caterers should
                       allow the complainant to tell the story, and continue to show dismay, but not
                       guilt. It is very important for caterers to notify their insurance carriers, who will
                       generally pursue an investigation or a settlement as appropriate. Off-premise
                       caterers should continue being polite to customers who are suing and remember
                       that caterers have rights too, and are entitled to a proper defense against what
                       may be an inflated or spurious claim.

Irradiation of Foods Irradiation of foods is a controversial topic and has been approved by the Food
                       and Drug Administration for chicken to destroy salmonella, as well as pork,
                       fruits, vegetables, and spices. This process, which destroys harmful bacteria, is
                       frequently compared to pasteurization. Instead of heat, irradiation exposes
                       food to energy in the form of gamma rays, machine-generated electrons, or X-
                       rays. The FDA is currently looking into irradiation as a way to fight *E. coli*
                       bacteria in beef. Other countries such as Canada, France, Italy, Japan, Ger-
                       many, Netherlands, and England permit irradiation for certain foods. There
                       certainly will be many advances in this technology as we near the twenty-first
                       century.

                       Readers wishing an in-depth knowledge of foodservice sanitation may wish
                       to read *Applied Foodservice Sanitation*, The Educational Foundation of the
                       National Restaurant Association (Wiley, New York, 1994)

SAFETY PROCEDURES

Each year there are over 250,000 on-the-job accidents in the food service
industry. On the average, 35 work days are lost when a food service employee
suffers a serious accident. Common causes of food service industry injures
include sprains, strains, cuts, and burns which are caused by slips and falls,
mishandling of knives and slicers, inadequate experience working with open
flames, steamers, and fryers, and overexertion from lifting and moving heavy
objects.

Off-premise caterers must make sure that their work places are safe for
employees, and teach employees how to avoid accidents. At off-premise sites,
caterers must be able to quickly recognize unsafe conditions and take corrective
action immediately.

According to Dean Anthony Marshall:

Responsibility for accidents at an off-premise event makes matters even more sticky. "The bottom line is that if someone is hurt, they're not going to care. They'll sue everybody involved whether they own the facility or they're the caterer. That person isn't going to get into the hassle of who's liable; they want compensation. A common defense taken by facility owners is to ask the caterer, or anyone involved in putting on the function to indemnify them against any losses. This can be handled easily by purchasing insurance specifically for that event."[8]

Following are some practices that will reduce accident risks for both employees and clients.

1. Floors must be kept clean, dry, and in good repair. Spills should be wiped up immediately, and "caution" and "wet floor" signs should be used as appropriate.
2. There should be adequate lighting in all areas where guests and employees walk. Dimly lit walkways at off-premise sites should be lit with temporary lighting. Employees never should be permitted to run, and they should be reminded to use extreme caution when working at off-premise sites with which they are not familiar.
3. Employees should be instructed in correct lifting and transporting methods. When lifting, it is best to lift twice, first mentally and then physically. By lifting mentally, one thinks, "Is the item too heavy or too bulky to see around? Is the path clean and is there a place to put the load?" Lifting heavy objects should be accomplished by first establishing solid footing, and checking that the floor is dry and clean. Next, stand close to the load, and spread feet to shoulder width. Place one foot slightly in front of the other to establish a focal point for the weight of the load. Keep the head over the body, and bend at the knees to reach the load. Grip the load with the whole hand, not just the fingers, and pull the load close while it is still on the ground. Tighten the stomach muscles. Arch the lower back in by pulling your shoulders back and sticking your chest out. Lift slowly, keeping the load close to the body with the legs taking the weight of the load. To set the load down, reverse the procedure.
4. Only staff trained to operate specific machinery should be permitted to use it. They should follow these procedures:
   ❑ Use equipment only for its designated use.
   ❑ Make sure the plug is disconnected and visible before disassembling and cleaning.
   ❑ Use equipment only with the guards in place.
   ❑ Remove jewelry, avoid loose clothing, and restrain hair.
   ❑ Turn off the equipment if distracted.
   ❑ Wear protective goggles, gloves, or clothing.
   ❑ Report any maintenance problem immediately to management.
   ❑ Use proper tools to feed the food product.
   ❑ Never operate equipment with loose wires or damaged switches or plugs.
5. Knives should always be kept sharp, since dull knives easily slip off foods and can cut people. When using a knife, cut away from the body, and cut

foods with fingers curled under. If a knife falls, don't grab for it, get out of the way. Knives should never be used to open containers, and they should be stored in a knife rack.

6. To prevent burns, off-premise caterers should train staff in the following manner:

> Remove lids from pots, pans, kettles (chafing dishes) carefully, allowing steam to escape away from the face and hand;
>
> Use dry, flameproof potholders;
>
> Turn the handles of pans inward on the range so that pans cannot be knocked off. Make sure the handles are not placed too near the heat;
>
> Move heavy or hot containers with enough help and know where the containers are going before picking them up;
>
> Be careful when filtering, changing (discarding) shortening in fryers. (Wait until the grease cools before handling.);
>
> Keep stove tops and hoods free of grease;
>
> Keep oven doors closed when not in use;
>
> Do not clean ovens and stoves until they have cooled;
>
> Keep papers, plastic aprons, and other flammable materials away from hot areas.[9]

Also, keep beverages away from fryer stations, since cold beverages, if spilled into the hot fryer, can cause a major eruption of hot grease. Deep fryers should not be set up in high-traffic areas.

It is imperative to properly train fry cooks. Inexperienced ones have been known to reach into hot grease with their hands for an accidentally dropped article.

7. Ovens, broilers, and grills that are fueled by the large tanks of propane should never be used indoors, or in any area lacking adequate ventilation. In some parts of the country, caterers also need special permits to use butane fuel and sterno indoors. Off-premise caterers should check with local authorities regarding these matters.

8. Folding tables and chairs should be checked before each use for damage. Folding table legs should be locked in place to ensure that the table does not collapse while in use by guests or staff. Chairs should be inspected for splinters, loose or missing screws and bolts, and other unsafe conditions.

9. All utility cords should be taped down, and/or covered with floor mats or some other protective covering so that staff and guests do not trip on them. Orange cords are the most visible. Warning signs should be placed in those areas where staff and guests could possibly trip over them.

10. Service staff should be trained in proper tray carrying procedures. Injuries to guests caused by careless staff have resulted in million-dollar lawsuits.

11. When working with charcoal, charcoal lighter fluid should be sprayed on the coals prior to lighting. It should never be sprayed on charcoal once it is partially ignited, since the flame could travel up the spewing fluid and cause a severe burn or explosion.

12. Flaming drinks and tableside flambés should not be permitted since there have been numerous injuries reported from the flames burning guests and staff.

13. Fire extinguishers should be located near each potential fire source. Smart off-premise caterers also carry at least one fire extinguisher in each catering vehicle. Staff should know how to use them, and extinguishers must be inspected in accordance with local laws.

14. First-aid kits should be located in all catering commissaries, and at all off-premise locations. All catering staff should be trained in the Heimlich Maneuver and some states require that a sign teaching this maneuver be posted in a conspicuous place in the catering commissary. The law does not require off-premise caterers to provide emergency assistance, but it does not forbid them from taking emergency action. No establishment or employee will be held liable for civil damage for an action that could be expected of any reasonably prudent person under similar circumstances. Having a staff member trained in CPR (cardiopulmonary resuscitation) techniques is not required, but is an excellent idea.

15. When emergencies arise, off-premise caterers should remain calm, determine the seriousness of the problem, quickly decide whether to call for help, make the accident victim as comfortable as possible, and administer basic first-aid in accordance with their first-aid guide.

    For burns, first remove whatever is causing the burn, use cool, running water to sooth *minor* burns, never apply ointments, sprays, antiseptics, or home remedies, and seek medical assistance in case of serious burns.

    For wounds, rinse with clean running water, apply pressure with a clean towel or napkin, use a first-aid kit, apply a water-resistant bandage, cover with a plastic glove (for hand wounds), and have severe wounds treated by medical personnel.

16. Accident reports must be completed for all accidents, and forwarded as appropriate to off-premise caterers' worker's compensation insurer, the Occupational Safety and Health Administration (OSHA), and the insurance company providing general business insurance.

17. After an accident, off-premise caterers should ask the injured how the accident happened. Obtain witness reports and inspect the scene for things such as lighting, cleanliness, dryness, and fallen objects near the injured person. It is never advisable to enter into a dispute with the injured person over the cause of the accident, reprimand any employee at the scene, offer to pay all medical expenses, admit responsibility, mention insurance, discuss the accident with strangers, nor permit photographs by anyone other than company representatives.

18. Fire can cause serious accidents, deaths, and major property damage. Off-premise caterers should train their staff to think fire safety and follow these procedures:
    ❑ Frequently check gas appliances for proper maintenance, and always check for the odor of gas buildups before lighting a match.
    ❑ Be sure that all cigarettes and cigars are extinguished before putting them in trash.

❑ All smoke alarms should be properly maintained.

❑ Grease to be discarded, oily rags, and other flammable or combustible materials should not be stored in the catering commissary.

❑ Power cords should be checked for damage, and water should never be splashed around electrical outlets.

❑ Hoods and exhaust filters should be cleaned at least weekly, and hot duct work at least twice a year by a professional company.

19. Off-premise caterers should be familiar with the various fire extinguishers to fight different types of fires. They should consult with local authorities regarding the number of extinguishers required, the types required, their placement, and their maintenance. Most local authorities will offer demonstrations for training purposes.

20. Off-premise caterers should have a planned evacuation procedure in case of fire, both at their commissaries and at off-premise sites. In the event of a fire, they should first call the fire department, advise their employees about the fire, and then calmly move all employees and guests from the building, tent, or party area.

21. Dance floors should be checked for cracks in which a woman's heel could get caught. Honoring requests from clients and guests to make the dance floor slicker could result in a serious slip and fall. Floors should be smooth, but have traction. Allowing guests to drink while dancing can also cause spills and subsequent accidents.

FEDERAL, STATE, AND LOCAL REGULATIONS

Federal agencies such as the Food and Drug Administration (FDA), U.S. Department of Agriculture (USDA), Centers for Disease Control (CDC), Environmental Protection Agency (EPA), National Marine Fisheries Service, and the Occupational Safety and Health Act (OSHA) all regulate the food service industry. Most of these regulations are enforced by state and local health departments.

Off-premise catering managers must be acutely aware of health regulations published by the local public health department or from the county commission. These agencies employ health inspectors who check for compliance with state and local laws. Caterers should correct any violations immediately to avoid fines and possible closure of their commissaries.

OSHA allows a compliance officer to enter a facility to determine adherence to standards and to determine if the workplace is free of recognized hazards. OSHA inspectors look for things such as accessibility of fire extinguishers, adequate handrailings on stairs, properly maintained and utilized ladders, proper guards and electrical grounding for food service equipment, lighted passageways (free from obstructions), readily available first-aid supplies and instructions, and proper use of extension cords. Fines are levied for serious violations.

SECURITY PROCEDURES

The FBI reports that in 1991 there were 687,732 robberies, with robbers grabbing $562 million in cash and property. Off-premise caterers are not immune from these robberies. Caterers who handle large amounts of cash are particularly vulnerable.

The cost for security systems such as closed-circuit television monitors, time-delay safes, and perimeter alarm systems is high, but will deter some burglars and thieves, as well as reduce insurance premium costs.

Many robberies are triggered by security leaks from current employees, or ex-employees who have learned the security system and quit, and return to rob the commissary.

Round Table Pizza, San Francisco, posts in its restaurants a list of safety tips for delivery drivers.
1. Enter and exit the restaurant through the front entrance after dark.
2. Drop excess cash after every delivery run in a secured drop-box located in the delivery area.
3. Carry only a minimum bank—no more than $20 or $30. This bank might include two $5 bills, 10 $1 bills and a few dollars in change. Order takers should tell delivery customers that drivers will not accept bills larger than $20 for payment of food.
4. If available, carry a two-way radio. It allows the driver to contact the restaurant or police in the event of a threatening situation.
5. Always lock vehicles and leave headlights and emergency lights on, and use a flashlight for a (night) delivery. After exiting the (vehicle) scan areas around the house, especially in darkened areas to the sides of the home.
6. Use extra caution in case of darkened homes or areas. If the situation seems threatening, do not make the delivery. Call the restaurant and have them phone the customer again, requesting they leave the front light on.[10]

Other loss prevention tactics include such procedures as depositing excess cash in a safe, varying cash-handling routines, counting money in a locked office, and never admitting any unauthorized personnel into the catering commissary.

INSURANCE PLANNING

When considering the purchase of insurance off-premise caterers should evaluate the size of the potential loss, the probability of the loss, and the resources to meet the loss if it should occur. Minor risks can be absorbed with the use of deductibles, while major risks should be covered. A good rule of thumb is not to risk more than one can comfortably lose.

Off-premise caterers should consult with reputable insurance brokers regarding the following types of insurance (some of these may not apply, while others are required by law).

Fire and extended property damage
Storekeeper liability
Business interruption
Crime coverage for burglary and robbery
Personal injury insurance for protection for libel, slander, defamation, or false
    arrest
Glass insurance
Product liability
Catering vehicle insurance
Fidelity bonds for employees who handle money
Liquor liability
Worker's compensation
Health and disability insurance for yourself and staff
Disability insurance for yourself

According to David Talty, insurance broker and lecturer at Florida International University, it is common knowledge in the insurance industry that the cost of insurance runs in two- to three-year cycles. It is always best to buy insurance when costs are lower. Talty also recommends:

> Be objective when purchasing insurance. Obtain bids, treat the various agents with respect and demand that they provide the best possible product at the lowest possible cost.
>   An insurance broker's job is to assist off-premise caterers in determining the right coverage and then to shop all of the insurance carriers available that underwrite off-premise caterers. It is always best to find a broker who represents a large number of carriers. Always insist on a strong and reputable insurance carrier with a high rating.[11]

It is always best to obtain bids from three or more brokers, and also look into the various insurance programs offered by associations, such as state restaurant associations.

In those instances where insurance is not available, or inordinately costly, restaurant owners have pooled their resources and become their own insurers.

CONCLUSION

Although the topics of sanitation and safety are mundane and basic, and perhaps not as exciting as making a sale, creating a fabulous buffet, or earning a sizable profit for the year, these topics cannot be stressed enough. Mistakes in these areas can cost off-premise caterers their reputation and their livelihood. Off-premise caterers should work closely with their local health departments and insurance carriers to insure that the highest standards of sanitation and safety are met on a daily basis.

NOTES

1. Joan Oleck, *Restaurant Business*, September 1, 1993, p. 57.
2. National Assessment Institute, *Handbook for Safe Food Service Management*, © 1994, p. 12. Reprinted by permission of Prentice-Hall, Englewood Cliffs, N.J.
3. National Assessment Institute, *Handbook for Safe Food Service Management*, © 1994, p. 23. Reprinted by permission of Prentice-Hall, Englewood Cliffs, N.J.
4. *New Miami*, July 1992.
5. National Assessment Institute, *Handbook for Safe Food Service Management*, © 1994, pp. 75–76. Reprinted by permission of Prentice-Hall, Englewood Cliffs, N.J.
6. National Assessment Institute, *Handbook for Safe Food Service Management*, © 1994, p. 77. Reprinted by permission of Prentice-Hall, Englewood Cliffs, N.J.
7. National Assessment Institute, *Handbook for Safe Food Service Management*, © 1994, pp. 92–93. Reprinted by permission of Prentice-Hall, Englewood Cliffs, N.J.
8. Steve Coomes, *NACE News*, National Association of Catering Executives, Louisville, KY, p. 3.
9. National Assessment Institute, *Handbook for Safe Food Service Management*, © 1994, p. 126. Reprinted by permission of Prentice-Hall, Englewood Cliffs, N.J.
10. Excerpted with permission of *Restaurants & Institutions* magazine, November 25, 1992, © 1992 by Cahners Publishing Company.
11. David Talty, Florida International University, verbal communications with author.

Chapter 13

Accessory Services, Theme Parties, Kosher Catering, and Weddings

This chapter serves as a vehicle for addressing topics that further enhance off-premise caterers' knowledge in areas that are critical to overall success in off-premise catering. Most clients rely on caterers' expertise in these areas as they plan special events. In many bidding situations, caterers with the most knowledge in these areas will gain the business, since clients can rely on them for the overall success of the event, not just for good food and service.

Aside from reading as much as possible on the topics covered in this chapter, experience serves as a wonderful teacher. Astute off-premise caterers will learn as much as possible from each event catered by taking copious notes, observing and evaluating accessory service suppliers during events, and starting files for excellent suppliers of these accessory services.

Accessory services contribute to the overall success of the catered event. They include such areas as:

Music and entertainment
Floral and balloon
Photography and videography
Valet parking
Lighting and audio-visual equipment
Ground transportation and limousines
Fireworks and lasers

Professional off-premise caterers are always knowledgeable in all of these areas, because clients rely on their judgment when selecting and planning for the use of these services. They realize that wonderful food and service at a wedding reception can be completely overshadowed by an inappropriate band, an impossible parking situation, or inadequate sound or lighting. At a minimum, caterers need to know who to recommend for these services. However, caterers who have more knowledge in these areas than their competitors will definitely have the advantage in most bidding situations.

While many off-premise caterers simply recommend suppliers of other services, some will engage these services for the client. Out-of-town clients frequently rely on caterers to recommend and book accessory services, while local clients usually choose to engage their own services. The key point to remember is for caterers to recommend only those suppliers who are professional, dependable, reliable, and who can meet the needs of each particular client.

Before specifically discussing each area of accessory services, it is necessary to talk about how off-premise caterers charge for their expertise in these areas. There are varying schools of thought ranging from no charges, commissions, and referral fees to actually marking up these services and adding them to the catering invoice.

Many caterers simply recommend services and allow clients to select from those recommendations. In these instances, caterers may or may not receive commissions or referral fees from these suppliers. Many feel that these fees are unethical while others look at this area as a free service to their clients. Some caterers feel that they make their income from the food, and that clients are entitled to the best price possible on the other services. Other caterers feel that they are sales representatives for the suppliers, and that they are entitled to the referral fee.

In cases where caterers book or engage accessory services for the client, they may wish to add markups to the price since they are in effect responsible for the performance of services, spending time screening, contracting, and paying these providers. The amount of markup will vary depending on each specific situation. Such things as overall budget, as well as amount of profits to be made in other areas of the party such as food, beverages, and rental equipment, will affect the markup. In some cases, caterers who agree to provide accessory services at their cost may take the party away from those who charge markups. Caterers must base their policies on their own unique situations.

Most off-premise caterers have developed excellent working relationships will certain accessory service suppliers. They have created a select team of winners who work well together to produce superb events.

MUSIC AND ENTERTAINMENT

Music is the "heartbeat" of the party. It can transform spectators into participants, and can truly "make or break" a party. A deejay playing the songs that everyone loves to hear will certainly make the party more enjoyable. On the other hand, a large party was ruined when a party planner hired a Michael Jackson impersonator to perform for a group of soft drink company executives. At that time, Michael was promoting a competitor's soft drink.

There are basically three general categories of music: background music, which is good during cocktails and dinner; music for dancing, which is best after dinner; and music for listening. Music at catered events can range from clients' stereos playing background music to large show bands. Harps and other strings produce excellent background music and music for wedding ceremonies. Deejays play a wide variety of prerecorded music at economical prices. Some deejays are also personalities who entertain between songs, and act as masters or mistresses of ceremonies. Popular too are party bands that play a wide variety of music that appeals to all age groups from the seniors to the teens.

Off-premise caterers should advise their clients to accomplish the following before engaging musical services:

1. Be sure that the music fits the event. A string quartet at a Country-Western party would not be appropriate.
2. Hear and see the group in advance.
3. Music should appeal to the group as a whole, rather than just satisfying the clients' own personal tastes. Included in the musical equation should be the purpose of the event, the average age of those in attendance, the range of ages, the part of the country in which the guests live, and where the party is held.
4. Always obtain and sign a written contract that includes such essentials as:
   Price
   Times of performances
   Break times
   Exact location of the party
   The type of party
   The type of music to be played
   The names of the musicians who will be playing (some leaders have a number of different groups playing under the same name)
   Musicians' attire
   Overtime charges, and who is authorized by the client to approve it
   Cancellation charges, deposit amounts, and payment terms
5. Settle on other areas such as:
   Where cases and personal belongings will be kept
   Policy on musicians' guests and potential clients who wish to hear them
   Food and beverage policies regarding musicians
   Changing and break areas

One main rule of thumb is that music should be playing when the guests arrive at the party. Strings may play softly as guests assemble for a wedding ceremony, rock music blasts as guests arrive for an outdoor barbecue, trumpets herald guests' arrival at an upscale dinner at a prestigious location, mariachis greet guests at a Latin-themed event, or the orchestra belts out an upbeat tune as guests enter the ballroom for dinner.

One trend in entertainment for corporations is to engage a "rapper" who performs a customized "rap" for the corporate clients including the clients' name, products, services, and personnel.

According to Lester Lanin, the noted New York band leader, the preferred number of musicians varies depending on the number of guests as follows:

NUMBER OF GUESTS	NUMBER OF MUSICIANS
125	5–7
250	7
500	12
750	12+ strings
1000	15–20

Off-premise caterers should be familiar with a few terms when dealing with musicians and their agents.

"Preheat" means cocktail hour music.

The term "noncontinuous" varies from city to city, but it generally refers to the time musicians will play, and the duration of their breaks. Common examples are: play 40 minutes, and rest for 20 minutes; or play for 45 minutes and rest for 15 minutes.

"Continuous" means that there will be music throughout the evening. There will be no breaks, or very short ones lasting no more than five minutes. When dealing with larger bands and orchestras, musicians will break at different times throughout the party.

Off-premise caterers should determine in advance the musicians' requirements such as:

- ❑ *Seating*—There are usually no extra rental chairs available.
- ❑ *Staging*—This can be expensive, and safety must be considered.
- ❑ *Tenting*—Many musicians with electrical amplifiers will not play unprotected from the rain and other elements.

Pricing for musical entertainers will be based on the following variables:

The number of musicians
The season
The night of the week
Regional factors
Other unique situations

Exhibit 13-1 lists many types of bands and other forms of entertainment. This should be helpful for off-premise caterers who are consulting clients regarding music and entertainment.

EXHIBIT 13-1
Suggestions for Music and Entertainment

BANDS

Wedding
Orchestras
Country and Western
Marching
Circus
Dixieland
Oompah
Mexican Mariachi
Greek

One-Man
Latin
Bagpipe
Israeli
Disco
Rock
Jazz
Chamber groups (strings)
Top 40
1950s and 1960s
All steel

EXHIBIT 13-1 (*continued*)

Calypso
Reggae
African
Strolling
Broadway show
Italian
Bluegrass
Easy-listening
Gospel
Rhythm and Blues
Folk
Polynesian
Drum and Bugle Corps
Brass ensemble
African jazz
Japanese Koto players
Japanese drum ensemble
Chowder marching
Strolling troubadour
Rockabilly
Beatlemania
Banjo
D.J.s
Video D.J.s
Opera performers

DANCE GROUPS

Teenage dance company
Oriental "Chinese Lion" company
East Indian dancers
American Indian dancers
Jazzercise groups
Schuhpattler dancers
Junkanou dancers
Israeli dancers
Tap dancers
Ballet dancers
Greek dancers
Belly dancers
Break dancers
Western swing dancers
Country cloggers
Square dancers
Polynesian dancers
Limbo and fire dancers
Japanese dancers

OTHER ENTERTAINMENT

Robots
Bellringers
Stuntmen
Mimes
Jugglers
Comedians
Impressionists
Magicians
Ventriloquists
Beatlemania band
Elvis show
Acrobats
Marionettes
Puppets
Celebrity look-alikes
Auctioneers
Champagne glass player
Trick roper
Stiltwalkers
Clowns
Costumed characters
Comic Santa Claus
Fortunetellers
Mentalists
Hypnotists
Caricature artists
Calligraphers
Emcees
Living images (walking plants, fish)
Live telegrams
Easter rabbits
Cigarette girls
Models
Rickshaws
Antique and custom autos
Motorcycle escorts
Armored cars
Talking parrots
Crab and frog races
Alligator wrestling
Motown review
Circus acts
Xanadu
Karaoke

FLORAL AND BALLOON DECOR

Off-premise caterers are often consulted about floral and other decor. Some caterers choose to create their own floral work (while creating additional profits) rather than referring the work to others. Others caterers recommend to their clients one or more floral designers.

As with music, off-premise caterers who understand decor will be perceived more favorably by uncommitted clients than caterers who have no clue regarding these areas. Following is a basic primer for those who wish to learn more about floral design:

1. Floral centerpieces should never be more than fourteen inches high, or they should be elevated on stands so as not to obstruct guests' views across tables.
2. For upscale events, a few exotic flowers are much nicer than are a large number of inexpensive blooms such as carnations, mums, and daisies.
3. When budgets are limited, a large, striking arrangement at the entrance is much more effective than a number of smaller arrangements placed around the party area.
4. For weddings and receptions, emphasis should be placed on the reception flowers and bouquets, rather than those at the church, since guests will enjoy them much longer at the reception than at the church.
5. Off-premise caterers should advise their clients that the florist they select should visit the party site first before preparing a proposal.
6. Whenever permitted, the flowers used at ceremonies should be used on buffet tables, or in other areas at the reception sites.
7. Off-premise caterers and their clients should be aware of extra fees charged by florists such as for delivery and setup. Also, as with the case of wedding cake fixtures, arrangements must be made between caterers, clients, and floral designers for the handling of such things as mirrors, special vases, arches, and other related items after the event has concluded.
8. When selecting flowers for catered affairs, caterers and their clients should understand the following:
   - ❑ For scent use roses, gardenias, narcissus, and tuberose.
   - ❑ For height use gladiolas, wildflowers, snapdragons, larkspur, and flowering branches.
   - ❑ For color use tulips, gerbers, lupin, irises, ranunculuses, and anemones.
   - ❑ For economy use sweet william, heather, miniature carnations, and Queen Anne's lace.
9. Always look for florists who understand the needs of off-premise caterers and their clients, and whether there is a very tight budget or one that is more liberal.
10. Clients should always have a plan for distributing the flowers upon conclusion of events. Some ways include drawings, hidden stickers under the chairs, or even a small bow tied to a piece of flatware. When flowers are left behind, off-premise caterers should control their distribution, rather than simply let their

staff take them at random. Many times, caterers can reuse floral arrangements, or break them apart and use the loose flowers for future displays. Under no circumstances should the staff be allowed to remove floral arrangements from the tables until approved by the off-premise caterer or party supervisor.

11. Live plants such as areca palms and ficus trees add dimension to certain off-premise locations. They work well to disguise tent poles, act as a backdrop for the stage and musicians, fill in corners of rooms, and line the entrance ways to create an aislelike effect.

Regarding floral costs, some off-premise caterers recommend that the cost of the florals should be approximately 10 percent of the food cost. Centerpieces can range in price from inexpensive bud vases to elegant, elevated works of art. Smart caterers and their clients realize that flower prices change dramatically depending on the time of year. Flowers are usually less expensive during the spring and summer, and are most expensive between Thanksgiving and Christmas. Roses are extremely expensive around Valentine's Day and Mother's Day. Many florists refuse to do weddings over these holidays since they are so busy with traditional holiday needs.

Balloons are an inexpensive way to decorate catered events. They add color, excitement, and a festive feel to the party. According to Carole Cotton of Happy Balloons in Miami, Florida:

> Many states have balloon release laws, which all reputable balloon suppliers follow. Clients need to be told that balloons may be used, guilt-free, as long as state laws are followed. Certain uses for mylar balloons are prohibited; however, latex rubber used in most balloons is natural and biodegradable within 10 years.[1]

PHOTOGRAPHY AND VIDEOGRAPHY

Off-premise caterers should establish relationships with good photographers and videographers. These professionals may be recommended to clients, and in return most of them will provide good photos and videos for caterers to show prospective clients.

The best photographers and videographers are those who are in control, efficient, and have a sense of humor. They are able to keep things moving so that events do not bog down as the rest of the guests await dinner while a photographer is still shooting photos. Professional photographers will want to know from the client the manner in which they wish the event to be remembered. Do they wish it to be "shot as it actually occurred; an editorialized version of the way it actually occurred, or loaded with group shots?"

Off-premise caterers should advise prospective brides and other clients wishing to use a photographer to evaluate photographers' work in the following manner:

❑ Review complete albums of work, rather than the best shots from a number of albums, so that the photographer's style may be visualized from start to finish.

❑ Select a particular photographer, rather than a "no-name" associate from a large studio.

❑ Inspect photographs for sharp shadows in the background (not good), and look for detail in areas such as the wedding cake icing and the wedding gown (good).

VALET PARKING

From time to time off-premise caterers are asked to assist clients with valet parking services. Many locations do not lend themselves well to self-parking, and at others, clients may wish to provide the valet service as an accommodation to the guests.

When recommending valet parking companies to clients, caterers should investigate the following:

❑ Is the company properly insured? Five million dollars is a good minimum for broad-spectrum liability insurance. Harm done to vehicles while the valet is driving the car is the responsibility of the valet service. Theft or vandalism that occurs when the car is parked usually is not covered.

❑ How does the service handle claims? How are they handled and how long does the process take?

❑ Does the service carry a business license and a valet permit to operate in the municipality where the party takes place?

❑ Are the personnel clean-cut, well-groomed, and immaculately attired?

❑ Are the personnel courteous? Usually, the valet attendants are the first people guests talk to upon arriving at an event. The first impression should always be outstanding.

❑ Are there letters of recommendation, or references to check?

❑ If possible, it is advisable to observe the company in action to see if there is a long wait for cars, whether they provide sufficient staff, and how well they treat the vehicles.

The number of valet parking staff necessary depends on these factors:

1. The number of expected vehicles—on the average there are 2.5 people per car.
2. How will they be arriving? Will they trickle in, like before a wedding ceremony, or will there be a tidal wave of cars as most of the guests arrive at the same time for a wedding reception after a wedding ceremony at nearby church.
3. How far do the valet parkers need to take the cars to park?

Professional valet companies can evaluate each situation and be able to recommend an adequate number of valet parking attendants to service an event. It is important to remember that when waiting in line for car parking, or waiting in line for car retrieval, each minute seems like ten minutes. Keeping this in mind, it is usually better to have too many rather than too few valet parking attendants.

On the evening of the event, the valet parkers should assemble at the party site one hour in advance of the arrival of the first guests. Their appearance should be checked by the off-premise caterer, and the details of the event should be discussed. The valets should be provided with a written script, telling them exactly how to welcome the arriving guests. An example might be, "Welcome to the Smith wedding reception. Please be sure to take your valuables with you, and follow the sidewalk to the reception."

Some interesting flairs to valet parking services can include free window washing by the parkers while the guests are at the event. Another would be to provide a party favor to each vehicle as a surprise farewell gift as the guests depart. For Saturday night parties, a complimentary copy of the following Sunday's local newspaper could help create a favorable impression.

LIGHTING AND AUDIO-VISUAL EQUIPMENT

Lighting is one of the most overlooked elements at catered events. Often, beautiful food displays are inadequately lit, or dangerous steps and other obstacles are barely visible. It is imperative that off-premise caterers visit party sites where events are to be held after dark, at a time when it is dark so as to gain a total picture of the situation and the requirements.

Good lighting is truly invisible. It can highlight attractive features, hide flaws, and provide for guests' safety. Many off-premise caterers handle some of their own lighting, while others work with light specialists who are expert in lighting special events.

According to Stephen Pollock, a Ft. Lauderdale lighting specialist, off-premise caterers should "have a basic knowledge of lighting so as to be able to professionally assist clients in this area."[2] Some tips from Mr. Pollock include the following:

1. Theatrical-type light fixtures can work wonders for buffets. These fixtures are easily mounted, adjustable, and can hold colored gels. They can be purchased or rented, and can provide illumination ranging from soft, diffuse lighting to a hard-edged, focused pattern.
2. For buffet lighting, a good instrument is the six-inch fresnel light, which puts out a soft light that can be spotted down to a narrow beam, or flooded to wash a wide area. The perfect color for lighting food is generally a "no-color" pink, which is a pale pink that almost appears white, yet it adds a rosy glow to a buffet. Buffet centerpieces can be lit with another color such as lavender. It is best to light buffets from the front, top, and back whenever possible.

Exhibit 13-2 is glossary of lighting terms prepared by Mr. Pollock.

Frequently, off-premise caterers are asked to provide audio-visual equipment such as podiums, microphones, slide and overhead projectors, movie screens,

---

EXHIBIT 13-2
Lighting Terms

Fresnel—A lighting instrument that uses a fresnel lens to produce a diffused, soft-edge beam. The spacing between the lamp and the lens can be adjusted to alter the beam spread from spot to flood.

Gobo—A metal template that, when inserted into a focusable lighting fixture, defines the pattern of light projected; it does for a lighting designer what a stencil does for a sign maker.

Leko—A slang term derived from lekolite, a lighting instrument manufactured by Century Lighting. A leko contains a movable lens that enables the beam to be focused with either a hard or soft edge. A group of internal shutters allows the beam to be cropped and many lekos have an adjustable iris that allows a variation of the beam's diameter. Lekos can accommodate a pattern holder containing a gobo for projection of a specific image.

Par lights—These are parabolic aluminized reflector lights. Unlike fresnels and lekos, the reflector and lens are built into the lamp, rather than being parts of the body. Par lamps are available in beam spreads from very narrow spots to wide floods.

Pin beam—A usually small, 25-watt lamp that projects a narrow beam of light up to 20 feet. It is used to light banquet table centerpieces, mirrorballs, and dance floors.

Wash—A broad, even, soft lighting over all or part of a room or stage, created by a group of floodlights, used to provide general illumination of one or several colors. More than one wash can be set up to cover an area, allowing for a choice of colors not only by changing washes, but also by blending them.

VCRs, rear-screen projectors, and a host of other technical equipment. Caterers who wish to be involved in this area should establish relationships with one or more audio-visual suppliers, and provide this additional service to clients. Many caterers add markups to their cost for this equipment, creating additional profits in exchange for their time spent dealing in these matters. Others simply recommend reliable audio-visual equipment suppliers to their clients and prospective clients.

Audio-visual technology can also be used in many aspects of special events such as theme enhancement, background music, foreground music, sound escape, and visual projection of theme elements. By the end of this century, much of the current technology will be outdated, and new technology will be available. New advances in technology can create any desired illusion through computers, even smells. Off-premise caterers should stay current on the latest advances in these areas so as to be in a position to lead the way into the next century serving more sophisticated clients who are looking for more than just food and beverage.

GROUND TRANSPORTATION AND LIMOUSINES

Occasionally, off-premise caterers become involved in securing ground transportation for clients, usually for out-of-town corporate clients who require transportation to and from the event site, and for wedding couples who need limousine service. Unusual requests include such things as horse-and-buggy rides, trolley rides, and rickshaw rides for wedding couples and their guests.

It is advisable for off-premise caterers to recommend such services but not to become involved in booking these services. Most caterers have learned that their time should be devoted to the event itself, rather than to worrying whether the buses or limousines arrive on time.

Off-premise caterers may wish to advise their clients using buses for transportation to event sites to be sure of the following:

❑ Greeter should meet the guests as they embark and disembark the busses.
❑ Refreshments are always welcome if the trip is longer than twenty minutes.
❑ The pickup time should be reconfirmed so that the transportation is present when guests are ready to leave the party site.
❑ Celebrity look-alikes, fortunetellers, magicians, or palm readers can provide entertainment during longer trips; Polaroid pictures of the guests are a welcome addition; sing-alongs with songsheets are excellent; and written or verbal travelogs along the way will create interest.

When recommending ground transportation providers, the main criteria are dependability and reliability. Caterers cannot afford to recommend a limousine company to a bride and groom that does not show up on time, or that breaks down on the way to the wedding reception.

The presidential stretch limousine seats up to six adult passengers and most come equipped with a telephone, beverage service, and a television. This is the most popular one but there are longer and wider ones available in some market areas. The unstretched Cadillac and Lincoln Town Car are becoming increasingly popular, but offer less room. Rolls Royce and Mercedes Benz conversions are also gaining in popularity among wedding couples.

FIREWORKS AND LASERS

Ted Walker, president of Add Fire, Incorporated, one of the nation's leading fireworks firms, says, "The use of pyrotechnics [fireworks] can cause the level of excitement of any event to heighten and continue throughout the event." Walker also states, "There are three ways to maximize the use of fireworks: outdoor aerial display, outdoor ground displays and indoor pyrotechnics."[3]

Outdoor displays are those with which most people are familiar. These are launched from the ground, produce their effects high in the sky, and require a large amount of room. Outdoor ground displays are normally used in conjunction with aerial displays to add to the dimension of the overall production and bring specific attention to a wide variety of subject matter (logos, trademarks, business phrases, and messages). Ground displays offer a greater arena for aesthetic demonstration and can be placed not only on the ground, but also on hot-air balloons, helicopters, stadium walls, mountain sides, floats, and ships. The name "ground display" means that it cannot be shot up into the air like an aerial shell. They explode while attached to an object. Indoor pyrotechnics can spice up an indoor event as long as safety can be assured. These can be placed on the ceiling to simulate outdoor aerial fireworks, or placed on a stagefront or on trusswork to create a fireworks waterfall.

Fireworks companies will inspect the sites for safety and aesthetic positioning of the fireworks in the environment, secure the necessary permits, and provide insurance and bonds as required.

Laser lightshows can also add excitement to a catered event. Laser light is a solid beam of light that when coupled with computer choreography can create complex displays that stimulate the senses. Indoor lasers, which include models such as variscan, dualscan, and smartscan, look like lasers but are less expensive. When this type of laser is used with a smoke machine, the audience believes that it is a real laser.

THEMES AND THEME PARTIES

There are hundreds of possible themes for parties. The American Rental Association in Moline, Illinois (800 334 2177) publishes two excellent brochures containing party ideas. They are: *Celebrate a Theme* and *365 Reasons to Have a Party*.

Chris Lee, President of California Leisure Consultants, in San Diego suggests that off-premise caterers and event planners consider these basic elements when choosing a theme:

Is the theme consistent with the overall theme and objectives of the meeting, convention, incentive program or fund-raiser?
Is the theme compatible with the demographics of the participants including age, sex, background and culture?
Does the menu (food and beverage) compliment the theme?
Is there enough participation for the group?

Lee further suggests when choosing a venue and location that planners:

Research all possible options.
Look for venues with built-in themes such as museums, etc.
Look for adequate access for motor coaches and other transportation.
How smoothly will traffic and people flow in and out?
Are there adequate utilities and power supplies?
Is there adequate space for guests to mingle once the stage, props, seating and food stations are in place? (Allow at least 30% of the space for staging, props and food stations.)

Is there a back-up location nearby in case of inclement weather?
Are there other scheduled events or holidays that may conflict?

Off-premise caterers may wish to consider the following when planning themed events:

❑ Theme the mode of transportation to the event to get them into the mood.
❑ Heavily theme entrances and exits since everyone will pass by them at least twice.
❑ For large events of 500 or more participants, use large props or place props well above eye level.
❑ Place some of the props and food stations into the middle of the event area to add dimension.
❑ Look into the areas of aromatherapy, special lighting, and soundscaping.
❑ Virtual reality software programs can add to a theme event as the participants become part of a video game and others can watch.[4]

Remember that a theme party can be visualized as an umbrella, with the spokes of the umbrella being the various elements that support the overall theme such as:

The invitation
The menu
The decor
The scripting of the event
The music and entertainment
The costuming of the guests and staff
The beverages

Astute off-premise caterers realize that if one or more of these umbrella spokes are weak, than the overall theme will be weakened.

One way to research a theme party is to rent several movies related to the theme to obtain ideas. A VCR with a pause button is excellent, so that the film may be stopped to look closely at decor, dress, props, and backdrops. Guests are more likely to relate to Hollywood's version of reality, than reality itself.

Libraries are filled with books that can offer further insight to theme ideas.

Before leaving the area of theme parties, let us examine fund-raisers. Every off-premise caterer is asked to cater fund-raisers for free, at cost, or at a sizable discount. Off-premise caterers who are just starting can gain good publicity and word-of-mouth from these events, as long as they are catered well. Established caterers know that involvement with fund-raisers creates a positive public image, but once the word gets out, everyone calls.

Off-premise caterers should carefully choose those fundraisers they wish to support. They cannot support them all, or there will be a disastrous bottom line. Some caterers have found that by charging the charity full retail price and then giving a donation to the charity they are able to maintain their food and labor costs, since the selling price is not discounted and the donations shows up on the income statement in the "charitable donation" category.

KOSHER CATERING AND BAR/BAS MITZVAHS

Kosher is a term that applies to all foods that observant Jews will eat or use that meet the specifications and the requirements of the Dietary Laws derived from the Old Testament. Kosher foods are distinguished as follows:

1. Kosher animals have split hooves and chew their cud.
2. Kosher fish must have fins and scales, and the scales must be easily removed so as to not harm the fish. Salmon is considered a kosher fish, while sturgeon is not.
3. Shellfish are not kosher.
4. Animals killed for sport are not kosher. With kosher beef, only the forequarters are normally used since the blood vessels are closer to the surface and can easily be removed.
5. Animals that are diseased or bleeding when brought in to kill are not accepted as kosher. Animals are inspected by a mashgiach, before being slaughtered by the shochet, the kosher butcher.
6. Kosher practitioners are not permitted to eat blood, so certain foods are salted to draw out the blood.
7. Kosher food items must be stored and cooked apart from nonkosher foods.
8. Meat and dairy products, as well as their dishes, can never be mixed together.

The mashgiach also plays the role of the overseer during the food preparation stages, ensuring that dairy and meat are never mixed together in the same bowls, ovens, sinks, etc. The mashgiach also checks to see that any food to be used is distinguished by proper kosher symbols.[5]

Here is a sample kosher menu:

Breakfast—Chopped eggs, herring, blintzes, bagels, lox, whitefish, cream cheese; basically a dairy breakfast.

Lunch—Knish, Waldorf Salad, brisket with prune sauce, duchess potatoes, steamed broccoli and baby carrots, fresh fruit salad for dessert.

Dinner—Smoked salmon mousse appetizer, Boston bibb with raspberry dressing, Chicken Veronique, any steamed vegetable, desserts, poached pear with mint sauce. Note: While presenting fish and chicken on the same menu, they are never served on the same plate or during the same course.

If lactose sugar, lactic acid, whey, or eggs come into contact with meat during cooking, the dish is no longer kosher. If any egg has a blood spot, it cannot be used.

> A true kosher kitchen will have at least two sets of all cooking tools and serving utensils to ensure the mix of items such as meat and dairy does not occur. However, one general exception to the rule is glassware, though many strict kosher Jews also choose to avoid this. ... Machines cannot be lubricated with pork-based oils or whale oils. If so, they are no longer kosher."[6]

Kosher style does not mean kosher. These foods may taste and look like kosher foods, but they do not meet the required high kosher standards. This type of menu may not include pork and shellfish, but the other dietary laws are not observed in the preparation.

Readers interested in learning more about kosher catering may wish to contact the following resources:

❑ *Kosher Outlook*—a kosher catering magazine published at 1444 Queen Anne Road, Teaneck, New Jersey 07666.
❑ Local orthodox rabbis.
❑ Orthodox Union—at 333 7th Avenue, New York, New York 10001.

The *bar mitzvah* is performed in a temple or synagogue on the Sabbath prior to a Jewish boy's thirteenth birthday. The *bat* or *bas mitzvah* is the female counterpart of the bar mitzvah. The key word to describe foods served after these events is "abundant." These events are hosted by the child's parents. Menus for these events must be designed so as to please both the teens and adults.

Today's bar mitzvahs feature DJ's that play songs that the kids hear on the radio, high-energy dancers to get everybody dancing, video games, laser lights, fog machines, roving video cameras that capture guests and flash their images on a big screen, and themes that change depending upon what is popular with kids at the time.

WEDDINGS AND WEDDING RECEPTIONS

These events can provide a large share of most off-premise caterers' revenues. Nearly all off-premise caterers cater these events, and some report that over 50 percent of their revenue come from them.

Caterers should be totally knowledgeable regarding wedding procedures for both Christian and Jewish ceremonies. Many times their knowledge in these areas can mean the difference between selling and not selling a wedding and reception.

Today, more and more couples are paying for their own receptions due to divorced parents and second marriages. Grooms are becoming more involved in wedding planning. Couples are looking for unusual venues such as mansions, gardens, and parks. Reception foods are lighter and more varied with buffets and food stations being the most popular. The one-sided, long head table is becoming less popular with many couples, who opt to sit at round tables with their bridal parties, or at a table for two (when they choose to not alienate family members by showing favoritism).

In 1992, the average age of brides and grooms was 28 and 31 respectively. Their combined median income was $45,747. The average wedding and reception was for 125 guests, and cost $16,144.

Overview Wedding plans begin with the engagement. Normally the bride's family determines the number of guests, but they should consult with the groom's family before determining this number. Usually only close friends and family are invited. Business acquaintances are not invited unless the wedding is to be extremely large. Wedding invitations are normally sent out approximately four weeks prior to the weddings.

Off-premise caterers who cater to bridal couples should be able to assist these couples in suggesting sites not only for the wedding and reception but also for engagement parties and the rehearsal dinner. Most young couples have never planned a catered event before, and their parents are only slightly more experienced in this area. Therefore, smart off-premise caterers should be able to advise them on suggested locations, and later on, make suggestions for music, photography, flowers, and the wedding cake. Many off-premise caterers assume the role of "wedding consultant," and handle many of the myriad details for the bride. In the nineties, many brides are busy with careers and just don't have the time to dedicate to all of details.

Additionally, off-premise caterers who are knowledgeable in the wedding procedures for both Christian and Jewish ceremonies will be able to assist couples and their families with the actual ceremony. These caterers further demonstrate their value to prospective clients, and some charge an additional fee for their services.

Exhibits 13-3 to 13-7 depict not only the order for processionals and recessionals, but also where the participants stand during the ceremony for both Jewish and Christian weddings. These exhibits are reproduced with the permission of Van Nostrand Reinhold and are taken from *How to Manage A Successful Catering Business* by Manfred Ketterer.

Additionally, Exhibit 13-8 illustrates where people stand in the receiving line and sit at the bride's and parents' table during the wedding reception.

A typical wedding reception includes a cocktail reception, usually with hors d'oeuvres, during which guests mingle and socialize while pictures of the bride, groom, and others are taken. The main meal usually follows cocktails, and is sometimes preceded by the first dance and the champagne toast.

The proper toasting procedures are:

1. The best man toasts the bride and groom.
2. The groom toasts the bride and her family.
3. The fathers toast the bride and groom.
4. The bride and groom toast each other.

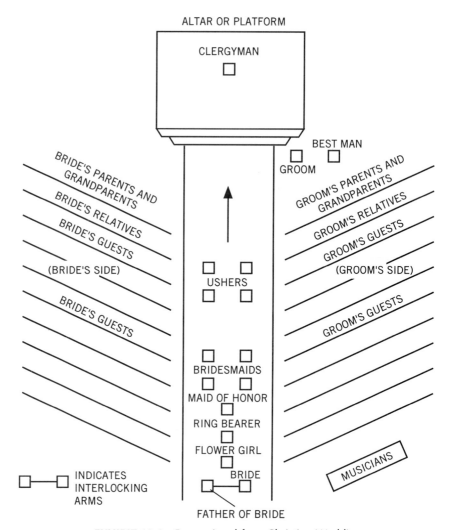

EXHIBIT 13-3   Processional for a Christian Wedding

For receptions where champagne is served only for the toast, it is best to save the toast until the time of the cake-cutting, so that guests will be less likely to go to bars for refills and be refused additional champagne.

Off-premise caterers are frequently asked to place party favors on the tables where guests are to be seated, provide a table for gifts (although most guests do not bring their gifts to the reception), and provide an escort table upon which the seating cards can be placed.

The main meal can be a seated, served meal, a buffet, one with food stations, or one with elements of all of these. An example of the last scenario would be

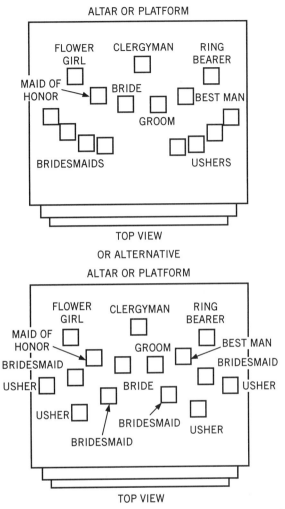

EXHIBIT 13-4 Positioning of Bridal Party for a Christian Wedding

one with food stations during the cocktail reception, and then a preset first course followed by a buffet.

Upon conclusion of the meal, it is best to offer dancing prior to the cake-cutting. This allows guests a chance to move around after the meal, and ensures that they stay in the spirit of the festivities. According to Jerry Wayne, a noted band leader and musician in South Florida:

The music mix can be magical to the success of the wedding. For most weddings, there are guests of all age groups, and wedding bands must be able to bridge the gap between dancers who love Cole Porter, George Gershwin and show tunes, yet

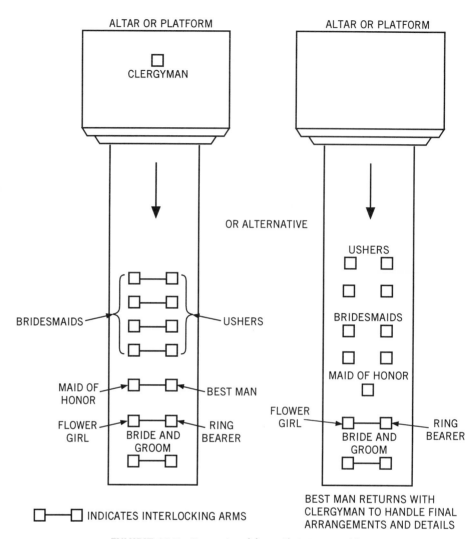

EXHIBIT 13-5   Recessional for a Christian Wedding

lure the young at heart onto the dance floor with today's hits and old time rock and roll.[7]

If it was not done prior to the meal, the champagne toast should be done prior to the cutting of the cake. The bride and groom cut the first piece of wedding cake together using a special, decorated cake knife. Off-premise caterers should provide at the cake table a plate, napkin, and two forks for the couple to use. First, the bride feeds a bite of cake to the groom, then the groom feeds a bite of cake to the bride. This symbolizes their willingness to share each other's lives. After this, the caterer's staff cuts and serves the cake to the guests. One nice

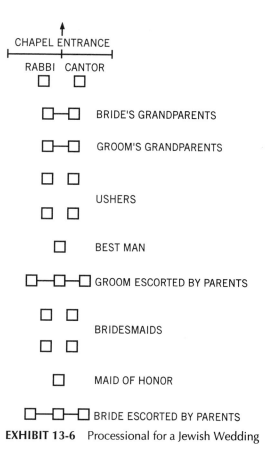

EXHIBIT 13-6   Processional for a Jewish Wedding

additional touch is to serve fresh fruits or another light dessert on the same plate as the cake. This creates interest, satisfies those guests who chose not to eat wedding cake, and generates additional profit for off-premise caterers. The top of the cake is first removed and saved for the couple to freeze and later eat on their first anniversary. A wonderful touch is for caterers to provide their own boxes with their name and logo, which will remind the couple of the caterer every time they open their freezer during the first year as husband and wife.

Most off-premise caterers do not produce their own wedding cakes, but they should be able to recommend one or more bakers who make excellent quality wedding cakes. Some caterers ask for a referral fee, while others receive a wholesale price for the cake, and charge the client retail. Some charge a cake-cutting fee in addition to the cake itself.

When ordering wedding cakes, couples should be prepared to tell the caterer or the baker the following:

The number of expected guests
The color and flavor of the icing and the trim

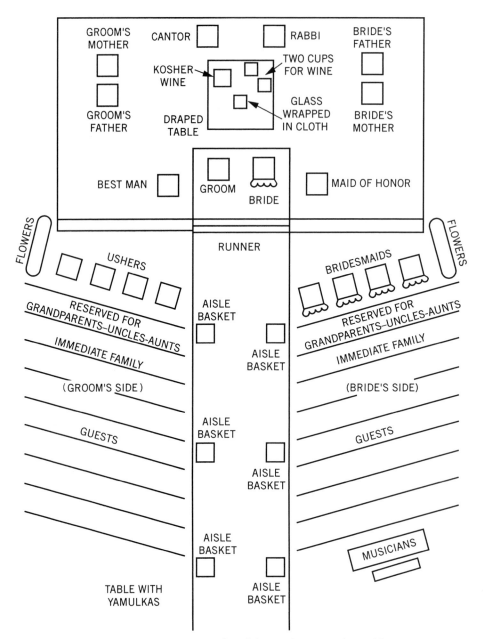

EXHIBIT 13-7   Positioning of Bridal Party for a Jewish Wedding

The flavor of the filling and the cake
What they wish on the top of the cake
Whether they want pillars
Other wishes

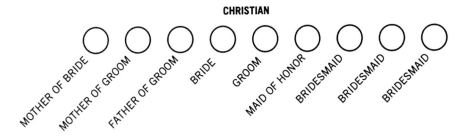

CHRISTIAN

MOTHER OF BRIDE · MOTHER OF GROOM · FATHER OF GROOM · BRIDE · GROOM · MAID OF HONOR · BRIDESMAID · BRIDESMAID · BRIDESMAID

(FATHER OF GROOM ACTS AS ROVING HOST AND USHERS CIRCULATE AMONGST GUESTS)

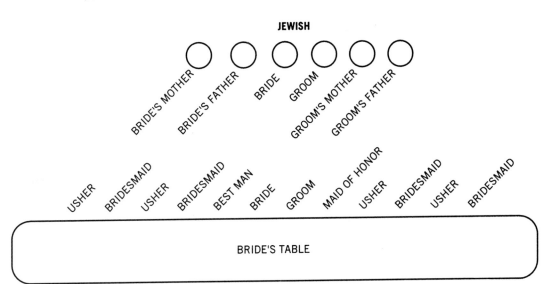

JEWISH

BRIDE'S MOTHER · BRIDE'S FATHER · BRIDE · GROOM · GROOM'S MOTHER · GROOM'S FATHER

USHER · BRIDESMAID · USHER · BRIDESMAID · BEST MAN · BRIDE · GROOM · MAID OF HONOR · USHER · BRIDESMAID · USHER · BRIDESMAID

BRIDE'S TABLE

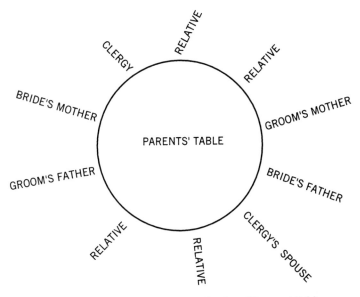

CLERGY · RELATIVE · RELATIVE · BRIDE'S MOTHER · GROOM'S MOTHER · PARENTS' TABLE · GROOM'S FATHER · BRIDE'S FATHER · RELATIVE · RELATIVE · CLERGY'S SPOUSE

EXHIBIT 13-8   Receiving Lines, Head and Parents' Tables

Off-premise caterers who are not involved in the cake order should find out in advance of the reception where the cake was ordered so that if it does not arrive on time they can call the baker without disturbing the bridal couple or their family.

When selecting wedding cake suppliers, off-premise caterers and wedding couples should sample cakes made by the baker to be sure that they are flavorful, attractive, and *moist*. The biggest complaint regarding wedding cakes is that they are dry. It is also advisable to see pictures of actual cakes made by the bakers and ask for recommendations.

One popular wedding cake has icing applied in the form of a basket weave and is decorated with fresh flowers. It is best to rely on the florist for the flowers rather than the baker, so that all of the flowers at the reception are color coordinated. Bakers who offer various flavors such as carrot cake, mocha, white chocolate, liqueurs, and fresh fruits are in demand.

Details such as delivery times and return of pillars and mirrors used underneath the cakes should be coordinated between the baker, the couple, and the off-premise caterer, to avoid confusion and losses.

After the cake-cutting, dancing usually resumes, and then as the event draws to a close the bride tosses her bouquet to the single ladies in attendance, and the groom removes the symbolic garter from the bride's leg and tosses it to the eligible bachelors. As the bridal couple departs, guests frequently throw birdseed or flower petals on them. Caterers need to know the rules of the facility regarding this. Some facilities do not permit any tossing at all. If birdseed or flower petals are thrown, the off-premise caterer should immediately see that they are swept up to avoid someone slipping. The throwing of rice is most often prohibited since rice will attract insects, and is slippery on hard flooring.

At the end of the reception, off-premise caterers should have the following cleaned, packed, and ready for the couple or family to take with them:

The cake top packed in a clean, attractive box
Any leftover foods or wedding cake as prearranged
Toasting goblets, cake knives, and any other accessories provided by the couple
    for use at the reception
The guestbook and pen in their original boxes

To avoid dealing with money on the night of the reception, off-premise caterers should provide wedding couples an invoice in advance, so that they simply need to bring the balance due in an envelope to the reception. Why ruin a romantic evening by having to discuss finances before the couple departs on their honeymoon?

Weddings in the 1990s include lush and opulent florals, hand-tie bouquets, colors such as burgundy, fuchsia, cranberry, plum, and orange, and fewer receiving lines or one-sided bride's tables. Popular are Victorian-themed receptions and destination weddings where 20 or 30 couples travel to a resort for the wedding. There tend to be fewer seated, served meals and more buffets and food station receptions; more vegetarian and ethnic foods, and less consumption of alcoholic beverages.

Depending on their circumstances, some couples will reduce the guest list in order to have a fabulous affair, while others choose not to come across as spending a lot. Couples who have well-established careers will spend what they can afford.

To characterize relationships with clients planning weddings, caterers find themselves acting as consultants and everyone finds himself/herself playing mother to the bride. Elise Shuman, director of catering at The San Ysidro Ranch in California, says there is an assumption by the bride that you'll do anything for her, and it's true. "If they want me to run out and get their bobby pins, I do, but I don't charge for that," Shuman says. Roberta Deem of Capers sums it up: "I'm more like a counselor than a caterer sometimes."[8]

NOTES

1. Carole Cotton, Happy Balloons, Miami, FL, verbal communication with author.
2. Stephen Pollock, lighting specialist, Ft. Lauderdale, FL, verbal communication with author.
3. Ted Walker, president, Add Fire, Inc., verbal communication with author.
4. Chris Lee, President, California Lesiure Consultants, San Diego, California (619-299-2200) Seminar 1992.
5. *NACE News*, May 1993, p 1.
6. *NACE News*, May 1993, p. 6.
7. Jerry Wayne, bandleader/musician, FL, verbal communication with author.
8. Mindy Sink, *Special Event*, November 1993, p. 36.

Chapter 14

Budgeting, Accounting, and Financial Management

Off-premise caterers who understand the financial aspects of their business will definitely increase their chances of success in this challenging field. They need knowledge in the areas of preparing budgets, producing accounting records, analyzing financial reports, effecting cost-control techniques, dealing with banks, and limiting tax liabilities, and need to understand how computers and software programs can assist them. Caterers who fail to understand the "numbers" will be more likely to fail in business.

Successful caterers know how the revenues and expenses from catered events flow through the business records and end up as profits or losses. They understand the difference between profits and cash. They know how to budget for sales and expenses as well as analyze financial results. They know how federal income taxes and other taxes impact their profits (bottom line). They also know how to determine if it is necessary to computerize their accounting records, or simply to maintain manual records.

BUDGETING, PRECOSTING, AND UNDERSTANDING CASH FLOW

A budget is a plan for operating a business expressed in financial terms. It includes sales and expense projections based on available information. No one should even consider starting an off-premise catering operation without first preparing a budget to determine the feasibility of the business venture. Off-premise caterers have lost millions of dollars by not first projecting their sales volume and relating these sales to actual overhead expenses.

One of the most common mistakes made by off-premise caterers is committing to large overhead expenses such as rent, utilities, and equipment financing without first determining how these expenses will relate to the projected sales. These caterers take on large financial obligations, too often assuming that large sales will follow. When these sales fail to appear, the expenses exceed the revenues and the business quickly fails. Planning realistically is essential.

For example, a startup off-premise caterer with no guaranteed sales or previous experience would more than likely be foolish to assume a $2,000-per-month lease and a $1,000-per-month payment for equipment financing. As a general rule of thumb, these two expenses should never exceed 10 percent of monthly sales. In this case, each month the caterer would need to average $30,000 in sales. A more realistic amount would be $300 to $500 per month for these expenses, since the required revenues would be significantly less, and obviously more achievable.

In this chapter, we will be referring to a hypothetical off-premise caterer who is starting a small catering business from a small kitchen equipped with basic equipment and utensils. This caterer pays annual rent of $5,000, is financing the business from personal savings and plans to rent the necessary front-of-the-house equipment from a local rental company. All examples and exhibits in this chapter will refer to this hypothetical caterer. Readers are cautioned at this point to not use the exhibits and figures in this chapter as "gospel." They are not. They are simply guidelines. Every off-premise caterer operates differently. The purpose of utilizing a hypothetical situation is simply to relate financial theory to reality.

Readers are not to assume that the various revenues, expenses, and profit are absolute numbers which all off-premise caterers must emulate. They are not. They are used only for demonstration purposes.

The first step in developing a budget is to project sales based on past and projected future performances. Obviously, startup caterers will have no past performances to evaluate, so they must make educated "guesstimates" as to their projected sales. When estimating sales, it is better to err on the underside, being conservative. Projected sales estimates should be based on the following input:

Number of projected catered events
Average selling price of each event
Seasonal variations
National and local economic indicators
Competitive factors
Industry trends

Once sales are projected on an annual basis, they can then be broken down by month. For example, a startup off-premise caterer who generally caters outside events in the South would generate more sales in the cooler months and fewer sales in the warmer months. This caterer, who projects $100,000 in first-year sales, could prepare monthly sales projections as follows:

January	$2,000	(first month in business)
February	3,000	
March	8,000	
April	6,000	
May	9,000	
June	5,000	(warmer months begin)
July	2,000	
August	4,000	
September	3,000	
October	10,000	(begins to cool down)
November	15,000	(reputation is building)
December	33,000	(excellent holiday season)
First year total	$100,000	

Why is it necessary to project sales on a monthly basis? Isn't it adequate to simply project them for the year? The answer is *No!* The reason is that it is imperative to determine profit and cash flow at least on a monthly basis in order to determine the amount of funding necessary to startup the business, and continue to fund it, until it becomes self funding. In the above example, it is more than likely that this theoretical off-premise caterer will lose money at least in the months of January, February, July, August, and September and hopefully generate a profit in the other months. In those months where there are losses, the business will be unable to pay its expenses from revenues; therefore, operating capital (cash) from the owner will be needed, to keep the business operating. A detailed discussion of this will follow later in this chapter.

The next step in preparing a budget is to estimate expenses. The four main expense categories are:

Cost of sales (food cost)
Payroll and related costs
Direct operating expenses
Administrative and general expenses

(A detailed discussion of the component expense categories for each of these expenses will follow in the accounting section of this chapter.)

Cost of sales is estimated by reviewing past performance results for this category, as well as current menu pricing and supporting costs. Off-premise caterers should know their desired cost of sales, based upon current pricing and costs. For example, an off-premise caterer whose overall pricing strategy is a markup of 3 times the cost of food should achieve a 33 1/3 percent cost of sales in the long run as depicted here:

Food cost for dinner is $5 times 3 = $15
Cost of sales % is $5 divided by $15 = 33 1/3%

A chart of markup factors and their associated food costs follows:

MARKUP FACTOR	PROJECTED FOOD COST/COST OF SALES
5	20%
4	25%
3	33 1/3%
2.5	40%

Most off-premise caterers operate between a 20 percent and 40 percent cost of sales. For budgeting purposes in this chapter, we will use 33 1/3 percent in our example.

Payroll and related costs such as payroll taxes, Worker's Compensation Insurance, and other costs directly related to payroll vary from caterer to caterer. Unlike costs of sales, which are much more variable in nature based upon the volume of business, payroll costs generally have components that are fixed, and components that are variable. Most off-premise caterers employ one of more employees on a permanent basis, who are paid to work regardless of the level of business. These people are essentially fixed payroll. Successful caterers know that the fewer employees in this category, the better. The main problem with large numbers of permanent employees is that when business drops off in slower seasons, these employees are still paid, which can quickly erode profits and create huge losses.

Every off-premise caterer should have as a major goal to keep payroll costs in check by keeping permanent employees at a minimum, and striving to staff parties with part-time staff who work only when needed. This type of staffing maximizes variable payroll costs.

Ideally, payroll and related costs as a percentage of sales should stay constant, rather than fluctuate wildly as sales increase or decrease from month to month. Off-premise caterers generally operate with payroll and related costs between 20 and 30 percent.

It is extremely important at this juncture to point out that those operators with high food cost percentages should have lower labor cost percentages, and vice versa. An off-premise caterer with a 40 percent food cost and a 35 percent labor cost will not stay in business long. Ideally, caterers should strive for a combined cost of sales and payroll percentage of 50 percent or less if they are to maximize their profitability.

The next budgeting step is to compute actual payroll and related expenses based upon available knowledge. In the above example, let us assume that the off-premise caterer employs a cook who works an average of 30 hours per week at an hourly rate of $7.50 per hour and a helper who works 20 hours per week at an hourly rate of $5 per hour. These two employees will earn $325 per week, or $16,900 annually. This off-premise caterer's related costs (employer's FICA expense, unemployment taxes, Worker's Compensation and other expenses that are directly related to payroll) are an additional 20 percent of actual payroll, increasing the $16,900 amount to $20,280 ($16,900 × 20% = $3,380 + $16,900). A short-cut to obtain the same result is to multiply $16,900 times 1.2, which will yield the same answer.

This off-premise caterer hires additional staff for parties, and this staff, *including related costs*, is 10 percent of total revenues in this example.

Operating and administrative and general expenses vary from one caterer to another; however, every off-premise caterer must always strive to keep these costs at a minimum in order to attain maximum profitability. A complete explanation of these expenses will follow later in this chapter. Both of these types of expenses contain portions that are fixed, and portions that vary depending on the level of business; however, to complete this illustration of the budgeting process, let us assume the following:

Administrative and General Expenses   = $800 per month
Operating Expenses   = $800 per month

Armed with the above knowledge it is now possible to complete an annual budget by month for this theoretical off-premise caterer.

REVENUE	COST OF SALES EXPENSE	PAYROLL & RELATED EXPENSE	OPERATING EXPENSE	ADMINISTRATIVE & GENERAL EXPENSE	PROFIT (LOSS)
$ 2,000	$ 667	$ 1,890	$ 800	$ 800	($ 2,157)
$ 3,000	$ 1,000	$ 1,990	$ 800	$ 800	($ 1,590)
$ 8,000	$ 2,667	$ 2,490	$ 800	$ 800	$ 1,243
$ 6,000	$ 2,000	$ 2,290	$ 800	$ 800	$ 110
$ 9,000	$ 3,000	$ 2,590	$ 800	$ 800	$ 1,810
$ 5,000	$ 1,667	$ 2,190	$ 800	$ 800	($ 457)
$ 2,000	$ 667	$ 1,890	$ 800	$ 800	($ 2,157)
$ 4,000	$ 1,333	$ 2,090	$ 800	$ 800	($ 1,023)
$ 3,000	$ 1,000	$ 1,990	$ 800	$ 800	($ 1,590)
$ 10,000	$ 3,333	$ 2,690	$ 800	$ 800	$ 2,377
$ 15,000	$ 5,000	$ 3,190	$ 800	$ 800	$ 5,210
$ 33,000	$11,000	$ 4,990	$ 800	$ 800	$15,410
$100,000	$33,334	$30,280	$9,600	$9,600	$17,186

In the above example it is interesting to note that the majority of the annual profits were generated in December, which means that in effect there was negative cash flow throughout the year. This particular off-premise caterer would be unable to extract any cash from the business until the end of the year, unless able to receive large advance deposits on future business, which is quite unlikely in the case of a first-year caterer.

Also of note is that it is apparent that on a monthly basis the caterer does not generate a monthly profit until sales reach the vicinity of $6,000. This is the break-even point, which will be discussed later in this chapter.

Is a profit of $17,186 an acceptable profit for a first-year caterer? This depends totally on the caterer. Is this a part-time or full-time venture? Was this caterer unhappily employed for a number of years and just happy to be on his or her own? What are the caterer's financial obligations? Are there savings from which to draw until the business becomes more successful?

START-UP EXPENSES

As pointed out earlier in this text, the best way to start an off-premise catering business is from an existing food service facility which operates for other purposes, such as a restaurant, club, or hotel. However, there are some instances where an individual may wish to rent a commissary to be used exclusively for off-premise catering.

How much will this cost? Although there are many regional and other factors which will affect this, a hypothetical estimate for a 2,000 square foot commissary with projected gross annual sales of $400,000 to $1,000,000 per year follows:

Advance rent and security deposits	$ 3,000–6,000
Equipment and fixtures	50,000–100,000
Leasehold improvements	10,000–20,000
Licenses, permits and impact fees	1,000–5,000

Marketing expenses	1,000–10,000
Utility and phone deposits	1,000–2,000
Accounting and legal services	1,000–4,000
Food staples	1,000–2,000
Preopening payroll	2,000–5,000
Supplies and uniforms	1,000–4,000
Prepaid insurance	2,000–8,000
Miscellaneous expenses	2,000–5,000
Contingency for unexpected	10,000–20,000
Total startup costs	$85,000–$191,000

These figures are simply very rough estimates of what it could possibly cost to setup and outfit a catering commissary. They are in no way to be used as definite figures for anything other than discussion purposes. Persons considering an off-premise catering commissary should calculate their own expenses and not use these numbers for anything but for hypothetical purposes. Startup costs will vary immensely depending on unique and individual circumstances.

CASH BUDGETS

Cash budgets account for the actual flow of cash in and out of the off-premise catering business. How do cash budgets differ from budgets for income and expenses? The answer is simple: Budgets for income and expenses do not account for cash flow. They simply record revenues and expenses, and do not take into account when the actual cash is received. For example, income from a catered event is recorded on the day the event occurs. However, for the same catered event, cash flow could be different.

Let's assume that an off-premise caterer books a party for March 15, and that the total price for the event is $1,000. This particular caterer requires a $250 deposit, which is received on January 15, $250 is paid on February 15, and the balance is paid on the day of the event. In this situation, cash is received during 3 months of the year, yet the sale (revenue) is not recorded until March 15. This is one way in which cash flow differs from basic budgeting.

A second way occurs on the expense side, when off-premise caterers purchase food and supplies on credit, and do not need to pay for these items until the tenth of the following month. In the above example, let's suppose that the food and supplies necessary to buy for the event were $250 at cost; however, this caterer need not pay for them until the tenth of the following month.

What about payroll costs? They are generally paid within one week of the party date, and although they do have some effect on cash flow, their effect is minimal in terms of this discussion.

Other factors separate income and expense budgets from cash budgets, for example, prepaid expenses such as insurance and utility deposits. In the insurance situation, many off-premise caterers finance their insurance premiums by paying anywhere from one-quarter to one-half of the policy in advance, and financing the remainder over a 6- to 10-month period. In the case of a $3,000 insurance policy, which will show on the records as a monthly expense of $250 during each of the 12 months of operation ($3,000 divided by 12 months), the actual cash flow could be as follows:.

On January 1 an off-premise caterer pays a $1,000 deposit toward an annual insurance policy and finances the remaining balance of $2,000 over the following 10 months. (Please assume that the $3,000 policy cost includes interest charges for the financed portion of the policy.) In this example the cash statement would show as follows:

MONTH	OUTWARD CASH FLOW
January	$1,000
February through November	200/month
December	None

Please realize that the income and expense budget would simply show an expense of $250 per month for all 12 months of the year.

Another major difference between cash and revenue budgeting occurs with the purchase of major equipment and fixtures. In the hypothetical example of startup costs, this off-premise caterer needed $50,000 in equipment and fixtures to get started. For cash budgeting purposes, let us assume that half of this amount was paid in advance, and the remaining balance was financed over three years.

In this case, the cash flow statement would show outward cash flow of $25,000 in January, and equal amounts of outward cash flow during the next 36 months for the remaining $25,000 that was financed plus interest charges.

However, the income and expense budget would show different figures equal to the amounts that can be depreciated under federal and state laws. (Off-premise caterers should definitely obtain professional advice from a certified public accountant and their attorney regarding this very technical accounting and legal aspect of the business.) Let us assume that the laws allow this off-premise caterer to depreciate this equipment over a five-year period (60 months). Therefore, the monthly depreciations charge would be equal to $50,000 divided by 60 months which equals $833.33 per month.

Startup off-premise caterers *must* project their cash flows annually, with the first year of operations being, of course, the most important. In the preceding example, where first-year sales are expected to be $100,000 let us determine the cash needs for this business using a basic cash budget system which projects cash receipts and payments on a monthly basis:

Cash receipts include:

Cash sales
Collection of accounts receivable
Advance deposits of future parties

Cash payments include:

Food purchases (cost of goods sold)
Payroll and related expenses
Direct operating expenses
Administrative and general expenses
Owner draw (amount owner takes from business)
Prepaid expenses (insurance)
Startup costs

In order to produce a statement of cash flow some assumptions must be made:

☐ All clients pay advance deposits equal to half the total bill during the month prior to the party, and they pay all balances due on the day of the party.
☐ Costs of goods sold and operating expenses are paid in the month following the event. Administrative and general expenses and payroll and related expenses are paid in the same month.

This example does not include any startup expenses. These will vary significantly from caterers with none to those with six-figure amounts. This example will simply address cash flows from operations.

This example does assume that our off-premise caterer purchased a $3,000 insurance policy, with payment terms as follows:

One-third down payment of $1,000 in January
Ten equal monthly payments of $200 per month from February to December

The cost of interest expense for this policy is included in the $3,000 total cost.

January Cash Receipts

Revenue	$2,000 (all of month's sales revenue)
Advance deposits	1,500 (half of February's sales revenue)
Total receipts	$3,500

January Cash Expenses

Cost of Goods Sold	-0- (all on credit, paid the next month)
Payroll and related	$1,890
Operating Expenses	-0- (paid following month)
Administrative and general	1,550 (adjusted for prepaid insurance)*
Total disbursements	$3,440

*This figure was determined by increasing the $800 per month charge for administrative and general expenses by $750 since it is necessary to prepay $1,000 of the insurance premium. Therefore, the cash disbursement was $750 more than the budgeted amount.

Cash Balance at the End of January

Receipts	$3,500
Disbursements	3,440

Cash balance at end of January without
   considering beginning cash balance $ 60

In January, although the records indicate a loss of $2,157, this hypothetical off-premise caterer actually generated a positive cash flow due to the receipt of advance deposits and not paying for cost of goods sold and operating expenses until February. The impact on February follows:

February Receipts
  Revenue (half of month's sales revenue)
    (First half was received in January
    as advance deposits for February) $1,500
  Advance deposits (half of March)   4,000
    Total cash receipts $5,500

February Cash Expenses
  Cost of goods sold for January   667
  Operating expenses for January   800
  February payroll and related   1,990
  February administrative and general   750*
    Total cash disbursements $4,207

*As in the previous example, the cash disbursement for administrative and general expenses is actually only $200, which is $50 less than the budgeted amount.

Cash increase during February $1,293
Cash balance at beginning of the month   60
  Cash balance at end of month $1,353

Again, in spite of a loss, a positive cash flow was achieved. Interested readers can continue this exercise throughout the year and project the positive and negative cash flows for the remaining ten months of the year.

It is important to understand the inherent differences between cash flow and income and expense accounting. Income and expense accounting is a true measure of the profitability of a business; whereas cash flow accounting simply keeps track of cash as it flows in and out of the business. Both are important. However, without positive cash flow, you will not stay in business.

BREAK-EVEN POINTS

All off-premise caterers must know their break-even points, whether they are just starting or seasoned veterans. The break-even point is the amount of revenue necessary for the business to cover its expenses; that is, neither earn a profit nor generate a loss. At the break-even point revenue equals expenses.

To calculate a break-even point, costs must be divided into fixed and variable costs. Referring to the preceding example we can separate these hypothetical costs as follows:

Variable Costs

Cost of goods sold	33 1/3% of revenues
Variable payroll and related	10 % of revenues

Fixed Costs

Fixed payroll per month	$1,690
Operating expenses	800
Administrative and general expenses	800
Total monthly fixed costs	$3,290

There are a number of methods for determining the breakeven point, some of which are extremely sophisticated, using such techniques as regression analysis. In this case, simplicity is the key, and one formula that can be used is:

The Break-Even Point = Fixed Costs divided by the Contribution Margin

The contribution margin is the difference between 1 and the variable costs. In this case it would be:

$$1 \text{ LESS } 43 \ 1/3\% \ (33 \ 1/3 + 10) = 56 \ 2/3 \text{ or } .5667$$
$$(1.0 - .4333 = .5667)$$

Using this formula, the break-even point can be calculated as follows:

$$\text{Break-Even Point} = \$3,290 \text{ (Fixed Costs) divided by } .5667$$
$$\text{(Contribution Margin)} = \$5,806$$

This figure can be verified by referring to the projected profits and losses. The financial projections for April show a profit of $110 on revenues of $6,000, while June's figures reveal a loss of $(457) on revenues of $5,000. Common sense proves that somewhere between these two revenues lies the break-even point.

Break-even points are targets for off-premise caterers to aim at. These targets give the caterer some indication of the level of revenues it takes to start generating profits. Potential investors and bankers will definitely need to know break-even points.

ACCOUNTING FOR REVENUES AND EXPENSES

The purpose of this section is to explain a basic accounting system that can be implemented by off-premise caterers on a daily basis without the need for learning a complicated computer system or engaging a high-priced accountant to keep basic business records. This system is easy to learn, and can quickly be taught to a qualified staff member. It does not eliminate the need for a Certified Public Accountant, particularly for year-end tax preparation, but it does provide the structure for documenting daily revenues and expenses, and the resultant records can be provided to an accountant for year-end tax preparation. This system will indeed save off-premise caterers thousands of dollars in expensive accounting fees when adopted and implemented.

It is important that off-premise caterers understand that records must be kept on a daily basis and on a timely basis. Revenues and expenses must be recorded daily, which will result in timely, up-to-date information. A major mistake that many small business owners make is that they do not keep their records up-to-date, which results in lengthy delays in obtaining financial results and can even lead to penalties when required governmental information and related fees are not submitted on time. Of course, it is always much easier to record transactions as they occur, rather than days, weeks, or months later.

The end result or bottom line of all record keeping is the Income Statement and Balance Sheet, which shows off-premise caterers their financial status. As noted earlier, the Income Statement shows the net profit or net loss for the accounting period. The Balance Sheet is essentially a snapshot of the financial status of the operations as of a particular date. The Balance Sheet depicts the assets and liabilities of the operation. The assets include cash, accounts receivable, fixed assets such as equipment and leasehold improvements, and food and supply inventories, and prepaid expenses such as prepaid insurance premiums. Liabilities include amounts owed to creditors, and employees, and other debts such as short-term and long-term loans. When total liabilities are deducted from total assets, the resulting figure is called the *net worth* or *equity* of the company as of a particular date. The balance sheet will be discussed in detail later in this chapter.

Readers are advised that this accounting system is not double-entry bookkeeping, and it does not replace Certified Public Accountants, but it does provide off-premise caterers with accurate figures that they can use to better manage their businesses.

Journals The basic components of this accounting system include journals used to record the various financial transactions such as sales, expenses, and other transactions:

- ❏ *Cash Receipts and Sales Journal*—This journal is used to record all cash receipts and revenues (sales).
- ❏ *Petty Cash Journal*—This journal is used to document all petty cash expenses.
- ❏ *Advance Deposit Journal*—This journal can be used in addition to the Cash Receipts and Sales Journal to record clients' advance deposits.
- ❏ *Client Invoice*—This is used to invoice clients for each event and used to record revenues in Sales Journal.
- ❏ *Cash Disbursements Journal*—This is used to record all cash disbursements for expenses other than payroll.
- ❏ *Payroll Journal and Individual Earning Records*—This journal is used to record all payroll expenses and payroll taxes.

By using these basic components of this accounting system, off-premise caterers will be able to easily prepare both income statements and balance sheets by simply recording totals and major figures from these journals.

Cash Receipts and Sales Journal. The cash receipts and sales journal is used to record cash receipts and sales information as it occurs. A simple, yet effective cash receipts form is to use a columnar accounting pad with sufficient columns to record the various categories of revenues and cash receipts, as well as any service charges, sales taxes, and gratuities. Some examples of revenue and cash receipts headings include:

Advance deposits
Food sales
Labor charges
Beverage setups, mixers, and corkage
Rental and other equipment
Florals and decor
Music and entertainment
Parking and valet services
Photography and video
Services charges
Gratuities
Sales taxes
Total amounts received

Many of these columns are used only when off-premise caterers actually provide services, or subcontract for these services for such things as music, parking, florals, and photography. When the clients directly pay the florist or the musicians, there is no need for off-premise caterers to record these transactions, since they do not affect the financial affairs of the business.

What are the input documents used as source documents for posting to this journal? Postings are made from a copy of the invoice provided to the client and upon receipt of advance deposits from clients. Please note that it is best to also keep an Advance Deposit Journal in addition to the Cash Receipts and Sales Journal so that advance deposits can be quickly found without going through page after page of journals.

To further explain this procedure please refer to Exhibit 14-1, which is a sample invoice for an off-premise event, and Exhibit 14-2, which is a sample Cash Receipts and Sales Journal. These two exhibits will show how sales are posted from the invoice to the journal.

Petty Cash Journal. The purpose of the Petty Cash Journal is to record expenses paid for from petty cash. Every off-premise caterer pays for miscellaneous expenses from petty cash. A last-minute purchase at the supermarket is but one example of a petty cash expense. Petty cash is not meant to pay for major purchases. Off-premise caterers wishing to establish a petty cash fund should first

EXHIBIT 14-1

Sample Client Invoice for Off-Premise Catering and Other Services

January 15, 19___
(Date of Invoice)

Mrs. James James
(Name of Client)
(Address of Client)

INVOICE FOR OFF-PREMISE CATERING SERVICES ON JANUARY 15.

30 DINNERS AT $15 PP	$450
30 BEVERAGES SETUPS, MIXERS, ICE AT $2 PP	60
STAFFING	200
FLORAL DECOR	100
RENTAL EQUIPMENT	400
TOTAL PRICE	$1,210
20% SERVICE CHARGE	242
6% STATE SALES TAX (VARIES FROM STATE TO STATE)*	87.12
TOTAL CHARGE FOR EVENT	$1,539.12
LESS: ADVANCE DEPOSIT PAID	600.00
BALANCE DUE	$ 939.12

1. In this example, sales tax is charged on the service charge, which is the law in most states.
2. It is highly recommended that off-premise caterers be paid in full no later than the day or night of the event, rather than extending credit. Even the largest corporations have ways to pay for things if required. Astute caterers will advise all clients that they require payment in full upon the completion of the event.
3. One way to do this easily, without disturbing the client on the night of the event, is to submit an invoice in advance of the event and ask the client to bring a check in that amount. (Some caterers require payment in full prior to the day of the wedding reception.) This is a much smoother procedure than disturbing a bride or her mother near the end of a wedding reception to write a check. Additional charges for extra guests or other unexpected costs can be invoiced.
4. Invoices may be prepared on preprinted invoice forms, or simply on the caterer's letterhead paper. It is highly recommended that invoices be prenumbered for control purposes, to insure that all invoices are accounted for and reconciled to cash receipts.
5. Math and other errors in invoices can be extremely costly and embarrassing. It is difficult to go back to a client one month after the party and ask for additional money due to an invoice mistake. Overcharges can be embarrassing, and can give some clients the impression that the off-premise caterer is deliberately overcharging.

EXHIBIT 14–1 (continued)

6. In the above example, state sales tax was charged on the service charge. What about charging sales tax on tips that the client pays? In most states, sales tax on gratuities need not be charged only when the following conditions are met:
   ❑ The gratuity or tip is 100% voluntary.
   ❑ All of the gratuity is distributed to employees.
   ❑ These two conditions are stated in the contract.

write and cash a check made payable to cash for the amount of the fund. Most funds range in size from $100 to $400, and even as high as $1,000 depending upon the size of the business and the expected uses. Petty cash should be kept separate from personal cash and kept at a minimum.

Off-premise caterers should retain receipts for all petty cash purchases, and the total receipts and the total remaining cash in the fund must always equal the total fund amount. For example, if after receiving an initial petty cash check for $500, and off-premise caterer has $250 cash remaining, there should also be $250 in receipts so that the total of the receipts and the cash total $500.

Once the petty cash funds are depleted to a point where they should be replenished, the receipts are recorded in the Petty Cash Journal as shown on Exhibit 14-3, and a replenishment check is written in the amount of the receipts. The Petty Cash Journal is simply a summary of each petty cash purchase and gives totals for each type of expense. The fund should always be replenished at the end of each accounting period to insure that all expenses for the accounting period are included in the same period.

One major point to emphasize is that all petty cash receipts must be marked paid once they have been reimbursed from the petty cash fund to prevent any fraudulent reuse at a later time.

Advance Deposit Journal. This journal simply lists the client's name, the amount and date of the advance deposit, and the date of the event. (It is good policy to include a copy of the client's deposit check, or a receipt in their file.) It is used in conjunction with the Cash Receipts and Sales Journal and simplifies searching when rendering final invoices to clients to ascertain the amounts paid in advance. Additionally, when preparing a balance sheet, the total amount of advance deposits is listed as *liabilities*, since the off-premise caterer has yet to perform the necessary service, and is liable for performance.

Occasionally, clients forfeit advance deposits. Forfeited advance deposits should be shown as *other income* on the financial statement. If the deposit is to be used toward a future party, then it must be duly noted in the deposit journal, along with the final date that it can be used. For example, a client plans an event for March 15 and gives the off-premise caterer a $500 deposit. On March 1 the client cancels the party and the caterer agrees to apply the deposit toward any event held by the client with the caterer until December 31 of the same

EXHIBIT 14-2
Sample Page from a Cash Receipts and Sales Journal

DATE	PARTY NAME	FOOD SALE	BEV SALE	STAFF	FLOW	EQUIP	MUSIC	SERVICE CHRG	SALES TAX	TOTAL	ADV. DEP.	AMT PAID
1-1	JAMES										600	600
1-15	JAMES	450	60	200	100	400	—	242	87.12	1539.12	939.12	
1-25	PEREZ	900	—	400				260	93.60	1653.60	1653.60	
1-29	SMITH										1500	1500
TOTAL		1350	60	600	100	400		502	180.72		3192.72	4692.72

NOTES:

1. Each column can be setup easily on columnar accounting paper.
2. Posting to this journal is made directly from the invoice.
3. The amount paid column is completed *only* upon receipt of payment.
4. At the end of the month, each column is totaled, and most of the totals are posted to the income statement for the month.

EXHIBIT 14-3
Sample Petty Cash Journal

Account to be Charged

Date of Purchase	Food	Beverage Mixers	Supplies	Laundry	Postage	Office Supplies	Total
1-15	25	25					$ 50
1-15			75				75
1-15				25			25
1-20					25		25
1-20						25	25
1-25	25	25					50
Total	$50	$50	$75	$25	$25	$25	$250**

*The total figures from the columns in the petty cash fund can be used to post expense to the Cash Disbursements Journal.

**$250 is the amount reimbursed by a check from the general checking account payable to cash for the petty cash fund. The fund must be reimbursed at the end of the accounting period.

year. This is noted in the Advance Deposit Journal and applied to any party held during the year or shown as other income on the December financial statement if not used. This and other sample advance deposit entries are shown in Exhibit 14-4.

Cash Disbursements Journal. The purpose of the Cash Disbursements Journal is to record all cash disbursement and expenses. An excellent system for small business operators is any "pegboard" or "one-write" check writing and record-

EXHIBIT 14-4
Sample Advance Deposit Journal

Date of Deposit	Name of Client	Date of Event	Amount of Deposit
1-1	James	1-15	$ 600*
1-29	Smith	2-14	1500
Other entries			
2-15	Rapp	3-15	500

(on 3-1 party cancelled—deposit valid until 12-31)

*Once a party is completed, and the deposit has been credited on the final invoice, a straight line may be drawn through the listing to reflect credit. For example, on January 15, after the James party, a straight line is drawn through the entry to indicate proper crediting.

keeping system. Many of these systems also include provisions for writing and recording payroll checks, although most caterers are usually better off engaging a computerized payroll firm for the payroll function to ease the bookkeeping load.

The pegboard is a simple system whereby a carbon imprint of each check written is recorded on the journal page, and there is a column for each class of expense. As each check is written, the amount charged to each expense account may be recorded. At the end of each journal page, and at the end of each accounting period, the columns are totaled and posted to the income statement summary.

For example, the journal page may include space for the following entries:

Date of the check
Check issued to
Amount of the check
Check number
Bank balance
Date and amount of deposits into account
Up to 33 columns for recording expenses

Invoices from suppliers are the basic input documents, which trigger the cash disbursement process, and there are a few basic rules to follow when processing invoices.

1. Invoices should be turned into the accounting office daily, rather than allowing them to build up and become a huge paperwork chore. When processed daily, they are easier to handle and errors can be corrected on a timely basis, rather than 30 days after the receipt of the merchandise.
2. All invoices should be checked for math errors, and particular attention should be given to returned merchandise, and merchandise that was on the invoice but not received.
3. Once checked, most bookkeepers and accountants file the invoices with those from the same vendor until they are due for payment.
4. At the end of the month, all invoices from each supplier are totaled, and compared with the monthly statement from the supplier. Differences are discussed until there is a mutually satisfactory resolution.
5. Off-premise caterers should always pay their bills on time, but there is no need to pay invoices early unless there is a discount offered for early payment, or if there are some special circumstances. In the case of vendors where there is only one invoice per month, some off-premise caterers prefer to write the check upon receipt of the invoice, address and stamp the envelope, but not mail it until the invoice is due.

Payroll Journal and Individual Earning Records. As indicated previously, off-premise caterers are advised to engage a computerized payroll firm for the preparation of payroll checks, journals, federal and state payroll tax reports, and individual earnings records. This work is very detailed and time-consuming, and can be more efficiently handled by firms specializing in this type of work at surprisingly inexpensive prices.

One key point for off-premise caterers to know is that off-premise catering personnel who receive cash tips of $20 or more in a monthly period must report those tips to their employer, the off-premise caterer, before the tenth day of the following month on IRS Form 4070. These tips are subject to FICA & MICA taxes for both the employee and the off-premise caterer, and are included in total wages for the purpose of computing payroll taxes, worker's compensation insurance and employee benefits.

CHART OF ACCOUNTS

Accounts used for recording revenues and expenses may include the following:

Revenue Accounts

Food Revenues
Mixers, Bar Setup Revenue
Equipment Revenue
Floral and Decor Revenue
Music and Entertainment Revenue
Revenues from Other Services as Appropriate
Sales Tax Collected

Expense Accounts

Cost of Sales Accounts

Cost of sales—food
Cost of sales—mixers, setups
Cost of sales—equipment
Cost of sales—floral and decor
Cost of sales—music and entertainment
Cost of sales—other services as appropriate

Payroll and Related Costs

Direct Operating Costs

Uniforms
Laundry
Replacement costs
Supplies
Transportation
Licenses and permits
Miscellaneous
Advertising and sales promotion
Utilities
Sales tax reimbursement to state

Administrative and General Expenses

Office supplies, printing, and postage
Telephone
Data processing costs
Dues and subscriptions
Insurance
Fees to credit organizations
Professional fees
Miscellaneous
Repairs and maintenance
Rent and lease expense

Revenues and Expenses Included in Each Account

Food Revenue—All sales of food. Many off-premise caterers who do not charge separately for staff include revenues from charges made to clients for staff in this account. Others create a separate account for revenue from staff.

Mixer and Bar Setup Revenue—All sales of mixers and bar setups when the client provides the alcoholic beverages, and the off-premise caterer provides the mixers, and so on. Of course, in states where off-premise caterers are licensed to sell alcoholic beverages, this account can be relabeled *beverage revenue* and include revenues from the sale of alcoholic beverages, as well as the mixers.

Equipment Revenue—All revenues from charges made for rental equipment and other equipment provided by the caterer. Of course, if clients deal directly with rental firms for equipment, this account is not used. Off-premise caterers who own equipment and rent it to clients would use this account to record the revenue.

Floral Decor, Music and Entertainment, and Other Revenue—All revenues from charges made for these services when provided by off-premise caterers.

Food Cost—All costs for food purchases less adjustments for inventory fluctuations and employee meals. A detailed explanation of this account will follow in this chapter.

Mixer and Bar Setup Cost—All costs for purchase of soft drinks, sparkling and still water, ice, juices, fruit, and other garnishes used for drinks served from bars or beverage stations.

Equipment Cost—All costs for renting equipment from rental firms.

Floral Decor, Music and Entertainment, and Other Costs—All costs for engaging floral designers, musicians, and so on as well as the cost of any purchases of flowers and items used to decorate parties.

Payroll and Related Expense—All wages paid to employees (including vacation pay, sick pay and holiday pay), employer's share of FICA expense, federal and state unemployment taxes as applicable, employee meal cost, and the cost for other employee benefits. Please note that the cost for Worker's Compensation insurance is included in this account, and not in the Insurance account.

Direct Operating Expenses

Uniforms—All costs for uniforms purchased and rented, costs for cleaning and repairing uniforms, and costs for uniform-related items such as name badges.

Laundry—All costs for laundering of table linens, napkins, towels, aprons, and other linens.

Replacements—All costs for purchase of china, glassware, flatware, tables, chairs, platters, trays, pitchers, serving dishes, chafing dishes, kitchen utensils, and serving utensils.

Supplies—All costs for the purchase of items such as sterno, charcoal, mesquite, cleaning compounds and supplies, silver and other polishes, soaps, detergents, disinfectants, brooms, mops, brushes, pails, portion cups, toothpicks, sword picks, doilies, cocktail and dinner napkins, paper towels, trash can liners, plastic flatware, aluminum foil, film wrap, disposable catering trays and bowls, matches, plastic drink glasses, plastic dinnerware, disposable containers and other applicable supplies.

Transportation—All costs to transport foods and supplies to the party site by off-premise caterers including the cost of leasing or renting vehicles, the cost of depreciation of owned vehicles, and all vehicle operating expenses such as gas, oil, repairs, and preventative maintenance.

Licenses and permits—Costs for all federal, state, and municipal licenses required to operate the off-premise business, as well as the cost for special permits and inspection fees.

Miscellaneous—All costs for minor purchases that are not included in any of the other direct operating accounts, and are directly related to serving the customer.

Advertising and promotion—All costs for newspaper advertisements (excluding help-wanted ads), magazine and trade journal advertising, brochures and menus, direct mail, signage, donations, client entertaining expenses, referral fees, complimentary food or other services, and any other expenses directly related to promoting or creating sales.

Utilities—All costs for electricity, electrical bulbs, water, sewage, waste removal, and propane and natural gas.

Sales taxes—Amounts paid to local and state governments for sales taxes. It is proper accounting to report these payments as reductions to the sales tax revenue account. However, in simplified accounting systems, it is not uncommon to show it as an expense, for easier comprehension.

Administrative and General Expenses

Office supplies, printing, and postage—All costs for printed matter not devoted to advertising and promotion such as accounting forms, stationery, catering forms and invoices, office supplies, and all postage except that related to advertising and promotion.

Telephone—All costs for telephone equipment rental, portable and vehicle phones, monthly service charges, other telephone charges, and long distance charges.

Data processing—All costs for data processing, such as preparation of payroll checks and reports and mailing lists.

Dues and subscriptions—Costs for dues paid for memberships in business organizations, as well as costs for subscriptions to trade papers and magazines.

Insurance—All costs for business insurance as described in chapter 12.

Fees paid to credit organizations—All costs for fees paid to Visa, Mastercard, American Express and other credit card companies.

Professional fees—All costs for legal fees, accountant fees, engineering firm fees, consultants fees, and fees for other professional services.

Miscellaneous—All costs for any minor charges of an administrative nature such as a bank charge.

Repairs and maintenance—All costs for painting and decorating, and repairs to all equipment and maintenance of grounds and gardens. Other charges to this account are for building alterations not in the nature of an improvement, such as plastering and upholstering. Costs for maintenance contracts on signs and equipment are also included.

Rent and lease expenses—All fees paid to the off-premise caterer's lessor for the use of the premises, plus any payment of local taxes or insurance which must be made by the tenant under the lease terms, as well as personal property taxes and sewer taxes.

INCOME STATEMENT SUMMARY

The Income Statement Summary is a worksheet used to summarize and calculate certain expenses prior to preparation of the Income Statement for the accounting period, which may be for one month, or in some instances for one quarter (three months). Most expenses can simply be posted directly from the Cash Disbursements Journal to the Income Statement; however certain expenses such as cost of sales, payroll and related expenses, and certain other expenses such as prepaid insurance require some intermediate calculations before posting to the Income Statement. Let us examine each of these calculations in detail as they relate to the Income Statement Summary.

Cost of Sales The basic formula for computing cost of sales is:
Calculation—Income
Statement Summary

> Beginning inventory
>   Plus purchases
>   Less ending inventory
>   Less employee meal and other credits
>   Equals cost of sales

Many off-premise caterers take inventories and calculate their values weekly, monthly, quarterly, or annually. Exhibit 14-5 is a sample inventory page that allows room for four inventories on one page, thereby, reducing paperwork and time spent preparing new pages each inventory period.

Most inventories for off-premise caterers would include enough pages in order to list all items to be inventoried or counted. Each of these pages is extended and totaled. Extension is accomplished by multiplying the number of units of an item times the unit cost. Totaling is simply adding all of the extensions on each page. Once each page is totaled, a grand total, or total inventory value is calculated by adding all of the page totals.

Inventory-taking is time-consuming, and for many off-premise caterers whose businesses are small and who are hands-on operators with small inventories, their time could be better spent working in other areas. For larger caterers, with significant fluctuations in monthly revenues and expenses, and for those that need to keep a very careful eye on costs, inventories are essential.

Once off-premise caterers take, extend, and total their inventories they use the grand total to post to their Income Statement Summary. The ending inventory for one month becomes the beginning inventory for the following month. For example, the inventory taken on January 31 is the ending inventory for January and the beginning inventory for February.

At this juncture, let us assume that our hypothetical off-premise caterer (addressed earlier in this chapter) took an inventory at the end of January, and calculated an inventory value of $200. How does the figure fit into cost of sales calculation on the Income Statement Summary?

Income Statement Summary Calculations for January

Beginning inventory for January	$0000
Food purchases for January	897
Less: ending inventory for January	200
Less: cost of employee meals for January	30
Cost of food sales for January	$ 667

Income Statement Summary Calculations for February

Beginning inventory for February	$ 200
Food purchases for February	1,140
Less: ending inventory for February	300
Less: cost of employee meals for February	40
Cost of food sales for February	$1,000

EXHIBIT 14–5
Sample Inventory Page

ITEM DESCRIPTION	DATE_____			DATE_____			DATE_____			DATE_____		
	QTY	PR	EXT	QTY	PR	EXT	QTY	PR	EXT	QTY	PR	EXT

PAGE TOTAL
FOR PERIOD _____   _____   _____   _____
Note: In the above sample:
  QTY = AMOUNT OF INVENTORY ON HAND FOR A PARTICULAR ITEM
    PR = UNIT PRICE FOR THE ITEM
  EXT = EXTENDED VALUE, WHICH IS THE QUANTITY MULTIPLIED BY THE UNIT PRICE.
For example, an off-premise caterer takes inventory and counts 10 pounds of sliced bacon, at a cost of
$1.75 per pound. This caterer would simply multiply 10 pounds times $1.75, and calculate an
extended value for bacon of $17.50.

Payroll and Related Cost Calculations- Income Statement Summary   Once the cost of sales is calculated for food, the next step is to calculate the payroll and related costs for the accounting period. This procedure is also best done on the Income Statement Summary since it involves a number of figures. The formula for payroll and related cost calculation is:

Gross wages
Plus: Employer's share of FICA & MICA expenses
Plus: Federal and state unemployment taxes
Plus: Cost of employee meals
Plus: Cost of other benefits
Plus: Cost for worker's compensation insurance
Equals: Total cost for payroll and related expenses

Calculations for payroll and related costs for January, using our hypothetical caterer are as follows:

Gross wages	$1,586
Plus: Employer's share of FICA and MICA at 7.65%	121.33
Plus: Federal and state unemployment taxes*	50.00
Plus: Cost of employee meals	30.00
Plus: Cost of worker's compensation insurance	100
Total payroll and related cost of January	1,887.33

*Please note that laws relating to unemployment taxes vary from state to state. Off-premise caterers are responsible for adhering to the laws in their states as well as federal statutes regarding unemployment.

**Please note that this amount is slightly under the budgeted amount for the month of $1,890 since the total cost for unemployment, FICA, and employee meals was less than 20 percent of the gross payroll for the month of January.

Prepaid Expenses Calculations— Income Statement Summary

Off-premise caterers frequently prepay expenses for insurance and other large dollar expenses. For example, off-premise caterers pay their total annual premium for the year in January. The insurance is in effect for the whole year, so the expense should be spread out over the twelve months, and not charged in total to January. Doing so would totally distort the financial results by overstating the January loss, and either understating losses or overstating profits in future months. This topic was addressed earlier in the cash flow section of this chapter. The calculation would be as follows:

Total cost for insurance for year	$3,000
Expense per month ($3,000 divided by 12 months)	250

Please note however, that the total disbursement for insurance expense will be $1,000 in January, which reflects the one-third down payment, and the remaining months through November will show a $200 disbursement; whereas the true month expense for insurance is $250 per month as shown above.

There may be other calculations unique to particular off-premise caterers that can be done on the Income Statement Summary. Once these are complete, work can begin preparing the Income Statement.

INCOME STATEMENT

The Income Statement for off-premise catering operations, if prepared accurately, will depict the profit or loss, as well as other key numbers for the particular period, whether it be for a month, quarter, or year. This statement is one excellent way to measure the success or failure of an operation. Exhibit 14-6 is a sample Income Statement for our hypothetical off-premise caterer.

An explanation of each Income Statement entry follows:

EXHIBIT 14-6
Income Statement

Year Ending December 31, 19____

	Food	Beverage	Equipment	Floral	Music/Ent.	Total
Revenue	$90,000	$5,000	$10,000	$3,000	$2,000	$110,000
Cost of Sales	30,000	1,500	8,500	2,500	1,800	44,300
Gross Margin	$60,000	$3,500	$ 1,500	$ 500	$ 200	$ 65,700
Payroll & Related	25,000	1,000				26,000
Direct Activity						
Profit	$35,000	$2,500	$ 1,500	$ 500	$ 200	$ 39,700
Direct Operating						
Expenses						
Uniforms	500					
Laundry	500					
Replacements	1,000					
Supplies	3,000					
Transportation	1,000					
Licenses	200					
Miscellaneous	500					
Adv and Promo	2,000					
Utilities	3,000					
Total	$11,700					$ 11,700
Administrative & General Exp						
Off Supp/Print	500					
Telephone	2,000					
Data Proc	1,000					
Insurance	3,000					
Fee to Credit	-0-					
Professional Fees	500					
Miscellaneous	100					
Repair/Maint	1,000					
Rent/Lease	5,000					
Total	$13,100					$ 13,100
Net Profit/Loss	$10,200	$2,500	$ 1,500	$ 500	$ 200	$ 14,900

Food revenue:

Food sales
Labor (staff) charges related to food sales
Services charges and sales taxes related to food sales

Beverage revenue:

Revenue from the sale of alcoholic beverages when permitted by law as well as
    mixers, ice, corkage, and other beverage-related charges
Labor charges related to beverages such as charges for bartenders
Service charges and sales taxes related to these sales

Equipment, floral and music revenue: all revenues, services charges, and sales taxes
charges for providing these services.

Total revenue: A total of the above revenues.

Food cost of goods sold: the amount computed on the Income Statement Summary.

Beverage cost of goods sold: the total amount of purchases for alcoholic and nonalcoholic beverages. Please note that larger catering operations may wish to adjust
these figures through the Income Statement Summary in a manner similar to
that for adjusting the food cost of sales.

Equipment cost of sales:

The total amounts paid to rental companies for equipment rentals that were pro-
    vided to clients
The cost of purchasing minor equipment for rental to clients
The cost of depreciation and amortization of major equipment and supply pur-
    chases that are rented to clients

Floral and music cost of sales: the amounts paid to florists and musicians for their
services when provided by the off-premise caterer.

Total cost of sales: a total of food, beverage, equipment, floral, and music cost of sales.

Gross margin figures: computed by deducting the cost of sales from the revenues
for each department.

Payroll and related figures: taken from the Income Statement Summary for each
department.

Direct activity profit: the amount remaining after deducting payroll and related
costs from the gross margin.

Operating and administrative and general expenses: posted to the Income Statement from the totals for these accounts in the Cash Disbursements Journal.

The totals of these expenses are then deducted from the Direct Activity Profit to determine the profit or loss for the accounting period.

Please note in Exhibit 14-6 that all of the Operating Expenses and the Administrative and General Expenses are charged to the food account. In theory, some of these expenses are directly attributable to the other accounts; however, for an operation of this size, generating $110,000 in annual revenues, in my opinion, it is not necessary.

BALANCE SHEET

Off-premise caterers should be familiar with Balance Sheets in order to gain a clearer picture of their business. Whereas an Income Statement shows the revenues, expenses, and profit/loss for a certain period of time, the Balance Sheet shows the financial condition of the business as of a particular time. It is essentially a snapshot of the assets and liabilities of the business.

Assets are things of value owned by the off-premise caterer such as:

Cash
Accounts receivable (amounts due from clients)
Food and other inventories
Prepaid expenses such as prepaid insurance
Fixed assets, including land, buildings-leasehold improvements to the building, vehicles and operating equipment

Accumulated depreciation on the above fixed assets is deducted from the assets' value. Computation of these amounts is best left to a certified public accountant. Basically, accumulated depreciation is a total of all depreciation charged to the business for income tax purposes. The laws in this area are strict and thorough.

Liabilities are obligations such as loans payable, advance customer deposits for parties yet to occur, amounts owed to vendors (accounts payable), payroll taxes payable and accrued payroll (amounts owed to employees as of a certain date).

The difference between the assets and the liabilities is called *equity*.

A simple example of the Balance Sheet for our hypothetical caterer at the end of the first year of operation could be as follows:

Balance Sheet of Hypothetical Off-Premise Caterer for the Period Ending December 31, _____

Current Assets

Cash		
In the bank		$5,000
In savings		2,000
Total cash		$7,000

Accounts Receivable	
Due from clients	1,000
Total accounts receivable	1,000
Inventories	
Food	500
Total inventories	500
Prepaid Expenses	-0-
Total current assets	$8,500
Fixed Assets	-0-
Total Assets	$8,500
Liabilities and Equity	
Current Liabilities	
Accounts payable	$1,000
Accrued payroll	500
Advance deposits-clients	1,000
Total current liabilities	$2,500
Long-Term Liabilities	-0-
Total liabilities	$2,500
Equity	$6,000
Total liabilities and equity	$8,500

RECORD RETENTION

How long is it necessary for off-premise caterer to keep records? Exhibit 14-7 is a Record Retention Checklist adapted from one provided by McBee Technologies. Since laws frequently change, off-premise caterers are advised to check with their certified public accountants before discarding any records.

ANALYZING FINANCIAL STATEMENTS

Off-premise caterers should understand how to analyze operational results as reported on Income Statements, Balance Sheets, and other financial records so as to be able to make good managerial decisions in the future, based upon financial results. It cannot be stressed enough that financial reports must be accurate and produced in a timely fashion so as to be useful.

Income Statements   Income Statements should include year-to-date figures, which are essentially totals of the results for the year. These totals are useful, and help to smooth out month-to-month fluctuations in revenues and costs, giving excellent totals which can be computed with the prior year's year-to-date figures.

EXHIBIT 14-7
Record Retention Checklist

NAME OF RECORD	NUMBER OF YEARS TO RETAIN
Bank Statements and Deposit Slips	3
Payroll Time Cards and Daily Time Records	6
Cancelled Checks	8
Individual Earnings Records	8
Paid Vouchers and Invoices	8
Mortgages, Notes and Leases	8
Corporate By-Laws, Charters and Minutes	Indefinite
Cash Receipts and Disbursements Journals	Indefinite
Checks for Taxes, Property and Major Contracts	Indefinite
Contracts and Agreements	Indefinite
Retirement and Pension Records	Indefinite
Tax Returns and Working Papers	Indefinite
Tax and Legal Correspondence	Indefinite
Expired Insurance Policies	4
Accident Reports	6
Fire Inspection Reports	6
Safety Records	8
Disability and Sick Benefit Records	6
Personnel Files for Terminated Personnel	6
Withholding Tax Statements	6
Sales Contracts and Invoices	3

Adapted from information provided by McBee Technologies

Monthly and year-to-date figures are compared with budgeted amounts to ascertain how well the off-premise caterer is doing in comparison with budget projections.

Percentage comparisons are done for revenues and expenses to see how well the caterer is doing at controlling expenses. Percentage comparisons are excellent, since percentages take into account fluctuations in revenues. For example, food cost of sales for one month might be $1,000 and the following month, $2,000. Does this mean that costs are rising, and becoming excessive? Not necessarily! It depends on the amount of food revenues. If food costs are budgeted to be 33 percent of sales, and sales for these two months are $3,000 and $6,000 respectively, then things look fine. However, if sales in the second month are only $5,000, this means that food cost has jumped to 40 percent of sales, and the caterer needs to investigate and perhaps take corrective action.

Another comparison is between revenues from month-to-month; year-to-date to gauge results. Are sales increasing or decreasing from the prior year and prior month? How do they compare to budgeted amounts? If sales are up from the prior periods, were prices raised? This could account for more revenue, but not necessarily more guests served or clients.

Another comparison is to divide total sales during a period by the number of guests served to determine a check average. Restaurants do this frequently to determine spending patterns, as well as how well their servers are selling the 'extras' such as desserts, drinks, appetizers, and other add-ons that increase the average check.

Another key computation is payroll percentage, which is determined by dividing food payroll and related costs by food revenues. Seasonal operators will see large variances in this percentage between busy and slow seasons. Many off-premise caterers experience large swings in monthly revenues that will affect this percentage greatly if certain key staff members are kept on the payroll during the slow season.

Prime cost is the combined cost of food and payroll. Many operators use this as a guideline. They realize that if their food costs are high, then their payroll costs must be low and vice versa. An off-premise caterer that operates with a 40 percent food cost will not stay in business long with a 40 percent labor cost. The total of the two is 80 percent, which is too high to generate a profit. Successful caterers operate with prime costs in the range of 40 percent to 65 percent.

After analyzing food and labor costs, operational costs and administrative and general costs should be compared in the same manner. Are any of these costs too high? Are any too low? If so, why? What changes can be made to counteract these results?

Of course, the most important figure is the net profit/loss amount. This is referred to as the *bottom line*. This, for many, is the true measure of their business success. How much did they earn after all expenses were paid? How much is enough? This depends totally on the individual caterer. In general, profit percentages for off-premise caterers are greater than those reported by restaurants. Another key point is that profits vary greatly from month-to-month for seasonal caterers. During slow periods, losses are common, but during peak season, profits are generous.

Balance Sheets   Balance Sheets for off-premise caterers also reveal operational successes and failures. The first account to check is cash in the operational account. Is there enough to pay all bills on time? If there is more than enough, excess cash should be deposited into interest-bearing accounts to generate interest income. Is there too little? If so, are accounts receivable high, meaning the clients are not paying their invoices on time, or perhaps the off-premise caterer's payment polices are too lenient? There are other reasons for too little cash:

❑ Business is not profitable over the long-run.
❑ Owners are withdrawing too much cash from the business.
❑ Inventories are too high.
❑ Business has seasonal fluctuations.

Some caterers who experience seasonal cash fluctuations obtain lines of credit from their banks from which to draw during the slow season, and pay back when business improves. Others borrow money in the form of loans. Caterers who are established and know that during certain seasons there will be a lack of cash will ask their clients for larger advance deposits during the slow season. This is very effective, since the caterer need not pay any interest expense, but there may in some cases be a need to give clients a slightly lower price or a discount on the event.

Accounts receivable should truly be nonexistent or kept at a minimum. Many businesses age their accounts receivable by separating them into the following time frames:

Less than 30 days past due
31–60 days past due
61–120 days past due
Over 120 days past due

The longer accounts are past due, the less likely it is that they will ever be collected. Astute caterers will not allow their accounts to become past due under virtually any circumstances. There are, however, those unpleasant situations where a check is "not good," or a caterer is duped into granting credit and then realizes that more than likely it will be impossible to collect. Some off-premise caterers establish a reserve account for this type of situation, by expensing small amounts each month to the operation as bad debt expense. This expense transaction does not involve cash, it is nothing more than a paper entry whereby the expense is charged against profits each month and an offsetting charge is made to the reserve for bad debt account. In this manner, when there is a bad debt, the financial statement for the month is not distorted by the bad debt. Off-premise caterers interested in learning more about this procedure, as well as the effect on their federal income taxes, should definitely contact a certified public accountant.

Food inventory turnover is determined by dividing the food cost of goods sold for the month by the average of the beginning and ending food inventory. However, as a practical matter, many caterers divide the food cost by only the ending inventory. If, for example, an off-premise caterer has food cost of goods sold for a month of $10,000, and the ending food inventory for the same month is $1,000, this caterer's food inventory turnover is 10 ($10,000 divided by $1,000). The higher the food inventory turnover figure the better, as long as there are sufficient foods on hand with which to operate efficiently. Restaurants operate with inventory turnovers of 3 to 5, but most off-premise caterers should have higher turnovers. Astute off-premise caterers will monitor their inventories, and promote or discount items that have been in stock for long periods of time as long as they are still fresh, and meet high quality standards.

Before leaving inventories, it is well understood among experienced off-premise caterers and restaurateurs that low inventories help reduce theft and pilferage. Thieves usually will steal items that are part of large inventories, thinking that the disappearance will be much less likely noticed than when items are missing from smaller inventories.

One other Balance Sheet analysis is to compare current assets to current liabilities. This comparison is known as the *current ratio*. A ratio of 2:1, where current assets are twice as large as current liabilities, is considered good. For the food service industry and off-premise caterers, a current ratio of 1:1 is acceptable since inventories and receivables are generally low, meaning that a large portion of the current assets is cash on hand.

CONTROLLING COSTS

Controlling costs is a daily function of all successful off-premise caterers. These caterers operate with their eyes wide open, always looking for waste, inefficiency, and other problems that will adversely affect profitability. There are some hands-on things that these caterers regularly do:

- ❑ Check garbage cans for product that has been discarded as waste yet could have been used, and flatware and other things that might be carelessly tossed away
- ❑ Count all rental equipment before and after each event
- ❑ Schedule enough staff so that the work will be completed on time; not so few staff that everyone needs to rush, doing a sloppy job, and not so many staff where people stand around waiting for something to do.
- ❑ Monitor utility costs, and turn things off when not in use.
- ❑ Buy labor-saving devices such as computers and kitchen equipment that will reduce daily payroll expenses.
- ❑ Inspect all areas for safety hazards.
- ❑ Carefully examine each operating cost and administrative and general cost at least quarterly to determine if there are any savings that can be made.

Of course, this list could go on indefinitely; simply being present at all events, watching and working will do wonders for reducing costs.

In addition to these hands-on techniques for controlling costs, there are myriad cost-control forms that off-premise caterers have developed to suit their own needs for projecting, analyzing, and controlling costs. Many of these can be done quickly and efficiently on computers. Let us examine three types of forms that can be used as effective tools for projecting and controlling costs.

Pre- and Post-Event Cost Form   The first form is the Off-Premise Catering Event Pre- and Post-Event Cost Form, and is shown in Exhibit 14-8. This form is completed at the time the first proposal is submitted to a potential client, up-dated as changes are made to the original proposal, and finalized upon conclusion of the event with actual expenses. This form is similar to a mini-Income Statement in that it includes projected revenues, food costs, equipment costs, labor and related costs, and operating costs.

The actual results from an event can reveal errors made in precosting and planning the party, thereby assisting off-premise caterers in understanding how to improve their profitability. It also reveals successful and profitable events, providing caterers with models to emulate.

EXHIBIT 14-8
Pre- and Post-Event Cost Form

Name of Client: _____

Date of the Event: _____

Minimum Number of Guests Expected: _____

Type of Cost	Projected Cost	Actual Cost
Food Cost-List Each Menu Item		
Total Food Cost	_____	_____
Labor Cost Calculations-List Costs for:		
Food Preparation at Commissary	_____	_____
Labor Cost for Delivery/Return	_____	_____
Supervisory Payroll	_____	_____
Kitchen Payroll		
Front-of-the House Payroll	_____	_____
Total Payroll	_____	_____
Add: Estimate Benefits %	_____	_____
Total Payroll & Related	_____	_____
Rental Equipment Expense	_____	_____
Direct Operating Expenses	_____	_____
Supplies	_____	_____
Transportation Vehicle(s)	_____	_____
Linens	_____	_____
Uniforms	_____	_____
Other	_____	_____
Total Operating Expense	_____	_____

EXHIBIT 14-8 (*continued*)

Calculation for Event Profitability

Revenue	Projected	Actual
Food/payroll		
Equipment		
Other		
Total		
Less Expenses		
Food Cost of Sales		
Equipment Cost		
Payroll and Related		
Other		
Total		
Operating Profit		

Daily Income Statement and Report

Another form that many larger off-premise caterers employ is a Daily Income Statement and Report. The advantage to this form, which is shown in Exhibit 14-9, is that it provides the operators with daily or weekly results, giving them timely information from which to correct problems, rather than waiting until the end of the month or quarter and then realizing that there is a major problem.

This report is completed by simply capturing information from client invoices, supplier invoices, time cards and time sheets, bank deposits, and checks written. Daily estimates can be used for expenses such as rent, utilities, insurance, and other expenses that occur regularly and without much variation from day to day. When this information is recorded in the Daily Income Statement, it will provide off-premise caterers with up-to-the-minute information that will enable them to make proper managerial and financial decisions.

This report should allow space for daily activity postings, as well as month-to-date columns. The month-to-date column will average out the results from the previous days in the month, which can vary immensely from day to day, and the monthly totals at the end of the month can be compared to the Income Statement for the month. Variances between the two statements can be reconciled at this point.

Ideal Food Cost Calculation Technique

Many off-premise caterers do not truly know if their food cost percentage is too high, too low, or on target. They know how their results compare to their budgets, prior years and prior months, but when it comes down to knowing exactly what their food cost should be, they do not know. Many would like to know, but

EXHIBIT 14-9

Daily Income Statement and Report

Date _____

	This Date	Month to Date
Revenues (posted from client invoices)		
Food		
Setups, mixers, ice, etc.		
Equipment		
Florals		
Music and entertainment		
Other		
Total revenue		
Cost of sales (posted from vendor invoices)		
Food		
Setups, mixers, ice, etc.		
Equipment		
Florals		
Music and entertainment		
Other		
Total cost of sales		
Cost of sales percentage of revenues		
Gross margin (revenues less cost of sales		
Food		
Setups, mixer, ice, etc.		
Equipment		
Florals		
Music and entertainment		
Other		
Sales tax		
Total gross margin		
Gross margin percentage of revenues		
Payroll (posted from time cards and time sheets. Calculate hours worked times hourly rate plus estimate for benefits.)		
Payroll and related percentage of revenues		
Activity profit (deduct payroll form gross margin)		
Activity profit percentage of revenues		
Operating expenses(caterers may use estimates or post figures directly from supplier invoices.)		
Uniforms		

EXHIBIT 14-9 (*continued*)

	This Date	Month to Date
Laundry		
Replacements		
Supplies		
Transportation		
Licenses		
Miscellaneous		
Advertising and promotion		
Utilities		
Sales tax submission to state		
Total operating expenses		
Operating expense percentage of revenues		

Administrative and general expenses (caterers may use estimates or post figures directly from invoices as appropriate.)

	This Date	Month to Date
Office supplies, printing, and postage		
Telephone		
Data Processing		
Dues and subscriptions		
Insurance		
Fees to credit organizations		
Professional fees		
Repairs and maintenance		
Rent and lease expense		
Total administrative and general		
Administrative and general expense percentage of total revenues		
Net profit/loss (activity profit less operating expenses and administrative and general expenses)		
Net profit/loss percentage of total sales		

Other information

Bank balance

	This Date	Month to Date
Beginning balance		
Plus: deposits this date		
Less: checks written this date		
Ending bank balance		

Accounts receivable

	This Date	Month to Date
Accounts receivable beginning balance		
Less: paid on account		
Plus: charges to accounts		
Ending accounts receivable balance		

since different menu items are sold with different food cost percentages, they need a formula from which to calculate the ideal food cost percentage, taking this into account.

The other problem is that revenues from various menu items change from month to month. For example, let us assume that an off-premise caterer sells both a chicken dinner and a steak dinner. The chicken dinner sells for $15, and has a 30 percent food cost, and the steak dinner sells for $20, and has a 40 percent food cost. What food cost should this caterer look for? It depends on the number of sales of each menu item. For example, if all sales during the month are chicken dinners, and the menu is designed for the chicken to generate a 30 percent food cost, then the food cost for the month should be 30 percent. If it is 35 percent, then this caterer may have a problem with controlling costs. On the other hand, if all sales are steak dinners, and the food cost at the end of the month is 40 percent, everything should be fine.

However, most caterers will sell some chicken dinners and some steak dinners. How can the ideal food cost be calculated? The answer is quite simple. All this caterer needs to do is determine what percentage of total sales are chicken, and what percentage of total sales are steak. This is done by dividing both the sales from chicken dinners and the sales from steak dinners by total food sales as follows:

Total food sales for the month are $5,000
Sales from steak dinners are $1,000
Sales from chicken dinners are $4,000
Steak dinner sales as a percentage of total sales are 20% (1,000 divided by 5,000)
Chicken dinner sales as a percentage of total sales are 80% (4,000 divided by 5,000)

The ideal food cost formula is simply to multiply the percentage of total sales for each menu item times the food cost percentage and total these extensions:

Steak dinner food cost percentage times percentage
of total food sales $.40 \times .20 = .08$

Chicken dinner food cost percentage times percentage
of total food sales $.30 \times .80 = .24$

Total of extensions $= .32$ (32%)

This is a simple example of how this calculation is made. Let us now determine an ideal food cost for an off-premise caterer who sells six different dinners, all at different food costs, as follows:

DINNER	FOOD COST %	% OF SALES	EXTENSION
Chicken dinner	25	20	.050
Roast beef dinner	30	15	.045
Italian dinner	20	10	.020
Seafood platter	35	20	.070

Broiled fish dinner	25	10	.025
N.Y. strip steak	35	25	.0875
Totals		100%	
			Ideal Food Cost = 29.75%

For off-premise caterers with licenses to sell alcoholic beverages, this same formula can be adapted to beverages sales and can be very useful since there often are large variances between costs for alcoholic beverage items. For example, martinis generally have higher cost-of-sales percentages than draft beer, making it difficult to determine the overall cost of sales based on various sales levels for these drinks.

MANAGING MONEY

There are some basic rules for off-premise-caterers regarding money management and dealing with banks and bankers:

1. *Pay all bills on time.* Never pay bills early unless there is a cash discount offered for early payment. There is clearly no advantage to early payment, and definitely a disadvantage when money paid early could possibly be earning interest in an interest-bearing account.
2. *Place excess cash not needed for day-to-day operations into interest-bearing accounts.* There is no reason not to take advantage of every opportunity to generate additional income. Off-premise caterers should pay particular attention to this during very busy periods of the year such as Christmas, when money piles up quite quickly in general accounts.
3. *It is rarely advisable to extend credit to clients.* Off-premise caterers are in the catering business, not in the banking business offering short-term loans. Caterers dealing with large corporations and organizations who say they take weeks to process invoices should develop the practice of providing early invoices in advance of the event for the estimated amount of the party, or a very large percentage of the expected amount due, and ask that they be paid prior to the day or night of the event. Any remaining small balances can be invoiced after the event.
4. *Under no circumstances issue a check when there are insufficient funds.* Caterers are almost always better off to approach creditors first, tell them of their financial difficulties, and also tell the creditors how they intend to satisfy payment on the account. A good rule of thumb is for checking account balances to average during the month about 30 percent of the total amount of the checks written during the month. For example, an off premise caterer who writes $10,000 worth of checks during the month should have an average checking account balance of $3,000.
5. *Establish a personal and trusting relationship with a banker.* Certainly, at some point a problem or need will arise when caterers will need a loan from a banker. It is far better to deal with a banker with whom one has an estab-

lished relationship than to try to find someone to loan money once there is a problem.

6. *All checking accounts must be reconciled once a month, immediately upon receipt of the bank statement(s).* Any delay can result in compounding of errors, and undue hardship in trying to unravel the financial disarray. Errors made by customers and banks can result in embarrassment when a supplier returns a check due to insufficient funds. One of the worst things that caterers can do is to let bank statements accumulate, and then try to reconcile many months at one time. It may be too late. Instructions for reconciling bank statements are on the back of most bank statements.

7. *Bank deposits should be made on a daily basis.* As soon as money is received, it should be deposited. It is not good policy to pay bills directly from cash receipts. Payment by check, or from the petty cash fund leaves a superior audit trail.

Selecting a Bank

Off-premise caterers should place their primary business accounts with the bank that can make the largest contribution to the business, even if it is not conveniently located. When searching, caterers should check with other business owners and suppliers and look for a bank that understands the foodservice business. Off-premise caterers must also feel comfortable when dealing with the bank and the bankers. Once these criteria are met, the off-premise caterer has more than likely found the right bank.

Loan Applications

When off-premise caterers need to borrow money they should first look to the financial institution where they keep their general, payroll, and other checking accounts. However, the problem with many banks is that they have very conservative lending practices, particularly toward foodservice businesses.

When requesting loans, good accounting work is paramount. Off-premise caterers should provide the bank financial statements in advance of requesting a loan. This helps to establish a relationship. Off-premise caterers should provide accurate and realistic figures, and also be prepared to answer bankers' inquiries about these figures. Astute bankers all know that it is a sure sign that someone is not on top of the business when they say that they need to "get with my accountant" for the answer.

Off-premise caterers needing assistance in completing loan applications and financial projections, at little or no cost, may contact local offices of the Small Business Administration (SBA) or the Service Corps of Retired Executives (SCORE).

Lenders consider the following factors when making loan determinations:

1. *Character*—Experience in catering, special skills, honesty, integrity, and willingness to pay back.
2. *Capacity*—The ability to pay back the loan with interest. Applicants must show projected Income Statements, Balance Sheets, and cash flow statements for three to five years.
3. *Capital*-Loans to off-premise caterers must be personally guaranteed by the owner.

4. *Collateral*—Since foodservice equipment depreciates quickly, and has no value to lenders, may lenders require that personal property be put up as collateral, which will be seized if the loan is not paid back. Examples of personal property are home equity, and personal savings accounts.

Prudent lenders usually look at the first or next three years of operation, and consider loan amounts of 8 to 10 percent of the total revenue. For example, an off-premise caterer who projects $750,000 in business during the next three years could perhaps obtain a loan for 8 to 10 percent of that amount or $60,000 to $75,000, which would need to be paid back over the next three years.

SBA-guaranteed loans are sometimes granted to entrepreneurs who cannot qualify for commercial loans. They offer an extended payment schedule of seven to eight years. Interested off-premise caterers may call the SBA.

Aside from banks, off-premise caterers may look to credit unions, real-estate developers, the SBA, investor groups, limited partnerships, and even friends and family members with deep pockets. However, borrowing should be kept at an absolute minimum in order to maximize profits and cash flow so as not to pay high interest expenses and debt service.

FEDERAL TAXES

What would business be like in the United States if there were no federal taxes? It would more than likely be more profitable, and would certainly require less paperwork. However, there are federal laws that must be followed by off-premise caterers. The major laws relate to payment of:

Federal income taxes (corporate and personal)
Federal Insurance Contributions Act (FICA)
Federal unemployment taxes

Of course, there are a number of state and local taxes on sales, payroll, income, and other areas.

Off-premise caterers *must contact a certified public accountant regarding payment of these taxes.* This text is meant only as an overview in this area, and represents general information regarding tax laws at the time written. Do no consider this as the final word in taxes. It is not!

Most off-premise caterers are incorporated, and must file a corporate income tax return at the end of the year. These returns are generally prepared on a calendar-year or fiscal-year basis. If based on a calendar-year, the return is due no later than March 15 of the following year. Six month extensions are available on request. It is imperative to properly report income and expenses. Overstatements of expenses and understatements of income can ultimately ruin a successful off-premise business. Off-premise caterers are advised to utilize the services of a certified public accountant and follow his or her advice when preparing tax returns. The penalties for errors and omissions are large, and the cost for professional tax preparation assistance is small compared with the consequences if done incorrectly. Some foodservice professionals who have not followed the tax laws have been incarcerated in federal prisons. Income taxes are serious business.

Employers are required to pay Social Security taxes and Medicare taxes for their employees. At the time of this writing, this tax is 6.2 percent of gross payroll for Social Security tax and 1.45 percent for Medicare tax. This amount is in addition to equal amounts withheld from employees' earnings. The maximum wage base for payment of Social Security tax is $60,600; however, all wages are subject to Medicare tax. Self-employed off-premise caterers must pay 15.3 percent Social Security taxes and Medicare taxes on their own pay from the catering firm.

Off-premise caterers are also required to pay federal unemployment insurance for their staff, which is usually in addition to state unemployment tax. Amounts for the state tax vary from state-to-state and normally the amount of tax due the federal government is reduced by the amount paid to the state.

Additionally, employers are required to withhold taxes from employees' pay checks in accordance with certain criteria published by the federal government. These monies must be deposited at certain intervals into banks, which in turn forward the money to the federal government. Many business owners with cash shortages are tempted to use these withheld wages for business expenses, and postpone their deposit until cash flow improves. This should never be done since the penalties for this are severe and it is a violation of federal law.

COMPUTERS IN CATERING

Computers are found in thousands of off-premise catering offices across the country. They are used by caterers for proposal and contract preparation, preparing pullsheets and packing lists, record keeping, maintenance of personnel files, and myriad other functions. It is interesting to note that most caterers use their computers only for a fraction of their total capabilities.

There are computer software firms that produce software exclusively for use by off-premise caterers. These software programs can accomplish the following:

Develop menus and recipes
Break down recipe ingredients for purchasing
List beverage items
List equipment needs
Produce staffing information
Produce cost-control forms
Generate packing lists
Compile production cost reports
Prepare production summary reports
Print food price update reports
Create bidder/purchasing lists
Process purchase orders

Generate receiving lists
Detail miscellaneous items

Some software programs such as those produced by Synergy Management Systems, CaterMate and Eatec Corporation include thousands of preprogrammed food, beverage, equipment, and miscellaneous items, as well as hundreds of recipes. These programs, when properly used and adapted, can save caterers significant amounts of time.

Every off-premise caterer should make a computer a high-priority purchase item. Even if the computer is used only for preparing proposals, contracts, basic forms, and perhaps a mailing list, it is well worthwhile. Off-premise caterers with existing computer systems should continually look for ways to maximize the use of their computers. There are no limits.

How does one go about selecting a computer system? Some caveats are:

❑ Never be the first to use a computer system.
❑ Check with a minimum of three other users of the system being considered.
❑ Decide in advance exactly what the system will be required to do.
❑ First find the appropriate software, and then look for the compatible hardware that will run the software.
❑ Be sure that the firm selected can provide adequate service and training.
❑ Use the computer before purchase to ensure that it is user-friendly and meets your need.

CONCLUSION

This last chapter could be the most important one for many readers, since financial knowledge is the key to business success. The bottom line is the end result. Fancy menus, beautiful linens, and flawless parties must generate profits, otherwise, their execution is in vain.

Readers are advised to thoroughly understand the financial aspects of this chapter before embarking on an off-premise catering career. Your future success will most definitely depend upon it.

Index